The Western Films of
Robert Mitchum

ALSO BY GENE SCOTT FREESE
AND FROM MCFARLAND

*Classic Movie Fight Scenes:
75 Years of Bare Knuckle Brawls, 1914–1989* (2017)

Richard Jaeckel, Hollywood's Man of Character (2016)

*Hollywood Stunt Performers, 1910s–1970s:
A Biographical Dictionary,* 2d ed. (2014)

*Jock Mahoney:
The Life and Films of a Hollywood Stuntman* (2014)

The Western Films of Robert Mitchum
Hollywood's Cowboy Rebel

Gene Freese

McFarland & Company, Inc., Publishers
Jefferson, North Carolina

LIBRARY OF CONGRESS CATALOGUING-IN-PUBLICATION DATA

Names: Freese, Gene Scott, 1969– author.
Title: The western films of Robert Mitchum : Hollywood's cowboy rebel / Gene Freese.
Description: Jefferson, North Carolina : McFarland & Company, Inc., Publishers, 2020 | Includes bibliographical references and index.
Identifiers: LCCN 2019044352 | ISBN 9781476678498 (paperback) ♾
ISBN 9781476637464 (ebook)
Subjects: LCSH: Mitchum, Robert—Criticism and interpretation.
Classification: LCC PN2287.M648 F74 2020 | DDC 791.4302/8092—dc23
LC record available at https://lccn.loc.gov/2019044352

BRITISH LIBRARY CATALOGUING DATA ARE AVAILABLE

ISBN (print) 978-1-4766-7849-8
ISBN (ebook) 978-1-4766-3746-4

© 2020 Gene Freese. All rights reserved

No part of this book may be reproduced or transmitted in any form or by any means, electronic or mechanical, including photocopying or recording, or by any information storage and retrieval system, without permission in writing from the publisher.

On the cover: cowboy hero Mitchum as Pecos Smith, with both guns drawn, in RKO's *West of the Pecos*

Printed in the United States of America

*McFarland & Company, Inc., Publishers
Box 611, Jefferson, North Carolina 28640
www.mcfarlandpub.com*

Table of Contents

Acknowledgments vii
Preface 1
Introduction 3

Bona Fides 9
The Films: 1940s–1970s 13
Off the Trail 179
The Films: 1990s 199

Adios, Amigo 209
Bibliography 217
Index 225

"I'm ridin' through!"
—Robert Mitchum's Jim Garry in
  Blood on the Moon (1948)

Acknowledgments

Putting this book together would not have been possible without the aid of those who pitched in, like long-time Mitchum friend Butch Huff and Mitchum's niece Cindy Azbill. Mitchum's co-star Robert Viharo and stunt double Dave Cass provided great, lengthy letters of remembrance revealing aspects of Mitchum's true character, and Mitchum's son Chris was kind enough to answer a few questions via e-mail. Esteemed western horsemen the likes of Fargo Graham and rodeo legend Chuck Henson shared their memories of working with Mitchum. I am also indebted to the cowboy stuntmen Rodd Wolff, Neil Summers and the late Jack Young, gentlemen who have been helpful in answering my questions going back now several years. Old Tucson Studios tour guide Marty Freese was instrumental in contacting cowboy character actor Don Collier and veteran western stuntman Bunker DeFrance. My TV personality pen pal Garry Armstrong provided not only his personal remembrance of interviewing and lunching with Mitchum but also his notes and Mitchum quotes from 1972. Thank you, Garry. I also owe thanks to the Motion Picture Academy Library for their help with research and to Boyd Magers of Western Clippings for providing lobby cards from Mitchum's earliest Hopalong Cassidy films.

Preface

Several books and countless articles have been written on silver screen legend Robert Mitchum. These focused on his adventurous life and personal complexity, offering little detail about the man's varied motion pictures. Mitchum made more than 100 films, a third of them westerns. Among these are many unique and darkly shaded characterizations. In-depth film detail is glossed over in the biographies in favor of personal analysis of the notorious aspects of Mitchum's stardom (drinking, fights, affairs, arrests). A private man, Mitchum didn't outwardly care about anything. His cool, reserved, often rebellious attitude toward authority endeared him to audiences but confounded movie executives. However, Mitchum was a deeply proud man and a respected professional beloved by the crews he worked with. He lived by the time-honored Cowboy Code and did consistently solid work. Hollywood never stopped hiring him, and his film career spanned over 50 years. Two decades after his death, he has relevance and staying power. Film retrospectives of his work are common.

When Mitchum started in Hollywood, it was in the western film. It's also where he ended. He adopted the rugged stoicism of the cinematic cowboy to his own lifestyle, carving out his tough guy image. He dressed the casual cowboy part off the set, breeding quarter horses at his personal ranch. Only a handful of cowboy stars became so absorbed in the western lifestyle. There remain actors, horse wranglers and western stuntmen able to share their memories. I've rounded up what I can for this look at Mitchum's western films and his significance to the genre. The broad range of Mitchum's cowboy career and the remembrances of his co-workers may shed new light onto one of Hollywood's most interesting, enigmatic and enduring characters.

Introduction

Robert Mitchum. The name immediately conveys the image of a sleepy-eyed, masculine presence clad in a trenchcoat and fedora, nose bent from some long-ago punch, a cigarette dangling from his lips as he stands in the shadows of a rain-soaked street in a black and white movie classic. Tough guy Mitchum was the quintessential film noir fall guy tempted by femme fatale Jane Greer in *Out of the Past* (1947). By the mid–1970s, he made for ideal casting as Raymond Chandler's world-weary, faded gumshoe Philip Marlowe in the period pieces *Farewell, My Lovely* (1975) and *The Big Sleep* (1978). He was the ultimate cool cynic, voicing his character's jaded narration in a crisp, deep, distinguished tone that had seen and done it all. Anti-heroic and reluctant to the nth degree, he drank whiskey like water and chain-smoked at a pace befitting a fiery furnace while waxing poetic on lost loves and luckless misfortune. Forces could disrupt him—beating him, shooting him, stabbing him, pumping him full of drugs—but by film's end, Mitchum would rise from the cinematic ashes, dust himself off, square the fedora on his head and pour himself a stiff drink. If there was a girl worth a damn in the story, he might pour one for her as well.

This is the screen image associated with Mitchum. However, he made a significant mark in the western genre, logging over 30 cowboy credits among his more than 100 film titles. The moody, hard-hitting entries *Blood on the Moon* (1948) and *The Lusty Men* (1952) are considered classics. *River of No Return* (1954) opposite Marilyn Monroe is a time-tested crowd-pleaser, and his Australian western *The Sundowners* (1960) was nominated for a Best Picture Oscar. A significant reason for these films' lasting success is Mitchum's solid performance in the lead parts.

Mitchum realistically handled horses and guns, his tight-lipped loners looking like they'd already rode dozens of hard trails. Those knowledgeable about the western genre and its important place in the history of film hold him in high regard. Allen Eyles' *The Western* rates Mitchum as "a performer of underrated ability; in westerns often the outsider without a cause, reluctantly involved in trouble." According to Paul Simpson's *The Rough Guide to Westerns*, "His quiet, brooding physical presence gave his many westerns a distinct flavor." Boyd Magers of the journal *Western Clippings* declares Mitchum "one of our most underrated stars." *"A" Western Filmmakers* author Henryk Hoffman notes of Mitchum, "He is tall, broad-chested and undeniably handsome, which makes him a perfect hero of the intellectual western…. Mitchum—with his absolutely original image—has certainly earned a position among the top dozen western stars." Kevin Grant and Clark Hodgkiss' *Renegade Westerns* calls Mitchum a "western superstar" on a par with genre stalwarts John Wayne, Clint Eastwood and Gary Cooper.

On-screen, Mitchum proved adaptable to any number of situations and looked extremely comfortable in cowboy boots and western wear. He played every kind of western role: lawmen, outlaws, soldiers, preachers, hired guns, lowly henchmen. The authentic period clothes seemed a second skin, and he learned to mount and sit a horse as well as anyone in the business. He was never better than when cast as a laconic drifter up against the weather,

On horseback at Sedona's Red Rock Crossing in *Blood on the Moon* (1948).

the terrain, advancing age and the odds—the essential ingredients for a true cowboy. When producers and casting directors had a need for an ambivalent American adventurer surviving bullets and bombs south of the border, Mitchum's name naturally rose to the top of the list. Most of these Mexican Revolution-era films were run-of-the-mill action pics, but Mitchum's presence in them was a welcome one. *Film Comment* called Robert Parrish's Mexico-lensed *The Wonderful Country* (1959) "arguably Robert Mitchum's best western."

Mitchum might not have dominated the genre the way America's favorite cowboy John Wayne did, but he shared the screen and star billing with The Duke himself in Howard Hawks' *El Dorado* (1967). That film is flawed and unambitious in its cinematic aspirations, but an entertaining outing beloved by fans of the stars. It's likely been seen by millions of

Holstered and ready as Jeb Rand in *Pursued* (1947).

people over the years, running regularly on television for decades since its initial theatrical release. The film is a treasured part of any western fan's DVD collection. Mitchum is one of the few actors who could go toe to toe trading punches and quips with the legendary, larger-than-life Wayne and not be blown off the screen. That is why Hawks cast him, and Mitchum delivered as he always did. No big deal. Just a job. Mitchum described himself as a hired hand who brought the needed tools. Nothing to it.

Mitchum's brave, terse western presence evoked real Montana cowboy Gary Cooper, the rangy acting legend who won an Academy Award for portraying Marshal Will Kane in *High Noon* (1952). Mitchum and Cooper were excellent technical actors praised for their professionalism before the camera. They could hit their marks and recite their dialogue line-perfect again and again with a minimum of scene-stealing theatrical gestures. They had great camera awareness and knew how to convey complex internal thought and emotion on the screen. Directors remarked that, on the set, they didn't realize how good these men were, but then they viewed the dailies. Takes where a director perceived the actors' energy level to be down were instead perfect for the camera. Most importantly, Mitchum and Cooper's strength of character registered strongly with audiences when they were up against superior forces. They had played the same leading role in 1927 and 1944 versions of Zane Grey's western *Nevada*, and strong similarities exist between Cooper's Kane and Mitchum's town tamer Clint Tollinger in *Man with the Gun* (1955), one of the 1950s' more underappreciated sleepers. Both men are pitted against shifty-eyed hired guns with little or no help from town locals, who instead offer varying degrees of friction. In each film, the love of a woman is at stake. Cooper died from cancer in 1961 at the age of 60. By the time Mitchum starred in the epic World War II mini-series *The Winds of War* (1983), *TV Guide* was running a profile on him proclaiming the aging star to be "Our Last Gary Cooper." Western icon Clint Eastwood has acknowledged Mitchum and Cooper as influences for his own silent but deadly, efficient cowboy characters.

While similarities exist between these men and their representation of the classic western formula that Wayne and Cooper laid the foundation for in *Stagecoach* (1939) and *The Westerner* (1940), respectively, there were marked differences. Mitchum added layers of depth and wrinkles of originality to his three-dimensional cowboy portrayals in the late 1940s and 1950s. In his book *The Quick, the Dead and the Revived: The Many Lives of the Western Film*, Joseph Maddrey notes that Mitchum "projected a very different persona from the likes of Gary Cooper and John Wayne. Whereas Cooper was simple and straightforward, Mitchum was cynical and suspect. Whereas Wayne was outspoken and dogmatic, Mitchum was cool and seemingly indifferent. He was a new type of hero for the postwar era."

Mitchum began his Hollywood career by playing nondescript heavies in squeaky-clean Hopalong Cassidy B-westerns. Bit parts. Little more than an extra. He was the third cowboy from the left, hired to fill the ranks. Yet he rose to stardom like a supernova in barely

As Jim Garry, the quintessential western-noir figure in *Blood on the Moon* (1948).

two years' time by showcasing a commanding presence and personality despite a penchant for underplaying. There was something emotionally complex smoldering under the surface that audiences and eventually critics picked up on; a strong hint of impending danger building within. Mitchum claimed that acting was little more than a paycheck to him, but he was professional in his naturalistic approach, carving a lasting career peppered with several above-average outings and some true classics. Mitchum's westerns were unique in that he worked with interesting writers and directors and generally steered away from the phoniness of the Hollywood back lot. Realism was key. Mitchum's robust oaters were filmed on location in authentic and beautiful Sonoran Desert and treacherous High Sierra locations that were as tough as they looked on screen. His morally ambiguous drifters and outcasts were rugged individuals, well-suited to the memorable landscapes and raging rivers they traversed. "I have two acting styles," Mitchum told *Time Out*. "With or without a horse."

The American cowboy is a simple man. He rode fence, herded cattle and broke horses. In comparison, Mitchum was anything but simple. He was a complicated man with a rare intellect who has rightly been called "a poet with an axe." Everything about him was as contradictory as east is to west. Mitchum could quote the great wordsmiths at length and mix in his own original prose, yet throughout his early life he worked as a day laborer with a pick and shovel. An honest day's work for an honest day's pay. The cowboy creed. He was married to the same woman for more than 50 years yet was notorious for extramarital affairs and bad boy behavior. He drank his fill and was often pleasantly stoned on marijuana reefer, yet he rarely if ever missed work because of it. He claimed he didn't care about the artistic merit of his projects but was always letter perfect on set, even in potboilers that were several rungs beneath his prodigious talents. He effortlessly sang and recorded calypso, folk and country-western music, punched out heavyweight boxing contenders, served time in jail, and bucked every convention of the Hollywood system while claiming he didn't give a damn about anything. He was "cowboy cool" and the first rebellious Hollywood hipster; yet he was a master craftsman and a smooth professional whose co-workers sang his praises for all to hear. An enigma.

Mitchum chose to hide his many complexities behind the cloak of a simple man. Hence, the role of a cowpuncher was a good fit. Westerns are morality plays full of myth. They're good vs. evil in the wide open spaces of the vanishing American West. When he began in the business in B-westerns, Mitchum only needed to know if he was wearing a white hat or a black hat. In time, he chose to wear gray. This gave the audience and the critics something to think about. Mitchum was coy that way. Before the cameras rolled, he'd innocently ask, "What are the lyrics?" The reality is, he knew the entire script and everyone's parts and their motivations. Sometimes they'd ask him to rewrite the dialogue himself, make it better using his astute ear for language.

By the end of World War II, westerns themselves were becoming more psychologically complex and Mitchum understood these

As Paddy Carmody in the "Australian western" *The Sundowners* (1960).

themes. Hollywood chose him to be their darkest star. He was the perfect actor to bring depth and shading to an increasingly analyzed cowboy characterization. Even when he was doing nothing, he was doing something by being himself within the storyline. His stillness spoke volumes. Had he been born 60 years earlier, it is very likely Mitchum would have been the anti-heroic characters he wound up playing: drifters roaming from town to town, sometimes with a price on their heads, sometimes with a badge pinned to their shirts. Men with a job to do.

There was no direct cowboy or rodeo work in Mitchum's background, but in his early years he lived as colorfully as any real-life Huck Finn or Tom Sawyer. Exact details of his adventurous life are hard to pin down as Mitchum was prone to telling tall tales and expanded on his own adventures through the years (especially when fueled by drink). Cowboys call this accepted behavior "telling a windy." This became especially evident after he found success in Hollywood and learned that part of the requirements of a movie star were answering the same insipid questions from a gaggle of reporters. Utilizing an expert gift for vocal mimicry and regional dialects, Mitchum would amuse himself and those close to him by jazzing up stories or inserting off-color humor for gullible reporters. He could do the same thing holding court on a bar stool at the local watering hole. Fellow actor Stuart Whitman of *Cimarron Strip* TV fame revealed in an A&E video biography on Mitchum: "He was a great storyteller…an incredible storyteller. Once you got him wound up, why, that was it. I mean, you could go out and saddle your horse and rub him down, come back, and he's still going on with the same story. And I never heard two stories twice."

Bona Fides

He was born Robert Charles Durman Mitchum in Bridgeport, Connecticut, on August 6, 1917. Before he turned two, Mitchum's father James Thomas Mitchum was killed in a railroad accident in Charleston, South Carolina. Young Mitchum had no direct memory of his father's death, but this was an important event physically and emotionally. Pure and simple, he became a fighter for his own survival, but a man given to an uncommon sense of introspection. There was always an underlying sense of abandonment in his being, a rootlessness that drove him to look over the next hill for something. His psychological make-up resembled the adventurous American frontiersman heading west for a better life on the open range. In a case of art imitating life, Mitchum portrayed that exact same character when he essayed the wagon train scout Dick Summers in *The Way West* (1967).

When he was young, his mother Ann exposed him to music and the literary arts, encouraging her child to write and recite poetry. On the margins of his many books, he drew self-portraits of a cowboy riding a horse, fantasizing that one day he could make that daydream a reality. In grade school, Mitchum authored an epic unpublished novel entitled *The Adventures of Sure Shot Shorty*, an example of the scope of his imagination. An avid reader of any subject of interest, Mitchum had the dual characteristics of his roughneck lineage. In addition to his Celtic and Scandinavian roots, his father had been part Blackfoot Indian, and young Mitchum was no milquetoast. He became a rambunctious troublemaker and prankster of legendary proportions, describing his childhood to *The Saturday Evening Post* as a history of "broken windows and bloody noses." At the age of six, he was wandering from home to play cowboy by pretend-lassoing a herd of horses stocked at the local rail yard.

The family moved around a great deal. Mitchum proved quick with his fists on the street and the schoolyard when challenged. He was never a bully but always stuck up for himself and the little guy, fighting each battle until it was won. Even when he wasn't guilty of some childhood transgression, his was the first name school officials looked to pin the crime on. The perceptive Mitchum saw the humor in that scenario but began to dislike bossy, bullying behavior represented foremost by authority figures, a trait that followed him throughout life. His younger brother John traced Robert's rebellious footsteps and the two became known wherever they went as "them ornery Mitchum boys."

Robert, nine, and John, seven, were sent to live with relatives on a Delaware farm to keep them out of trouble and instill an honest work ethic. It was on that Delaware farm that Mitchum sat his first equines; plow horses named simply Jim and Harry. He began hunting in the woods with a single shot bolt-action Winchester rifle. These childhood actions would give him at least some level of experience to draw from in his subsequent career as a cowboy actor. After two years of farm life, they were sent to Philadelphia to live with their sister Julie (aka Annette, a dancer and actress). Bored with school and seeking adventure, the restless and independent Mitchum began traveling from home for extended periods of time. He wasn't trying to get away from anything as much as he was attempting to satisfy his curiosity regarding the world and the images his dedicated reading of authors Thomas Wolfe, Joseph Conrad, Jack London, W.H. Davies and Jim Tully conveyed. He always maintained a loving relationship with his mother, and she was complicit in these jaunts, packing clothes or wiring him a little money at predetermined locations.

In the early 1930s, the two brothers were living with their mom and her third husband in a tough section of Hell's Kitchen in Manhattan's Lower West Side. Mitchum routinely ditched school, preferring to visit the Museum of Natural History or read books at the New York City library. A favorite hangout was mobster Waxey Gordon's Riding Stables. It was soon back to Rising Sun, Delaware, where Mitchum learned to box from light-heavyweight champion Tommy Loughran at a church camp on the Indian River. He built his muscles by attaching a pole to a pair of suitcases and filling them with an increasing number of books as he gained strength in his various lifts. Mitchum attended school at Felton High, claiming to have completed the school's curriculum by the age of 14. He didn't stick around to graduate. Grown up beyond his years, in 1932 he had a summer job as a deckhand on the salvage ship *Sagamore* out of Fall River, Massachusetts, until the skipper found out he was underage.

Like many in the dirt-poor Depression Era America, Mitchum took to riding the rails to seek work and life experience. It was a decision of self-sacrifice as these extended journeys essentially meant he was not burdening his family with another mouth to feed. In his story "Desperate Youth," writer Daniel Ahern called young men like Mitchum "the wild boys of the road." On one early trip to see the Okefenokee Swamp, he jumped off a boxcar in Savannah, Georgia, only to be nabbed by police and arrested for vagrancy. He was sentenced to roadwork on a chain gang at Chatham County Camp No. 1 and began looking for any opportunity to get back home. The 15-year-old Mitchum managed to escape with the sound of gunshots whizzing past his ear. Traversing the swamps, mountains and woodlands of several states, the young fugitive finally made it home by hitchhiking to Delaware with blood poisoning and gangrene from his shackled leg threatening the loss of the lower limb. His mother nursed him back to health with homemade poultices. During his time recovering from the leg wound, he met young Dorothy Spence and told her one day he'd return for her. He was true to his word.

Mitchum made a total of nine trips across the United States by freight train during the years of the Great Depression seeking his own Manifest Destiny. Oftentimes with no definitive destination on his young mind, he hit every state there was to see under the stars. All the time he was riding the iron horse, he'd study the various characters he met in the hobo jungles. However, it wasn't always such an idyllic and romanticized existence. Mitchum had to stay one step ahead of the brutal sap-carrying rail yard bulls who sought to kick him off his latest train. Survival was never guaranteed, and many tramps perished: crushed under the force of the policeman's clubs, the train's wheels, or at the clawing hands of their fellow hoboes. The older 'bos would look to roll a young bum for anything of value in his pocket, and there was constant competition for the claim of an empty boxcar whose walls could cut the wind. Mitchum developed a sixth sense for danger and learned to live by his fists. He claimed he once skinned a squirrel for dinner with the sharp edge of a soup can lid and rolled his own marijuana cigarettes as the plant grew wild along the rails. Many nights he had to line his pant legs with newspapers to stay warm. One Christmas Eve found him huddled around a mesquite campfire with two strangers in Yuma, Arizona, after he was turned away from entering the state of California. It was moments like these that formed and toughened his character.

Initially Mitchum rode to see the scenery, but as he became older, he took on what jobs he could find. He drove a truck, operated a punch-press in Toledo, Ohio, picked fruit in Georgia, and mined coal in Libertyville, Pennsylvania. He was a mechanic's apprentice and a Civilian Conservation Corps ditch digger. There was more manual labor in Chico, California, and a brief period spent as a prizefighter in Sparks, Nevada, and Redding, California. Mitchum claimed 27 professional bouts with a few more amateur fights added while working as a bouncer in a West Coast bar. He landed at his sister's new home in Long Beach, California, briefly laboring as a longshoreman but generally relaxing at the beach. During this period, he worked on improving his physique, adding needed muscle to his impressive bone structure. Mitchum had especially broad shoulders, a narrow waist and trim hips. Standing close to 6'1", the now adult Mitchum weighed in at a lean and athletic 180 pounds.

With his sister's encouragement, Mitchum entertained the idea of becoming a writer and occasionally stepped onto the stage to act with the Long Beach Players Guild. His best showcase at Long Beach was playing mobster Duke Mantee, terrorizing a Black Mesa, Arizona, diner in a 1938 staging of Robert E. Sherwood's *The Petrified Forest*. The 1936 film version had gone a long way to elevating Humphrey Bogart's film career, and Mitchum likewise did justice to the part of the fugitive killer. There's even a connection to the Old West: The aged character Gramp Maple tells tales of encountering Apache Indians and once being shot at by Billy the Kid. Creative director Larry Johns, who later made his career in B-westerns and TV shows like *The Lone Ranger* and *Death Valley Days*, noticed Mitchum's acting potential immediately. Years later, he told Mitchum biographer George Eells, "He was born into it. I found he needed only the merest hint and he could find his way from there."

Some references suggest Mitchum picked up work as a film extra during this period along with his actor pal John "Jack" Shay. They would take turns wearing the same well-worn suit to casting calls. Alfred Hitchcock's *Saboteur* (1942) is acknowledged as a film where Mitchum did an uncredited walk-on. According to actor Robert Cornthwaite, Mitchum's first film work might have occurred a few years earlier on a western. In Paul Zollo's *Hollywood Remembered*, Cornthwaite says: "I never played myself in films. I always played characters. But if you have an attractive enough personality, you can do very well playing yourself. Robert Mitchum did that, and he could, because he was Robert Mitchum. He was a highly intelligent guy. I knew and worked with him on stage in 1940 before either of us were in pictures. He got a day's work in a western while we were working on that play."

Despite picking up solid notices for his stage performances, Mitchum was determined to be a writer. The idea of being a stage actor didn't hold any appeal outside of a place to meet girls. He hated makeup and didn't consider the acting vocation manly enough. Mitchum fashioned himself a writer in the adventurous tradition of Ernest Hemingway and Jack London, though he revealed a talent for dashing off quick and witty rhymes. He wrote ad copy, songs, plays, burlesque stories and pulp fiction. He even sold a few. For a while he shared a Hollywood apartment with a group of struggling actors led by Anthony Caruso, Steve Brodie, John "Dusty" James and Jack Shay that was dubbed El-Rancho Broke-O. When they weren't looking for work, they were hanging out in the local saloons and hip jazz clubs like the Hangover. Mitchum even hit the open road as a ghostwriter for traveling astrologist Carroll Righter.

Mitchum kept his promise to Dorothy Spence and returned to Delaware to marry her. He brought his new wife west with him and in 1941 they welcomed their first son, James (nicknamed Josh). The responsibility of being a husband and father prompted Mitchum to take a full-time factory job as a sheet metal worker at Lockheed Aircraft. This was a vital occupation at the outset of World War II. Mitchum worked the graveyard shift, and the odd hours created a case of chronic insomnia. When on the clock, Mitchum took No-Doz caffeine pills and chewed on tobacco laced with Tabasco sauce to keep himself awake. For a year, he couldn't get more than a few minutes of sleep at a time; his frayed nerve endings constantly astir. The whirring blades and buzzing noise of his Lockheed machine wore on his state of mind to the point that Mitchum felt himself physically going blind. On a doctor's recommendation, the heavy-lidded Mitchum was forced to quit the job at Lockheed. His sister suggested he give the motion picture business a try, reminding him that agent Paul Wilkins had once expressed interest in the rugged, unconventionally handsome Mitchum when he was on stage in Long Beach. A tired Mitchum decided he'd be happy for a while even being an extra in the movies, knowing full well that eventually his draft number would be called for the war effort now that he wasn't employed at Lockheed.

Agent Wilkins took one look at Mitchum's impressive physique, high cheekbones, cleft chin and razor blade–thin smile, then listened to the way his deep baritone negotiated the English language. He agreed to take Mitchum on as a client and asked if the young man had experience with horses. Mitchum told him about working on his family's Delaware farm. Wilkins sent Mitchum to the Gower Street office of Harry "Pop" Sherman, the producer of over 40 Hopalong Cassidy films starring William Boyd. They were based on author Clarence E. Mulford's popular novels and short stories. In 1942, Sherman moved his Hoppy outfit from Paramount to United Artists and increased his film budgets to between 80,000 and 100,000 dollars. The result was some of the best produced and remembered Cassidy films.

Wilkins fibbed to Sherman that Mitchum had busted broncos in Laredo, Texas. Mitchum played along, realizing that his hiring might depend on his familiarity with livestock. He expounded on his various rough-hewn jobs and his history of riding the rails. Sherman thought he looked sufficiently mean around the eyes and told him not to cut his hair or shave. He had a job playing what was known in the industry as a "dog heavy." Mitchum borrowed $55 from his grandfather's "coffin fund" and paid for his Screen Actors Guild card. He was about to head down a long Hollywood trail.

The Films: 1940s–1970s

Border Patrol (United Artists, 1943)

Cast: William Boyd (Hopalong Cassidy); Andy Clyde (California Carlson); Jay Kirby (Johnny Travers); Russell Simpson (Orestes Krebs); Claudia Drake (Inez); George Reeves (Don Enrique Perez); Duncan Renaldo (Commandante); Pierce Lyden (Loren); Bob Mitchum (Quinn); Cliff Parkinson (Barton); and Victor Adamson, Roy Bucko, John L. Cason, Bert Dillard, Joe Dominguez, Art Felix, Herman Hack, Earle Hodgins, Bob Kortman, Johnny Luther, Merrill McCormick, Leo J. McMahon, Charles Murphy, Bill Nestell, Hugh Prosser, Dan White, Henry Wills.

Crew: Harry Sherman (Producer); Lesley Selander (Director); Michael Wilson (Scriptwriter); Russell Harlan (Photographer); Irvin Talbot and Paul Sawtell (Music); Ralph Berger (Art Director); Earl Moser (Wardrobe); Sherman A. Rose (Editor); Glenn Cook (Assistant Director); Ted Wells, Clem Fuller, Henry Wills, Aline Goodwin, Leo McMahon, Cliff Lyons, Cliff Parkinson (Stunts); Mike Nimeth, Cliff Parkinson (Wranglers).

65 minutes; Released April 2, 1943

A trio of Texas Rangers led by Hopalong Cassidy (William Boyd) attempts to free a group of Mexicans being forced to work as slave labor in the Silver Bullet mine. Cassidy and his fellow Rangers (Andy Clyde, Jay Kirby) are captured and placed on trial by crooked town boss Orestes Krebs (Russell Simpson) for crimes they didn't commit. Krebs' jury consists of his own henchmen and hired guns (including "Bob" Mitchum as Quinn). At one point, juror Mitchum is called as a witness against Cassidy and his crew. Although the odds are stacked against them, Cassidy and his trailmates escape from Krebs' jail and prevail in a final shootout on the streets of the town. Among those who catch lead from Cassidy's six-shooter is Quinn.

Border Patrol was filmed on location in Kernville, California. The Kern River Valley was a popular site for low-budget B-westerns due to its rugged landscape, breathtaking scenic panoramas and proximity to Hollywood. Many a Tom Mix, Buck Jones and Bob Steele film was shot there, as well as the river-crossing scene of John Ford's classic *Stagecoach* (1939). Located approximately 160 miles north of Los Angeles, Kernville was home to the Kern River, a wild waterway bordered by large, imposing granite slabs and boulders. The river offered an assortment of rapids for scenes of cinematic adventure. Nestled in the southern Sierra Nevada range, Kernville lay at roughly 2500 feet elevation with summer temperatures approaching 100 degrees at midday. Death Valley and the Mojave Desert lay 90 miles to the East. Mornings were the best time to shoot in Kernville, but these quickie outfits used every available moment of sunlight they could. Oftentimes they were still going until sunset, placing the actors and camera wherever there was available natural light.

Upon his hire by "Pop" Sherman, Mitchum was instructed to ride a bus to Bakersfield and then travel 40 miles to the Kernville location via clapboard truck. When he arrived at the Hollywood bus stop with cardboard suitcase in hand, he came across a familiar sight: mustached western movie bad-man Pierce Lyden, one of Mitchum's former roommates at Anthony Caruso's El Rancho Broke-O on Highland Avenue. Former writer Mitchum explained to the surprised Lyden that he was now an actor. Lyden accepted that answer. Practically everyone in Los Angeles aspired to be rich and famous on the big screen. Mitchum, however, saw it as a job and one that he needed.

He'd bummed around enough to know the many things he didn't want to do, and he was now faced with the responsibility of providing for his family. He'd be a lowly extra if it paid a few bucks. "It sure as hell beat punching a time clock!" Mitchum told biographer Mike Tomkies of his new vocation. Mitchum signed a photo for Lyden claiming that "Pop" Sherman "illuminated my early path" while Lyden "witnessed my deflowering."

Determined to make a good initial impression, Mitchum had little idea what to expect from a western location film-set except what Lyden told him on their shared bus ride. He was relieved that he wasn't expected to provide a horse of his own. Making things uncomfortable for the cowboy neophyte, his arrival in Kernville was met with a somber mood by the cast and crew. Sixty-year-old actor-stuntman Charlie Murphy had died in Bakersfield on June 11, 1942, after falling under a wagon in the recently completed Hoppy film *Lost Canyon* (1942). Mitchum was essentially filling Murphy's spot in the Hoppy crew, so he could understand why he wasn't greeted with open arms. At least he had Pierce Lyden to pose questions to. Mitchum claimed he was given Murphy's blood-stained hat by wardrobe man Earl Moser, who was seen scraping dry, crusted gunk off the brim. Mitchum told *Rolling Stone* he made his movie debut in "a dead man's hat."

The crew sensed Mitchum might be a bit greener than he initially let on, so wrangler Cliff Parkinson gave him an unruly steed to test his mettle, a horse that had once allegedly killed a man in a rodeo. Mitchum recalled for the *Tucson Daily Citizen* that the horse had "hooves like rocking chairs" and a nasty disposition. This was no farm horse, and Mitchum was quickly thrown off. He gamely climbed back on, only to be thrown again. "That fool came back for me, his hooves wind-milling," Mitchum said. "I rolled around on the ground throwing rocks at that horse until he calmed down." Legend has it a frustrated Mitchum, feeling that his employment might be at stake, whacked the horse on its nose before mounting the saddle a third time. "I hit him smack in the snout with my gloved fist," he said. "And we got along together after that."

Once he was astride the animal and staying in the saddle, Mitchum's greatest concern became getting the horse to start and stop on time. All the cowboys watched his brave battle. Breaking in a new boy was a common source of amusement for the group, but their laughs soon gave way to a growing admiration. Many greenhorns couldn't pass muster. That wouldn't be the case with Mitchum. Stunt actor Parkinson, a rodeo veteran, took a liking to Mitchum's determination and gave needed tips, informing him that for the motion picture business he only needed to be able to look like he could ride. Naturally, the easier Mitchum sat in the saddle, the less skittish the horse became. Initially saddle-sore, the self-described "Connecticut Yankee" was soon riding around like a natural and able to effectively "fork a horse." In time, he became extremely knowledgeable about equines and the breeding of quarter-horses. Regarding his Hoppy apprenticeship, Mitchum told *The Evening Capital*, "By the time I was done with 'em, I was a real western actor with all his tricks."

Various versions of this story have surfaced over the years, many attributed to Mitchum himself changing details or adding embellishments. From John Ford's film *The Man Who Shot Liberty Valance* (1962) comes the line, "This is the West. When the legend becomes fact, print the legend!" In an interview with Charles Champlin, Mitchum claimed the horse threw him 40 feet in the air! In his autobiographical book *Them Ornery Mitchum Boys*, actor brother John Mitchum related a first-person account from William Boyd where the actor says the horse assigned to Mitchum was responsible for Charlie Murphy's death. Boyd verifies that Mitchum slugged the animal after being thrown, causing its eyes to roll back, and that Mitchum "rode him well for the rest of the picture."

Mitchum's son Chris has a version that is in line with Boyd's account. He says of his dad and the horse:

> When he arrived on set, they asked him if he could ride. "Sure," he said, having never been on a horse. The horse was skittish and wouldn't let him mount. He took it around a building, sided it up to the wall, hit it behind the ear, and said, "I need this job," and mounted. No problems the

Lobby card featuring (from left) Andy Clyde, Jay Kirby, William Boyd, Russell Simpson and a relaxed Mitchum making his film debut in *Border Patrol* (1943).

rest of the day. At the day's end when he turned in the horse, the wrangler said, "I'm surprised you could ride that horse.... That hat you're wearing, that was worn by the man that horse killed yesterday. That's why you got the job."*

Striking an animal might seem like cruelty on Mitchum's part, but sometimes it's a necessary resort for an especially mean-spirited horse. Even the great stuntman and rodeo champion Yakima Canutt admitted in his autobiography to arming himself with a bullwhip and a sawed-off pool cue when faced with the notorious stallion Rex when they made *The Devil Horse* (1926). Like Mitchum's horse, Rex had killed a man by stomping him to death. When Rex charged, Canutt defended himself, and the horse was soon manageable in his presence. "I hate to have to go to extremes like that," wrote Canutt. "But in truth, I think I saved a beautiful horse. Maybe a few actors. And probably myself." Mitchum eventually became the owner of several horse farms and developed a special relationship with his horses. In motion pictures he worked multiple times with legendary animal trainer Ralph Helfer, even developing a friendship with Helfer's lion Zamba when they were making the jungle adventure *Rampage* (1963). Helfer described Mitchum as "a natural animal lover."

On location, Mitchum learned a great deal from listening and hanging out with what had become known in movie circles as the Gower Gulch cowboys. "We worked with a tough bunch," Mitchum said in *Western Clippings*. "Real cowboys and some ex-outlaws. Those men could really ride. I could not." The corner

---

*Chris Mitchum (e-mail correspondence, May 2018).

of Gower Street and Sunset Boulevard in Hollywood was where cowboy extras congregated in front of Brewer's Saloon, hoping to be hired for the day by the nearby studios like Republic and Columbia. These included the Bucko brothers (Roy and Ralph), Ben Corbett, Art Dillard, Herman Hack, Blackjack Ward, Rube Dalroy, Gentleman Jack Evans and Hal Taliaferro, who used to star in cowboy films as Wally Wales. Pierce Lyden had grown up on a ranch in his native Nebraska, spent time cowboying, and even performed in a Clyde Beatty Wild West Show. Prolific character player Bob Kortman trained horses for the U.S. Cavalry before beginning as a heavy opposite cowboy star William S. Hart in silent films.

Many of these stuntmen and riding extras were veterans of numerous cattle drives and rodeo events. They had drifted into film work after mechanization and changes in transportation forced them out of their natural vocation. When working on a Hoppy film, they referred to themselves as the "Bar 20 Boys." In Kernville, nights were spent sharing whiskey around a campfire or in the nearby Bucket of Blood saloon. Accommodations included a shared toilet at the end of the hall at the bare-bones Dow Motel. Mitchum was quick to pick up on these real cowboys' mannerisms and style of speech. As a creative writer, he could identify with their rounds of cowboy poetry and humorous colloquialisms. He would use these characteristics to inform many of his own western portrayals in later years. In *Them Ornery Mitchum Boys*, John Mitchum wrote, "Bob met many of these men before I did and regaled me with exciting tales. I was thrilled whenever I would finally work with one of these obscure stalwarts."

Mitchum's assigned character Quinn is identified as a desperado wanted for robbery in three states. His first appearance on film is shooting a gun on horseback with the lines, "Come on! Let's get out of here!" In some trimmed versions of the film, his initial appearance becomes a bushwhack ambush of Cassidy and the star's white horse Topper (trained by Mike Nimeth) from rocks above. In the courtroom he is relaxed and nonchalant as he leans against the bar exhibiting no apparent camera shyness. When seated in a chair, he has his leg comfortably crossed and gives easy line readings that would come to define Mitchum's casual acting style. He appears completely natural and believable in this setting. When he stands beside Boyd's Cassidy in the saloon, there's a brief antagonistic bump between the actors, foreshadowing their future battles on camera. Boyd initially took umbrage at Mitchum's unscripted contact, asking director Lesley Selander after the take who the new guy thought he was. When Selander instructed Mitchum to stick to the script, the young actor apologized to Boyd. The star accepted and the two developed a quick professional friendship that would greatly benefit the young actor. Thirty years later, a grateful Mitchum told Boston TV's Channel 7 reporter Garry Armstrong, "Bill Boyd was a standup guy."*

In a shootout near the film's end, Mitchum is fatally shot by Hopalong and falls off a porch on Kernville's western street. Mitchum does his own stunt here, beginning from an initially crouched position and slowly guiding himself through the air to land on his back in the dirt as gently as possible. No doubt Pierce Lyden told him that actors who could do their own action worked more in these films because the producers didn't have to hire stuntmen to double them. As a star, Mitchum would become renowned for his willingness to do a great deal of his own stunt work. These B-westerns didn't bother with special effect squibs or fake blood on the wardrobe. In many ways, they were like children playing cowboys and Indians.

Border Patrol finished shooting in one week. At one point, it was titled *Missing Men*. During the filming, Mitchum had impressed director Selander. (The former assistant director, known for his professionalism and flair for action scenes, had helmed nearly 40 formula westerns in the previous six years.) Word got back to producer Sherman, and Mitchum was asked to appear in the movie outfit's next production, *Hoppy Serves a Writ* (known as *Texas Law* before release). It was an invitation he gladly accepted.

---

*Garry Armstrong (e-mail correspondence, August 2017).

Mitchum became a permanent fixture in that season's Hoppy films. In all, Mitchum made seven Hoppy flicks that were released in 1943. He didn't make Hopalong Cassidy films exclusively but freelanced around the Hollywood studios, taking what "day player" parts his agent Paul Wilkins could arrange. Mitchum worked constantly and had an incredible 19 films released in 1943 alone. The Hoppy films were essentially his training ground. He was on them for the duration of their location shoots and saw the size of his parts grow considerably in stature as the series progressed. "I got a hundred bucks a week and all the horse manure I could take home," he told Mike Tomkies.

Hoppy Serves a Writ (United Artists, 1943)

Cast: William Boyd (Hopalong Cassidy); Andy Clyde (California Carlson); Jay Kirby (Johnny Travers); Victor Jory (Tom Jordan); George Reeves (Steve Jordan); Jan Christy (Jean Hollister); Hal Taliaferro (Greg Jordan); Forbes Murray (Ben Hollister); Bob Mitchum (Rigney); Byron Foulger (Danvers); Earle Hodgins (Jim Belnap); Roy Barcroft (Colby); and Roy Bucko, Bob Burns, Ben Corbett, Art Felix, Herman Hack, Art Mix, Cliff Parkinson, Edward Peil, Sr.

Crew: George Archainbaud (Director); Harry Sherman (Producer); Gerald Geraghty (Screenwriter); Russell Harlan (Photographer); Irvin Talbot and Paul Sawtell (Music); Ralph Berger (Art Director); Earl Moser (Wardrobe); Sherman A. Rose (Editor); Glenn Cook (Assistant Director); Henry Wills, Clem Fuller, Cliff Parkinson, Warren Fiske (Stunts); Mike Nimeth, Cliff Parkinson (Wranglers).

67 minutes; Released in March 1943

Mitchum's second Hoppy filmed was the first to be released to theaters, so some references are correct calling it his film debut. Even Mitchum sometimes referred to it as his first film. Mitchum claimed the "Hoppies" were the only films of his own that he ever saw at the theater, no doubt due to initial curiosity. Mitchum was never one given to ego. He couldn't care less about seeing himself on the screen. "I punch in. I punch out," he told *Rolling Stone* in 1983. "I don't worry about the film." That detached, flippant attitude opened the shooting gallery for critics to take aim at him, with *Time* magazine's James Agee once famously describing Mitchum as having a "curious languor" about him. The truth was that when he was "punched in," few Hollywood actors were more professional or better equipped mentally and physically to handle the material. Professionalism became a point of pride for him.

There's not a lot of Mitchum to see in *Hoppy Serves a Writ*, considered one of the top Cassidy films. It's full of solid action and well-lensed outdoor scenery from future Academy Award–nominated cinematographer Russell Harlan, who went on to film such classics as *Red River* (1948), *The Big Sky* (1952) and *Rio Bravo* (1959). Character actor Victor Jory, cast as an Oklahoma Territory cattle rustler, is an excellent adversary for Texas lawman William Boyd. In addition to the presence of Mitchum, the film boasts top B-western heavy Roy Barcroft and future TV Superman George Reeves. Like Mitchum, young Reeves appeared in a variety of roles within the Hoppy series. At one point in the film, Mitchum lifts comic-relief sidekick Andy Clyde so that fellow bad guy Reeves can slug him, a cowardly action certain to rile youngsters in the audience. These "dog heavies" were so mean they'd even stoop so low as to kick a dog if there was one around, hence their name.

Mitchum recalled that the imposing Barcroft initially came across as "a mean dude" and "thought I was too pretty."* However, Barcroft was known in the business as a big softy and was beloved by the crews. He and Mitchum became friends on location and worked together again years later in Oregon on *The Way West* (1967). Barcroft talked up Mitchum in Bobby Copeland's biography on the veteran character actor:

> I remember I worked the first show Bob Mitchum ever worked in, which was a Hopalong Cassidy. We both did henchmen, and I think I was getting quite a bit more money than he was at the time. But he developed a real independent attitude, and I know when salaries used to be $250 a week for a leading man, he wouldn't take it; he wanted $300 a week. I know Republic tried to get him for $250, and he held out…. The next time I saw him over there, he was getting $7000 a week. Mitch was a tough guy and didn't let anything get

---

*Garry Armstrong (e-mail correspondence, August 2017).

William Boyd's Hopalong Cassidy (left) is about to encounter Mitchum's Rigney in *Hoppy Serves a Writ* (1943).

in his way. I remember one time he was having trouble with a horse. He slapped that horse right across the nose with his gun. When he was told he shouldn't do that, Mitch told the man that he was being paid to ride the horse, and he would slap the horse or anyone else who got in his way. That's just the way Mitch was, and I respected him for standing up for himself.

Henchman Mitchum (in the background and out of focus) was witness to a blistering saloon fight scene between Boyd and the dastardly Jory. Star Boyd used a stunt double for the brawl, but Jory did all his own fighting. Screen action was a point of pride for tough guy Jory, a former boxing and wrestling champion. He had done so many movie fights that he could enact a bout of fisticuffs for the camera as well as established stuntmen. This greatly aided the filming of his fights and made him a popular bad guy with producers and audiences. Because of Jory performing his own

fight scenes, newcomer Mitchum erroneously thought only the star of the film was afforded a stunt double. When it came time to do his own fights in the Hoppy series, Mitchum took Jory's lead and performed his own action, unaware that he could have asked the director for a stuntman and saved himself some bruises. "I was big, and it looked like I could handle myself in a brawl," he explained to Cork Millner.

At one point in the film, a bearded Mitchum hides behind a cabin's door with his gun drawn, waiting to ambush Boyd's Cassidy upon his entry. A perceptive Boyd shoves the door open and knocks Mitchum down. Mitchum has a few brief lines of dialogue but is visible until the end of the picture. He is once again shot dead by Boyd in the climactic shootout. Mitchum shocked the cast and crew with his improvised death. He dramatically rolled off a tall boulder and took a dangerous ten-foot fall into the rocks below. He managed to protect his face from hitting a small boulder beneath him by falling on his hand, but not so that it would look like anything except a body going slack in a dead fall. The stunt surprised director George Archainbaud and the actors he was working with, who would no doubt have alerted him to established safeguards and stunt pads. Mitchum could easily have broken his neck or cracked his skull. They didn't need another fatality after Charlie Murphy.

Mitchum continued to absorb the experience of being a motion picture cowboy and *de facto* stuntman. He had a great respect for the cowboy culture and was more than willing to learn the western character. He shared the cowboys' whiskey and sat with them at their poker table, watching their interactions. Calm and observant, he was a quick study and a hard worker who made the assimilation look easy. He had spent his entire life up to this point fitting into different environments for his own survival. The boots and gun rig with iron hanging against his leg began to feel comfortable, the scruffy stubble on his face less itchy. His natural athleticism aided his broadening skill-set. When he wasn't busy filming, he'd practice his fast-draw, roping and riding skills. "The horse was a crucial accessory to his film apprenticeship as a desperado bit-player," wrote *Sight and Sound*. In no time at all, he was passing himself off as one of the gang. He found he enjoyed the experience. "It was very pleasant company, the old Pop Sherman–Bill Boyd Hopalong Cassidy group," Mitchum told interviewer Jerry Roberts.

Part of his come-and-go absence throughout the film might have been calculated by Mitchum, who was being paid for his time regardless if he was directly in front of the camera or not. Career-minded young actors want to be seen on the screen, especially if it's in the same camera shot as the star of the film. Mitchum, however, took an opposite approach and preferred to observe the action being shot from the sidelines. He told Johnny Carson on a 1978 *Tonight Show* appearance: "I learned when I first started with Bill Boyd on the Hopalong Cassidys that as long as I stayed away from Bill Boyd—a good distance from the star—when they came in on sort of a medium close-up, I could be goofing off 'over there' because I'm not in the shot. And I tried to maintain that all the way through."

Although he might have laid claim to "goofing off," he was no doubt taking the whole experience in. Throughout his career, Mitchum downplayed his own behind-the-scenes effort, but insiders would reveal he was one of the hardest workers in the business. During the making of *Hoppy Serves a Writ* in Kernville and Lone Pine, Mitchum was given a better opportunity to observe Boyd, paying attention to the veteran actor's underplaying and camera technique. Boyd, a silent film star for Cecil B. DeMille, was in his 40s with white hair and a build that was less than imposing, yet audience attention was riveted to him when he was onscreen due to his all-black outfit and considerable screen presence. While he didn't perform a great deal of action (especially any involving horses), Boyd hit his marks and didn't bump into the furniture. His voice was low enough that other characters had to hang on his every word to hear him. He came across very well on screen, and Mitchum made mental notes for his own eventual screen image and technique. There wasn't a lot of chance to make an impact outside of his crazy death scene, but what he did do decked out in his nondescript rolled-up jeans, plaid shirt and light neckerchief, he did well. Regarding individual demands made upon his person by the film, Mitchum told interviewer Dick Cavett in 1971 his part was "all beard, very little dialogue."

The Leather Burners (United Artists, 1943)

Cast: William Boyd (Hopalong Cassidy); Andy Clyde (California); Jay Kirby (Johnny); Victor Jory (Dan Slack); George Givot (Sam Bucktoe); Ellanora Needles (Sharon Longstreet); Bobby Larson (Bobby Longstreet); George Reeves (Harrison Brooke); Hal Taliaferro (Lafe); Forbes Murray (Bart); Bob Mitchum (Randall); and Victor Adamson, Roy Bucko, Bob Burns, Jack Casey, Tommy Coats, Art Felix, Kit Guard, Herman Hack, Chick Hannan, Bob Kortman, Merrill McCormick, Art Mix, George Morrell, Bill Nestell, Cliff Parkinson, Christian Rub, George Sorrell.

Crew: Joseph Henabery (Director); Harry Sherman (Producer); Jo Pagano (Scriptwriter); Bliss Lomax (Story); Russell Harlan (Photographer); Irvin Talbot and Samuel Kaylin (Music); Ralph

Berger (Art Director); Earl Moser (Wardrobe); Carrol Lewis (Editor); Glenn Cook (Assistant Director); Frosty Royce, Tommy Coats, Cliff Parkinson, Henry Wills, Clem Fuller, Jack Casey (Stunts); Mike Nimeth, Cliff Parkinson (Wranglers).

66 minutes; Released May 28, 1943

Hoppy and cohorts take on a gang of cattle rustlers hiding their stolen wares in the Buckskin Mine. There are few surprises in a storyline provided by prolific western novelist Bliss Lomax (aka Harry Sinclair Drago). This routine Hoppy adventure concludes with a shootout and cattle stampede through a mine shaft. Unbilled in the opening credits, Mitchum's initial appearance as the character Randall hinted at a significant role. He is paired with villainous Victor Jory as the "brains heavy" outlines his plans. This was perhaps a test by the filmmakers to see how the promising Mitchum fared against an established actor like Jory. Star Bill Boyd reportedly bet Mitchum he'd blow his dialogue in his first attempt. Mitchum accepted Boyd's bet and nailed his lines in one take to collect.

Mitchum comes off well. He's not afforded any more generous screen moments during the film, but his strong baritone was already lending itself to authoritatively barking orders among the other henchmen. This time out, Mitchum is clad in a lighter shirt with accompanying hat and a dark vest. He had gained familiarity with his gun belt rig and looks entirely comfortable in the part. He was gaining notice.

He earned the respect of fellow heavy Jory, who was quoted in *Western Clippings* detailing the challenges inherent in making outdoor action pictures:

> The best actors in pictures play in westerns. They have to be good because perfect timing and spacing is required in the various scenes. They have to learn how to deliver dialogue from the back of a horse and under unusual conditions. I have never worked in a picture with so many good fellows, both men and women, as I have discovered in the Harry Sherman unit. Everybody is pleasant and there's not a laggard in the outfit. It's just one happy family and now I understand why so many people are anxious to work with "Pop: Sherman."

Filming of the Hoppy pictures was fast-paced but with a sense of fun. Everyone got along and pitched in to get the job done. The Gower Gulch gang could laugh at a new cowboy like Mitchum trying to stay on his horse as easily as they could a classically trained actor rushing in a haste to get dialogue before the camera. "I remember a picture I was doing with Andy Clyde, who played Hopalong Cassidy's sidekick," Mitchum told Joseph DiMona. "The only area of sunlight left at the end of the day had a big muddy ditch in it, and Clyde, who was doing the scene, fell right into the ditch. He stood up, brushing the mud and glop off him, and said with dignity, 'This isn't the theater.'"

In *Hollywood Corral,* Don Miller wrote about Mitchum in the Hoppy programmers: "Even cloaked in anonymity, there was something about him—his manner, the unusual structure of his face—that attracted and held the attention." It's hard to believe that Mitchum is in his mid-20s here. As Kirk Honeycutt of *The New York Times* notes, "His face already looked older, tough, broody, hardened by experience." Character actor George Givot explained the appeal further, commenting to Mitchum biographer George Eells regarding Mitchum on *Leather Burners*:

> He was a handsome guy, but he photographed better than he appeared on the set. He had photographic charisma that few people seem to have, and if they have that, they don't need much else. That's the secret of screen success—to have that certain something that makes people look at you when you're doing nothing, watch you, remember you and wait for you to come back when you're off screen. Even in small parts in cheapie productions, he had that.

Director Joseph Henabery's career stretched back to D.W. Griffith's *Birth of a Nation* (1915) where Henabery portrayed Abraham Lincoln. Jory and George Reeves had important roles in the MGM classic *Gone with the Wind* (1939) but were slumming in the eyes of the industry by being reduced to B-westerns. Considering William Boyd's past as a major DeMille star, Mitchum took stock regarding how quickly and to what depth one's fortunes could fall in the business. He had no illusions about attaining stardom in the film industry. He simply wanted to do a professional job and collect his paycheck. Looking back at this film, Hopalong

Cassidy chronicler Francis M. Nevins calls its subsidiary casting of Jory, Reeves and Mitchum "especially rich."

In addition to the incredibly scenic rock formations in the Alabama Hills of Lone Pine, *Leather Burners* features location work at Bronson Caves and Bronson Canyon in Los Angeles' Griffith Park. That's where the climactic shootout in the mine occurs. Western fans will identify the former construction quarry as the same location used for the climax of John Ford's *The Searchers* (1956). Filming at this sea level locale provided a cooler climate for the cast and crew to work in, as well as a chance to sleep in their own beds at night. In comparison, toil in the arid high desert of Lone Pine could be excruciating in the late summer heat. Come evening, Mitchum and the cowboys felt the need to cool off with a round of well-earned beers. At roughly 3700 feet elevation, the dry, volcanic rock and granite badlands of the Alabama Hills stood in stark contrast to the foreboding Sierra Nevada peaks and Inyo Mountain range surrounding them. Within the Hills, one could look in any direction and see no sign of civilization. Regarding the memorable Lone Pine movie location, Mitchum told Charles Champlin of *The Los Angeles Times*: "I remember the Dow Hotel and a place up the street we called the Bucket of Blood. Don't know what its real name was or whether it's still there, but we kept it busy.... Once we shot on the Alkali desert east of Lone Pine. And the heat! Unbearable, unforgiving. The cowboys would toss a handful of dust at the camera as they rode by. It took four hours to clean the damned thing, so you could sit in the shade of a cactus for a while."

Colt Comrades (United Artists, 1943)

Cast: William Boyd (Hopalong Cassidy); Andy Clyde (California); Jay Kirby (Johnny); Lois Sherman (Lucy Whitlock); Victor Jory (Jeb Hardin); George Reeves (Lin Whitlock); Douglas Fowley (Joe Brass); Herbert Rawlinson (Varney); Earle Hodgins (Wildcat Willy); Bob Mitchum (Dirk Mason); and Ralph Bucko, Roy Bucko, Tex Cooper, Jim Corey, Art Dillard, William Gould, Fred Kohler, Jr., Cliff Lyons, Jack Mulhall, Tex Phelps, George Plues, Dewey Robinson, Phil Schumacher, Jack Shannon, Russell Simpson, George Sowards, Hal Taliaferro, Blackjack Ward, Henry Wills, Bill Wolfe.

Crew: Lesley Selander (Director); Harry Sherman (Producer); Michael Wilson (Screenwriter); Bliss Lomax (Story); Russell Harlan (Photographer); Irvin Talbot and Paul Sawtell (Music); Ralph Berger (Art Director); Earl Moser (Wardrobe); Fred W. Berger (Editor); Glenn Cook (Assistant Director); Dick Johnston (Production Manager); Ted Wells, Clem Fuller, Cliff Lyons, Henry Wills, George Sorrell, Jack Shannon, George Plues (Stunts); Mike Nimeth (Wrangler).

67 minutes; Released June 18, 1943

Outlaw Dirk Mason (Mitchum) opens the film at Lone Pine Station, killing freight carrier Hal Taliaferro and stealing a mail pouch. With a $5000 wanted dead or alive price on his head, he's chased non-stop by Texas Ranger Hopalong Cassidy and his sidekicks California and Johnny (Andy Clyde and Jay Kirby). Desperate, Mitchum seeks sanctuary with chief "brains heavy" Victor Jory but is rebuked. Jory attempts to shoot Mitchum to silence him, but the outlaw escapes. Mitchum is finally cornered in a saloon and felled by a Cassidy punch. This leads to conflict with the hotheaded locals led by Jory cohort Douglas Fowley, who wants to immediately string Mitchum up. The wily Mitchum gets hold of a gun and is shot down by Fowley. Mitchum takes a face-first fall to the floor, one of the trickier stunts to execute as he offers a quick, nearly imperceptible bracing with his palms and takes the brunt of the drop on his lead shoulder with his head turned.

Mitchum bites the dust before the film reaches the eight-minute mark, but he has made a significant impression in his brief screen time and holds his own in a stare-down with master villain Jory. This was Mitchum's fourth Hoppy feature to be released to theaters in less than three months. The Saturday afternoon B-western matinees were extremely popular with the juvenile market. The kids loved their heroes and loathed the bad guys. They were starting to notice Mitchum lurking in the background of a saloon or falling before the camera in exciting action scenes. He might not have generated catcalls like beloved cowboy heavy Charlie "Blackie" King, but he was on his way. In his *Biographical Dictionary of Film*, David Thomson writes of Mitchum: "For a big man he is immensely agile, capable of unsmiling humor, menace, stoicism, and above all, of watching other people as though he were waiting to make up his mind."

Leading lady Lois Sherman (better known as Teddi Sherman) was the daughter of producer Harry Sherman. She later distinguished herself as a screenwriter of western TV shows and films like *Four Faces West* (1948). Teddi has earned a place in Mitchum lore regarding his Hollywood discovery as told by veteran Paramount producer A.C. Lyles on the Mitchum TV documentary *Hollywood Greats*. Lyles said,

> Bob was hitchhiking or something. And Teddi Sherman gave Bob a lift some place and told "Pop," her father, about this wonderful handsome fellow that she met who should be a big movie star in things. "Pop" got in touch with him and brought him in, and that was the start of how he got into Hopalong Cassidy pictures.... Bob had that quality. He could have stood on the corner of Hollywood and Vine and something would have happened for him that would have brought him into stardom.

Because these Hoppy films were geared for the younger set, there were few on-screen deaths that would make the kids squeamish. By film's end, Hoppy had usually managed to round up the bad guys with a minimum of bullets fired. Mitchum, however, was somewhat of an anomaly in the Hoppy universe. His hardcase characters wound up pumped full of lead. He had suffered on-screen deaths in *Border Patrol* and *Hoppy Serves a Writ,* and now he was a goner in the opening reel of *Colt Comrades*. The fatalistic aspect of Mitchum's low-rung Hoppy characters hinted at the complex western screen image that would soon follow. John Wayne played mythic heroes, and fans could count his on-screen deaths on one hand. Mitchum played real men treading dangerous territory. They were apt to end up a denizen of Boot Hill by picture's end. Mitchum biographer John Belton wrote, "Wayne has to climb down from Mt. Rushmore to become human. Mitchum's climb is always upward: He is forever mortal."

Mitchum's *Colt Comrades* wardrobe looks like the outfit he wore in *Border Patrol*. There's the same light shirt, slightly darker vest, black kerchief and dark chaps. He has managed to get out of "a dead man's hat," as Charlie Murphy's

As Dirk Mason with a bounty on his head in *Colt Comrades* (1943).

blood-stained headpiece has been swapped for the lighter Stetson he wore in *Leather Burners*. These films were essentially budget westerns, and if it fit, wardrobe man Earl Moser saw you wore it again and again. Pierce Lyden revealed that many of the Gower Gulch players provided their own togs. The western clothes look good on Mitchum. Not too tight or baggy, they adhere to his rugged physique with functionality. They appear to be the outfit and gear of a man who would ride the range, ready for a fight at a moment's notice. Toward the end of his career, Mitchum poked humor at his screen image, telling *Parade* magazine that the only thing he changed in 50 years in Hollywood was his socks and his underwear.

Because they were his start, these economy oaters held a special place in what became Mitchum's later cynical worldview. Although he had little formal education, Mitchum held the equivalent of a master's degree in the school of hard knocks. He was blessed with a photographic memory and a highly capable brain that could decipher and comprehend complex thought. He was said to possess an IQ of 160. Mitchum had already tried every hardscrabble job and quickly came to appreciate earning a decent wage for playing a kid's game for the cameras. He reflected on western films in a 1971 French TV interview:

> I enjoy westerns because they're very simple…. Playing cowboys and Indians out in the fresh air. Free lunch, you know. It's better than working, I discovered that. They're very singularly uncomplicated. Sometimes they're physically demanding and occasionally physically hazardous because after all, falling from horses and jumping from trains and back again can sometime be a little uncomfortable. But yeah, I like it. It's uncomplicated, and as I say it's a good outdoor exercise. I enjoy that.

The Lone Star Trail (Universal, 1943)

Cast: Johnny Mack Brown (Blaze Barker); Tex Ritter (Fargo Steele); Fuzzy Knight (Angus McAngus); Jennifer Holt (Joan Winters); George Eldredge (Doug Ransom); Michael Vallon (Jonathan Bentley); Harry Strang (Sheriff Waddell); Earle Hodgins (Mayor Cyrus Jenkins); Jack Ingram (Dan Jason); Bob Mitchum (Ben Slocum); Ethan Laidlaw (Steve Bannister); Jimmy Wakely Trio (Musicians); and Victor Adamson, Cyrus Bond, Bob Burns, William Desmond, Denver Dixon, Billy Engle, Fred Graham, Scotty Harrel, Reed Howes, Carl Matthews, Art Mix, Eddie Parker, Bob Reeves, Henry Roquemore.

Crew: Ray Taylor (Director); Oliver Drake (Producer and Writer); William Sickner (Photographer); Hans J. Salter (Music); Jack Otterson (Art Director); R.A. Gausman (Set Decorator); Ray Snyder (Editor); Melville Shyer (Assistant Director); Carl Matthews, Fred Graham, Eddie Parker, Tom Steele (Stunts).

58 minutes; Released August 6, 1943

After his early exposure to the acting business in the Hoppy series, Mitchum began playing a wide variety of bits and supporting parts at all the major studios. Among his 19 titles released in 1943: nearly half of them westerns, plus the war films *Aerial Gunner, We've Never Been Licked, Corvette K-225, Cry "Havoc," Minesweeper, Doughboys in Ireland* and *Gung Ho!* While playing a soldier in *The Human Comedy* (1943), Mitchum sang a snippet of Roy Rogers' popular cowboy song "The Last Roundup" (aka "Git Along Little Doggie").

One of his showiest roles of the year was in Universal's *The Lone Star Trail* where he played Ben Slocum, yet another western bad guy. This time he wasn't a henchman but an actual mustached "dress heavy" responsible for framing rancher Johnny Mack Brown. A "dress heavy" was the well-attired banker, businessman or town boss whose overwhelming greed sets a plot in motion. This film's stars Johnny Mack Brown and Tex Ritter were popular performers at the Saturday matinee, and the exposure helped solidify Mitchum's growing reputation.

Filmed in September 1942, *The Lone Star Trail* pairs Brown and Ritter to double the box office draw by appealing to fans of both actors. Former University of Alabama football star Brown handled the action workload as a man trying to clear his name but singing cowboy Ritter wasn't afraid to get his hands dirty in a saloon brawl. The film boasts a major minute-and-a-half fight that fans still talk about today. Brown and undercover U.S. Marshal Ritter go up against bad guys Mitchum, Jack Ingram and Eddie Parker in a humdinger that *The Hollywood Reporter* called "a whale of a scrap." Ingram and Parker were prolific actor-stuntmen. Parker was best known for doubling John Wayne in the epic fight in *The Spoilers* (1942) while Ingram went on to become the proprietor of the popular western movie location Ingram Ranch. In his encyclopedic book *The Western,* author Phil Hardy writes, "A big plus is the film's finest sequence, a lengthy, realistic scrap between Brown and Mitchum that leaves Mitchum on the floor and Brown bruised and bloodied." Herb Fagen's *Encyclopedia of Westerns* states, "This was one of the first films to give real notice to Robert Mitchum, and his fight scene with Brown is a real gem." According to the studio retrospective *The Best of Universal,* the film is "well remembered by western buffs thanks to the savage barroom brawl between Brown and a young villain named Robert Mitchum." Biographer Alvin H. Marill declared that the fight "ranks among the very best in the eyes of B-western enthusiasts." Boyd Magers' cowboy journal *Western Clippings* ranks it among the "great screen fights," and this author includes it in the book *Classic Movie Fight Scenes.*

The film concludes with Mitchum on the losing end of another tussle with the stars. Mitchum was assigned a stunt double for these fights: the legendary Tom Steele, a top fight man who unfortunately looks little like Mitchum. Steele doubled B-western stars Allan

"Rocky" Lane and Wild Bill Elliott on many Republic films. The fact that cult figure Steele is easily identifiable to fans of the genre makes his presence more apparent and detracts slightly from the film's blazing action sequences. Being asked to step off-camera during a movie fight scene was new for Mitchum, but he quickly set aside any sense of macho pride. He realized that when he was on the bottom of a pile of stuntmen, he was taking a job away from one of them and they'd all be happier and a little less rough with him in the close-ups if he let them do their job. Mitchum can still be seen slugging away for a good deal of the action save the moments when he goes over the top of a bar or a table. These were stunts he proved more than willing to perform in the Hoppy series, but if it was Steele's job, then Mitchum was happy to let him do it. *Lone Star Trail*'s outdoor location was Corriganville, a 1500-acre movie ranch in Simi Valley, California, owned by B-western star Ray "Crash" Corrigan.

Mitchum was developing and cultivating his image, finding that he excelled as a glowering menace. Audiences began identifying favorably with his volatile presence and squint-eyed, sideways glances. "I came at a fortunate time," he explained in David Downing's book *Robert Mitchum*. "They wanted ordinary guys who looked ugly, and there I was, all broken up." He described his screen image to the *Deseret News* as "dissolute, brutal, untrustworthy, a general ne'er-do-well." The nostalgic journal *Favorite Westerns* noted: "The unique screen style and presence of Robert Mitchum would never place the actor in the conventional western star category. No viewer would confuse Mitchum's threatening anti-hero persona with white hat Saturday matinee heroes riding the straight and narrow. However, Mitchum westerns rank among his finest efforts."

Lobby card featuring (from left) mustached bad guy Mitchum, Tex Ritter, Johnny Mack Brown, Jennifer Holt, Harry Strang and George Eldredge in the Universal B-western *The Lone Star Trail* (1943).

In director John Badham's Hollywood memoir *I'll Be in My Trailer,* Mitchum revealed his fondness for playing western movie black hats:

> I loved playing villains, especially as a young actor. A villain doesn't get cut out of the picture and he generally has a contract that runs through the course of the movie. If the hero and the screenwriter and the director do any kind of half-ass job, your work as a villain is almost done with just a little effort on your part. Plus, more women are attracted to the bad guys than they'll admit. It's good pay for basically showing up and acting like you would if someone threw a bucket of water on you while you were sleeping.

Mitchum's presence as the new gun in town was creating whispers behind the scenes of these modest westerns. As he became known within the industry, there's proof the potential for stardom was already being noted by those he encountered on film sets. Mitchum himself didn't have any illusions of fame and fortune. He was simply trying to get by and provide for his family. He might have been picking up the occasional shift at Lockheed even as he started making waves in his western picture career. Singing cowboy Jimmy Wakely appeared in *Lone Star Trail* with his music trio a year before launching his own heroic B-western career at Monogram. In David Rothel's *Those Singing Cowboys,* Wakely remembered Mitchum's arrival upon the set:

> I heard this booming voice. Oliver Drake was doing the picture and he had brought in this actor who was working at Lockheed all night. It was Bob Mitchum. I always said that's where Mitch got those sleepy eyes, working swing shift over at Lockheed and making westerns during the day. He was playing heavies then—third heavies; he was not even number one heavy.

Wakely sensed something special about Mitchum and began telling people the new guy was going to be a big star.

Beyond the Last Frontier (Republic, 1943)

Cast: Eddie Dew (Johnny Revere); Smiley Burnette (Frog Millhouse); Lorraine Miller (Susan Cook); Bob Mitchum (Trigger Dolan); Harry Woods (Big Bill Hadley); Ernie Adams (Sarge Kincaid); Richard Clarke (Steve Kincaid); Charles Miller (Major Cook); Kermit Maynard (Clyde Barton); and Rudy Bowman, Ralph Bucko, Wheaton Chambers, Art Dillard, Curly Dresden, Eddie Juaregui, Jack Kirk, Cactus Mack, Kansas Moehring, Frank O'Connor, Post Park, Jack Rockwell, George Sowards, Al Taylor, Ted Wells, Henry Wills.

Crew: Howard Bretherton (Director); Louis Gray (Producer); John K. Butler and Morton Grant (Screenplay); Bud Thackery (Photographer); Mort Glickman (Music); Russell Kimball (Art Director); Charles Craft (Editor); Derwin Abrahams (Second Unit Director); Tom Steele, Ted Wells, Art Dillard, Eddie Juaregui, Kermit Maynard, Post Parks, Henry Wills (Stunts).

60 minutes; Released August 18, 1943

Eddie Dew launched a short-lived western series for Republic as the largely forgotten cowboy character John Paul Revere. The film itself is now considered a rarity and difficult to come by, though it's rewarding for fans of Mitchum as he has a large supporting part and makes the most of it. Fourth-billed, he dominates the proceedings as main heavy Harry Woods' hired gun, chosen to infiltrate the Texas Rangers to unmask the spy in their own gang (Dew). Mitchum decides he likes the way the Rangers do business and is malleable to joining up with the lawmen. Veteran B-western director Howard Bretherton, who helmed the earliest Hopalong Cassidy films, was quick to catch on to Mitchum's ease in front of Bud Thackery's camera and showcases him to advantage. There's plenty of fights, chases and saddle falls involving Mitchum. He even guns down a rattlesnake.

Beyond the Last Frontier lacks the technical polish seen in Mitchum's Hoppy films, but it's a more than passable B-western filler. Filmed in the summer of 1943 at Corriganville, the Walker Ranch near Placerita Canyon in Newhall, and Iverson Ranch in Chatsworth, it failed to develop a connection between the star Dew and the paying audiences. Dew made so little impact that when he changes costumes midway through the film, it's hard to recognize him at first. Part of the problem with Dew is that he lacked sufficient leading man charisma and was overshadowed in his debut film by the film's heavies, as well as his own comic sidekick Smiley Burnette.

Phil Hardy noted in *The Western,* "What attention Burnette didn't bag went to Mitchum as the reformed baddie." Boyd Magers of *Western Clippings* opined, "Good/badman Robert Mitchum walked away with the honors in this film. It's a real star-turn for the sleepy-eyed actor. It may be Dew's debut as a cowboy star, but it's Mitchum's movie all the way." In *Hollywood Corral,* Don Miller wrote, "Dew was hamstrung by the cumbersome screenplay, and to add insult to injury, a supporting character, a good-bad type, attracted more notice than did the star. The role was played by the intriguingly odd-looking Bob Mitchum, he of the Hopalong Cassidy heavies." According to *Western Movies'* Michael R. Pitts, "This one fails to do much other than have the hero take a backseat to villain Bob Mitchum."

At the time of the film's release, the *Motion Picture Herald* wrote, "Mitchum's presence is far more appealing than the star's," and *Motion Picture Daily* noted that Dew was "overshadowed by the comedy of Smiley Burnette and the workmanlike job of Bob Mitchum." *The Hollywood Reporter* stated, "Bob Mitchum shows up well in the supporting cast as an adventurous young gunman who finally swings the balance to the Rangers." After one more film, *Raiders of Sunset Pass* (1943), Republic pulled the plug on Dew and replaced him in the series with former Three Mesquiteers star Bob Livingston.

Mitchum's character Trigger Dolan claims, "I can shoot the eyebrows off a coyote at 50 yards," leading to his recruitment by gunrunner Harry Woods. Mitchum assumes the identity of his friend Steve Kincaid (Richard Clarke), a newly signed Ranger captured by outlaw Woods. Mitchum agrees to get the information on the Rangers' inside man under the condition his friend Kincaid is safely released. Once inside the Ranger compound, Mitchum plays straight man to Burnette's antics, even garnering a laugh or two himself with his hip jargon like "No, soap, dope," "So long, sis," "That's a hot one" and "Not so fast, suckers." He knocks out Burnette with a single punch, so he can chase Dew on horseback in one of the film's best action moments. Mitchum is seen riding hell-bent for leather in profile before Dew escapes by jumping off a cliff into a lake. Continuing to play both sides, the savvy Mitchum is wise to Dew's identity and unveils him to veteran bad guy Woods. Mitchum eventually has a change of heart during the action climax when Woods won't release the real Kincaid. Woods has

Early publicity photograph as Trigger Dolan in Republic's *Beyond the Last Frontier* (1943).

henchman Kermit Maynard (himself a former B-western star) put a bullet in Mitchum's back, but Mitchum rises wearily, claiming, "He just winged me." Mitchum has his arm in a sling for the final scene, where Dew and Burnette recommend he be allowed into the Rangers while female lead Lorraine Miller bats her eyelashes.

With the increased responsibilities of his parts in *Lone Star Trail* and *Beyond the Last Frontier* came a healthy uptick in Mitchum's required dialogue. It was at this juncture in his career that audiences became aware of the great Mitchum voice. There was nothing else like this low, smooth, richly hypnotic rumble being spoken on the screen. And when needed, Mitchum could convincingly make it *boom* like a crack of thunder on the plains. The voice sounded entirely authentic to the western period save for the hip slang heard here. He didn't like being caught having done so, but the well-read Mitchum always did his homework. In *Western Films,* Brian Garfield wrote, "Among actors who have appeared frequently in westerns, there are surprisingly few who possess a good range of accents and speech patterns, and there is only one who excels: Robert Mitchum."

By branching out from the Hoppy films,

Mitchum continued to establish his credentials with audiences as a western actor specializing in playing bad guys. And this was no run-of-the-mill "dog heavy" but a man with a strong moral compass who finds himself on the wrong side of a fight. Three-dimensional heavies exhibiting internal conflict as well as physical charisma are always interesting, especially when played by an actor on the rise like Mitchum. Cerebral and guarded, his character tastes his words before spitting them out. In hindsight it's easy to be swayed by the power of his personality and performance, seeing the star that he would eventually become.

Mitchum's presence in this and *Lone Star Trail* opened eyes. His career was one to watch. Had he continued mining the bad guy vein in B-westerns, it's highly likely he'd still be considered a cult personality by genre aficionados. Mitchum wrote in *Modern Screen* that he "planned my career as a character actor, wrestling with beards and dialects."

Bar 20 (United Artists, 1943)

Cast: William Boyd (Hopalong Cassidy); Andy Clyde (California); George Reeves (Lin Bradley); Dustine Farnum (Marie Stevens); Victor Jory (Mark Jackson); Douglas Fowley (Slash); Betty Blythe (Mrs. Stevens); Bob Mitchum (Richard Adams); Francis McDonald (Quint Rankin); Earle Hodgins (Tom); and Roy Bucko, Bob Burns, Art Felix, Kansas Moehring, Cliff Parkinson, George Plues, Henry Wills.

Crew: Lesley Selander (Director); Harry Sherman (Producer); Morton Grant, Norman Houston and Michael Wilson (Screenplay); Russell Harlan (Photographer); Irvin Talbot (Music); Ralph Berger (Art Director); Earl Moser (Wardrobe); Carrol Lewis (Editor); Glenn Cook (Assistant Director); Ted Wells, Clem Fuller, Henry Wills, George Plues (Stunts); Mike Nimeth, Cliff Parkinson (Wranglers).

54 minutes; Released October 1, 1943

Producer Harry Sherman and director Lesley Selander began experimenting with the Hoppy formula for the last of the 1942–1943 filming season. Sidekick Jay Kirby was dropped, replaced by George Reeves. Their greatest deviation from the norm was to take the promising Mitchum out of his villain clothes and see how he cleaned up as a good guy. The *Bar 20* plot has cattle buyer Hoppy uncovering a scheme to rob earnest young land owner Mitchum. Cast against type as the second romantic lead, Mitchum is clean-shaven and wears a suit and a white hat. He is engaged to Dustine Farnum but set up to be robbed by his friend and best man Victor Jory (at his most conniving). Mitchum is more suspicious of interloper Hoppy and his friends. Tension is introduced between Mitchum and Reeves, who fancies Farnum himself. At one point, Mitchum is dropped by a straight left fist from Reeves. Mitchum later saves Hoppy's life and marries Farnum. The film was made in Lone Pine's Alabama Hills, an impressive backdrop.

Mitchum recalled that two Hoppies would be made back to back over a 21-day period. There would be five days in the studio on the first picture, followed by location shooting for both films, then back to the studio to do the interior shots of the second film. Such a breakneck pace required talent in front of and behind the camera. Sherman hired professional production staff members and actors who didn't waste time between set-ups. Character actor Douglas Fowley was a versatile pro who had lent support to Victor Jory in the western hit *Dodge City* (1939) and in the 1950s memorably played Doc Holliday on TV's *The Life and Legend of Wyatt Earp*. Selander and his cinematographer Russell Harlan are held in high regard. Assistant director Glenn Cook later made his mark on the western genre as a production manager on the TV westerns *Gunsmoke*, *Have Gun—Will Travel* and *Death Valley Days*. Henry Wills became one of the genre's best stunt coordinators, setting up impressive western action on *The Magnificent Seven* (1960) and TV's *The High Chaparral* (1967–1971). This film's co-writer Michael Wilson went on to win an Oscar for *A Place in the Sun* (1951) and co-wrote the ingenious *Planet of the Apes* (1968). Due to the Hollywood blacklist, Wilson penned such highly regarded films as *The Bridge on the River Kwai* (1957) and *Lawrence of Arabia* (1962) without proper screen credit. The Hoppy films were regarded as B-pictures and rarely rated mention by the major trades. They were not recognized by the likes of the prestigious *New York Times*.

Mitchum acquits himself admirably as Richard Adams, who at varying times in the storyline is too trusting and overly suspicious. It was the most dialogue he'd been given to this

28   The Films: 1940s–1970s

Mitchum, with the craggy rocks of Lone Pine behind him, incurs the wrath of George Reeves in *Bar 20* (1943).

point and he handles it flawlessly. He had come a long way in a few short years. His potential as a leading man is apparent, despite his unusual somnambulistic appearance. Part of what was intriguing about Mitchum and attracting notice were those heavy-lidded eyes. The perpetual tired, hangdog look has been attributed to a lengthy number of factors, among them his chronic Lockheed insomnia, getting battered in the boxing ring, being hung over, smoking marijuana and oftentimes simple boredom or lack of interest at the scripts sent his way. All these things may have contributed to some degree, but the truth is that his trademark saddlebag eyes were largely genetic. In his autobiographical book *Them Ornery Mitchum Boys*, brother John wrote of a 1929 photo of the brothers, "Bob chose merely to look sleepy-eyed, a condition he carried over into his professional pursuits and which he continues to affect to this very day."

False Colors (United Artists, 1943)

Cast: William Boyd (Hopalong Cassidy); Andy Clyde (California Carlson); Jimmy Rogers (Jimmy Rogers); Douglass Dumbrille (Mark Foster); Tom Seidel (Bud Lawton/Kit Moyer); Claudia Drake (Faith Lawton); Bob Mitchum (Rip Austin); Glenn Strange (Sonora); Pierce Lyden (Lefty); Roy Barcroft (Sheriff); and Victor Adamson, Roy Bucko, Bob Burns, Jack Evans, Sam Flint, Al Haskell, Earle Hodgins, Elmer Jerome, Ray Jones, Tom London, Jack Montgomery, George Morrell, Frank O'Connor, Cliff Parkinson, Tex Phelps, George Plues, Tom Smith, Glen Walters, Dan White.

Crew: George Archainbaud (Director); Harry Sherman (Producer); Bennett Cohen (Screenplay); Russell Harlan (Photographer); Irvin Talbot and Paul Sawtell (Music); Ralph Berger (Art Director); Earl Moser (Wardrobe); Fred W. Berger (Editor); Glenn Cook (Assistant Director); Ted Wells, Clem Fuller (Stunts); Mike Nimeth, Cliff Parkinson (Wranglers).

65 minutes; Released November 5, 1943

The serviceable opener for the ninth season of Hoppy films finds Mitchum playing hired gun

Rip Austin, one of a solid quartet of dog heavies that included Roy Barcroft, Pierce Lyden, and the 6'5" Glenn Strange (a handy, well-liked former rodeo cowboy, stuntman and musician best known for playing Sam the bartender on TV's *Gunsmoke*). Douglass Dumbrille portrays the "dress heavy" banker embroiled in a nasty squabble over water rights against a Lone Pine backdrop. The town scenes were filmed on the western street at California Studios on the corner of Bronson and Melrose, a set Harry Sherman used for several of the Hoppy films. The producers displayed their confidence in Mitchum's acting ability but weren't ready to bestow him with the lead heavy part. Mitchum looked too rugged, cold-blooded and immoral to be cast as a simple townie businessman. In his dusty cowboy clothes and sandpaper-rough five o'clock shadow, he was perfect casting as the dog heavy. Mitchum is given a couple of good scenes, coming off well in a poker game and a fast-paced barroom brawl with Hoppy. Considering the upward trajectory of Mitchum's career, producer Sherman was happy to have him. Despite modest box office returns for the previous season, moneyman Sherman upped the budgets to over $100,000 a picture. The film was rereleased in 1949 with Mitchum's name above Boyd's and proved to be a cash cow.

Mitchum was beginning to distinguish himself as a solid picture fighter, and his *False Colors* battle is arguably his best to this point of his career, meriting inclusion in the book *Classic Movie Fight Scenes*. Caught cheating at poker, he threatens Hoppy's aged sidekick Andy Clyde with chilling matter-of-factness: "I'll break every bone in your body." Mitchum grabs Clyde by the nose until Hoppy intervenes. They engage in an energetic fight. However, it's not blocked out smoothly for the camera. The Hoppy films were still transitioning from the old-school fights of the silent days where the camera simply aimed at two actors or stuntmen throwing punches into one another's arms and shoulders. In the mid–1930s, John Wayne and stuntman Yakima Canutt developed the idea of "the pass system," which took advantage of different camera angles and post-production editing to give the appearance that missed punches were connecting. Mitchum would soon learn these carefully rehearsed actions. Mitchum's screen bouts were especially convincing due to his believable movements and reactions. "I was always being slammed against barroom walls by Hoppy," he recalled for *Memories* magazine.

The *False Colors* fight is captured in a medium shot with Mitchum doing his own stunts. Mitchum proves more than willing to throw his body to the floor, over chairs and across the bar top to make the film's hero Boyd look good. Boyd was no doubt pleased to work with such a giving and able actor. "Bill showed me some of his moves from his days in silent movies," Mitchum recalled in the early 1970s. "He was so cool."* Mitchum was no stranger to real-life fights. He'd been scrapping since his childhood and his abbreviated boxing career gave him a solid base of experience off which to work. He knew how to throw an effective punch, not necessarily a prerequisite for fake film fisticuffs but handy knowledge to possess. His timing was expert, as was his judgment of force and distance, especially important when working with the star. In Mitchum's mind, it was more than all right to lose a picture fight to a nice guy like William Boyd. Taking a fist to the arm or shoulder beat taking a fist to the nose or the eye. Mitchum was content in his own knowledge that he could probably mop the floor with all the Hollywood heroes if push ever came to shove.

The film concludes with Boyd taking on Dumbrille, and there's at least a moment or two in that fight where it appears it might be Mitchum doubling the older heavy for flips and falls. Poor quality due to the age of the print makes it difficult to get a clear picture, but it seems to be a job the obliging Mitchum would step in and do. Various sources through the years liked to refer to him as a stuntman on these early productions, and Mitchum himself told Garry Armstrong that he had stood in or doubled for Boyd and Roy Barcroft in rehearsals or camera set-ups.† Mitchum proved to be

---

*Garry Armstrong (e-mail correspondence, August 2017).
†Garry Armstrong (e-mail correspondence, August 2017).

A surprised Andy Clyde watches William Boyd's Hopalong Cassidy beat Mitchum's bad guy Rip Austin bloody in a top-notch barroom battle from *False Colors* (1943).

one of the best physical actors around and seldom needed to be doubled unless a stunt had an element of true danger to it. The fact he could do virtually all his own brawling action as well as stuntmen made his fights especially memorable. "Mitchum has more courage, guts, stamina and physical strength than any other movie star I know," claimed writer Lloyd Shearer. "Stuntmen and stand-ins have refused to act in dangerous bits he has pulled off."

In his book *Those Saturday Serials,* cast member Pierce Lyden recalls Mitchum's toughness and willingness to undertake all the required action in these early assignments. While attending the 1990 Sierra Film Festival at Lone Pine, Lyden recalled:

> Sitting there through the program brought back many memories. One was the time on a Hopalong Cassidy with Bob Mitchum. It was his first picture. We were making two pictures at a time then and had done some work at Kernville and Red Rock Canyon. Then we came up to the "Bama Rocks." A new boy on the Hoppies just had to be broken in by the "Bar 20" boys. Bob wasn't what you would call a cowboy yet. He had been on and off the horses that they gave him, front, back and sideways. And to make matters worse, they had outfitted him with a beginners' stove pipe chaps. Hard and stiff as a board. After two weeks of dirt, sand, rocks and fights, he was tired, dirty and bruised. So, when poor Bob saw the "Bama Rocks" he said, "Oh no, not these too." Bob was a friend and I couldn't help but feel sorry for him. But "Them Ornery Mitchum Boys" had guts. He was a cinch to make it.

Riders of the Deadline (United Artists, 1943)

Cast: William Boyd (Hopalong Cassidy); Andy Clyde (California Carlson); Jimmy Rogers (Jimmy Rogers); Frances Woodward (Sue Mason), William Halligan (Simon Crandall); Bob Mitchum (Nick Drago); Richard Crane (Jim Mason); Anthony Warde (Gunner Madigan); Hugh Prosser (Deputy Sheriff Martin); Herbert Rawlinson (Capt. Jennings); Jack Rockwell (Tex); Earle Hodgins (Sourdough); Montie Montana (Pvt. Calhoun); and Bill Beckford, Roy Bucko, Art Felix, Herman Hack, Ray Jones, Pierce Lyden, Cliff Parkinson, Robert Walker.

Crew: Lesley Selander (Director); Harry Sherman (Producer); Bennett Cohen (Screenplay); Russell Harlan (Photographer); Irvin Talbot and Paul Sawtell (Music); Ralph Berger (Art Director); Earl Moser (Wardrobe); Walter Hannemann and Carrol Lewis (Editors); Glenn Cook (Assistant Director); Ted Wells, Clem Fuller, Montie Montana, Henry Wills, Cliff Parkinson (Stunts); Mike Nimeth, Cliff Parkinson (Wranglers).

70 minutes; Released December 3, 1943

In the fiftieth film in the Hopalong Cassidy series, the star shocks his sidekicks by quitting the Texas Rangers to join a gang of bad guys. Hoppy has really gone undercover to find the murderer of a friend. Mitchum, in black hat, is swaggering bad guy Nick Drago, who smokes cigarettes and has a history with the Texas Ranger. Cassidy had sent him to jail, and the sneering Mitchum refuses to believe the Ranger has gone over to the dark side. When Mitchum gets too jumpy, Boyd quick-punches him. They have an extended saloon brawl near the end of the film with Mitchum knocked unconscious on a toppling card table. It's not up to their fight in *False Colors*, but it's still one of the best fights in a Hoppy film. Mitchum is revived by his outlaw mates with a bucket of water to the face. In the finale, Mitchum is shot dead by Hoppy's sidekicks.

The movie was once again lensed in the parched landscape of Lone Pine's Alabama Hills and at the nearby Anchor Ranch. Seen in the background in several shots is Mt. Whitney, at 14,500 feet the highest summit in the contiguous United States. Mitchum told Charles Champlin the Hoppy location films were his "road game." Whenever he was between jobs at the movie studios, he knew he could get hired by "Pop" Sherman's outfit. "Thanks to Bill Boyd, there was always a role for me in the 'Hoppy' films," he told Dick Cavett. This film gained him his first-ever notice in the industry bible *Variety*, which wrote, "Bob Mitchum is a tough customer who continually tangles with Boyd."

However, Mitchum was well-served career-wise to get out of the Hoppy series before he became typecast as a B-western heavy. With *Bar 20* he showed the extent of his range and heroic potential, but few of the actors employed in these low-budget horse operas worked outside of that genre despite the level of their talent. The major studios looked down on the independent units and even snubbed their noses at the second feature product coming out of their own gates. Victor Jory was perhaps the exception. He could play a heavy anywhere, having already established in *Dodge City* (1939) and *Gone with the Wind* (1939) before dipping into the Hoppy films.

As for Mitchum, in his first full year in the industry he'd hit the ground running with his diverse array of screen appearances and proved himself an actor adept at performing action scenes. His masculine presence, rich voice and unique, sleepy-eyed naturalness were serving notice within the industry that he was a genuine talent. While working on the MGM war film *Thirty Seconds Over Tokyo* (1944), where he played one of star Spencer Tracy's pilots, Mitchum caught the attention of noted director Mervyn LeRoy. After screen tests were finished, LeRoy knew Mitchum possessed something unique and indefinable that worked well in front of the camera. During filming on location at Pensacola, Florida's Eglin Air Force Base, Mitchum had his first taste of notoriety as a Hollywood tough guy. There was a real sergeant who took delight in harassing what he considered pantywaist actors. When the sergeant stepped over the line with Robert Walker, Mitchum laid into him in the barracks, completely knocking a door off its hinges as he administered a humbling beat-down. "It took three of us to stop it," cast member Steve Brodie recalled for George Eells. "Mitch just came unglued."

Observing Spencer Tracy at work, Mitchum took note of that star's ease before the camera and lack of histrionics. The movie camera could pick up the slightest gestures and a mere suggestion of thought when in a tight frame. There was no need to play to the rafters as a stage actor would. The esteemed veteran Tracy had it down, and Mitchum decided his own deep baritone and heavy-lidded nonchalance was everything he needed. All that was called for in this industry was to say the lines and hit the marks. That seemed easy enough to Mitchum. He'd learned the same thing from William Boyd on the Hoppy films, and Tracy reinforced it. "Learning to act is like learning to be tall," was a favored Mitchum expression he repeated in

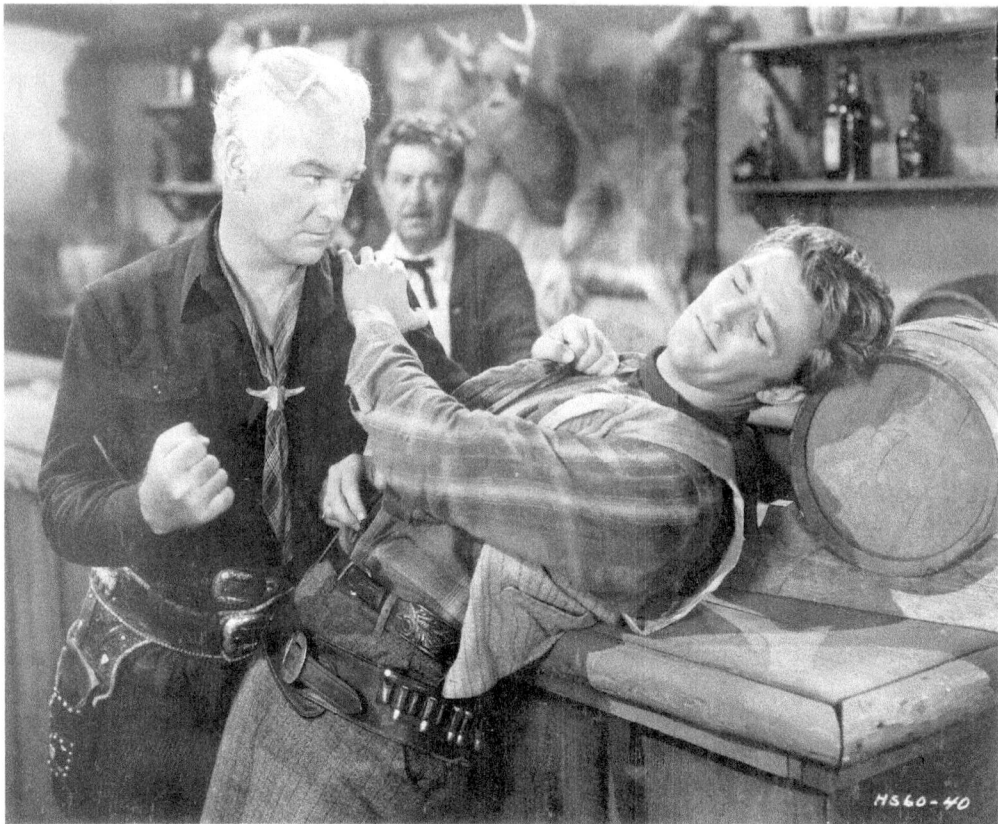

William Boyd doles out more punishment to Mitchum's bad guy Nick Drago in *Riders of the Deadline* (1943).

The Reluctant Star, suggesting one either had an interesting screen presence or they didn't.

Mitchum appropriated something else from Tracy and Boyd, an ability to drink alcohol and maintain star status without serious repercussion. In Tracy's case, drinking was relegated to when he wasn't filming. In that environment, he was completely out of control, skirt-chasing and bar-fighting. Tracy's wild and lawless escapades were covered up by his home studio MGM and its celebrated "fixer" Eddie Mannix. Mitchum learned the local law was willing to look the other way. Boyd's career faltered because of drink in the early 1930s before he redeemed himself with the Hoppy films. Most accounts say Boyd had his drinking under control, limiting himself to a single drink at the end of the day. However, in a quote appearing in Bobby Copeland's *Trail Talk*, Mitchum suggests Boyd never stopped drinking. "He drank more than any man I ever saw," Mitchum said.

"Boyd kept quarts of whiskey on the set. He drained one every day." It didn't make him any less a man in Mitchum's eyes. He was a star to Mitchum and the "Bar 20 Boys."

Publicity declared that Mitchum made nine Hoppy films. An ad placed by Paul Wilkins in the 1944 *Motion Picture Almanac* pegs the number at eight. History shows that Mitchum is credited with seven plus *Lone Star Trail* and *Beyond the Last Frontier*. Regarding his time spent with Boyd, Mitchum was appreciative. He told *The Washington Post*, "He's one of the few people I ever asked for an autographed picture. He wrote on it, 'To my favorite actor.' Ha. I bet he wrote that on everybody's."

Girl Rush (RKO, 1944)

Cast: Wally Brown (Jerry Miles); Alan Carney (Mike Strager); Frances Langford (Flo Daniels); Vera Vague (Suzie Banks); Robert Mitchum (Jimmy Smith); Paul Hurst (Muley); Patti Brill (Claire);

Sarah Padden (Emma Mason); Cy Kendall (Honest Greg Barlan); John Merton (Scully); and Ernie Adams, Bobby Barber, Virginia Belmont, Chris Willow Bird, Sammy Blum, Eddie Borden, Jack Casey, Wheaton Chambers, Greta Christensen, Rita Corday, Hal Craig, Kernan Cripps, George DeNormand, Abe Dinovitch, Byron Foulger, Raoul Freeman, Sherry Hall, Duane Kennedy, Diana King, Paul Kruger, Rosemary LaPlanche, Margaret Landry, Bert LeBaron, Jack Low, Sam Lufkin, George Magrill, Cy Malis, Glenn McCarthy, Frank Mills, Tex Mooney, Charles Morton, Stub Mussellman, Merlyn Nelson, Paul Newlan, Bud Osborne, Jasper Palmer, Lee Phelps, Joe Rickson, Suzanne Ridgeway, Elaine Riley, Gail Robinson, Robert Robinson, Dick Scott, Ray Spiker, Ken Terrell, Michael Vallon, Dale Van Sickel, Max Wagner, Chalky Williams, Chili Williams.

Crew: Gordon Douglas (Director); Robert E. Kent (Screenplay); Nicholas Musuraca (Photographer); C. Bakaleinikoff (Music); Albert S. D'Agostino and Walter Keller (Art Directors); Duncan Mansfield (Editor); James Casey (Assistant Director); George DeNormand, Bert LeBaron, George Magrill, Jack Casey, Glenn McCarthy, Merlyn Nelson, Ray Spiker, Ken Terrell, Dale Van Sickel (Stunts).

65 minutes; Released October 21, 1944

As the rising Mitchum's name began to be bandied about by the various studios, Mervyn LeRoy contemplated giving him the starring role as the gladiator Demetrius in the big-budget Biblical epic *The Robe* (finally made a decade later with Victor Mature in the part). With that buzz in place, there was suddenly a clamor for somebody to get him signed to a long-term deal. Columbia offered a term contract and RKO (where *The Robe* was in development) became determined to lock him up first with a seven-year offer that would top out at a wage of $2000 a week by contract's end. There was one catch. Studio executive Herman Schlom didn't like the name Mitchum and wanted to rename him either Robert Marshall or John Mitchell. Mitchum had been easygoing up to this point

(From left) Paul Hurst, Mitchum and Frances Langford attempt a western-comedy with mixed results: RKO's *Girl Rush* (1944).

in his young career but flatly refused to change his name, countering the less than glamorous name Schlom would be seen on screen. Agent Paul Wilkins argued successfully that Mitchum was already being recognized under his own name and was beginning to receive fan mail. It made no sense to change. Schlom and the RKO studio heads eventually gave in. He'd be billed as Bob Mitchum.

Movie studios created stars, molding them to fit a preconceived homogenized image. That way, a performer could always be replaced or threatened to be replaced by a similar type. It gave the studios power over the talent. Mitchum was different and knew it. He was an individual and wasn't changing anything. He stuck to his guns. Take it or leave it. He was the only Robert Mitchum type in town. One RKO executive was especially turned off by Mitchum's burly physical presence, droopy eyes and crooked nose, thinking he looked more like a monster than a potential movie star. The notion of having cosmetic surgery to enhance his features was introduced. "A casting office asked me if I'd ever thought of having my nose fixed," Mitchum recalled for *The Los Angeles Times* in 1994. "I said, 'It's already been fixed, by about four left hooks.'"

RKO looked to put the new contract player to work on their Encino Ranch Western Street. Producer Sid Rogell's first assignment was a curious one: a back lot cowboy comedy from director Gordon Douglas, *Girl Rush* (1944). Douglas requested Mitchum for one of the film's co-starring leads.

Mitchum, cast as the film's action hero Jimmy Smith, was billed fifth behind the comedy team Alan Carney and Wally Brown and leading ladies Frances Langford and Vera Vague (aka Barbara Jo Allen). Despite the below-the-title casting, Mitchum, clad in a cowhide vest and featuring a pompadour, is given numerous opportunities to shine and plays romantic scenes with Langford as the vaudeville leads introduce a gaggle of women to an 1849 town full of gold miners. Langford sings several songs, including the Harry Harris-Lew Pollock original "When I'm Walking Arm in Arm with Jim." Stephen Foster's "Oh! Susanna" can be heard over the opening credits.

The brawling climax has the male leads, Mitchum included, masquerading in drag to take down a gang of claim jumpers. The film's notoriety stems from the lone opportunity to see Mitchum in a blonde wig and a frontier woman's dress, but he proves a good sport about it as he punches out bad guys Cy Kendall and John Merton to save the day and the community of Red Creek. Mitchum contributes to the absurdity of the situation by refusing to alter the pitch of his deep voice when miner Paul Newlan takes a shine to him. "I like 'em big," says the tall miner, sizing Mitchum up. Mitchum doesn't bat a false eyelash. "They don't come too big for me either, bud," he says in response. It's a nice touch and reveals that Mitchum didn't take himself too seriously. He had a sense of humor regarding the movie business. This is the kind of film stars would be embarrassed by, but Mitchum poked fun at himself over the years regarding *Girl Rush*. In a 1978 *New York Times* interview, he said, "I've played cowboys, old Chinese laundrywomen, anything but midgets. My first picture at RKO, a Zane Grey western [sic], I was in drag."

In its review, *Variety* commented, "Robert Mitchum catches attention with a smooth performance and a likable personality," while *Motion Picture Daily* wrote he was "decorative in a masculine sort of way." *The Hollywood Reporter* was hopeful about his future: "Mitchum displays plenty of potentialities with an easeful and personable performance as the young miner." Barrie Hanfling's *Westerns and the Trail of Tradition* notes, "The film was average, but Mitchum caused excitement." In his entertaining Mitchum biography *Baby, I Don't Care*, Lee Server wrote, "The film proved to be a good showcase for RKO's new contract player. Mitchum exuded a maximum of masculine charisma throughout, did charming love scenes with Frances Langford, displayed a breezy sense of humor, and maintained his cool aplomb even in a bonnet and gingham dress."

Tom Weaver's book *Wild Wild Westerners* quotes RKO contract player Robert Clarke saying of Mitchum, "People working with him could tell that he was headed onward and upward." *Girl Rush* cast member Elaine Riley recalled Mitchum in *Ladies of the Western*: "The first time I ever saw him he came on the set of that Frances Langford picture and somebody said he's going to be the next big star. And I thought, oh? And he certainly turned out to be." After working together on *Lone Star Trail*, Jimmy Wakely was still putting in a word for Mitchum wherever he went. Wakely told David Rothel, "When I went over to Columbia later, I talked with Jack Fier who was my boss there. I said, 'You've got to sign up Bob Mitchum. He's going to be a big star.' He said, 'Ah, hell, he'll never amount to anything. He's just a henchie.' A henchie was an also-ran heavy. Then Mitch did a picture with Hoppy that I saw at the Hitching Post Theatre in Hollywood. In about five minutes Mitch got killed and the picture might as well have ended right there. The next morning, I went in to see Fier. I told him I had seen Mitch and said some good things about his performance.... Fier called his secretary and said, 'Get Mitchum's agent.' Well, they offered him $300 a week for a 40-week contract, but the agent said, 'RKO just called and we're going with them....' You knew you were looking at a future star."

There's more evidence of Mitchum's eventual stardom occurring in this film, and that's the way director of photography Nicholas Musuraca's camera captures his physical movement. Mitchum had one of the great Hollywood walks—chest puffed out, chin and shoulders back, eyes fixed ahead to maintain balance—as he determinedly strode forward under his powerful legs while casing out any situation. Nothing like John Wayne's halting, hip-rolling, pigeon-toed strut, Mitchum's walk was a manly stride that could fill up a room and draw all eyes his way. It even had a name. They called it "the Mitchum Ramble." *Washington Post* writer Paul Hendrickson once described the movement being "as languid as a boa's glide." When cowboy boots were added into the mix, the increased height made him look even more imposing and dangerous. Mitchum's walk meant business. He could be laidback and nonchalant to the point of lethargy, but when he exploded panther-like and focused, it seldom failed to impress. His direct-line path and dead-eyed stare could close a room and offer no options of escape for his prey when he drew back his massive clenched fist.

Mitchum found humor in people's reactions. He told Earl Wilson of the *Los Angeles Herald Examiner*, "People think I have an interesting walk. Hell, I'm just trying to hold my gut in."

Nevada (RKO, 1944)

Cast: Bob Mitchum (Jim "Nevada" Lacy); Anne Jeffreys (Julie Dexter); Guinn "Big Boy" Williams (Dusty); Nancy Gates (Hattie Ide); Richard Martin (Chito Rafferty); Craig Reynolds (Cash Burridge); Harry Woods (Joe Powell); Edmund Glover (Ed Nelson); Alan Ward (William Brewer); Harry McKim (Ed Ide); Larry Wheat (Ben Ide); Jack Overman (Red Berry); Emmett Lynn (Comstock); Wheaton Chambers (Dr. Darien); Philip Morris (Ed Nolan); Russ Hopton (Henchman); Sammy Blum (Bartender); and Virginia Belmont, Patti Brill, Ralph Bucko, George DeNormand, Tex Driscoll, Mary Halsey, Ben Johnson, Jack Kenny, Bert Moorhouse, Philip Morris, Sammy Shack, Margie Stewart, Sid Troy, Bryant Washburn.

Crew: Edward Killy (Director); Sid Rogell and Herman Schlom (Producers); Norman Houston (Screenplay); Zane Grey (Story); Harry J. Wild (Photographer); Paul Sawtell (Music); Roland Gross (Editor); Harry Mancke (Assistant Director); Ben Johnson, Fred Graham, George DeNormand, Ralph Bucko, Sid Troy (Stunts); Allen Lee, Kenny Lee (Wranglers); Clarence "Fat" Jones (Livestock Provider).

62 minutes; Released December 24, 1944

Mitchum's signing at RKO, and arguably his entire career up to this point, was made possible because he had not yet been called off to fight the Germans or the Japanese in the service of his country. At the outset of World War II, Mitchum received a deferment from military service because he had been working in the defense industry at Lockheed and was the breadwinner for his immediate and extended family. Some discrepancy exists as to whether he failed his initial physical due to the odd sag of his eyelids. Subsequent studio distributed press bios, rarely a source for accurate information, would claim the military turned him down due to an astigmatism in his eyes brought on by his boxing background. Mitchum rarely bothered to clear up any inaccuracies about his own life and career, realizing the intermingling of truth, lies and rumor created an effective smokescreen he could hide behind. "It's all true," he would say when questioned, telling Roger Ebert in 1969, "Make up some more if you want to."

Mitchum as Jim "Nevada" Lacey and Richard Martin as his guitar-slinging saddle partner Chito Rafferty in *Nevada* (1944).

Regarding the military deferment, the same couldn't be said for a great deal of the hale and hearty male population. One of those inducted was RKO's resident cowboy hero Tim Holt. The son of silent film star Jack Holt, Tim had replaced the popular but aging cowboy actor George O'Brien in 1940 and subsequently turned out 18 better-than-average oaters for the studio. Raised on movie sets and at the Culver Military Academy, the stoutly built, medium height Holt was well-suited for the assignment. He could ride expertly and was athletic enough to handle plenty of his own picture-fighting and gunplay. When he needed a stuntman, in stepped Dave Sharpe, one of the best action doubles in the business. All was well with Holt's well-produced cowboy series at RKO until his draft number came up.

The studios were not keen on losing their biggest moneymakers. Republic, resistant to John Wayne entering the military, encouraged him to seek deferments based on a combination of old injuries and family responsibilities.

This pressure from above had to have been unsettling for an actor like Wayne seeking to answer the call of duty yet retain the star status it had taken so long to achieve. In addition to the inherent danger of entering a war, there was no guarantee a top spot at the studio would be open upon his return. Wayne began making patriotic war films which served to boost morale for the overseas effort. Clamor for his induction died down. However, his non-service during the war was a point of personal regret for Wayne throughout the rest of his life. Wayne became a super-patriot, even recording a spoken-word album of songs penned by John Mitchum, *America, Why I Love Her*. To this day, his harshest critics still refer to him as a draft dodger.

At RKO, the studio began looking in-house at actors already under contract as a replacement for the departing Tim Holt. They didn't have to look far. There was rough-hewn Bob Mitchum all duded up and looking impressively photogenic on the range in their very own *Girl Rush* (1944). Studio memos note Mitchum as a "rugged, underplayed type" who, on- and off-camera, "is proving himself a team player." Tall, dark, deep-voiced and ruggedly handsome, he seemed a perfect fit. He even had more than a half-dozen cowboy credits to his name playing bearded heavies, so he'd be familiar with horses and western props. The studio cleaned him up further and ran their tests. It wasn't hard to determine that RKO had themselves a new cowboy full of action-hero promise. The studio was producing a series of formula films based on the writings of popular western scribe Zane Grey, and Mitchum pulled on his boots ready to go to work. The *Nevada* credits would read: **Introducing Bob Mitchum as Jim "Nevada" Lacy**.

Due to a combination of Norman Houston's screenplay and his own unique persona, Mitchum came across as atypical in comparison to the usual cowboy hero blueprint. His character Nevada was realistically tough and honest but basically a somewhat lazy, good-natured cowpoke looking for a sizable payday through a roll of dice or the striking of gold. No sense busting horses or herding cattle for the rest of his life at $20 a month when a man of the west had other means to entertain a good-looking woman. It lent his easygoing character an interesting shading. Anne Jeffreys is cast as a good-bad chorus girl and Nancy Gates as the sweet ingénue, but the storyline doesn't link Mitchum up with either romantically. "I worked mostly with donkeys and brood mares," Mitchum told reporters when asked about any romantic entanglements from this period. Mitchum was protective of his real-life leading ladies and was not one to kiss and tell. Even if he did have a roving eye, he was respectful enough of his wife not to flaunt it to the press. The females are on screen and Mitchum notices, but more pressing matters exist as he is chased by crooked gam-

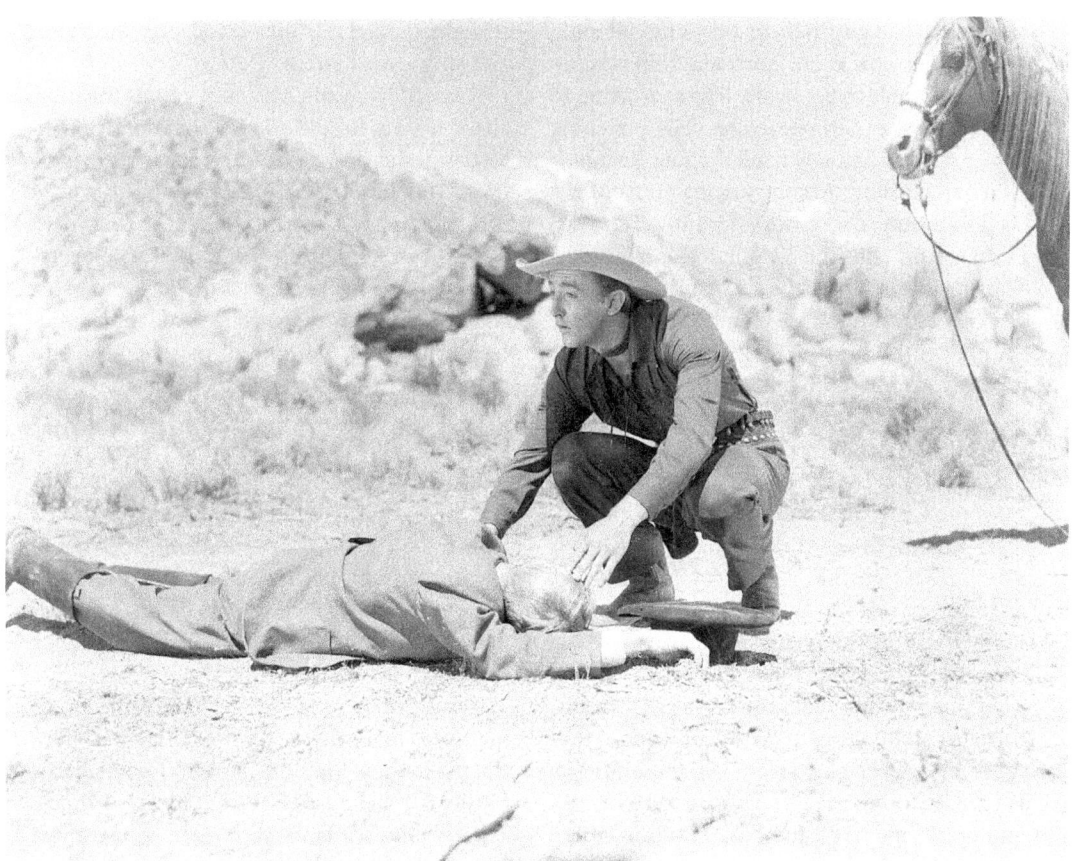

Finding the body of Harry McKim in RKO's *Nevada* (1944).

blers and the law after being unjustly framed for the murder of Gates' father.

The part of a man on the run with no place to call home became consistent with the subsequent Mitchum western output. He was routinely seen as the independent, laconic stranger who drifts from one place to the next like any rawhide roustabout worth his salt. Spartan, yet resourceful in his surroundings. Fast with his fists and his irons. He'd face down danger if need be but chose to circumvent it if possible until the final reel. Mitchum's cowboy characters were like the man himself. In 1974, he described his own rambunctious nature to the *Daily Mail* as "a constant motion of escape."

For the demands of the various action scenes, the neatly tailored Mitchum is dressed simply and effectively in a Nudie Cohn design, not adorned in any flowery drugstore cowboy outfit. He sports a low-hanging two-gun Colt rig suggesting he's quick when forced to draw. His accuracy with a firearm is so pinpoint that he shoots a bad guy in the hand while galloping away on horseback. His horsemanship is superior as he is able to heroically leap into action to save Jeffreys' runaway carriage. His punching power flattens bad guy banker Craig Reynolds with a single blow. Accompanying him at times on his adventures are two appealing sidekicks, burly Guinn "Big Boy" Williams and Richard Martin, the latter as the colorful Irish-Mexican character Chito Jose Gonzales Bustamante Rafferty. Both actors make sensible saddle partners for Mitchum, unlike the typical comic-relief antics of an aged Gabby Hayes-Andy Clyde or portly Smiley Burnette-Andy Devine. Taking photographic advantage of the high skies and fantastic granite and monolithic rock formations of Lone Pine's "Alabams," *Nevada* is a perfectly acceptable B-western. Its star makes an impressive debut, although he was still finding his way in the western milieu riding the trail of the Lonesome Pine.

In some scenes, Mitchum seems slightly uncertain regarding his performance, more tentative and uncomfortable than the audience is used to seeing him. The posture is a bit stiff and erect, and even the bass baritone comes off an octave high. He resorts to smiling a lot, which endears him to the audience but seems odd coming from a Mitchum character (many think of him as dour-faced, forever bored and inherently cynical). Veteran B-western director Edward Killy was likely more concerned the lighting was sufficient and the dialogue spoken cleanly. He wasn't worried with the intricacies of performance from a cowboy actor. The straightforward Mitchum compares favorably to fellow B-western stars like Wild Bill Elliott and Allan "Rocky" Lane. Outside of one comment regarding Jeffreys' beauty, Mitchum is squeaky-clean in the film and doesn't smoke tobacco or drink liquor on screen. He's exactly what a virtuous B-western cowboy should be for America's youthful audience: highly sanitized and infinitely capable. Early western star Tom Mix explained Hollywood's interpretation of the mythic do-no-wrong cowboy: "The Old West is not a certain place in a certain time. It's a state of mind, whatever you want it to be." In the 1940s, Hollywood wanted their cowboys to be smiling, colorfully attired, and generic straight shooters. If they could play the guitar and sing, even better.

It's curious seeing Mitchum cast as the moralistic hero as he had seemed so natural and effortless in his down-and-dirty supporting parts up to this point. Perhaps carrying the weight of a starring role on his shoulders found its way at least temporarily into his psyche. A few years before *Nevada,* he was in danger of being rousted off a boxcar traveling through the middle of nowhere and now all these lights, cameras, reflectors, microphones and Hollywood people scurrying about were for him. It had to be ironic if not slightly unsettling. He adjusted quickly. Mitchum is slick and charismatic, displaying a calm toughness and a unique profile before the cameras. Brief mention is made of his unconventional appearance for a leading man, with co-star "Big Boy" Williams of *Dodge City* (1939) fame remarking, "Your eyes look like a couple of poached eggs."

Texas-born cattle-puncher Williams broke into films as a cowboy stuntman. He was given the nickname "Big Boy" by Will Rogers based on his 6'2" height and thickly muscled frame. The affable Williams starred in many silent westerns and early talkies like *Thunder Over Texas* (1934) and *Law of the 45's* (1935) before taking on character roles. He was a solid horseman with a reputation as a top polo player. He was also one of the strongest and toughest men in Hollywood, once reputed to have knocked down a horse with a punch after it bit him. On *Nevada,* he and Mitchum were running through the blocking of a fight scene and Mitchum accidentally slugged Williams with a mighty blow. It didn't faze Big Boy. "That was the best shot I ever threw," an amazed Mitchum told Mike Tomkies.

A long-time drinking buddy of John Wayne and Errol Flynn, Williams became legendary for his rowdy exploits. He fell asleep dead drunk on Boot Hill while on a promotional tour in Kansas for *Dodge City.* Williams hoisted a few with Mitchum between the time they appeared together in *Nevada* and *Home from the Hill* (1960). Williams' vast cowboying experience in both real life and Hollywood oaters rubbed off on Mitchum, especially his insistence that real cowboys dress plain without all the Hollywood flash. Williams had a large ranch in Texas in addition to a home near San Diego where he created a "gallery of stars" on his property. Friends such as Mitchum and Flynn etched their names there into concrete blocks for posterity. Williams died of uremic poisoning in 1962 after appearing in supporting roles in *The Alamo* (1960) and *The Comancheros* (1961). He was 63.

Transitioning from B-western heavy to stoic cowboy hero was largely unprecedented. The lone comparable actor to Mitchum is former Olympic swimming champion Buster Crabbe, who ironically enough portrayed the exact same Jim "Nevada" Lacy character in a 1935 Paramount version of Zane Grey's *Nevada.* Crabbe got his start playing heavies opposite Randolph Scott in *To the Last Man* (1933) and Gene Autry in *Colorado Sunset* (1939) before portraying a heroic Billy the Kid in a string of bottom-of-the-barrel Poverty Row quickies throughout the 1940s. Even then, Crabbe was a known heroic commodity with audience recognition as he had made his name through serials as Flash Gordon and Buck Rogers. On the other hand, a few former B-western stars became heavies. The most notable of these were Tom Tyler and Bob Steele. So, Mitchum's journey from Hoppy heavy to RKO cowboy star was unique.

Regarding horsemanship, the improvement in Mitchum's western riding ability is noticeable. This was aided in great part by a perfect movie horse. Mitchum rode the Quarter-type stallion Steel, a well-regarded chestnut-sorrel who featured a distinctive flowing mane, wide blaze and three white stockings. Horse and rider were in complete harmony—an extension of one another—with Mitchum able to keep a slack rein. Hailing from the Fat Jones Stables, Steel was the favored steed of actors ranging from John Wayne in *Tall in the Saddle* (1944) to Joel McCrea in *Buffalo Bill* (1944). He was calm in the face of movie commotion and always made the star atop him look good. After *Nevada,* Steel was ridden in future westerns by Gregory Peck, Clark Gable and Gary Cooper. Rodeo champion Ben Johnson famously rode Steel (and stunt horse Bingo) across Monument Valley in *She Wore a Yellow Ribbon* (1949) and *Rio Grande* (1950). When the required riding in *Nevada* involved the added danger of a saddle fall or the traversing of especially rugged terrain, expert horseman Johnson served as Mitchum's stunt double. "I kept telling them I couldn't ride a horse or anything," Mitchum told Mike Tomkies in 1973, "But they went through all the old Hopalong Cassidy movies, then dressed everyone else up very badly and marched me out there before the cameras in a tailor-made outfit. After that, I was sort of on the hook. RKO opened the door for me, and I became their workhorse."

Ben Johnson is apparent doubling for Mitchum in a fight scene with veteran heavy Harry Woods (doubled by Fred Graham). Now that Mitchum was a star, it was sensible that RKO would protect its investment by using a double for any rough stuff. However, the barn fight in *Nevada* was a piece of action Mitchum was highly capable of performing himself, and his presence would have improved the film immeasurably by showing off his toughness in close-up. No doubt speed and economy were at work here. It was far easier to let two professional stuntmen throw together a quick routine for a master shot than go to the trouble to choreograph time-consuming multiple action set-ups for the film's star. If you had to use a double, Ben Johnson was a good one to have.

The cowboy from Oklahoma went on to become a western icon as a multi-layered heavy in *Shane* (1953) and he garnered an Academy Award as Best Supporting Actor for *The Last Picture Show* (1971). Regarding his early stunting days, Johnson is quoted in Richard Jensen's bio, saying, "I was doubling for people like John Wayne, Jimmy Stewart and Joel McCrea, and I would watch the way they did things. I never really had a desire to be an actor. I always had something else to do.... I could always make a living working on a ranch or in a rodeo." Like Mitchum, Johnson was a natural actor without affectation. Both men spent their lives playing characters true to their own nature. There's little argument they borrowed from one another in this film to the mutual benefit of their careers. At the end of the fight, Mitchum's shirt is ripped to shreds, eliciting a collective sigh in theaters around the country from admiring females. In quick order, Mitchum would have his own fan club dubbed "The Mitchum Droolettes." His female fans referred to him as "the riot on the range."

When Mitchum told "Pop" Sherman he could ride on his first Hoppy, film it was not an uncommon boast. Virtually all actors were instructed by their agents to say they could handle a horse if it meant landing a part. Jack Palance in *Shane* (1953), Leo Gordon in *Hondo* (1953), Ernest Borgnine in *The Stranger Wore a Gun* (1953), Claude Akins in *Bitter Creek* (1954) and Henry Silva in *The Tall T* (1957) are a few examples of Eastern-born actors who couldn't ride on their initial hire but learned and became strongly identified with the western genre. In *Nevada,* the same theory held true for juvenile actor Sammy McKim, cast as Nancy Gates' younger brother. In a scene where Mitchum is at the reins of a buckboard, they are attacked by an outlaw gang. Mitchum hands the reins to McKim so that he can fend the bad guys off with his gun. When director Edward Killy asked McKim if he could handle a buckboard, McKim volunteered he could. Untrue. With the cameras running, McKim lost control of the horses, and he and Mitchum had to bail out of the runaway buckboard.

Mitchum was making the most of his opportunity, yet even at this early juncture he could do things that were perceived as outlandish behavior simply on principle when bucking authority. Because he wasn't yet deemed important enough by RKO's "suits" for his own dressing room, Mitchum completed one dusty day's work by shedding his western outfit to his boxers and spraying himself down with a garden hose beneath the studio head's office window. He was quickly given his own dressing room and personal shower. That was the extent of his "star trip" and it gave him one of the first of his many amusing behind-the-scenes anecdotes to tell over the years. A Mitchum dressing room was a curious achievement. This was a man who'd spent his life sleeping under the stars atop rumbling trains, on available couches and floors, or even in a converted chicken coop. It was obvious he didn't need many frills. When the day concluded, crew members were left scratching their heads as the star of the film exited the studio gates and hitchhiked home to his wife and kids.

By many accounts, eternal non-conformist Mitchum was slightly embarrassed and uncomfortable at headlining a film. He was friendly and professionally courteous to his castmates, but in off-hours on the Lone Pine location he'd retire to a local watering hole and pull his hat down over his eyes. "There was a mystique about Mitchum, even then," leading lady Anne Jeffreys told Lee Server. On this film, Mitchum preferred to be a quietly brooding lone wolf staring into his drink rather than a back-slapper fraternizing with cast and crew. "I never had or wanted an entourage," he told Mike Tomkies. "I'm a loner." Killy spent a total of ten days shooting in Lone Pine with an additional two weeks of interiors at RKO. The end couldn't come quick enough for the restless Mitchum. He eventually loosened up on the movie set, but his basic nature was a solitary one. Regarding his sudden stardom, Mitchum told *The Montreal Gazette* in 1978, "I always wanted to be anonymous. I still do."

Co-star Richard "Chito" Martin spoke to author David Rothel about his initial impression of Mitchum in the 1984 book *Those Great Cowboy Sidekicks*:

> I still see Bob Mitchum occasionally. When I first met him, I looked at him and said, "You surprised me; I didn't expect you to become a lead-

ing man; I expected you to be a character actor." He didn't look to me like what a leading man was supposed to look like in those days. When we did those two Zane Grey pictures, Bob was making $150 a week and I was making $75. We used to hide behind the rocks and hope they picked up our options. We were concerned about it; both of us wanted to stay alive.

Anybody who worked with Bob Mitchum and knew him, liked him. He was a great guy. I got along with him; every one of us did, but he was controversial. If you didn't like Bob Mitchum, you just didn't like him. He wasn't going to change himself in any way to fit what anybody else might expect of him, and he's still the same today. The last time I saw him, he ran into the back of my car on purpose. It cost me a hundred and fifty dollars. I was at a stop signal on Wilshire Boulevard when it happened. I looked into my rearview mirror and there was Bob. He yelled, "Hi, Chito! How are you?" I hadn't seen him in about five years…. He said, "Oh, I just wanted to say hello." That's the way Bob Mitchum is; he's just a crazy guy. Sometimes he'd rather go out the window than through the door.

The critical reaction to *Nevada* was positive for a B-western. *Film Daily* wrote, "Bob Mitchum for the first time is presented as the star of a western. The actor certainly justifies the faith placed in him, delivering a performance that is smack in the groove. The fellow does himself pretty, dishing out the heroic stuff." *The Motion Picture Herald* labeled Mitchum "a good draw," adding, "Mitchum has what it takes to put over a picture like this…. If he could sing he would be the leading cowboy in a short time." *Motion Picture Daily* noted, "[His] laconic performance is somewhat reminiscent of John Wayne." Kasper Monahan of the *Pittsburgh Press* proved especially perceptive: "Remember the name: Bob Mitchum, for you'll be hearing about him. He's been swaggering around in boots and 10-gallon sombreros for some years now, but I have a notion that his days of obscurity are over." Looking back at the starring debut, Ed Hulse in *Filming the West of Zane Grey* opined, "Mitchum had undeniable screen presence, and his vaguely menacing look added an edge to his persona." According to Don Miller in *Hollywood Corral*, Mitchum "carried off his role in fine style, with all the equipment needed for top billing."

West of the Pecos (RKO, 1945)

Cast: Robert Mitchum (Pecos Smith); Barbara Hale (Rill Lambeth); Richard Martin (Chito Rafferty); Thurston Hall (Col. Lambeth); Rita Corday (Suzanne); Russell Hopton (Jeff Stinger); Bill Williams (Tex Evans); Harry Woods (Brad Sawtelle); Bruce Edwards (Clyde Morgan); Perc Launders (Sam Sawtelle); Bryant Washburn (Doc Howard); Philip Morris (Marshal); Martin Garralaga (Don Manuel); Sammy Blum, Robert Anderson (Gamblers); Italia DeNubila (Dancer); Ethan Laidlaw (Lookout); Jack Gargan (Croupier); Larry Wheat (Butler); and Alfredo Berumen, Eumenio Blanco, Archie Butler, John Eberts, Edmund Glover, Carmen Grenada, Herman Hack, Carl Kent, Allen Lee, Frank O'Connor, Cliff Parkinson, Jose Portugal, Paul Ravel, Joe Rickson, Jason Robards, Sr., Robert Robinson, Ariel Sherry, Jack Tornek, Virginia Wave, Henry Wills.

Crew: Edward Killy (Director); Sid Rogell and Herman Schlom (Producers); Norman Houston (Screenplay); Zane Grey (Story); Harry J. Wild (Photographer); Paul Sawtell (Music); Albert S. D'Agostino and Lucius Croxton (Art Directors); Roland Gross (Editor); Harry Mancke (Assistant Director); Archie Butler, Cliff Parkinson, Jack Tornek, Henry Wills (Stunts); Allen Lee, Kenny Lee, Cliff Parkinson (Wranglers); Clarence "Fat" Jones (Livestock Provider).

66 minutes; Released August 10, 1945

This entertaining, humor-filled RKO horse opera features a fine cast giving likable performances against the scenic backdrop of Lone Pine. The movie is an entirely pleasant way to spend an hour.

In a solid follow-up to his first starring role, Mitchum is cast as amiable cowpoke Pecos Smith, a character that's not a long stretch from his Jim "Nevada" Lacy in the previous year's *Nevada*. Sitting tall in the saddle, he's perhaps a bit more virtuous this time out and every bit as tough and masculine. Exuding self-confidence and courage, he is the perfect B-western cowboy for the kids in the balcony to look up to. His improved riding skills, including smooth mounts and dismounts on Steel, showcase the quick transition he had made to being on the range. He handles his guns and fists efficiently when the plot demands. Mitchum enjoyed being a cowboy so much that one fan magazine claimed he carried his lasso with him to the local market and roped the goods he wanted off the shelf! Mitchum is paired once again with Richard Martin as good-natured side

Astride the famous movie horse Steel in *West of the Pecos* (1945).

kick Chito. Fellow trail rider Guinn "Big Boy" Williams did not return from *Nevada*, which means that even more of the film's storyline is carried by Mitchum. He's up to the task.

West of the Pecos takes place in Texas as businessman Thurston Hall and his daughter Barbara Hale travel from the east to set up a hacienda in the western territory. It's a lawless area ruled by vigilantes. Their stagecoach is robbed and the bandits kill stage guard Bill Williams, a good friend of Mitchum's Pecos. Mitchum vows to find the men responsible as well as transport Hall and Hale safely across the terrain. Because Hale has disguised herself as a tomboy to avoid unwanted advances, Mitchum thinks she is an odd, crazy boy, and this leads to some of the film's more amusing moments. They have good chemistry together in these scenes. Eventually Hale lets her hair down and she and Mitchum are arm in arm by film's end, after he's punched out chief bad guy Harry Woods. Despite Mitchum's character's apparent motivation, the film is no tale of revenge. He is never presented as anything except

a cowboy hero who sets a good example for the children in the audience save for the lone instance of him rolling a tobacco cigarette (what cowboys called a quirly). It's a wonder RKO allowed that bit of authenticity into the film. Roy Rogers and Gene Autry never smoked in their films.

Handsomely produced, it's yet another beneficial showcase for Mitchum. The reviews came back even stronger than those for *Nevada*. "Remember Mitchum's name…he's destined for stardom," claimed the *New York Daily News*. "Robert Mitchum is the cowboy and a find," said *The Hollywood Reporter*. "Westerns can use a guy like that to the advantage of audiences and exhibitors." *Film Daily* remarked, "Mitchum plays the hero extremely well," while *Variety* concluded, "Robert Mitchum, with the help of Richard Martin, does the riders of the range proud." *The Motion Picture Herald* called it "[o]ne of the best westerns to come from RKO in a long time…. Bob Mitchum is great in this feature," and *Film Bulletin* chimed in, "The lanky, two-fisted and not-too-handsome

Robert Mitchum is likable and capable." From *The New York Post*: "If the western art form is to be reconstructed into a brand-new kind of structure with a nuclei of adventure and sex, Mitchum is the man to do it."

Years later, Brian Garfield in *Western Films* declared, "Mitchum carries it valiantly," while Don Miller's *Hollywood Corral* reported, "Mitchum ambled through the heroics, making it all look like a snap, which it wasn't." In *The Encyclopedia of Western*, Herb Fagen wrote that Mitchum "revealed many of the qualities that would one day propel him to the front ranks of major movie stars." According to Mitchum biographer John Belton, "Mitchum captures the primitive diamond-in-the-rough quality of Grey's heroes." But film noir writer Imogen Sara Smith opined, "Mitchum was wasted on these cardboard heroes and boy's-adventure stories, which had no use for his undercurrents of melancholy, disaffection and skeptical intelligence." She wanted more seriousness from the intriguing actor, who soon moved into the noir genre.

With his second starring role as an RKO cowpuncher, Mitchum began to relax a bit more on the set, but he wasn't changing who or what he was as a man for anyone. He could take this version of Hollywood stardom or leave it. During this time in his life, it's what was paying his bills, but he'd as soon drive a truck. Supporting players like Richard Martin (who married Mitchum's *Girl Rush* co-star Elaine Riley in 1946) accepted this common-man attitude and spoke highly of him. At the Lone Pine Film Festival, Martin said they always hoped the RKO executives wouldn't show up on location because, "If they ever saw how much fun we had here in Lone Pine, they wouldn't pay us *any*thing, and we got precious little as it was." Star Mitchum was earning $350 a week, Martin $75. "For a while, it looked like I was going to be stuck in westerns," Mitchum told Erskine Johnson in 1946. "I figured I could make six a year for 60 years and then retire." Leading lady Barbara Hale recalled in *Western Clippings*, "Robert Mitchum never changed. He was the dearest, most wonderful man." Hale went on to marry this film's featured player Bill Williams, who later starred in the TV western *The Adventures of Kit Carson* (1951–1955).

A fighter for the common man, Mitchum considered the RKO crew an extended family. If he felt the studio was treating them with disrespect by skimping on the morning meal, he dipped into his own pocket to buy his co-workers breakfast and coffee. If a crew member was fired, Mitchum calmly walked off the set until the person was rehired. If his stand-in was feeling a little too hung over, Mitchum stood in for his stand-in. On one occasion, Mitchum was having a palm tree trimmed on his property. When he learned that the tree-trimmer was an out-of-work stuntman, he got the man hired on at RKO. The crews were loyal to their star and several common names appear on the credits of the films Mitchum produced in the 1950s. Mitchum's RKO makeup man Holly Bane went on to a successful career as a western supporting player under his own name and the stage name Mike Ragan. One of Mitchum's behind-the-scenes film technician friends was Donald Paul Haggerty, the father of future animal trainer and *Grizzly Adams* TV star Dan Haggerty. At the 2014 Western Film Festival in Glendale, Arizona, the rough-hewn Dan Haggerty revealed, "Robert Mitchum was my godfather. He was a great guy."*

When he wrote his 1934 novel *Code of the West*, Zane Grey became the first to acknowledge the unwritten rules of behavior and core values demonstrated by the men who rode the range. These principles became known as the Cowboy Code and were further popularized in print by western writers Max Brand and Louis L'Amour. Cowboy stars John Wayne and Gene Autry trumpeted these feelings to the youth of America on and off the screen. Mitchum did so by his actions behind the scenes at RKO, exemplifying the cowboy way as he earned the trust and loyalty of the men and women he worked with. He was never above pitching in to get the job done with a little grunt work. He'd gladly wrangle the horses any day over fussing about his profile in the makeup chair or worrying about his lighting in front of the camera. At the *Cowboy Ethics* website, writer James P. Owen

---

*Dan Haggerty (western festival appearance, October 2014).

has summarized the Cowboy Code as (1) Live each day with courage; (2) Take pride in your work; (3) Always finish what you start; (4) Do what has to be done; (5) Be tough, but fair; (6) When you make a promise, keep it; (7) Ride for the brand; (8) Talk less and say more; (9) Remember that some things aren't for sale; and (10) Know when to draw the line.

The American cowboy symbolizes freedom and the great outdoors. They were stoic by nature, and not given to overt displays of emotion—like Mitchum. The B-western genre defined right and wrong for an entire generation, which is why they remain beloved to this day. Mitchum intrinsically understood this Cowboy Code of being a good American while promoting beneficial life lessons. Cowboys didn't quit, and they didn't shirk responsibility. You could bank on them. He absorbed the character traits and values of the western men he portrayed. Mitchum believed in self-reliance and personal freedom and let his actions define him rather than any lip service. He displayed honesty, integrity and a strong work ethic for his employers.

However, Mitchum was a study in contradictions. While he possessed and represented all the admiral qualities of a cowboy hero, he drank liquor, smoked like a chimney, and got into bar fights when challenged. In 1945, he broke a cop's nose in a fight on his property and was thrown into the lockup. The fact is that several Old West lawman legends once rode the outlaw trail. Men like Pat Garrett, Tom Horn and Henry Brown had checkered pasts. Movies created myth and invented the virtuous singing cowboy. The lines between good and bad were complicated by true survival and the reality of the situation. Among Hollywood cowboy actors, Mitchum was far closer to reality than myth.

In Darrell Arnold's *The Cowboy Kind*, renowned stuntman Richard Farnsworth said, "For many of us, the cowboy is still the most interesting of all our American heroes. It is sometimes difficult to separate the cowboy of legend from the real cowboy—a man who works on horseback, lives in the wide-open spaces, makes his living from the land, and performs skillful tasks like riding and roping." Rodeo legend Slim Pickens explained to Jerry Buck in *The Advocate*, "The cowboy was a dropout. He was somebody who would rather be out punching cows than be around people in a city. Back in those days, nobody ever wanted his daughter to marry a cowboy." These men lived by their Code, as horse wrangler turned stuntman Ben Johnson explained to *American Cowboy* magazine. A true cowboy was a man of his word, polite to women, soft with children, kind to strangers, and loyal to his horse. "I was raised on an Osage reservation on the same side of the creek where Will Rogers was a boy," Johnson says. "We were taught to stick to what you believe in."

Cowboy stars who were targeted as role models for the youth of America needed to toe the line in their personal lives or risk being ousted, and Mitchum was on a rocky ledge with uncertain footing in that regard. Sunset Carson is a perfect example of a cowboy actor whose vices led to his erupt departure from Republic. Mitchum was different. He understood that stardom could be short-lived and he wasn't given to ego or self-inflation. He would not create false artifices for the sake of career. He could be replaced easily enough, and he un-

As Cowboy hero Pecos Smith, with guns drawn in *West of the Pecos* (1945).

derstood this. "One of the greatest movie stars was Rin Tin Tin," he would say in *The Reluctant Star*, referring to the famous German Shepard canine. "What the hell. It can't be too much of a trick."

With his name first in the B-western credits and advertising, he was bound to gain greater notice. One odd novelty piece was *Hollywood's Make-Up Magic*, a promotional short he did for Max Factor's makeup studio. Mitchum's segment is called "How to Put Hair on a Cowboy's Chest." It's speculated that this bit was filmed as far back as 1942, although Mitchum appears in a heroic cowboy outfit strongly resembling those he wore during his RKO tenure. In the spot, makeup technician Fred Frederick applies a thick thatch of fake hair onto a smiling Mitchum's chest using spirit gum. The promotional ad was shown in theaters around the world and can be glimpsed in the Mitchum–James Stewart documentary *Two Faces of America*.

"I'm very fond of Mitchum" Robert Aldrich related in a Richard Combs biography on the film director. "I was an assistant when he was doing those Zane Grey westerns at RKO. I think he's a marvelous actor." Aldrich also worked with Mitchum as an assistant director to William Wellman in *The Story of G.I. Joe* (1945) and to Lewis Milestone in *The Red Pony* (1949). He directed such noteworthy westerns as *Apache* (1954), *Vera Cruz* (1954) and *Ulzana's Raid* (1972) in addition to directing Mitchum in *The Angry Hills* (1959). Some sources claim it was Aldrich who pointed out Mitchum's abilities to Wellman. Legend has it that Wellman himself spied Mitchum walking down the street and was intrigued enough by his masculine gait to bring him in for an interview. Syndicated columnist Harold Heffernan even wrote that *Story of G.I. Joe* producer Lester Cowan discovered Mitchum from his Max Factor ad!

Wellman, an Oscar-winning director with a larger-than-life persona, had Mitchum read for the important part of Bill Walker in his dramatic World War II film *The Story of G.I. Joe*. Mitchum told Charles Gentry, "I've faced a lot of tough things in my life, but the worst was getting through my first interview with Bill Wellman…. He was harder than any tough sergeant." Wellman grilled Mitchum on his height, weight and acting background. Mitchum answered honestly but told Wellman he didn't care for the director's gruff line of questioning. Wellman was accustomed to haughty actors embellishing their height and accomplishments and was impressed with Mitchum's candor. They proceeded to a screen test. Mitchum stunned Wellman with the sincerity of his portrayal. The scene in question, war-weary Mitchum's composition of letters to the parents of dead soldiers, led to a Best Supporting Oscar nomination and a farewell to any sense of anonymity in his life or work.

Mitchum's name immediately shot to the A-list of movie stars. "All this that is happening to me is an accident," he told Florabel Muir of *Photoplay*. "I just happened to get a part in a good picture and a role I could handle. It was right down my alley." Mitchum credited everything but his own talent. He felt it was impossible not to generate audience sympathy during the film's memorable ending when his dead body is brought back from battle draped over a mule in front of his silent soldiers. "I got an Academy Award nomination for playing a corpse," he told the *Newark Star Ledger*. "If the captain in that picture had lived and turned out to be a hero, nobody would ever have heard of me again." To the *San Francisco Chronicle* he said, "I'm just a boy out of the gallopers. I've made ten westerns, and nobody ever heard of me." Over the years, Mitchum continued to exhibit cowboy modesty and to downplay his success, explaining in David Downing's bio, "Up there on the screen you're 30 feet wide, your eyeball is six feet high, but it doesn't mean that you really amount to anything or have anything important to say."

The release of Wellman's celebrated war film coincided with Mitchum's own inevitable military service in the U.S. Army. Mitchum served stateside as a drill instructor and medical assistant from April 12, 1945, until the end of the war, and earned a sharpshooter's medal on the rifle range. He received his discharge papers on October 11, 1945. Mitchum's service to his country was never something he went into detail about with the press, preferring to leave that aspect of his life private. When asked, he would play off his involvement by taking a few comic jabs regarding his duties checking soldiers for hemorrhoids during their physicals. He ended up making nearly as many war films as he did westerns, with titles like *Heaven Knows Mr. Allison* (1957), *The Enemy Below* (1957), and *The Longest Day* (1962) highly recommended. The epic mini-series *The Winds of War* (1983) and *War and Remembrance* (1988) defined the latter portion of his career as a tough military man. Regarding his dual 1940s image of cowboy and soldier, Mitchum reckoned he was physically suited for the work, telling the *Cleveland Plain Dealer*, "I could crawl on my belly with a rifle better than the other guys."

Upon his return to the studio, RKO had far greater plans for their hot new star than to return him to the B-western fold. James Warren replaced Mitchum in the Zane Grey series, starring in *Wanderers of the Wasteland* (1945) opposite Richard Martin as Chito. *Sunset Pass* (1946) and *Code of the West* (1947) followed with John Laurenz taking over the Chito part. Warren was then replaced by Tim Holt when RKO's previous cowboy hero returned from the Armed Forces. Richard Martin came back as Chito for 29 entertaining adventures with Holt that lasted into the early 1950s. Mitchum humorously claimed he got himself canned by blinking his eyes every time he fired off his six-shooters. "I might have wound up a western star," Mitchum told *Time Out* of his early tenure at RKO. "You get conditioned, you know. I was their horseshit salesman."

Pursued (Warner Bros., 1947)

Cast: Teresa Wright (Thor Callum); Robert Mitchum (Jeb Rand); Judith Anderson (Mrs. Callum); Dean Jagger (Grant Callum); Alan Hale (Jake Dingle); John Rodney (Adam Callum); Harry Carey, Jr. (Prentice); Clifton Young (The Sergeant); Ernest Severn (Young Jeb); Charles Bates (Young Adam); Peggy Miller (Young Thor); Norman Jolley, Lane Chandler, Elmer Ellingwood, Jack Montgomery (Callums); and Erville Anderson, Walter Bacon, Hank Bell, Virginia Brissac, Russ Clark, Ben Corbett, Jack Davis, Lester Dorr, Tom Fadden, Carl Harbaugh, Scotty Hugenberg, Kathy Jeanne Johnson, Al Kunde, Harry Lamont, Mickey Little, Ian MacDonald, Charles Miller, Ervin Richardson, Sherman Sanders, Paul Scardon, William Sundholm, Ray Teal, Louise Volding, Eddy Waller, Slim Whitaker, Crane Whitley, Ian Wolfe.

Crew: Raoul Walsh (Director); Milton Sperling (Producer); Niven Busch (Screenplay); James Wong Howe (Photographer); Max Steiner (Music); Ted Smith (Art Director); Christian Nyby (Editor); Leah Rhodes (Wardrobe); Russell Saunders (Assistant Director); Allen Pomeroy, Terry Wilson, Glen Thompson, Audrey Scott, Louise Volding, Vivian Nalder, Robert "King" Sterling (Stunts); Terry Wilson (Wrangler).

101 minutes; Released March 2, 1947

Following Mitchum's Oscar nomination, the clamor for his services became intense. At RKO, there seemed no role more suited than that of one of three G.I.s (Guy Madison, Bill Williams, Mitchum) readjusting to the States after World War II service in Edward Dmytryk's drama *Till the End of Time* (1946). In *The Reluctant Star,* Dmytryk said, "He was born with what we call film-style acting. A really fine film actor does not give a performance. He creates a person. Mitchum was one of the very best at that." Mitchum's choice role as a former rodeo rider strongly reinforced his already established western screen image. "We're all a case of mistaken identity in this business," he told Louella Parsons. "I play in Texas pictures, and everybody thinks I come from Texas. The only time I've ever been in Texas was when I've ridden a freight car across the state."

Mitchum donned a Stetson, Levi's 506 Denim jean jacket and cowboy boots for the film. He even sang a snippet of Tex Ritter's cowboy song "I Got Spurs" and participated in a barroom brawl. His William Tabeshaw in *Till the End of Time* is an early example of a fatalistic Mitchum character doomed by circumstances. He experiences severe headaches from his war-related injuries and can never return to the rodeo because of a steel plate holding his skull together. There are few things worse than a young cowboy being told he can no longer cowboy and Mitchum completely captures that angst. Regarding the class production, *Newsweek* wrote that Mitchum "lassos top acting honors."

RKO saw dollar signs in their ability to loan Mitchum out to other studios as well as place him in high-profile roles for themselves. RKO's first loan-out was for Warner Bros.' psychological A-western *Pursued*. This complex adult-themed story from *Duel in the Sun* (1946) screenwriter Niven Busch is considered the first noir-western. It's the first Freudian oater, full of elements of Greek tragedy and repressed events from Mitchum's childhood affecting him as a grown man. Director Raoul Walsh was an action master by reputation, but by relying on the brilliant black and white location photography of James Wong Howe, he created one of the screen's most striking westerns even if several elements of characterization don't add up. They lensed on breathtaking rock-wall vistas in Red Rock Canyon near Gallup, New Mexico, between August and October 1946. The story of a deadly family feud and the toll it takes on one surviving son (Mitchum) is told in flashback by the star as he pieces together nightmares from his haunted past to Max Steiner's pulsing score. Trying to help him is new bride Teresa Wright, so confused by family allegiances that she has plotted to kill Mitchum on their wedding night.

The marriage has an incestuous feel as Wright's mother Judith Anderson raised them in the same home as brother and sister since they were children. This scenario creates a growing tension between Mitchum and Wright's real brother John Rodney who is fed decades of built-up hatred by elder relative Dean Jagger. The motivations and actions of Wright, Anderson and especially Rodney never develop sufficiently and are the weakest element of the otherwise absorbing film. These three characters behave irrationally and force the increasingly confused Mitchum to react to them.

Mitchum's recent return from fighting in the 1898 Spanish-American War drives plot points into action. A pressed-upon Mitchum is forced to kill multiple times in self-defense with his rifle in the wilderness and his sidearm on a shadowy back street when Wright's suitor Harry Carey, Jr., draws on him. On the run due to circumstances beyond his control, he's a tiny dot on horseback in a vast landscape with multiple pursuers closing in. This is an especially well-constructed scene from Walsh and editor Christian Nyby. Here, the impressive Gallup location greatly benefits the visual look of the film. These formidable cliffs and towering sentinels of northwestern New Mexico had rarely been seen in a western outside of *Billy the Kid* (1930). By story's end, the existential outsider Mitchum has returned to his isolated burned-out childhood cabin at the fictional Bear Paw Butte, which triggers his memory sufficiently to piece together why events have unfolded in such a manner.

Teresa Wright (screenwriter Busch's real-life wife) is given top billing, but Mitchum dominates with his brooding, intense and sexually charged performance. It is by far his most troubled and vulnerable screen character, a man with intimate knowledge and awareness of his own impending doom. His character describes the feeling as "a black dog riding my back." His smoldering sensuality is played up for the females in the audience by Howe's appreciative camera in this stylish, edgy, fatalistic western noir crossover. He wears open-neck shirts displaying his chest or is clad in a rugged buckskin Indian jacket. Reports from the set were that Wright felt very nervous working around him due to the presence of her husband and her own sense of attraction to her alternatively tough and tender co-star.

When he got out of the Army in late 1945, Mitchum filled out his lean, genetically gifted frame by taking bodybuilding workouts at the Easton Bros. Gym. He also sparred in the Hollywood YMCA boxing ring with pugilists turned actors Steve Brodie and Robert Ryan. The result was that the strapping 190-pound Mitchum never looked better than he did in this film. As was becoming typical of Mitchum and his iconic male bravado, he downplayed any hard work on his part to the press, proclaiming the sole exercise he undertook was breathing in and out. Given his new physical maturity and fully realized self-confidence, he was creating a new individual prototype for Hollywood stardom that could not be bent, shaped or whittled away by the studios. He was the original cowboy rebel whose hip swagger anticipated the coming of Elvis Presley and rock'n'roll. Co-star Harry "Dobe" Carey, Jr., forever beloved by western fans for his roles in John Ford's *3 Godfathers* (1948), *She Wore a Yellow Ribbon* (1949) and *The Searchers* (1956), described Mitchum to Lee Server as "an overwhelming personality... the coolest guy that ever lived."

"Dobe" was the son of actress Olive Carey (*The Searchers*) and original Hollywood cowboy Harry Carey, John Wayne's screen hero. The young Carey won the part in *Pursued* (his first important role) over 25 other actors, including Montgomery Clift. "Dobe" got his nickname due to his adobe-red hair. He would become a Mitchum friend and drinking buddy for the next two decades, although the two drifted apart when Carey swore off alcohol in the 1970s. They were still friendly at that point; they simply had less in common. Carey had a small part opposite Mitchum in *Blood on the Moon* and a character role in *The Way West*. He always spoke highly of Mitchum on the film festival circuit. In *Feature Players*, Carey reflected on *Pursued*: "Mitchum's terrific. I've worked with him three or four times and he's never changed. He was very easy to work with. I was nervous, and he was always calming me down. A very laid-back guy."

Walsh filled the film with veterans of the Hollywood western, many with stunt riding careers dating back to the silent movie days, including "Smiley" Ben Corbett, "Handlebar" Hank Bell, Charles "Slim" Whitaker, Jack "Monty" Montgomery and "Bear Valley" Charlie Miller. Solid character actors Lane Chandler and Ray Teal (best known as Sheriff Roy Coffee on TV's *Bonanza*) were western film vets, and Mitchum continued to absorb the experience and knowledge surrounding him. Mitchum became friends on this film with his on-screen brother John Rodney. Mitchum got such a kick out of seeing the Brooklyn-born Rodney's discomfort in the saddle that he playfully called him "Roarin' Horse Rodney" for the rest of the picture. When Raoul Walsh fretted about storm clouds threatening to ruin a day's shoot, Mitchum produced a local Navajo medicine man who claimed he could ward off the rain for the sum of $5. It still rained, to Mitchum's delight.

Mitchum gives his character of Jeb Rand a strong degree of authenticity and moves in the western surroundings like he belongs. One especially smooth display of agility stands out during a canyon ambush. Mitchum leaps from his horse, and in the same motion withdraws his rifle from its sheath on his saddle before landing on his feet to return gunfire. It's a revelation for those who buy into the notion that Mitchum walked through performances under the influence of alcohol or lack of energy. He was, in fact, a fine athlete. In his book *The Noir Western—Darkness on*

With leading lady Teresa Wright on location in Gallup, New Mexico, for *Pursued* (1947).

the Range, David Meuel noted that Mitchum was the rare actor "who could do just about anything extremely well."

Joe Carducci wrote of the typical Hollywood cowboy and his lack of dexterity in *Stone Male*:

> It is worth watching mounts and dismounts of horses in westerns. The dudes and old-timers often require a cut so that they are suddenly up in the saddle or at least can grab hold of the stirrup to get their foot into it off camera. [Charles] Bronson and some others jump up directly into the saddle, then put their boots into stirrups. The most impressive mounts involve a single jump up and the insertion of the boot into stirrup mid-air. Of the big stars, one can see Robert Mitchum pull this off.

Another physical highlight of the film is a fistfight between Mitchum and Rodney on their home front porch. Veteran stunt coordinator Allen Pomeroy, fight choreographer and stuntman for Randolph Scott in the memorably epic brawl in 1942's *The Spoilers,* was using two brand new stuntmen, Terry Wilson and Glen Thompson. Pomeroy had placed several World War II veterans into training and used footage from the tough fight scene in *Pursued* to showcase their action abilities. The ironic thing is that it is clearly Mitchum himself doing a great deal of the impressive screen fight against his director's wishes. Mitchum's double Wilson did execute a horse jump over a fence for Mitchum, but the star was a seasoned hand at performing the bulk of his own screen fights. "We could do fight scenes in one or two takes and nobody got hurt," Mitchum said in the early

In a Navajo coat, Mitchum finds the remains of his childhood home in *Pursued* (1947).

1970s. "Walshie tried to play tough guy, but we ignored him."* Wilson went on to become one of the top stuntmen of the 1950s and made his mark as an actor on the long-running TV series *Wagon Train* (1957–1965) as scout Bill Hawks.

Walsh and Mitchum were an interesting pairing in *Pursued*, their lone film together. One-Eyed Walsh was famous for discovering Marion Morrison, rechristening him John Wayne, and starring the former USC football player in *The Big Trail* (1930). Walsh and Mitchum nearly worked together a second time: The director wanted Mitchum to star as the cowboy outlaw who breaks jail with a murder rap hanging over his head in *Colorado Territory* (1949), a western remake of Walsh's own classic *High Sierra* (1941). Studio head Jack L. Warner preferred hiring the safer choice of Joel McCrea, the scandal-free, dependable star of such high-profile westerns as *Union Pacific* (1939), *The Virginian* (1946) and *Ramrod* (1947). Mitchum's eight-year-old son Jim did end up appearing unbilled in *Colorado Territory*.

When Walsh got a look at the film's fight scene footage, he realized how effective it could be having a handy lead actor capable of doing his own stunts. Walsh demanded a lot out of his star physically despite Terry Wilson and a local rodeo cowboy named King Sterling being available to double Mitchum on horseback. In one *Pursued* scene, Mitchum came out of a box canyon bareback and the animal spooked. It rolled over Mitchum, knocking the wind out of him and injuring his hip. Walsh didn't miss a beat, asking Mitchum to bring the horse out a little faster the next take. Mitchum shook off the dust and obliged. In another scene, Mitchum handled a live, defanged rattlesnake. In his 1974 autobiography *Each Man in His Time*, Walsh praised his star: "Robert Mitchum impressed me as being one of the finest natural actors I ever met." Mitchum was equally fond of Walsh, telling Dick Lochte, "He's a double-tough mother and a great man. I have a great respect for him." Mitchum delighted in revealing Walsh's hands-off directing style. He frequently told the humorous story of Walsh unsuccessfully rolling his own tobacco while scenes were going on, spilling the fixings out on his blind side as he paced around. If the dialogue sounded okay, he'd yell "Print!," rip out the script's pages for that scene, and move on.

Pursued provides the first real opportunity to hear Mitchum sing more than a snippet on screen. With John Rodney, he duets on the Irish folk song "Danny Boy" to the arrangement of "Londonderry Air." On his horse, Mitchum offers a few solo lines of the sad cowboy standard "Streets of Laredo." His singing style is extremely relaxed and pleasing to the ear. Mitchum's vocal talents were called upon repeatedly throughout his career, especially in the western genre. He plays a wandering minstrel in *Rachel and the Stranger* (1948), and debate still rages if it's him or Tennessee Ernie Ford doing the opening credits theme song to *River of No Return* (1954). For *The Night of the Hunter* (1955), Mitchum offered an especially chilling on-screen version of the hymn "Leaning on the Everlasting Arms." In 1957, he released the infamous album *Calypso Is Like So*, a fascinating glimpse into his time spent in the Caribbean making *Fire Down Below* (1957) and *Heaven Knows, Mr. Allison* (1957). A song Mitchum wrote and sang, "The Ballad of Thunder Road," for *Thunder Road* (1958) became a mild pop hit with that film's release. The song became such a notorious outlaw anthem that legendary Gonzo journalist Hunter S. Thompson requested it be played at his wake (leading to his cremated ashes being shot out of a cannon by actor Johnny Depp). Mitchum also wrote and sang "Whippoorwill" for *Thunder Road*.

Mitchum performed the Irish lullaby "Too Ra Loo Ra Loo Ral" with the Ames Brothers on *The Ed Sullivan Show* in 1957 and sang Australian drinking songs on-screen throughout *The Sundowners* (1960). In 1968, he made country and western recordings for Nashville's Monument Records and Roy Orbison producer Fred Foster. These included the single "Little Ole Wine Drinker Me," a song by Bakersfield cowboy singer Charlie Walker that Mitchum liked. Mitchum's version reached

---

*Garry Armstrong (e-mail correspondence, August 2017).

#9 on *Billboard*'s Hot Country Singles Chart. Other songs Mitchum tackled on the *That Man* album were "Wheels (It's Rollin' Time Again)" and "Gotta Travel On," appropriate titles for the eternal nomad. He also sang the title song to the western *Young Billy Young* (1969), which later showed up on the 1990s Mitchum compilation album *Tall Dark Stranger* alongside the *Rachel* songs and various jazz-flavored demos of standards and traditional folk songs like "Roving Gambler."

Fred MacMurray and John Garfield were originally attached to star in *Pursued* before Mitchum landed the part. Up-and-comer Kirk Douglas was also under consideration. However, leading lady Teresa Wright wanted and got Mitchum. He is rock-solid sorting through his repressed memories and critics took note of the complexities he conveyed. *The New York Herald Tribune* said, "Mitchum gives a modulated characterization of the man pursued by fugitive memories and very real enemies," while *Newsweek* praised all the leads, calling their collective work "superior to those performances usually associated with gunplay and the great open spaces." *The Hollywood Reporter* wrote, "Mitchum makes his characterization outstanding under the punchy direction by Walsh." According to *The Los Angeles Times,* Mitchum and Wright "both have potent assignments." *Esquire* flat-out declared, "The picture moves Robert Mitchum into the front ranks of stardom." But *The New York Times*'s prickly Bosley Crowther took Mitchum to task for his dark probing gazes into the past and his extreme underplaying: "Mitchum is a very rigid gent and gives off no more animation than a Frigidaire turned to defrost."

More recently, *Western Films* author Brian Garfield wrote, "The acting by all four principals is splendid," while Henryk Hoffman of *"A" Western Filmmakers* said that Mitchum gave "[a]n outstanding performance." According to *The Encyclopedia of Westerns*, "The casting is superb, with Robert Mitchum so natural that he makes his complex character totally believable," while *The Rough Guide to Westerns* said that Mitchum "gives one of his most impressively low-key studies in fatalism." From *The Western Reader*: "The film rests on Robert Mitchum's deeply weary way of moving, his passive way of waiting for mysteries to unravel around him, as put to such good use in so many later film noirs." *Renegade Westerns* found *Pursued* was "the perfect template for Robert Mitchum's fatalistic outsiders; the physique and swagger of a champion offset by the mien of an eternal loser." At the site *Buddies in the Saddle,* blogger Ron Scheer wrote, "Mitchum portrays well the emotional dislocation surely felt by a generation of returning soldiers, especially as he loses the ranch and the girl he plans to marry. His sense of lonely resignation is re-

With pistol drawn, striking a studio pose with Teresa Wright in *Pursued* (1947).

flected in Mitchum's unsmiling, almost sullen expression, always masking what seems to be hurt and confusion." *Western Clippings* determined *Pursued* to be "the ultimate film noir western," while according to Lincoln Center's *Film Linc Daily*, "*Pursued* opened up new paths for the western and remains one of Mitchum's great achievements."

Ever the non-conformist, Mitchum took his performance seriously but downplayed any great talent on his part. To him, acting was an un-masculine profession, and in the documentary *The Reluctant Star* he derisively called himself "a movie actress." He told biographer Mike Tomkies, "I got three expressions, looking left, looking right, and looking straight ahead." He was, however, building up his screen image as a restless outcast prone to extended runs of bad luck. On two occasions in *Pursued*, he loses a pivotal coin toss that severely affects his future. He accepts these fateful losses with a typical Mitchum nonchalance, announcing he hopes "to lose more slowly" in the future. Gambling hall owner Alan Hale later manipulates the odds on a roulette wheel so Mitchum will win for a change, eventually taking him in as his business partner. Hale, an extremely likable sidekick to Errol Flynn in *Dodge City* (1939), *Virginia City* (1940) and *Santa Fe Trail* (1940), is the lone character in the film who isn't gunning for the luckless westerner.

Professional whenever the cameras were ready to roll, Mitchum was already beginning to garner a reputation for his interactive nightlife. It was hard for anyone not to notice his capacity for relentless self-destruction. The cast and crew were housed on location at the El Rancho Hotel in Gallup along historic Route 66 and the Santa Fe Railroad, and rising star Mitchum was easily the center of attention. Plagued by restlessness and insomnia, he could operate on far less sleep than the average human being. Resembling a drover entering a new town, Mitchum unwound like any cowboy worth his spurs. He rough-housed with the stuntmen, played cards, and drank at the local watering holes until the wee hours. Accepting a challenge from the town bully, he met the braggart back of the hotel and knocked him down and out with two well-placed punches. If there was anything else of interest, he'd find it before grabbing a few hours of shut-eye. He'd answer the morning call to the bleary-eyed astonishment of all those attempting to keep up with him, be they cast, crew or local recruits. His favored hangover cure was a couple of ounces of bourbon blended with orange juice, eggs and honey. Another remedy was a Ramos Gin Fizz consisting of gin, lemon juice, lime juice, egg white, sugar, cream, orange-flower water and soda water. Mitchum called it "Mother's Milk." Throughout the day he downed Fernet Branca, an Amaro bitter herbal elixir from Italy that some felt was a magic hangover cure. A bottle of Fernet Branca itself consisted of 39 percent alcohol.

Mitchum had tremendous recuperative powers and the willpower to get up and go. Cowboys who couldn't get out of their bunk didn't keep jobs for long, but Mitchum met each daily challenge. Location filming interested him and temporarily satisfied his inquisitive wanderlust. It was like a field trip for Mitchum where he absorbed the local Navajo Indian culture and discovered their customs; what they ate, what they drank, what they smoked. It was processed to inform his portrayal or be used later as part of the vast Mitchum tapestry. Some actors learned their craft in classrooms. Mitchum learned his craft through real-life interaction traveling first the United States and later the world. "I like people and I like towns," he told *Photoplay*. "A strange town is always exciting. Every new place is an adventure. I'd get into a new town and wouldn't know what to expect. There would always be a new, interesting person to talk with."

Mitchum followed *Pursued* with a strong role complimenting Robert Young and Robert Ryan in Edward Dmytryk's bigotry-in-the-military drama *Crossfire* (1947) and an outright lead in Jacques Tourneur's definitive film noir *Out of the Past* (1947). His iconic modern-day performance as ill-fated detective Jeff Bailey placed him in the ranks of the big stars and solidified his image for the rest of his career as a man undone by his love for bad girl Jane Greer. Before a trenchcoat and fedora became his permanent calling cards, he made three more interesting, high-quality westerns in quick succession: *Rachel and the Stranger* (1948), *Blood on the Moon* (1948) and *The Red Pony* (1949). Biographer Derek Malcolm quoted Mitchum as saying, "I was now a leading man. A cause for apprehension and embarrassment. It was much too late to begin following any design or direction."

Mitchum continually confounded the established Hollywood press machine with his blunt talk and/or vague philosophical allegories. Reporters expecting cowboy simplicity were flummoxed by the intellectual before them. He was bored by their questions, and fatigued insolence became his favored expression. However, his spicy answers and colorful language proved great copy. "The columnists and reporters all just loved him because he'd say anything," stand-in Boyd Cabeen told George Eells. They weren't sure what to believe. Early movie cowboy Tom Mix created a studio bio so fantastic that holes were easily punched into its fabric. Mitchum's entertaining stories about hobos, chain gangs, youthful miscreants and boxing matches had a ring of truth. He quickly dispelled RKO publicists' stories that he performed in vaudeville as a child, broke horses in Texas, sailed on a freighter to South America, and studied at Duke University. "I didn't write the darned thing," he told Hedda Hopper in 1947 regarding untruths in the RKO bio.

Despite his work ethic, Mitchum showed no fear of disrupting the business suits who signed his paychecks. He complained that David O. Selznick, who owned part of his contract with RKO, made $200,000 loaning him to Warner Bros. while Mitchum made $163 a week after taxes for starring in *Pursued*. Legend has it Mitchum relieved himself on Selznick's office carpet as a show of his lack of appreciation. Mitchum merely claimed that he really had to go. At one point they had him working around the clock on three films at the same time. It was rare that he ever saw a script before being told to report. Mitchum requested that his contract be amended to allow him to make one film of his choice every 18 months. He told columnist Hedda Hopper, "The rest of the time I'll crawl through any picture on my hands and knees and bark if necessary. I just want one film in which I'll have time to learn my role before going before the camera."

To stay connected to his working-class roots, Mitchum could be seen stocking shelves at the Crescent Heights Market or scrubbing dishes at the Chateau Marmont, down-to-earth activities no headliner would think to engage in. He loafed at the market with a group of actors who called themselves "the grocery store cowboys." His pals remained rugged character actor types the likes of Steve Brodie, Tom Munroe and Peter Coe. In 1946, cowboy heavy Dick Curtis completed building the western set Pioneertown near 29 Palms in Yucca Valley, and Mitchum attended the premiere event for his movie friend.

Mitchum sometimes hiked to a secluded Hollywood Hills cabin dubbed "The Hangout," owned by western actors Pierce Lyden and John James. Mitchum welcomed the opportunity to share a drink and shoot the bull there with cowboy buddies like Douglas Fowley. "It was high on the side of a hill, surrounded by trees and brush," Lyden told the *Orange County Register*. "You had to park on a one-lane road and walk up a path about 300 yards. In fact, you had to have a road map to find the place. And when it rained, forget it. Bob Mitchum used to drop by for a drink and to relax after a day's work.... It was a place for tired actors to get away from it all." It was at "The Hangout" that Mitchum met stuntman turned western character actor Richard Farnsworth, later an Oscar nominee for *Comes a Horseman* (1978). Farnsworth became another lifelong acquaintance and co-worker.

Mitchum never bought into the need to be seen at the swankiest Hollywood clubs and hot spots for the paparazzi cameras. He couldn't care less about advancing his career by meeting the so-called right people. To him, the cowboy types were his stock and the men he was comfortable spending down-time with. Mitchum was forever threatening to quit the business, always claiming to interviewers (like Cameron Shipp of *Collier's*) that he was "between trains" in this part of his rambling life. In *The Reluctant Star*, he confessed that he expected to one day be telling another old hobo about "that time when I was a Hollywood movie star." His ancestors had been the earliest settlers in South Carolina of the 1640s. Some had gone west on the Lewis and Clark expedition and returned scandalously with Blackfoot Indian brides. "I'm from the low-down Mitchum line," he told *Modern Screen*. "But I'm kind of proud of it. They didn't believe in rules, my ancestors, and they didn't give a damn. And every one of them could look after himself wherever he went, which was often a pretty far piece."

Rachel and the Stranger (RKO, 1948)

Cast: Loretta Young (Rachel); William Holden (David Harvey); Robert Mitchum (Jim Fairways); Gary Gray (Davey); Tom Tully (Parson Jackson); Sara Haden (Mrs. Jackson); Frank Ferguson (Mr. Green); Walter Baldwin (Gallus); Regina Wallace (Mrs. Green); and Frank Conlan.

Crew: Norman Foster (Director); Richard H. Berger (Producer); Waldo Salt (Screenplay); Maury Gertsman (Photographer); Roy Webb (Music); Albert S. D'Agostino and Jack Okey (Art Directors); Les Millbrook (Editor); Harry Mancke (Assistant Director); Dewey Starkey (Unit Manager).

80 minutes; Released September 20, 1948

A delightful, overlooked gem, *Rachel and the Stranger* features one of Mitchum's most accessible performances. The simple, well-told story has proven to be an audience favorite for those lucky enough to come across it. *Rachel* was a surprise hit for RKO.

The film is set in early 1800s Ohio but was filmed in and around heavily wooded areas of Springfield and Eugene, Oregon, in the late summer and fall of 1947. Locations include Fox Hollow Road, Spencer Butte, the McKenzie River and the Fern Ridge Reservoir. The unjustly forgotten black and white film presents Mitchum to great advantage as a buckskin-clad frontiersman and is an excellent first viewing choice for those unfamiliar with his overall western catalogue. He is first seen wandering into director Norman Foster's frame leading a horse and strumming a guitar with nary a care in the world—a perfect Mitchum introduction. It had the working titles *Rachel* and *Tall Dark Stranger*. The Waldo Salt screenplay (from the writings of Howard Fast) provides a fine mixture of drama and pathos. "My role in that was fairly well-threaded," Mitchum told the *Milwaukee Sentinel*, "with a very good grade of sardonic comedy plus some corn and veritable slapstick."

Mitchum is Trapper-Indian scout Jim Fairways, the stranger of the title. It's a complicated scenario as Mitchum and William Holden are friendly rivals going back to the courting of Holden's first wife, who has recently died from sickness. Mitchum heads to the high country for the hunting season and upon his return is surprised to see that Holden has quickly taken on a new wife, Rachel (Young), to help raise his son (Gary Gray). The reality is that Holden bought indentured bondwoman Young from the local fort and there's no love between them. A perceptive Mitchum picks up on this and decides the earthy Young might be a better fit for him. His not-so-subtle courtship of Young is filled with gentle doses of humor. This wakes Holden up from his stupor and the rest of the film has the men vying for Young. A comic fistfight is a highlight. The turning point comes when Holden's isolated cabin is attacked by a band of Shawnee Indians, and all parties must join to save the homestead.

As part of the courtship of Miss Young, Mitchum doffs his buckskin outfit for his Sunday clothes, looking like the evil preacher he would play so memorably in *The Night of the Hunter* (1955). Mitchum and Holden performed

As frontiersman Jim Fairways in *Rachel and the Stranger* (1948).

a wonderfully choreographed fight scene with a pack of hound dogs nipping at Mitchum's heels. "We played it for comedy," Mitchum recalled in the Holden documentary *Golden Boy*. "Bill had a sense of merriment with him all the time." The action-filled climax involving the Indian attack on the cabin is far darker and an exciting counterpoint to the film's earlier action. Mitchum excels with his physicality, although RKO trimmed portions of these scenes during the film's 1950s reissue. Realizing that Holden and Young are indeed a good match, Mitchum leads the members of the fort off into the wilderness to track down the remaining Indians at the film's conclusion.

Ideally cast as the vagabond frontier balladeer, the wild and woodsy Mitchum describes himself as a loner who always has an itch in his boots. The roguish actor is at his most laidback and charming as the man of the wilderness, a close counterpart to his real-life persona. Mitchum liked hunting and fishing and was known to get away from the hustle and bustle of Hollywood to be one with nature. Oregon suited him. "My heart goes where the wild goose flies," he told Roger Ebert in 1969, quoting "Mule Train" singer Frankie Laine. Unlike many social creatures, Mitchum was content in his outdoor solitude. He enjoyed the location and *Rachel and the Stranger* was one of the few films he confessed delight in making. He had a sufficiently adventurous crony in stand-in Boyd Cabeen and made a new drinking partner in his fellow leading man. "Holden and I used to drift off to the side for quick pick-me-ups," Mitchum told Garry Armstrong. "Holden had stashes everywhere, but he was professional. Always knew his lines. Some of the PR guys were tryin' to brew trouble between me and Holden. We got a hold of one of the little bastards and corrected him."*

The mischievous men got on well with Loretta Young, a strictly raised Catholic they jokingly termed Mother Superior or Thin because of her bony body. In later years, Mitchum referred to her as Sister Mary after her TV character on *The Loretta Young Show*. They took

Showcasing his musical talents in *Rachel and the Stranger* (1948).

delight in watching how she always meticulously positioned herself in front of the camera to capture the best light. "Holden and I liked to prank Sister Mary," Mitchum said in 1972. "We would look at her cross-eyed in some [extreme close-ups]. We'd stay cross-eyed until the cameras rolled. Sister Mary would giggle or frown, but there was never any evidence to back up her behavior. She'd come into our trailers full of vim and vigor. We'd just smile at her. Holden could look so angelic."†

Holden biographer Michelangelo Capua writes that Young invited her leading men to dinner on a Saturday night and Mitchum and Holden each drained a bottle of whiskey. Young was shocked and told them their insides would rot. Mitchum said. "You worry too much." She implored her co-stars to mind their off-hours activities and initiated an infamous "curse box" on the set: Each crew member who swore was to contribute a nickel, dime or quarter depending

---

*Garry Armstrong (e-mail correspondence, November 2018).
†Garry Armstrong (e-mail correspondence, November 2018),

upon the severity of the swear word. Mitchum deposited several dollars into the box at once, then announced loudly for all to hear, "What I want to know is, what does Miss Young charge for a fuck?"

Mitchum pleasantly sings folk songs throughout the film including "O-he, O-hi, O-ho," "Foolish Pride," "Just Like Me," and "Rachel." He fingers the chords and strums the guitar while singing but didn't have to worry about playing the instrument during shooting: The guitar's strings were made of cotton and merely decorative. Decca Records released the Mitchum recordings and discussed making an entire album of songs. Kirk Douglas was tested for the Fairways part but exiting RKO head Dore Schary requested that Mitchum be given the role. Eastern-raised Douglas was not yet comfortable in a western setting, although his later performance in *The Big Sky* (1952) revealed a kinship to Mitchum's "great white trapper" character in this film. Joel McCrea was originally offered the Holden part.

It was not an easy location. Snakes and wild animals were present, and the water in the McKenzie River was ice-cold. All the stars received bee stings and needed shots for exposure to poison oak. A fire intentionally set to the cabin and barn went out of control, with Mitchum and Holden pitching in to help the Lake County fire department. The increasingly westernized Mitchum rode a bucking horse on a dare, spraining his wrist when inevitably thrown. While fishing during his off-hours, he caught a 42-inch Chinook Salmon, a point of great pride. Between camera set-ups, Mitchum liked to throw a baseball around, leading to a humorous moment. A group of Mitchum-obsessed bobbysoxers rode their bicycles more than ten miles to the location to get a close-up look at their hero. Mitchum promptly split the backseat of his buckskin pants when throwing a pitch, leading to a hail of laughter from the girls as Mitchum ambled to his dressing room. Child actor Gary Gray, interviewed in *Wildest Westerns*, recalled Mitchum on the location pitching in to help an older crew member who was having difficulty chopping wood: "Robert Mitchum was one heck of a good guy, big and brawny, and nice," said Gray. "Bob felt sorry for the old guy, as he wasn't doing very well; so, Bob took off his shirt and took the ax away from him and chopped it up for him."

Reviews were strong with *Variety* writing, "Everyone concerned do good if not outstanding jobs. ...[Mitchum's] role fits him naturally as he makes it entirely believable." *The Los Angeles Times* singled Mitchum out for praise: "Mitchum provides an impressive portrait of a happy-go-lucky wanderer who turns into a backwoods Cupid." *The New York Times* found the three leads "lend stature and conviction to their roles," and *Box Office* declared, "[The] performances generally are excellent." The *Evening Independent*: "Robert Mitchum gives a terrific performance as the stranger." *Modern Screen* wrote, "Mitchum is amazingly like Bing Crosby, believe it or not—he has that same effortless grace, that same almost carefully casual delivery." *Film Bulletin* noted the resemblance, writing, "Robert Mitchum scores as a gallivanting, buckskin playboy crooning six songs that sound like early American ballads in a Crosby-toned voice." *Western Clippings* believed the film "showed Mitchum's acting abilities beyond his usual brooding sternness," while *Western Films* cites the "lovely performances by the three stars."

Mitchum was peaking in his film career but not without concerns. He earned $3000 a week from RKO during the picture. He appreciated the pay but wanted little part of the trappings of fame, particularly regarding his personal privacy. "Bob has the rugged independence of an Army mule," his wife told *Photoplay*. He still dressed like a simple ranch hand and favored dive bars and gin joints over glitz and glamor establishments. He liked to kid that he was the worst dressed man in Hollywood. Forever frugal when it came to his own clothes, he saved and wore his Navajo and rawhide jacket wardrobe from his westerns *Pursued, Rachel and the Stranger* and *Blood on the Moon*. Mitchum defiantly marched to the beat of a different drummer, extremely ill at ease at being asked to attend press gatherings and studio promotions that played up his beefcake body or his "immoral face." The sudden influx of money had repercussions. Hangers-on began appearing with regularity at their modest Oak Glen home, mostly people Mitchum knew from the Army, the movie studio or bars he frequented (Lucey's near RKO, Boardner's on Hollywood Boulevard, Barney's Beanery on Santa Monica Boulevard, Victor's [later the Saratoga], Ye Coach & Horses, and the Cock 'n' Bull on the Sunset Strip). These new people in his life wanted him to share drinks, hospitality or more. Mitchum tried to oblige, finding some semblance of a macho energy outlet to counteract an otherwise un-masculine profession. Women and would-be starlets began throwing themselves at the big screen's newest sex symbol with little concern that he was a married man. Mitchum was given to moments of moral weakness as he attempted to accommodate all concerned at the expense of a normal home life. The buzz and commotion placed a great strain on his marriage as the parties sometimes ended up back at the Mitchum homestead. "It sometimes took 36 hours to outdrink them," Mitchum told Peer J. Oppenheimer. "And it nearly killed me—but in the end, they went."

A friend, Paul Behrmann, became Mitchum's business manager and promised to look after his finances. Soft-touch Mitchum was allotted a $20 a week allowance so that he wouldn't have money in his pockets to hand out to those who hit him up for loans or freebies. After a year of making movies continuously, Mitchum thought he had $68,000 in the bank. Dorothy was dismayed to find they had a little over $50 in their checking account. Mitchum's friend had stolen all his money and refused to give an accounting for the missing nest egg. A disappointed Mitchum did not press charges but was ultimately called to testify against Behrmann for another case where the money manager had bilked a client. An angry Dorothy wanted to leave Hollywood altogether and took the children home to Delaware.

Mitchum was suddenly at a crossroads in his career, half-ready to ditch it all but bound by the studio to soon begin a new film. He needed the upcoming money. In his idle hours, he hoisted more drinks and rolled pakalolos to relax. He wasn't the lone actor in Hollywood who smoked marijuana: Republic stuntman Duke Taylor was busted in 1945 and John Ireland's part in 1948's *Red River* was cut by director Howard Hawks because of the actor's pot use. But Mitchum became the first high-profile actor busted for it. At the time, it was widely perceived to be a career-killer.

On August 31, 1948, Mitchum was out for drinks with a bartender buddy turned real estate agent, Robin "Danny" Ford. The two men stopped off at a tiny Laurel Canyon bungalow on Ridpath Drive to meet actress Lila Leeds and her roommate Vicki Evans. No sooner had Mitchum been handed a joint than the cops busted in with tipped-off press quickly in force at the police station to document the arrest of a major Hollywood star. Ironically, one of the cops in on the arrest was Arizona-born Mescalero Apache Rudy Diaz, who after retiring from the force became a character actor in movies like *Bandolero* (1968), *Coogan's Bluff* (1968) and *Mackenna's Gold* (1969). A suspicious Mitchum sensed a set-up. When queried by the police what his occupation was, a downtrodden Mitchum sighed, "Former movie actor."

Mitchum took his punishment like a man, benefitting from the expertise of studio lawyer Jerry Geisler who determined that time served was needed in the eyes of the public. Mitchum was ultimately sentenced to 60 days in jail and two years of probation. Mitchum served his time at the County Jail and the Castaic work farm, which he described in David Downing's bio as "the finest vacation I've had in seven years…. It was a relief to get away for a while." In his book *The Tough Guys,* James Robert Parish famously quoted Mitchum likening the experience as being "like Palm Springs, without the riffraff." The so-called medical experts assigned to his case determined Mitchum to be "psychologically ill-equipped for his sudden rise to fame." He used his incarceration to clear his head and get himself in shape with hard work and regular exercise. They even had him milking cows on the farm. Mitchum claimed that jail provided the best sleep he'd had in his life. He still had the promise of an RKO film to be made in the form of the breezy Don Siegel action flick *The Big Steal* (1949). Part of this modern noir film was shot at the western movie location Iverson Ranch, where a notably craggy stone providing cover in a shootout became known among film fans as Mitchum Rock.

Warding off a Shawnee attack in a dark moment from *Rachel and the Stranger* (1948).

New RKO studio head Howard Hughes had a vested interest in Mitchum's fate. Hughes took a liking to Mitchum's screen image and paid a visit to him in jail to reassure Mitchum that RKO would stand behind him. He offered to front Mitchum a $50,000 loan at five percent interest so Mitchum could pay off his legal fees and buy a new home for his family. It meant, however, that Mitchum was bound to turning out schlock product for the studio for the next several years. "The dialogue in most of them is so bad you have to spit it out like dirt in your teeth," Mitchum told *Motion Picture* magazine. This unfortunately built up his image as a listless, bored leading man who'd walk through whatever part he was given.

The release of *Rachel and the Stranger* was bumped up to gauge audience reaction and formulate a plan for the rest of the films awaiting release. When Mitchum appeared on screen in *Rachel,* a collective cheer went up in movie theaters around the nation. Mitchum's bad boy image was reinforced and audiences were okay with it. They couldn't get enough of "Hollywood's Cowboy Rebel." His Hoppy films were dusted off with Mitchum's name now above the title, and he was elevated to co-star status with western star Randolph Scott for reissues of their 1943 World War II films *Corvette K-225* and *Gung Ho!* In the *Hollywood Greats* documentary, RKO actress Jane Russell says of Mitchum, "Everybody that knew him loved him and stuck by him. When he came out [of jail], the audience loved him just as much if not more when he flashed on the screen." Even Lila Leeds, whose career was ruined by the arrest and its publicity, couldn't say anything negative about Mitchum. "Bob was a very down-to-earth fellow," she stated in her memoir. "Everyone liked him, everywhere we went."

The notoriety of the marijuana bust made Mitchum a hip icon for the dope-smoking counterculture of the late 1960s and early 1970s. The rebellious jean-jacketed Mitchum image merged over time with the dirty, long-haired marijuana smoking "outlaw country" movement fronted by highwayman musicians the likes of Kris Kristofferson, Willie Nelson, Waylon Jennings, Mickey Newbury and the ever-dangerous Johnny Cash. To them, the influential Mitchum was a societal outcast they could relate to.

But not everyone let Mitchum off so easily in the conservative late 1940s and early 1950s era. The president of the United States, Dwight D. Eisenhower, was a western fan and watched more than 200 cowboy films while in the White House. However, Eisenhower refused to watch any starring the real-life reefer-smoking miscreant Robert Mitchum.

Blood on the Moon (RKO, 1948)

Cast: Robert Mitchum (Jim Garry); Barbara Bel Geddes (Amy Lufton); Robert Preston (Tate Riling); Walter Brennan (Kris Barden); Phyllis Thaxter (Carol Lufton); Frank Faylen (Jake Pindalest); Tom Tully (John Lufton); Charles McGraw (Milo Sweet); Clifton Young (Joe Shotten); Tom Tyler (Frank Reardon); George Cooper (Fred Barden); Richard Powers (Ted Elser); Bud Osborne (Cap Willis); Zon Murray (Nels Titterton); Robert Bray (Bart Daniels); and Erville Alderson, Ruth Brennan, Harry Carey, Jr., Iron Eyes Cody, Ben Corbett, Joe Devlin, Al Ferguson, Clem Fuller, Robert Malcolm, Ted Mapes, Chris-Pin Martin, Al Murphy, Hal Taliaferro.

Crew: Robert Wise (Director); Sid Rogell and Theron Werth (Producers); Lillie Hayward (Screenplay); Luke Short (Story); Nicholas Musuraca (Photographer); Roy Webb (Music); Albert S. D'Agostino and Walter E. Keller (Art Directors); Samuel E. Beetley (Editor); Edward Killy (Production Manager); Ted Mapes, Clem Fuller (Stunts); Tim Wallace, Dick Dickinson (Stand-ins); Lee Doyle, Bob Bradshaw (Wranglers).

88 minutes; Released November 9, 1948

"When there's blood on the moon, death lurks in the shadows," promised the RKO ad campaign, suggesting a darker-than-normal Hollywood oater. Based on Luke Short's 1941 story *Gunman's Chance,* the noir-influenced *Blood on the Moon* is a moody, atmospheric Robert Wise western buoyed by Mitchum's subtle, melancholy work as the lonely cowboy experiencing a long run of bad luck. The tightly crafted adult western was effectively lensed among the beautiful red rocks of Sedona, Arizona, by noir master Nicholas Musuraca. Filmed in a shadowy black and white, the movie doesn't take advantage of the vibrant colors of the area, but Musuraca is a master of lighting, visual images and overall mood. He perfectly captures the unique qualities of the location. It's one of the best filmed noir westerns, its lone visible weakness a sequence with obvious rear projection shots of a cattle stampede.

Set in the days following the Homestead Act of 1862, *Blood on the Moon* is a fascinating psychological character study of a tired man with conflicted morals about using his gun skills for profit. Mitchum's ambivalent character Jim Garry tried to be a cattleman, but his herd took sick and now he's drifting aimlessly. When we're introduced to him in a great opening shot, he's riding his horse through a rainstorm, cold and alone. Stopping to remove his mud-caked boots and enjoy a cup of coffee under the temporary sanctuary of a tree, he suddenly finds his entire camp scattered by a raging stampede of cattle. Herd cowboy Robert Bray rides up and is immediately suspicious of Mitchum's presence in this off-the-wagon-road location. Bray takes Mitchum to cattle boss Tom Tully's camp where they are hospitable but feel the stranger to the area is a gunman hired by interloper Robert Preston. At this early point in the story, Mitchum himself doesn't know that's what he is.

With his horse in front of Sedona's Red Rock Crossing in *Blood on the Moon* (1948).

James Stewart was originally courted to star in the film, but Mitchum is perfect casting. No western actor comes to mind who is better in the part of the independent, cagily reticent outsider. There existed a strong element of mystery to his screen portrayals that stemmed from his own real-life qualities and how he was perceived. He was gaining a reputation in Hollywood as an enigma on- *and* off-screen. He could be cynical and aloof, particularly with the media, and that antisocial persona fits the requirements of this dark western. Film critic Roger Ebert has called Mitchum "the soul of film noir." No one was better suited for the darkest existentially cast shadows. Intrigued by the character and the execution of the subject matter, Mitchum told the magazine *Trail Dust* that *Blood on the Moon* was his favorite western.

Character actor Walter Brennan, a three-time Oscar winner (including one for 1940's *The Westerner*), had been making westerns for over 20 years and was a student of the Old West. When he got his first look at Mitchum in costumer Joe De Young's western wardrobe and the attitude he carried with it, Brennan was moved to remark, "That is the goddamnedest realest cowboy I've ever seen." Outfitted in range-worn chaps and high Stetson, Mitchum was dirty, ungroomed, unshaved, and completely looked and felt the part of his rogue cowboy character. He wore a single Colt on his hip positioned midway between his hanging wrist and elbow for the quickest and smoothest access. E.C. Abbott writes in his authentic tome of western trail life *We Pointed Them North: Recollections of a Cowpuncher*, "A cowboy with two guns is all movie stuff, and so is this business of a gun on each hip."

Jim Garry is the quintessential enigmatic Mitchum drifter, a somber, unsmiling cowboy with a conscience. The wayfaring stranger. He finds himself drawn into a feud over grazing rights by old friend Tate Riling (Preston). Preston says differently, but Mitchum quickly realizes he's little more than a hired gun and, based on Preston's current behavior, doesn't like the side he's fighting for. He's more interested in steadfast cattleman Tully and his daughter Barbara Bel Geddes (replacing a late-scratch Anne Jeffreys). Mitchum takes a shine to the feisty Bel Geddes after the couple fire a series of warning shots at one another during an early face-off at a creek crossing. It's a case of love at first shot.

Mitchum has some fantastic action moments in the film, including his best fight scene. In the town of Sun Dust, he comes to the aid of Tully and Bel Geddes when they're threatened by Preston's other gunmen Zon Murray and Tom Tyler. (Tyler was a former B-western star. Murray went on to become one of the busiest of the TV western heavies until he injured his back in a horse fall on a 1960s episode of *The Virginian*.) The hired guns are leery of Mitchum and the reputation Preston has crowed about. Mitchum takes a step forward and decks Murray with a right cross that sends him over a hitching rail. Tyler, infamous for his gun bat-

Wardrobe capturing the look of a real cowboy in *Blood on the Moon* (1948).

tle with John Wayne in *Stagecoach* (1939), is a distance away and momentarily thinks of reaching for his gun. Mitchum begins striding toward him, commanding "Drift!" Tyler wisely turns and shows his yellow streak in the face of Mitchum bearing down. It's one of Mitchum's definitive tough guy moments.

Even better is his face-off with the shifty, conniving Preston when they meet in an outpost commissary cantina (filmed on a shadow-heavy RKO soundstage). Preston played a similarly not-to-be-trusted friend the same year opposite Alan Ladd in the western *Whispering Smith* (1948). Preston excels as the slick talker. Superb tension is created by Wise with low-key lighting enhancing the scene's visual impact. Preston is aware that Mitchum has already turned on his two gunmen and is testing his allegiance. As a backup, he has gunman Tyler outside ready to fire a chicken-hearted bullet into Mitchum's back depending on his old friend's choice. Mitchum makes his decision clear: He's disgusted at Preston's dirty tactics and the use of romancing Tully's other daughter Phyllis Thaxter to gain an advantage over her father. "I've seen dogs that wouldn't claim you for a son, Tate," Mitchum seethes.

These words lead to an outstanding fight scene. Mitchum and former amateur boxing champion Preston did the bulk of the brutal brawling themselves over the course of three grueling days. They wore protective elbow and knee pads under their clothing but sustained real injuries, including a broken finger for Mitchum. Preston accidentally connected with Mitchum's nose in one take, but the star shook it off and claimed his stuffy sinuses were suddenly clear. Outside of a brief exchange of real punches with former professional heavyweight boxer Jack Palance on *Second Chance* (1953), it was the toughest movie fight Mitchum ever had. Mitchum recalled: "Preston was in pro-fighter shape and damn serious about the fight scenes. I cut back on the hooch because 'Prest' wasn't holding much back. The dude was *too* serious. Whoo-ee, I earned my bread on that show."*

Wise wanted things to look spontaneous on screen, with both men bloody and exhausted by fight's end. The two actors perfectly understood what Wise was seeking even when the film's stuntmen wanted to enact a more traditionally slick and choreographed fight routine. Wise bowed to Mitchum's experience in such matters. "I think he probably knew more than I did about barroom fights like this one," Wise said in *Focus on Film*. Due to the actors' gritty effort, it's one of the best fight scenes in the western genre or any type of film, earning high praise in the book *Classic Movie Fight Scenes*. Mitchum, his long hair flying, cuts his hand on a broken bottle during the fight and ends the brawl sitting atop Preston while pounding his bloody fists into his former friend's face. When Tyler enters the cantina with his gun on a breathless Mitchum, rancher Walter Brennan arrives to save him. Brennan watches as Mitchum wearily picks up his pistol and struggles to gain his balance, his every muscle aching and spent in exhaustion. Mitchum's body language in this scene is spot-on. He has won the fight, but his strength and stamina have been sapped by the experience.

One of the earliest films lensed in Sedona, *Blood on the Moon* benefits greatly from the picturesque location and such Arizona landmarks as Cathedral Rock, Red Rock Crossing, Coffee Pot Rock, Little Horse Park, Boynton Pass and the Van Deren cabin in Dry Creek Basin. Mitchum and pals Preston and Charles McGraw stayed at the Sedona Lodge and shared drinks at the wooden-walled Oak Creek Tavern (now known as the Cowboy Club). They had fun together on the set, gently teasing and ribbing their female co-stars. Barbara Bel Geddes, later famous as the matriarch Miss Ellie on the popular modern TV western *Dallas* (1978–1990), was still moved to call Mitchum "a fine guy" when queried by *Motion Picture* magazine. *Blood on the Moon* was Mitchum's first collaboration with stand-in Tim Wallace, a burly Irishman who continued with him as friend and drinking companion for the next 30 years. Mitchum made sure Wallace was paid twice the going rate for a stand-in, humorously referring to the loud, uncouth Wallace as his

---

*Garry Armstrong (e-mail correspondence, August 2017).

drama coach. In his spare time, RKO publicity had Mitchum choose the prettiest girl from nearby Flagstaff's Arizona State College (now Northern Arizona University) to serve as the Yearbook Queen. When it looked as if an approaching snowstorm might trap Mitchum in Flagstaff, RKO tried to back out of the commitment. Mitchum would have none of it. He had given his word he'd be there to present the award, and he was. When Mitchum expressed interest in a Colt revolver owned by a local Indian, the native gifted Mitchum the pistol with a specially made bone handle and holster. The firearm shows up in other Mitchum films.

Mitchum's continually improved horsemanship aided him during location and studio-shot portions of the film. At RKO, his shod horse slipped on the slick soundstage floor and nearly fell, but Mitchum stayed in the saddle. Humorously, the horse began to loudly eat a cellulose boulder while Mitchum and Barbara Bel Geddes played a love scene. The horse was

Barbara Bel Geddes and Mitchum pose in front of the Sedona landscape in an RKO publicity photograph for *Blood on the Moon* (1948).

then repositioned and the undamaged portion of the fake rock turned away from the camera. Mitchum suffered a minor injury on the Arizona location when he dove into a bush and his hand landed on and was pierced by the fang of a rattlesnake's skeleton. The latter half of the film is set in the high country of the Coconino National Forest near Flagstaff and the San Francisco Peaks, with the bundled-up actors braving the ice and snow as they ride amongst the Ponderosa Pines. Many of the close-ups for these scenes were shot on a studio set due to an abundance of ski tracks visible to the camera on location. Some scenes were filmed at the RKO Ranch in Encino, California, while others were done at Monogram Ranch in Newhall. Additional second unit photography was done in Colorado.

The choice to film in Sedona during the dead of winter presented several weather-related challenges, including snow and simulated rain which froze in the air and did not provide a called-for slush on the ground. This necessitated that the water be heated before being sprayed over the actors by fire hoses. The steaming water remained liquefied long enough for the takes to be completed. The ominous clouds overhead did provide an unexpected visual bonus. Director Wise elaborated on further challenges in an audio commentary for the film's 1990 laserdisc release:

> When you go out on your locations, one of the things you're always concerned about is the weather. We used to chase the sun around this whole valley of Sedona with these red buttes and all that, because it would change so fast. We would cover one end of the valley at one location and it would cloud up; then we'd see the other end of the valley, it looked clear. So, we'd move out to the other end of the valley to get that clear light, and by the time we got there the clouds all shifted and now the sun was back where we had been. It was just a maddening problem we had all the way through the film.

Wise, formerly a film editor under Orson Welles, didn't have any problems with his leading man, whom he worked with again several years later in the comedy-drama *Two for the Seesaw* (1962). Wise was especially intrigued when he snuck a glance at Mitchum's script

As noir cowboy Jim Garry in *Blood on the Moon* (1948).

and noticed that in several places Mitchum had written the acronym NAR in the margins. "No Acting Required," explained Mitchum. "I don't need a line. I'll give you a look."

Wise told *Focus on Film*:

> Bob was just fine to work with. He likes this part and he contributed a number of ideas.... He never wanted to do too much. Just enough and then hold back a little, leave something a little unspecified. He was very bright, very facile; quick with language. But he likes to give the impression that he somehow wasn't articulate. I always thought he was a little embarrassed to be an actor. That this was sissy stuff. He should be a stevedore or fireman or something. He never said this, but it was a feeling I had about him.

Mitchum got some of his best reviews yet. *Newsweek* wrote of the film:

> The only thing that distinguishes it from the "gallop and gun-belt" sort of thing is the presence of Robert Mitchum in the cast. But that makes a considerable difference. Afoot or on horseback, the slow-voiced, sad-faced RKO star moves with the feline grace of a mountain lion, and despite his appealing diffidence, belongs to that rare

breed of Hollywood cowhand—he not only acts tough but looks as though he really could use his rifle or six-shooter if necessary [and] is equal to the task of making even the preposterous circumstances that lead up to [the climax] convincing."

The New York Times opined, "Robert Mitchum carries the burden of the film and his acting is superior all the way," while *Variety* wrote Mitchum "handles with skill" his assignment. *Film Bulletin* called him "convincingly hard-bitten as the terse, sleepy-eyed cowpoke from Texas," while *The Hollywood Reporter* stated, "Robert Mitchum gives a strong, vigorous portrait of the individualistic westerner." *The New York World Telegram* wrote the film "might have turned out to be just an ordinary western…but the presence of Robert Mitchum in the cast raises it several notches above that level." *Cue* called Mitchum "among the best of the steely-eyed, tight-lipped heroes of Hollywood hoss operas."

Some began to see a trend in Mitchum's screen image. According to *Motion Picture Daily*, "Mitchum gives a typical Mitchum performance—quiet, icy, unruffled, seemingly lethargic." *The Los Angeles Times* said, "He's a good actor, saturnine but sympathetic." *The L.A. Daily News* offered a rave review for Mitchum's western work: "Mitchum has hardly ever had a role in which he didn't underplay. That's his stock in trade, and that's all right with us. But this role seems to fit him much better than any he's done. The boy can be awfully tough in a quiet, menacing way. He sits a horse with more flair than anybody in pictures, with the possible exception of John Wayne."

Philip Armour included *Blood on the Moon* in his book *The 100 Greatest Western Movies of All Time*: "One of the biggest reasons for its success is the way Robert Mitchum embodies the character of the surly-looking stranger who's ridden into town to go to work for his old friend." *Cowboys & Indians* magazine placed it on their top 100, writing, "Mitchum, a shifty character in any setting, plays moral relativism so well that even when he does the right thing, you still don't trust him." According to Lincoln Center's *Film Linc Daily*, "Mitchum flourishes amid Wise's assured direction." Brian Garfield's *Western Films* praised the "flawless performances," saying, "Mitchum, Preston, Bel Geddes and Tully are outstanding," while Michael R. Pitts' *Western Movies* said the film was "greatly helped by its trio of stars, especially Robert Mitchum." *Western Clippings* termed it "an often overlooked but truly classic western, most likely Mitchum's best." *The Rough Guide to Westerns*: "Mitchum excels as the brooding drifter with a conscience," and *Westerns and the Trail of Tradition* adds, "Mitchum is marvelous in his sleepy-eyed way." *Renegade Westerns* noted that Mitchum "shows far greater range than he had in *Pursued* in a role that fits him equally snugly."

Mitchum chronicler Jerry Roberts praised the film's bone-rattling action, writing, "The violent fistfight between Mitchum and Preston remains one of the screen's most startling sequences of fisticuffs." Lee Server called the fight "the film's most memorable sequence." In *Arizona's Little Hollywood,* Sedona location expert Joe McNeill said it was "still one of the most brutally realistic bare-knuckle brawls ever filmed." Writing on Mitchum in *The Village Voice,* Carrie Rickey observed, "Mitchum could defend himself with a truly terrifying physical strength." Roger Ebert added, "When he was in a fight in a movie, you felt like you were watching a fight. Not a skillful exercise in choreography, constructed out of pseudo-karate, special effects and stunt man. But a fight, in which one guy's fist hits another guy's gut, and it hurts, and is surprising and definitive, and is over in a flash."

The story throws the audience a curve in the final reel after Mitchum has suffered a knife wound from Indian assassin Iron Eyes Cody, veteran of dozens of westerns. Sweat-soaked with fever and infection, Mitchum is tended to by Bel Geddes in Brennan's cabin as Preston and his remaining guns close in. Mitchum rises wearily to take them on. Surprisingly, he emerges from the shootout intact and all ends happily for the Mitchum and Bel Geddes characters. Given his high-profile death scenes in *The Story of G.I. Joe* (1945) and *Out of the Past* (1947), audiences were not associating the Mitchum screen persona with happy endings. It would not have been out of the question for the totally spent Mitchum to have died in this final shootout. The finality of death seemed the sole answer for his tumultuous internal conflict. Filmgoers were beginning to sense there was something dark and dangerous about this actor and his cinematic output. He was a long way from the relaxed, smiling days of *Nevada* and *West of the Pecos*. Mitchum was noir, and in the subgenre of the edgy noir-western he was the undisputed king.

The Red Pony (Republic, 1949)

Cast: Myrna Loy (Alice Tiflin); Robert Mitchum (Billy Buck); Louis Calhern (Grandfather); Shepperd Strudwick (Fred Tiflin); Peter Miles (Tom); Margaret Hamilton (Teacher); Patty King (Jinx Ingals); Jackie Jackson (Jackie); Beau Bridges (Beau); Little Brown Jug (Little Brown Jug); Nino Tempo (Nino); Tommy Sheridan (Dale); and Eddie Borden, Dolores Castle, Wee Willie Davis, Joan Delmer, Alvin Hammer, Gracie Hanneford, Poodles Hanneford, Bill Quinlan, George Tyne, Max Wagner.

Crew: Lewis Milestone (Director); Lewis Milestone and Charles K. Feldman (Producers); John Steinbeck (Screenplay); Tony Gaudio (Photographer); Aaron Copland (Music); Victor Greene (Art Director); Harry Keller (Editor); Robert Aldrich (Assistant Director); Bobbie Dorree, Chuck Roberson (Stunts); Glenn Randall (Wrangler).

89 minutes; Released March 28, 1949

Lewis Milestone's *The Red Pony* was Republic's well-intentioned attempt at handling a serious literary classic, John Steinbeck's tragic coming-of-age story, penned in 1933. *The Red Pony* was comprised of four short stories with Steinbeck himself handling the screenplay. Esteemed cinematographer Tony Gaudio shot in Technicolor on beautiful Agoura, California, locations (primarily the Morrison Ranch), and composer Aaron Copland of *Billy the Kid* "cowboy ballet" fame offered a rare film score. With Myrna Loy heading the cast as young Peter Miles' mother and scene-stealing Louis Calhern as his grandfather, the sad story of a boy and his horse was one of the most prestigious projects Republic ever took on. The 81-day schedule was the longest for a film from the studio with shooting finishing in August 1947. Loy was paid $200,000 and Mitchum, a fan of Steinbeck's writing, $130,000. It has all the proper ingredients for a classic but is a slight misfire despite worthy moments from its fine cast.

Second-billed Mitchum comes off best as common-sense ranch hand Billy Buck, a heroic cowboy figure to the precocious young boy. Miles' character idolizes Mitchum's affable masculinity, once fantasizing that Mitchum is an Arthurian knight in shining armor. In Steinbeck's original story, Billy Buck was an older character with a droopy mustache. However, it's hard to go wrong with the casting of Mitchum. He has a natural rapport on screen with the youngster Miles as he shares his vast knowledge of horses and offers life lessons. "I'm half horse myself," Mitchum says, relating how his mother died at birth and his dad raised him on mare's milk. Mitchum worked closely with horse trainer Glenn Randall to accustom himself to the feel and lingo of the character. Mitchum looks the part of a modern cowboy clad in black Stetson, boots and jeans. His cowboy mannerisms are authentic. When he places straw between his teeth, slips his hands into his back pockets, or sits on a fence, it looks like reflex action he's been displaying all his life.

The leisurely paced story involves Miles' prized dark chestnut pony Galiban (named after a nearby Salinas Mountain range) becom-

As ranch hand Billy Buck in *The Red Pony* (1949).

ing sick with respiratory problems when it gets out of the barn and stands in the rain overnight. The pony escaped because Miles taught it to open the door, yet the child foolishly blames Mitchum for the illness. The steady Mitchum determines to right himself in the eyes of the boy, but the pony worsens. Seeing no other course of action, Mitchum is forced to give the pony a tracheotomy so it can breathe. This saves the horse, but that night it once again gets out of the barn (this time under the eye of Miles). When the boy tracks the pony down the next morning, he finds its dead body being ravaged by vultures in a shocking visual. Mitchum promises Miles he can have his own prized horse's pony but is worried it might be born breach. Mitchum will risk the life of his own horse for the safe birth of the boy's new pony.

The Red Pony was shown in schools for years as a learning aid for those youngsters assigned to read Steinbeck's books. However, the scene where Peter Miles was attacked by a vulture was unsettling for many kids at the time of the picture's original release. The effect was achieved by having the trained pony lie still while vultures pecked at raw meat attached to its side. A subsequent scene with Mitchum in a barroom that lent character development and action to the storyline was cut from the final print as the filmmakers feared it would upset the tone of the picture. The violent scene in question was a bar fight with 6'5", 290-pound pro wrestler Wee Willie Davis. Those who saw footage of the brawl proclaimed it one of the greatest screen fights, on par with the famous battle between John Wayne and Randolph Scott in *The Spoilers* (1942). Republic director Joseph Kane obtained a copy of the fight for his personal film library and showed it to interested parties through the years. It no doubt helped bolster Mitchum's tough guy legend in Hollywood circles.

Due to that violent scene being snipped, we don't learn anything about Mitchum's life outside of his interaction with the boy. How did he end up there? Why does he stay? What kind of a social life does he have? At one point he humorously tells Miles all the photos of lady friends decorating his room are his cousins. "We're a big family," he explains with a smile. But that is the extent of personal info about Mitchum's Billy Buck. Given the relationship struggles on-screen of Loy and the boy's citified father Shepperd Strudwick, the audience suspects a possible subplot developing between co-star Mitchum and leading lady Loy. However, nary a hint of amorous behavior is present in the family-oriented film despite Republic pairing Mitchum and Loy for a series of publicity photos. Ultimately Mitchum proves to be more of a father figure to the boy than his real dad before the movie's climactic happy reconciliation. The Old West is referred to during the film by the long-winded grandfather's stories of leading settlers across the plains and mountains in younger days. In this sense, Mitchum could be a modern surrogate for the trailblazer, who acknowledges Billy Buck's skill with horses.

Aspiring writer Mitchum occasionally penned a guest piece for newspaperman Jimmie Fidler's regular column. On westerns, Mitchum was becoming an expert, although he had not yet developed the deep appreciation for his equine co-stars outside of a willingness to trade places. He felt they had it better than him on the set and humorously told his audience about his current love-hate relationship. He wrote,

> After serving as a somewhat reluctant saddle-partner of Hollywood horses for years, I have come to the conclusion that our positions should be reversed. If a screen cowpoke like myself wants the finer things in life, he had better change places with his horse…. Fortunately for me, I do not have to maintain the horses I ride in pictures. If I did, there would be a passel of ragged Mitchums running around while their old man begged alms outside the studio parking lot. I hear from guys like Gene Autry, Roy Rogers and Hoppy that the bills I foot for my wife, three kids, 12 relatives, two cats, one dog and a recently arrived houseguest from Far Rockaway are just a little under what a single movie horse requires for Spartan living. That ain't just hay, brother, no sir. That's oats, alfalfa and wheat germ oil besides.
>
> Getting an actor to work in the morning is no problem. He simply is pushed out of bed and into his car. But movie horses rate royal treatment. After a brisk rubdown and nourishing breakfast, they are chauffeured to the set in streamlined trailers. The actors, having mem-

orized dialogue and sweat out rehearsals, then leap on these educated chargers and expect to be galloped away. They are—usually too far beyond the camera and into a protruding two-by-four which the crafty horse has correctly figured should knock the mime right off the saddle…. Several, following these painful encounters, have refused point blank to recognize the Cowboy's Code which requires the hero at picture's end to give his loyal and ever-loving steed a kiss…. Many a movie mount has learned to steal scenes by prancing, mincing, strutting, waltzing, undulating, gyrating, and otherwise ambulating. This looks great on the screen and undoubtedly wins fan letters for the horse, but all it gets for the guy astride him is headaches and a loosened upper plate…. Any actor who can manage even a faint smile while this is going on deserves a special Academy Award. I refrain from suggesting what the horse deserves…. I am ready, any time he is willing, to trade places with my horse. He never will though. Too smart. He's got it made and he knows it.

It wasn't only motion picture horses Mitchum made folly with. During filming, Mitchum teased the prim Miss Loy on the set about her perfect complexion and buttoned collar until it was time to roll film. When columnist Hedda Hopper visited the production, Mitchum told her the script had Loy performing the provocative dance of the seven veils. In her 1987 autobiography *Myrna Loy: Being and Becoming*, the actress remembered:

> Bob clowned around, but when it came to actually working he was all business. He is one of those artists that make it look easy, a fine actor and intriguing man with many sides to him. He has that smooth, masculine face, seemingly without a care in the world, yet you saw an underlying sensitivity and intelligence. And it was typical of his contradictory nature that this macho man who loved deviling me should ask me to sign a photograph for him at the end of the picture.

Loy biographer Emily Leider wrote, "Robert Mitchum is compelling as Billy Buck. Broad-shouldered, laconic and unsmiling, he is at ease with the horses he grooms, sharing their elemental grace." Mitchum biographer Mike Tomkies added, "Mitchum delivered his most sincere performance of the period." Reviews for Mitchum at the time were strong despite the rash of negative press regarding his marijuana bust. *Box Office* crowed, "Mitchum turns in one

With horse Galiban in *The Red Pony* (1949).

of his best performances," while *The Hollywood Reporter* praised his "silent strength." *The Los Angeles Times* wrote, "Performances are of high-caliber, particularly by Robert Mitchum as taciturn Billy Buck," while *The Hollywood Citizen News* remarked, "Robert Mitchum makes of the hired hand a virile character who beneath his rugged appearance has many commendable virtues." *Variety* wrote, "Robert Mitchum underscores a likable role with a finely drawn portrayal of a grownup who understands both kids and horses. Mitchum once again demonstrates his flair for apt characterization without overplaying the faculty of getting at the emotional core of his audience." According to *Motion Picture Daily*, "Mitchum's performance, like the picture itself, is well done, but restrained," and *The San Francisco Chronicle* wrote, "Robert Mitchum plays Billy Buck as an easygoing, reliable man who has been around horses for years, which is exactly as he should be played." However, Bosley Crowther of *The New York Times* found Mitchum "strangely laconic—too much so—as the hired man."

The Red Pony provided a nice change of pace from the dark action characters Mitchum had been essaying, and he recalled its making with fondness. To promote the film, Republic created a nine-story billboard of Mitchum on 47th Street in New York City, and a photo feature with Mitchum entitled "How to Train a Horse" appeared in *Life* magazine. His western persona had become fully realized. The understanding character showed the actor's range and intelligence, proving a nice counterpoint to his now wild public image. RKO further tried to soften the bad boy image, arranging for Mitchum to emcee a June 25, 1949, program at the Knickerbocker Hotel in Hollywood for country singer Eddy Arnold. On the show were western stars Gene Autry, Pat Buttram, Carolina Cotton, Hank Thompson, Nick Lucas and Hill and Range music publisher Julian Aberbach. Mitchum was a jazz proponent and amateur saxophonist but enjoyed country and western music. Cowboy crooner Jim Reeves became one of his favorite artists. Mitchum's co-workers recalled the star softly singing sad country tunes to himself between scenes.

The Lusty Men (RKO, 1952)

Cast: Susan Hayward (Louise Merritt); Robert Mitchum (Jeff McCloud); Arthur Kennedy (Wes Merritt); Arthur Hunnicutt (Booker Davis); Frank Faylen (Al Dawson); Walter Coy (Buster Burgess); Carol Nugent (Rusty Davis); Maria Hart (Rosemary Maddox); Lorna Thayer (Grace Burgess); Burt Mustin (Jeremiah Burgess); Karen King (Ginny Logan); Jimmie Dodd (Red Logan); Eleanor Todd (Babs); and Emile Avery, William Bailey, Barbara Blaine, Hazel Boyne, Jack Braddock, Robert Bray, Ralph Bucko, Roy Bucko, Paul E. Burns, Bob Burrows, Wayne Burson, Benny Burt, Mary Jane Curry, Lane Chandler, Dick Crockett, Richard Farnsworth, Sam Flint, Bob Folkerson, Roy Glenn, Chick Hannan, Don Happy, Carol Henry, Paul Hielbich, Riley Hill, William Holms, Leroy Johnson, Alice Kirby, Mike Lally, Emmett Lynn, Frank Matts, John McKee, Edward McNally, John Mitchum (as John Mallory), Dennis Moore, Nancy Moore, Fox O'Callahan, Charles Parkinson, Joe Phillips, Denver Pyle, Mike Ragan, Joey Ray, Marshall Reed, Bob Reeves, Richard Reeves, Sam Reynoso, Chuck Roberson, George Ross, Wally Russell, Les Sanborn, Louise Saraydar, Carl Sepulveda, Rocky Shahan, George Sherwood, Ralph Stein, Glenn Strange, Jean Stratton, Jack Tornek, James Van Horn, Ralph Volkie, George Wallace, Dan White, Chili Williams, Sheb Wooley, Sally Yarnell.

Crew: Nicholas Ray (Director); Jerry Wald (Producer); Tom Gries (Associate Producer); David Dortort and Horace McCoy (Screenplay); Lee Garmes (Photographer); Roy Webb (Music); Albert S. D'Agostino and Alfred Herman (Art Directors); Ralph Dawson (Editor); Edward Killy (Assistant Director); Bob Burrows, Wayne Burson, "Cowboy" Tug Carlson, Fred Carson, Dick Crockett, Ross Dollarhide, Richard Farnsworth, Don Happy, Carol Henry, Leroy Johnson, Dan Poore, Chuck Roberson, Gerald Roberts, Rocky Shahan, Kenneth "Blackie" Stephens, James Van Horn (Stunts); Casey Tibbs (Technical Advisor).

114 minutes; Released October 24, 1952

After his hyped jail sentence, Mitchum went over three years without making a new western. During this period, RKO concentrated his work in the modern noir films *Where Danger Lives* (1950), *His Kind of Woman* (1951), *The Racket* (1951), *Macao* (1952) and *Angel Face* (1952). This routine trenchcoat product seemed to transition Mitchum away from his cowboy image and reestablish him as an eternally bored modern fatalist playing opposite the feminine wiles of Faith Domergue, Jean Simmons and Jane Russell. He had opportunities to star in *A Streetcar Named Desire* (1951) and

As veteran rodeo cowboy Jeff McCloud in *The Lusty Men* (1952).

From Here to Eternity (1953), but Hughes and RKO kept him on a never-ending shoot on the inconsequential *His Kind of Woman*. Every day he spent on this film saw his character beaten and pummeled to a pulp as Hughes tinkered and toyed with the production, bringing in new directors and co-stars to watch Mitchum bleed. After more than a year on the needlessly demanding film, the star finally kicked up a storm in a fight scene, flinging stuntmen against the walls and tearing apart the set in a blind rage. When the dust finally settled, the legend of Big Bad Bob Mitchum was rekindled and set aflame within the industry.

He was grateful for Hughes' support after his arrest, but the by-the-numbers studio assignments were undermining his once promising career and he hated being forced into a box. He began calling them "gorilla pictures." As he explained to the press, "apes" would beat on him for 90 minutes of screen time until they finally tired, and the heroine lifted him from the ground and declared him her hero. Story was always secondary to the action of Mitchum being beaten senseless. There was one RKO western he was slated to do that had to be abandoned due to his legal troubles. That was *Roughshod*

(1949), where he was replaced by Robert Sterling. Leading lady Gloria Grahame and screen heavy John Ireland wound up co-starring in the Mark Robson film about a wrangler transporting a quartet of dance hall girls through the Sonoran Desert with a killer on his tail. Generally forgotten, the black and white sagebrush saga would have been elevated by Mitchum's steely presence.

In his personal life, Mitchum moved his family away from bustling Hollywood to rustic Mandeville Canyon in Brentwood, situated among the Santa Monica Mountains. The land was once occupied by the Chumash and Tongva Indian tribes. Mitchum now lived near old pal Anthony Caruso along sycamore- and oak-lined horse trails. Gregory Peck and Richard Widmark joined him as neighbors, and the actors became known as "The Mandeville Canyon Gang." Caruso recalled this period for *Wildest Westerns*:

> Bob and I went to Long Beach High School together. I loved him, just like I loved Alan Ladd. Two o'clock in the morning Mitchum would be yelling outside our front door, "Let me in! Let me in! The bandits are after me! The bandits are

As a bronc rider in *The Lusty Men* (1952).

after me!" He lived around the corner from us and was a character. I'd let him in and he'd have a jug of wine or a bottle of booze with him and sit down and not leave until it was all gone. I'd just have one drink and stay up and talk with him.

Herbie McDonald was a Howard Hughes–RKO liaison who operated under various titles in the developing city of Las Vegas. For several years he served as the entertainment director at the western-themed El Rancho Resort where he became famous for designing the $1.00 Buckaroo Buffet. When RKO needed to keep Mitchum out of the public eye after his 1948 arrest, Hughes enlisted McDonald to keep the actor spirited away on a private boat on Lake Mead. McDonald arranged for food to be delivered to Mitchum and saw to his needs. In a KNPR interview, McDonald recalled Mitchum returning the favor when McDonald was in Los Angeles. McDonald describes an early a.m. phone call to his hotel room and a Mitchum invite to his new digs: "He says, 'Now, Herbie, I haven't got any furniture, but I'm going to cook you breakfast because I still owe you.' So, my first wife, Phyllis, and I went out to his house. He had no furniture in this lavish home. And he fed us breakfast, and I ribbed him.... He was a neat guy."

RKO tried their best to keep Mitchum on the straight and narrow, forbidding bad influence Boyd Cabeen from working on any more Mitchum films as his stand-in. The two of them together were too much testosterone to handle. Whenever Mitchum went into the city, he was shadowed by an ex-cop turned Howard Hughes employee, Kemp Niver, whose job was to keep the unpredictable Mitchum out of trouble and prevent fans from trying to pass him outlaw weed. Mitchum called him The Shamus. Eventually, Niver's presence was no longer needed, as the courts decided that Mitchum's celebrated Laurel Canyon bust was a frame-up. His record was quietly cleared in 1951. Free to roam, Mitchum began showing up in old haunts and new ones like the Fog Cutter steakhouse on La Brea and the Villa Capri on Yucca Street in Hollywood. Dorothy held down the home front.

Mitchum had several unrealized western projects. RKO tried to mount a frontier flick on explorers Lewis and Clark in 1947 with Mitchum as one of the leads. In 1948, producer Bryan Foy wanted him to star in a film version of the 1938 stage play *Missouri Legend* about Bob Ford, the former outlaw who shot and killed Jesse James for the reward. Foy's film about this dark character never got off the ground. Producer Sol Lesser wanted Mitchum for a series of western films based on Frank H. Spearman's railroad detective Whispering Smith, even after Alan Ladd played the role. In 1950, silent film cowboy star Broncho Billy Anderson's sister tried launching a biopic of his life with Mitchum as the star. Mitchum was under consideration to headline Stuart Heisler's *Dallas* (1950), but Gary Cooper wound up taking the part of gunman Blayde Hollister. In 1951, RKO announced plans to pair Mitchum and Jane Russell in *The Wild River*, a story of the Mississippi from screenwriter David Dortort, but the project sank like a stone. Jacques Tourneur's Argentine-set *Way of a Gaucho* (1952) was a title originally announced for Mitchum. Rory Calhoun ended up playing the South American cowboy. Tourneur tried landing Mitchum again for the Colorado-set western *Great Day in the Morning* (1956), but Robert Stack wound up in the part.

In 1952, *Collier's* published prolific western writer Louis L'Amour's short story "The Gift of Cochise." The producing team of John Wayne and Robert Fellows bought the story from L'Amour and assigned screenwriter James Edward Grant to develop it into a film. Mitchum and Glenn Ford were approached to portray the lead character Ches Lane. When they proved unavailable, Wayne stepped into the starring role of what became Hondo Lane. *Hondo* (1953) remains one of Wayne's most popular films, and L'Amour's same-titled novelization is one of his best-selling books. Another film that was announced as ready to begin shooting in early 1953 was *The Gambler's Moon* with Edmund Grainger producing a script by Thames Williamson. Robert Ryan, Ursula Thiess, Arthur Hunnicutt and Mala Powers would have starred with Mitchum. In 1955, actress Rhonda Fleming acquired a script titled *Hardrock* and tried to interest Mitchum in playing her leading man, a two-fisted miner. The film was never made. That same year, Mitchum and Carol Ohmart were the projected stars for the Michael Curtiz western *The Maverick*. The retooled film turned up the following year as Rudolph Mate's *Three Violent People* (1956) with Charlton Heston and Anne Baxter. Mitchum was courted for Delmer Daves' Sedona-lensed *The Last Wagon* (1956) but couldn't line up his film schedule. Richard Widmark ended up starring as Comanche Todd, an Indian scout accused of murder.

Director Nicholas Ray had wanted Mitchum to play the Native American heavy Chicamaw in his noir film *They Live by Night* (1948), and Mitchum lobbied for the part. But RKO nixed that type of role for its rising star, and it went to Howard Da Silva. Under contract to the studio, Ray unofficially directed some scenes of John Cromwell's *The Racket* and Josef von Sternberg's *Macao*; so he and Mitchum became familiar to one another. Mitchum was soon attached to Ray's next RKO project, the realistic rodeo drama *The Lusty Men*. Ray landed the film after Robert Parrish, Raoul Walsh and Anthony Mann all passed. Based upon a 1946 *Life* magazine article by Claude Stanush, the story examined the day-to-day un-romanticized and dangerous life of a modern-day rodeo cowboy. Mitchum felt strongly about this western character, and it became a personal project that he backed creatively.

Under the working title *Cowpoke,* the picture filmed authentic action at real rodeos in Los Angeles, Phoenix, Tucson, Denver, Spokane and Pendleton during the latter half of 1951. Even though the original screen treatment clocked in at 17 pages, Ray correctly felt it was vital to the film's authenticity to capture footage at these real rodeo events while the script was being finished. When Susan Hayward became attached on a loan-out from 20th Century-Fox, her part was expanded by writers Horace McCoy and David Dortort (later the creator of the TV westerns *Bonanza* and *The High Chaparral*). Her scenes were rushed into production due to her limited availability. Mitchum was the star but generously let Hayward take first billing in the credits. However, there's no mistaking it is Mitchum's film as he commands every frame of action with his virile manliness.

He has never been better on screen than as the veteran bronc-busting, bull-riding cowboy Jeff McCloud.

Clad in Stetson, boots, jeans, rodeo buckle and Wrangler Blue Bell 11MJ jacket, a tired, bone-weary Mitchum looks and feels the part. He lives and breathes this sad-eyed, middle-aged cowpoke. After being thrown and kicked by a brahma bull, there's a tremendously evocative opening scene shot by cinematographer Lee Garmes of a busted-up Mitchum limping alone across an empty arena amongst wind-swirled papers. He is favoring a broken rib and his step has a hitch in it. All his worldly belongings are in a bag slung over his shoulder, the result of 20 hard years spent on the rodeo circuit and in sawdust-covered honkytonks. Roy Webb's score perfectly complements Mitchum's pained gait. The funny thing is, he is considered a legend among his fellow cowboys: the former World Bronc Busting Champion. However, it is an empty, lonely life and Mitchum has come to that realization. He never married and hasn't any money to his name. Drifting, he makes his way to his childhood home in Texas where he crawls under the rundown house to find a toy cowboy gun, a rodeo flyer and a tobacco tin from a youthful hiding place. It's his past, but he now realizes he has no future.

Old man Burt Mustin finds him under the house and makes him back out at gunpoint, but after learning he grew up in the home invites him in for a cup of coffee. The dialogue, a portion devised on the set before filming by Mitchum and Ray, is superb. Lyrical and low-key, Mitchum earns instant audience sympathy as he volunteers he has no prospects and only enough sense "to come in out of the rain." Having spent a fortune of winnings on good times, he sums up his life as "broken bones, broken bottles, broken everything."

A young married couple (Arthur Kennedy and Hayward) arrives. Their goal is to purchase Mustin's home, but ranch hand Kennedy's nest egg is a long way from complete. A rodeo novice, he latches onto Mitchum and the latter begins to see a future in training the promising apprentice for half his earnings. However, with success Kennedy becomes swept up in the alluring rodeo lifestyle and Mitchum begins to feel a

Learning how to be a rodeo cowboy for *The Lusty Men* (1952).

strong attraction to Kennedy's neglected wife. Director Ray claimed the film wasn't necessarily a western but a film about longing for and finding a home. Mitchum conveys this conflicted angst as well as anyone when he locks eyes with Hayward. They have superb screen chemistry. However, Hayward had a reputation for being difficult and sulking on sets when she didn't get her way. Mitchum teasingly called her "the old gray mare" in front of reporter Aline Mosby, referencing the well-known folk song concerning the aging horse Lady Suffolk who wouldn't undertake more than a slow trot on the track. It's been reported that Hayward didn't care for Mitchum because he ate garlic prior to a kissing scene. She returned the favor. Mitchum, however, thought their on-set relationship was fine.

Hayward ultimately proves loyal to her husband and their shared dreams, leaving Mitchum on the outside looking in. Branded by the now egotistical Kennedy as a has-been and a hanger-on, Mitchum sees little choice except to return to the rodeo himself. He's out not only to prove his own manhood but to serve as a martyr for Kennedy. Out of practice and with slowed reflexes, his veteran savviness can't prevent a tragedy. Caught in a stirrup during a surprisingly successful eight-second bronc ride, Mitchum is dragged under the horse's hooves and has his lung pierced by a broken rib. Struggling for breath, he is unceremoniously carted out of the rodeo arena, so the next event can go on. As the final act of his life, he buries his head into a sobbing Hayward's breast.

This contemporary western was one of the few movies and characters that truly interested Mitchum, and he worked extremely well with Nicholas Ray. He asked Ray to see an early assemblage of the completed scenes and for once was impressed and happy with the work at hand. Mitchum strongly identified with this luckless drifter and displays extraordinary range. Strong, stubborn, sexy, sage, witty, lived-in, lonesome, moody and detached…it's an Oscar-caliber performance. However, there was no such recognition from the Motion Picture Academy in the wake of his pot bust. They were still seething at his no-showing at the ceremony for his *Story of G.I. Joe* nomination and his apparent disregard for the craft of acting.

"There never was a bronc that couldn't be rode, there never was a cowboy that couldn't be throwed," Mitchum says throughout the film in displaying his cowboy wisdom. When Hayward asks what happened to Mitchum's substantial earnings from his years on top, he volunteers it just "floated away." He eloquently explains why he is who he is in describing the feeling of sitting on a powerful bull or bronc with the rodeo audience cheering and the anticipation the ensuing few seconds of skill could mean life or death for the cowboy. "Some things you do just for the buzz you get out of it," he says. That line might be an apt description of Mitchum's own wayward indulgence throughout his life. Chasing a feeling. When a movie wrapped Mitchum got into his car and drove aimlessly for days across the country. His wife and children accepted his lifelong wanderlust as a strong part of the man. It's who he was. "I guess I'm just a bum at heart," he told *Modern Screen*. "Been chasing rainbows all my life and suppose I always will."

Ray's true-to-life filming style used celebrated world champion bronc rider Casey Tibbs as a technical director and bulldogging champ Dan Poore as Mitchum's double. Ironically, former Mitchum stuntman Ben Johnson briefly quit the film business around this time to dedicate a year to pursuing a World Championship in team roping. Johnson ultimately won his champion buckle but wound up flat busted after a year on the road fronting entrance fees to all his broke pals. Johnson returned to motion pictures. Rodeo legend turned western character actor Slim Pickens might have worked on *The Lusty Men* had he not been busy as Rex Allen's sidekick at Republic. The film was populated with an assortment of real cowboys and rodeo veterans like Gerald Roberts, Jerry Ambler, Les Sanborn, Pete Crump, Ross Dollarhide and Eddy Akridge. These were rough-hewn men in a macho profession Mitchum could relate to. Many of the stuntmen he knew had rodeo backgrounds as well. Blackie Stephens credits Mitchum with discovering him on this film, telling the *Spokesman Review* he made $100 for each bronc and bull he rode: "That was pretty good money, so I decided to stick with movie cowboying." Rodeo legends Tibbs and Jim Shoulders became Mitchum's spirited drinking pals in the ensuing years. Mitchum occasionally took in rodeo events either announced or unannounced. In 1954, he made a personal appearance in Estes Park, Colorado, for the rodeo social at the Riverside Dance Hall.

On the *Lusty Men* set, Mitchum was surprised to find that his brother John Mitchum (using the stage name John Mallory) had a small part as a cowboy. John told *The San Francisco Chronicle* in 1976,

> A lot of people think I got into this business because of my brother Robert. But that's a lotta bull roar. I was walking down Santa Monica Boulevard one day, when a casting agent saw me and said I should become an actor. I was a handsome guy then, so I listened to him and found myself in a little western called *The Prairie*. The director, Frank Wisbar, told me to take a punch at Alan Baxter. Hell, I didn't know anything about movie fighting. But I did know about boxing from my Army days. So, I slugged Alan. Hard. Very hard. Took three stitches to close up a rip around his eye. I had a helluva lot to learn about movies. And movies had a lot to learn about me.

Familiar western actors Glenn Strange, Marshall Reed, Lane Chandler, Sheb Wooley, Richard Farnsworth and Denver Pyle fill the smallest of parts, further adding to the film's sense of time and place. Mitchum was especially glad to be wearing casual, comfortable western wear in the great outdoors as opposed to toiling under hot studio lights in moth-eaten, sweat-stained, smelly RKO suits. It was largely a fun set for Mitchum despite the meddling of producer Jerry Wald. Mitchum was always opposed to bottom-line businessmen. The colorful rodeo personalities and stunt players present, like "Bad" Chuck Roberson, caused Mitchum to exhibit his own rowdy cowboy behavior with the crew as he horsed around with water pistols until it was time to film. "They're so serious," Mitchum told reporter Aline Mosby of the new generation of actors. "Why doesn't everyone have fun?"

Mitchum dubbed his director Nicholas Ray "The Mystic" due to his deep, studious concentration before directing a scene. Mitchum was initially concerned Ray wasn't providing any technical marks to hit. Ray was more concerned with discussing character background, motivation and improvisation. However, when Ray was finally ready to roll, so was Mitchum. "Nick Ray was a fine man," Mitchum told *Time Out*. "He was a drinking fellow, you know. Very intense." Ray found Mitchum to be a natural actor on par with the legendary Humphrey Bogart. In his autobiography *I Was Interrupted*, Ray wrote:

> The quality of being and acting at the same time was perhaps as true of Bogart as of anybody I've seen on film. He was always very well prepared—he knew what the scene was to be, he knew his action, and the details came naturally to him—but he wouldn't learn his lines until the last moment. But Bogie, like Bob Mitchum, had a truly photographic memory. When word got out about how he and Mitchum took advantage of this ability to achieve spontaneity, soon every new actor who had touched the fringe of the Actors Studio was asking for his lines, saying, "I never rehearse lines because it interferes with my spontaneity." Then we'd have to go 12 takes....

Physically Mitchum is at his broad-shouldered peak of rugged manliness. He never ceased to be a strong attraction for the women in the audience and those on the set. Co-star Carol Nugent (aka Carol Adams) portrayed the teenaged daughter of Mitchum's broken-legged rodeo mentor Arthur Hunnicutt. She told *The Prescott Courier*: "When I did *Lusty Men* with Bob Mitchum, I had a crush on him. On my first scene on the first day, I am to run and jump into his arms. He is a very sexy man. I forgot what I had learned. I couldn't say any dialogue." Veteran character lead Arthur Kennedy said of his co-star, "I like Bob.... He's highly intelligent but doesn't like to reveal it."

Publicity played up Mitchum's $100-a-week Hopalong Cassidy past and the fact that he was now earning $4250 a week from RKO to once again play a big-screen cowboy. Before the film's theatrical release, *Cowpoke* was known under such titles as *This Man Is Mine*, *Rough Company* and *The Losers* before Howard Hughes decided upon the lurid title *The Lusty Men*. Mitchum, Kennedy and Hunnicutt attended the world premiere at the Majestic Theatre in San Antonio, Texas. While there, Mitchum downed Lone Star Beer at the Menger Bar, the area's oldest continuously operating saloon, located on the grounds of the Battle of the Alamo between the Mexican Army and Texans led by Davy Crockett and James Bowie in 1836. Teddy Roosevelt organized his Rough Riders at the historic Menger in 1898. Mitchum crowned "Texas' Most Luscious Cowgirl" after beauty contest winners from Fort Worth, Dallas, Houston and San Antonio faced off.

The critical reception was overwhelmingly positive with Manny Farber of *The Nation* writing, "Mitchum is the most convincing cowboy I've seen in horse opry, meeting every situation with the lonely, distant calm of a master cliché-dodger." *Variety* noted, "Robert Mitchum gives what many will term his best performance yet," while *Film Bulletin* wrote, "Robert Mitchum checks in with one of his better performances as an ex–rodeo champion on the skids." *The Hollywood Reporter* hailed the performance as his "best to date" and offered: "Mitchum does an outstanding job, endowing the character with warmth and sincerity." *The Los Angeles Times* called Mitchum and Kennedy "both excellent" as contrasting types, and *Box Office* said Mitchum's character was "splendidly played." Even Bosley Crowther of *The New York Times* was won over by this performance: "Mr. Mitchum is most authentic as a hard-bitten rodeo 'tramp' who has gone on the shelf because of injuries...." *Newsweek* weighed in with, "Robert Mitchum is excellent as a jaded former world champion," and *Saturday Review* contributed: "Robert Mitchum, as the rodeo has-been, is outstanding in a generally superior cast."

According to Brian Garfield's *Western Films*, Mitchum gave an "awesome portrayal... [Y]ou can feel every one of his broken bones," while *Western Clippings* praised the "excellent performances," noting of Mitchum that it's "good to see him back in western garb." In *Rodeo Cowboys in the North American Imagination*, Michael Allen opined, "Robert Mitchum's gripping 1952 performance ... marked the first effective portrayal of the rodeo hero in popular culture.... The performances of Robert

Mitchum in *The Lusty Men* and Steve McQueen in *Junior Bonner* have never been equaled in rodeo literature." Mitchum chronicler Bruce Crowther wrote, "For *The Lusty Men* he found a touch of sadness which never degenerates into pathos, a characteristic which he rightly saw would sit ill upon the shoulders of a tough rodeo rider." *The Rough Guide to Westerns* compared Jeff McCloud to Mitchum's other past-his-prime cowboy in *El Dorado* (1967): "He gave near-definitive studies of dignified, worn-out, broken-down heroes." David Thomson in the *Biographical Dictionary of Film* called it "a beautiful study in independence brought to a realization of loneliness without a trace of sentimentality, never far from humor, and never separating manliness from intelligence."

The idea of formal rodeos originated in 1850s California as a way for ranches to separate horses and cattle based upon the skilled practices of Spanish vaqueros. Buffalo Bill Cody began staging rodeo exhibitions in his Wild West shows during the 1880s to thrill paying audiences. Eventually the breaking and branding became competitive and took on a sporting nature, with black cowboy Bill Pickett becoming a celebrity in the early 1900s demonstrating his unique steer wrestling abilities (he'd bite down on the steer's lip when he tackled it from his horse). By the 1920s, annual rodeo round-ups in Cheyenne, Wyoming, and Pendleton, Oregon, were considered by promoters to be World Championships with legendary movie stuntman Yakima Canutt claiming the title of overall champ on four occasions. As organized rodeo events took shape with dozens of skilled competitions in play, the Rodeo Cowboys Association emerged in 1945 to bring order to the chaos and identify true individual champions of the sport. Six events became standardized features for male competitors. They are saddle bronc riding, bareback bronc riding, bull riding, tie-down roping, steer wrestling and team roping. Barrel Racing emerged as a male and female competition.

Many rodeo cowboys began riding in their youth, forging the skills they would need to compete to an elite level. Mitchum had none of that childhood muscle memory to draw from. However, the role of a modern rodeo cowboy fit him well and served as a strong reminder to film audiences that Mitchum was one of their most believable western stars. Despite being a neophyte to the rodeo life, his every action and reaction in the film looks genuine; a true testament to his natural physical talents and adaptability. Publicity claimed that Mitchum did his own riding, calf-roping and bulldogging for the film and was lobbying RKO to join the rodeo circuit so he could compete professionally. The latter sounds like studio fluff, but there was no denying that the actor rode bulls and broncs against the studio's wishes and got a taste of what it was all about. He suffered a bad leg bruise roping a calf and rode a randy cayuse Indian pony named High Voltage out the chute. When rodeo tutor Les Sanborn found himself in trouble with a bull, it was Mitchum who dragged the cowboy to safety while others distracted the animal. Ray's opening shot where Mitchum straddles the bull Razor and lowers himself onto its back sets the tone for the picture. It's tough and uncompromising with no false glamour. It's as gritty as sand between the teeth. "You eat a little dirt if you have to," Mitchum explains to protégé Kennedy.

"Pretty physical," Mitchum told *Time Out* regarding the making of the film and his game attempt at staying on a bucking bronco. He elaborated:

> All those guys on their broncs, they just look like they're on rocking chairs. I get on a horse and they all say, "It's okay, he's just a retired old bronc." And this thing is turned loose, and I can't get off him. Bloody hell! They'd go in and try to pick me off, and my horse would turn around and kick the pick-up horse. He's heading for the fence and I just can't fall off him. I'm bleeding from the hair by the time they blow whistles and fired guns and everything.

Mitchum had hoped for the opportunity to sing a cowboy tune in the film but agreed with Nicholas Ray that they couldn't find an appropriate reason for his character to do so. Mitchum did have approval of Jimmie Dodd singing "Chilly Winds" at a rodeo party in the film. At producer Jerry Wald and RKO's request, an alternate happy ending had Mitchum hook up with an old girlfriend, but all involved talent-wise found it false and the antithesis of what they were trying to achieve with the movie. After filming the scene per the requirements of his contract, Mitchum claimed he had his secretary Reva Frederick throw the reel in an incinerator. This must have been okay with Nicholas Ray, who shared Mitchum's vision for the character. Ray subsequently wanted Mitchum to play the title character in the western *Johnny Guitar* (1954) but RKO refused to loan him out for that cult favorite. Sterling Hayden, a scowling ocean-farer turned actor who held as much scorn for Hollywood as Mitchum, played the part. Hayden begrudgingly accepted roles that first went through John Wayne and Mitchum. Other westerns during this period for which RKO refused Mitchum loan-outs were *Lone Hand* (1953) and *Saskatchewan* (1954). Those roles were played by Joel McCrea and Alan Ladd, respectively. RKO did, however, loan Mitchum out to 20th Century–Fox for the poor Congo adventure *White Witch Doctor* (1953) opposite Susan Hayward. It was their repayment to Fox for giving them Hayward. In that embarrassing film, Mitchum had to wrestle a man in a gorilla outfit.

River of No Return (20th Century–Fox, 1954)

Cast: Robert Mitchum (Matt Calder); Marilyn Monroe (Kay Weston); Rory Calhoun (Harry Weston); Tommy Rettig (Mark Calder); Murvyn Vye (Dave Colby); Douglas Spencer (Sam Benson); and Fred Aldrich, Claire Andre, Hal Baylor, Don Beddoe, Ralph Bucko, Roy Bucko, Larry Chance, John Cliff, Edmund Cobb, Cecil Combs, John Doucette, Tex Driscoll, Geneva Gray, Al Haskell, Chuck Hicks, Ed Hinton, Michael Jeffers, Dick Johnstone, Mitchell Kowall, Richard Lamarr, Anthony Lawrence, Jarma Lewis, Jack Low, Hank Mann, Jack Mather, Ann McCrea, Harry Monty, Fay Morley, Charles Morton, Paul Newlan, Barbara Nichols, George Patay, Jack Perrin, Joe Phillips, Robert Robinson, John Roy, Danny Sands, Ralph Sanford, Harry Seymour, Arthur Shields, Cap Somers, George Sowards, Constantine Stavropoulos, Jack Tornek, Jack Veitch, Bob Whitney, Harry Wilson, Will Wright.

Crew: Otto Preminger (Director); Stanley Rubin (Producer); Frank Fenton (Screenplay); Joseph La Shelle (Photographer); Cyril J. Mockridge (Music); Addison Hehr and Lyle Wheeler (Art Directors); Louis Loeffler (Editor); Charles Le Maire (Wardrobe); Paul Helmick (Assistant Director); Pat Anthony, David Bald Eagle, Norman Bishop, Jim Brewster, Len Carroll, Harry Froboess, Mac Graham, Dan Heather, Bob Herron, Robert Hinkle, Robert F. Hoy, Roy Jenson, Harry Monty, Bob Morgan, Arvo Ojala, Ronald St. Clair, Helen Thurston, Tim Wallace, Fred Zendar (Stunts); Thomas Koehler Biggs, Bud Brewster, Jim Brewster, Len Carroll, Louis Delorme, Mac Graham, Dan Heather (Wranglers); Ike Mills (Livestock Provider); Ralph Helfer (Animal Supervisor).

91 minutes; Released April 30, 1954

For a guy who wanted little more than to get away, Mitchum was feeling increasingly trapped by stardom and the binding RKO contract. Everywhere he went, would-be tough guys wanted to try their chances with him, and Mitchum was sometimes forced to oblige. When pushed past his own point of no return, Big Bad Bob would resort to a savage street-fighting mentality and rarely gave opponents a sporting chance. Hollywood stuntmen voted him the man they wanted on their side in a barroom brawl. While dining with Robert Preston in a New York City restaurant, Mitchum was sucker-punched without provocation while standing at a urinal. He promptly deposited the bold puncher in a garbage can in the back alley.

The legend of his toughness continued to grow, particularly after he broke the jaw of heavyweight boxing contender Bernie Reynolds in a Colorado Springs tavern while making the Korean War flick *One Minute to Zero* (1952). "The public and many movie producers are sold on the idea that I live 90 percent of my life in a bar with a pair of broads around my neck and my right hand cocked for anyone who breathes hard in my direction," Mitchum complained to the *Los Angeles Herald Examiner*. He told William Otterburn-Hall of the *San Francisco Chronicle*: "I just want a quiet time, but wherever I go, some goddamn guy has to come up and start something—even if it's just a conversation. Seems like the only place I can be alone is a john with a good lock on it." Any chance to escape to the great outdoors and the wide-open spaces of a location like Alberta, Canada, was fine with him. He was perfectly content to wade in a quiet stream with a bag of ice-cold beer and a fishing pole in his hand. He took 20 pounds of angling equipment with him on location for *River of No Return*.

Mitchum grew especially tired of being paraded by RKO as a hunk of beefcake. He spent the latter half of *His Kind of Woman* (1951) bare-chested and beaten, then had to train with pro handler Ralph Volkie at Terry Hunt's Hollywood gym for boxing scenes in *Second Chance* (1953). He'd already refused to shave his chest for the studio. Mitchum intentionally slacked off in his exercise routine and gained a few pounds around his waist so he wouldn't be asked to do any more gratuitous shirtless scenes. It was easy enough for him to suck in his gut when the camera was rolling. The new heft in his midsection did the trick. There was a single unbuttoned shirt scene in *River of No Return* after Mitchum fights off a mountain lion (animal trainer Pat Anthony doubled Mitchum for the attack, supervised by Ralph Helfer). Mitchum thought the added weight made him resemble a Bulgarian wrestler.

He now weighed a solid 205 pounds. Biographer John Belton wrote, "He is built like a Great American Bison: his massive head, shoulders and chest taper down to a narrow waist. Directors find him difficult to dress. Indeed, they prefer to undress him; he takes his shirt off in most of his films and his bare chest in movie ads still sells tickets." Mitchum's 48" chest now took on a barrel-like thickness. The joke in Hollywood became that Mitchum's chest entered a room several seconds before he did. "I always made the same film," Mitchum complained to Mike Tomkies of the string of repetitive RKO films and loan-outs. "They'd just keep moving new leading ladies in front of me. I'd close my eyes and when I opened them again, there was a new leading lady. I woke up once and there was Marilyn Monroe."

River of No Return opposite iconic sex symbol Monroe is one of Mitchum's most popular and enduring titles, not a classic by any means but an entertaining, entirely pleasant and colorful film to view. It was a 20th Century–Fox loan-out, shot in CinemaScope and stereophonic sound in the expansive wilds of Banff National Park and Jasper National Park near Devona Flats and Lake Louise in the heart of the Canadian Rockies. Filming was done on the Athabasca River, the Cascade River and the Bow River. They are all meant to be the Salmon River which flows down through Idaho into the Snake River. It's beautiful country, well-captured by cinematographer Joseph La Shelle, who went on to shoot *How the West Was Won* (1962).

The film opens with Mitchum on horseback in the mountains, the river in the distance behind him. It's a perfect beginning but a cinematic height the rest of the film touches in brief instances. A great deal of the action takes place on a wooden raft on the raging river of the title with a soaked Mitchum grimacing as he poles through the rapids and dodges Indian arrows before going over the Bow Falls. It sounds exciting, but many of these action scenes were too obviously done in the studio and suffer for it. Otto Preminger was an odd choice to direct the picture. It was his lone western.

The role of Matt Calder is the prototypical Mitchum societal outsider, a widowed ex-con returning from a jail sentence and a nasty reputation for shooting a man in the back. ("What does it matter how you kill a snake?" he asks.) It's obvious the reputation isn't warranted as Mitchum cares deeply about his abandoned

Mitchum as Matt Calder and Marilyn Monroe set off sparks in the popular outdoor drama *River of No Return* (1954).

(From left) Mitchum, Tommy Rettig and Marilyn Monroe brave the rapids in 20th Century–Fox's *River of No Return* (1954).

son (Tommy Rettig) and seeks to make amends with the youngster for the time he missed as a father. In early scenes, Mitchum is in a mining camp to pick the boy up. Mitchum envisions living on the edge of the wilderness with his son where they can farm and be left alone. Into their lives come gambler Rory Calhoun and his saloon singer girlfriend Monroe. Mitchum rescues them from the river, which the inexperienced Calhoun has no business being on. Calhoun claims he's headed to pick up a mining claim he won, but it's obvious he's no good. He steals Mitchum's gun and his horse to make haste for his claim. Outside of shooting a man in the back, no worse deeds can be done in the West, and this leaves Mitchum and his boy defenseless against the local Cree Indians. Calhoun leaves Monroe behind so she won't slow him down. When the Indians descend upon their cabin, Mitchum, Monroe and Rettig have no recourse but to brave the rapids of the River of No Return. Mitchum, his cabin burned to the ground, is now bent on revenge against Calhoun.

Outside of the physicality of the part, no great acting demands were made on Mitchum by the film except projecting his usual quiet strength. For Mitchum, the role was as comfortable as an old shirt. He teaches life lessons to the boy, tangles with heavies Calhoun, Murvyn Vye and Hal Baylor, and clinches romantically with Monroe. He'd done it all before. "Calhoun had a good punch and didn't need a double," Mitchum said of his friend.* Baylor, another pal, used to be the California Heavyweight Champ when he was known as Hal Fieberling. At 6'3" and 230 pounds, Baylor was cast as villains who engage in fisticuffs with film heroes because he never needed to be doubled. Interviewed by *The Daily Herald*, Baylor

---

*Garry Armstrong (e-mail correspondence, August 2017).

rattled off the names of Mitchum, John Wayne, John Payne and Robert Ryan as on-screen adversaries. "You name the actor, he's beaten me up," Baylor says. Mitchum said that he, Baylor and stuntman Roy Jenson undertook fight rehearsals themselves in their off-hours, so they could get a print easily once the cameras rolled. The actor commented:

> Guys got hurt when you had to do myriad takes on fight scenes. The chances of missing an angle on punches and punch reactions increased with each take. Baylor and Jenson were savvy pros who did their best before liquid lunches. Both were very light on their feet despite their size. We always looked for little "tells" with each other when we set up fight scenes. The directors usually didn't know about the "tells," and we didn't bother sharing the info.*

Mitchum did reveal that his screen fight with veteran tough guy Murvyn Vye of *Whispering Smith* (1948) infamy deviated from the planned choreography:

> Murvyn Vye was a tough son of a bitch. He was used to playing nasty guys. …Murv tried to butt me in the head. I ducked. He was pissed. I think Murv might have been a little wasted…. I was supposed to hold him in a headlock until Otto called "Cut." So, I'm holding Murvyn, he's wheezing, and I had to sneeze. I loosened my grip a little bit and son of a bitch Vye bites me! I tightened my grip again and held it for a few minutes until Otto finally called, "Cut." I look at Vye and he's got an evil grin. Never could figure out what the hell happened. Always thought Preminger was behind it.†

One interesting bit of western survivalist lore is presented as Mitchum bakes a fish packed in mud in the campfire. He also lassos an elk in the river from the raft. Regarding his chemistry with Monroe, the film relies on their growing desire for one another as they begin to see the other in a different light. That wasn't good enough for Fox executive Darryl F. Zanuck, who requested that Preminger add a body massage and an aggressive kissing scene that appears out of character for the extremely laid-back Mitchum. The grotto scene, with a randy Mitchum angry at Monroe's attempts to sabotage the journey, is tantamount to an attempted rape. It is a harbinger of the sexual menace he would later display in *Cape Fear* (1962). Already out of his element on the film and on to another project, Preminger refused to film the scene. Director Jean Negulesco helmed the footage of physical contact between the stars in the late fall of 1953. At the Hollywood studio, Mitchum's star contract stipulated that he would work until five p.m. and no later. Negulesco was up against the clock and concerned that his leading lady was taking ill under the studio lights. Fearing costly overruns if Monroe called in sick the next day and thereafter, Negulesco approached Mitchum and asked if he would film one more scene despite the late time. Mitchum agreed without hesitation. They got their shot while a runny-nosed Monroe was able. As he took her to the ground, Mitchum managed a single kiss on the squirming Monroe, complaining that it was hard to take aim with all her undulating. "She actually bit me in our little wrestle scene," Mitchum said. "I didn't mind it."‡

Monroe was impressed by Mitchum and talked of their passionate embrace in the film's pressbook: "This is a brand-new experience for me. I have never had a romantic love scene with a rugged he-man. It's quite enjoyable." By the end of the story, Mitchum walks into Monroe's saloon performance and throws her over his shoulder to take her with him into the great wilderness to be surrogate mother to his son. Some in the audience liked the take-charge aspect of Mitchum's character. The part played into his established bad boy image. He performed a near-repeat of the scene with Angie Dickinson in *Young Billy Young* (1969).

Monroe was happy for the opportunity to wear shoes on the film due to Mitchum's height. She usually had to go barefoot because of being paired with short male co-stars, but Mitchum towered above her throughout. She expounded on Mitchum in the pressbook, revealing:

> He's one of the most fascinating men I have ever known. He's a man's man, the outdoor he-man

---

*Garry Armstrong (e-mail correspondence, August 2017).
†Garry Armstrong (e-mail correspondence, August 2017).
‡Garry Armstrong (e-mail correspondence, August 2017).

type, but he possesses a great inner strength in addition to mere physical prowess. He is what he wants to be, and he doesn't cater to anyone else's taste or ideas. As a professional he was a pleasure to work with. For all his seeming indifference, he is a hard worker, rarely missing a line, delivering his best. This is the challenge that affects every other member of the cast to excel too. And then, he is generous with his time, energy and help. I had always heard that he was one of the nicest guys in the business. It was wonderful to discover that the legend was not only true—but an understatement.

Mitchum had known Marilyn Monroe back when she was a teenager named Norma Jean Baker and married to his Lockheed pal Jim Dougherty. Dougherty would sometimes share the egg sandwiches she made for him with Mitchum, who rarely brought his own lunch to the factory. Due to their previous knowledge of one another, Mitchum tended to treat Monroe like a kid sister and looked out for her. There had been rumors of Mitchum straying romantically with his leading ladies, notably with Ava Gardner in the 1890s bayou romance *My Forbidden Past* (1951). "I think every girl who ever worked with Bob fell in love with him," Gardner wrote in her autobiography. "And I was no exception." Fox no doubt wanted to play up the smoldering physical attraction between sex symbols Mitchum and Monroe, but for some of the filming Monroe's baseball player boyfriend Joe DiMaggio was present. Mitchum maintained that he never found Monroe sexy despite her screen image. To him, she was a sad and confused soul.

Mitchum was entirely content to spend his time in Canada pitching horseshoes and fishing with local outfitter Del Davis or imbibing in the Banff Springs Hotel bar with Rory Calhoun, Tim Wallace, Murvyn Vye and stunt double Roy Jenson (who braved the rapids on the raft with stuntwoman Helen Thurston and midget Harry Monty for the movie's impressive long shots). Local horse wranglers and outfitters like Jim Brewster, Mac Graham, and Len Carroll were recruited to work from the Rafter Six Guest Ranch and Seebe Guest Ranch and found themselves handling the livestock and at times standing in for Mitchum in long shots. Midway through the film, the crew of the western *Saskatchewan* (1954) began shooting nearby, and the females on that project began clamoring for Mitchum. Some stuntmen (including Bob Hoy) came over from *Saskatchewan* to help fill out the Indian attack scenes. While shooting in Jasper, the stars stayed at the Jasper Park Lodge and received nightly entertainment with the locals at the Speros dancehall.

Roy Jenson, 6'2" and 215 pounds, was between seasons for the Calgary Stampeders in the Canadian Football League and talked his way onto the film as a double for Mitchum. He had previously worked on films as an extra while playing college ball for UCLA but had little to no experience in westerns. In *Them Ornery Mitchum Boys*, John Mitchum claimed that his brother and Jenson nearly got into a fight on this initial film. Jenson became known as one of the toughest men in Hollywood, and Brother John was glad the argument didn't end in violence for the sake of both men. Jenson eventually became a Mitchum drinking buddy and appeared with him on screen in *5 Card Stud* (1968). Jenson made his mark in westerns as a supporting actor with memorable turns in *Waterhole #3* (1967), *Will Penny* (1968), *Big Jake* (1971), *The Life and Times of Judge Roy Bean* (1972), *Breakheart Pass* (1976) and *Tom Horn* (1980) in addition to all the major TV shows. "When I started doing stunts, I had to go buy a horse to learn how to ride," Jenson told *Western Clippings*. "I never became a 'horseman,' but I could get on, get there and get off…. The river was treacherous. I just about got killed three times."

If 20th Century–Fox was unable to play up a love affair between the two stars, they could emphasize the dangers of the location. The production lost three shooting days within the first week of filming due to inclement weather. Mitchum took an unintentional dip in chilly water and grew sick. At one point on the river, Monroe's wading boots filled up with water and Mitchum had to rescue her from drowning, to the delight of the publicists. On another occasion, the stars were on a raft that became lodged on a rock on the rapids after a safety cable snapped. Stuntman Norman Bishop had to go out in a lifeboat and rescue the actors

Mitchum takes aim at attacking Indians in *River of No Return* (1954) as Marilyn Monroe and Tommy Rettig try to stay afloat.

before their raft capsized. Mitchum, suffering from the flu with a fever of 102, tried to send Monroe and Rettig to safety first, but Monroe insisted she wouldn't get on the boat unless the ill Mitchum did at the same time. Publicists again attributed the rescue to Mitchum. Finally, Monroe slipped on a stone in the riverbank and sprained an ankle. When she was outfitted with a leg cast, Mitchum started calling her Hopalong.

Back in Hollywood, the film's action was redone in close-up with the principals in a studio water tank being blasted from all directions by buckets and fire hoses, the better to keep Monroe's wardrobe wet, tight and clingy. Mitchum played up the CinemaScope danger for the press, saying:

> This new medium is going to turn a lot of actors gray overnight. The new lens brings you so close to the audience it's impossible to use doubles or stuntmen. I've done things in this picture which would give some stuntmen the shivers. The amazing thing is how Marilyn and Tommy Rettig, who plays my son, have done them. We've dodged arrows in mountain streams and poled an awkward wooden raft over fast stretches of rough water. I was so struck with admiration for my two companions. I almost forgot to be frightened for myself. But there's no question that close views of actors struggling against danger will make action movies more entertaining.

Feeling that Monroe had a personality that was too fragile for Hollywood, Mitchum tried to look out for her in other ways. The greatest hurdle for Monroe to overcome on the film was a constant reliance on instruction and positive analysis from acting coach Natasha Lytess. Lytess would have her over-enunciate syllables and placed an emphasis on motivation for every single action in the script to the consternation of Preminger. Upon completing a line of dialogue, Monroe looked off-camera to Lytess rather than her director, infuriating the short-tempered Preminger. Mitchum thought Lytess was a fraud and the production was held up while Monroe readied herself physically and mentally for the cameras. As Preminger and the studio-approved Lytess were at great odds, Mitchum and assistant director Paul Helmick became go-betweens for Monroe and the director. "For quite a while it was Mitchum who made things work," Helmick recalled in his autobiography. However, the making of the picture dragged on interminably, and Mitchum became bored with the endless waiting around. Throughout the extended delays, he tended to drink, even wandering off for a beer with the locals at times. He took to calling the movie *The Picture of No Return*. "I thought we'd never get back," he told columnist Bob Thomas.

Preminger forbade alcohol on the set, unless it was specifically targeted for his leading man. As was tolerated at the time with contemporary stars like Clark Gable, Errol Flynn and Humphrey Bogart, Mitchum's mild day-drinking was allowed if he was on time and knew his lines. His punctuality and knowledge of the script was never in question. Nips of vodka throughout the day kept him nice and relaxed for the cameras. He was the least of Preminger's worries. At one point, Mitchum had to slap Monroe on her backside to bring her into a scene for the cameras. "Stop the nonsense!" he barked so they could begin filming. Director John Huston later wanted Mitchum to star opposite Monroe in the modern western *The Misfits* (1961), but Mitchum turned down the physically and mentally exhausting part of broken-down cowboy Gay Langford. Clark Gable took the film instead and had a fatal heart attack by the end of that stressful experience.

"She was very shy, very pleasant, very sweet," Mitchum said of Monroe in a 1980s WEDU TV interview. He continued:

> But she was not too comfortable around people because I suppose her background had not prepared her for sort of easy sociality. She was convinced that she was not terribly pretty or sexy. As a matter of fact, she didn't have an aura of sexiness about her. The drama coach Natasha Lytess came into her life because I'm sure that Marilyn thought there was some magic in Natasha. She felt she needed someone to support her, to tell her what she was doing was right when she did do something right. She felt that this whole lark of being a sex symbol or a glamour queen was just that. She would play it if that's what they wanted, and she burlesqued it really because she thought the whole thing was very, very funny. At that time, I didn't think she knew too many people who were very friendly to her. Growing up in an atmosphere of agents, directors and journalists, she seemed like a lost child.... Her position in this atmosphere was like Alice in Wonderland. The whole thing was through the looking glass and she could not believe that anyone was very serious about her.

Mitchum had worked with Preminger before on *Angel Face* (1952) where the director demanded Mitchum slap leading lady Jean Simmons repeatedly for the camera. Legend has it that with Simmons in tears and Preminger saying she needed to be hit harder, Mitchum turned on the director and slapped him to get his attention. Mitchum asked if that was hard enough or should the next one be harder. Preminger suddenly decided the last take was plenty hard and would be a print after all. So Mitchum could deflect at least some of the bullying tyrant's criticism aimed at Monroe to make her more at ease. Preminger, entirely different away from the stresses of a movie set, knew what Mitchum was doing and came away from *River of No Return* impressed by his leading man. Mitchum chronicler Alvin H. Marill quoted Preminger saying:

> I remember Bob as a man of professional integrity, and I would like to work with him again whenever it's possible. Beyond that, while I see him too rarely, when I do it's as if we had parted only yesterday. Bob has a warmth, a feeling apart from his intelligence that makes him a friend for life even if you've only had a fleeting experience of work or personal contact with him.

The film's producer Stanley Rubin spoke of Mitchum's behavioral dichotomy in a radio interview for WMPG:

> I had an immediate and very favorable impression of him as a man who was unlike the image he portrayed on screen. I found him to be a

very likable, very on the surface, easygoing guy, though later on with further experience with him I did get evidence of his volatility. There was one particularly bad night…. I have very fond memories of Mitchum. I want to make that statement. I like him a lot. I respected him as an actor. He was indeed when sober a very nice man, but he had his drinking moments.

Rubin went on to reveal that one night after filming on the Fox lot, an angry Mitchum tore up a dressing room and ripped a phone from the wall. "In spite of that, he was on the set the next morning at the appointed time. He was there, got his makeup, proper wardrobe, and knew his lines perfectly and delivered a first-rate performance."

The film's bad guy Rory Calhoun was one of Mitchum's pals. When Calhoun and Lita Baron renewed their wedding vows on location in Alberta, Mitchum served as their best man. Mitchum nicknamed Calhoun, "Smoke," as he tended to tag his buddies with a variety of catchy monikers. Professional film extra George Fargo was "Grey Cloud," character player Robert Rothwell was "Wing Commander," bit player Desmond Slattery was "Dusty Dirty," Cedric Onstatt was "Seed Sacker," Long Beach pal Elmer Elsworth Jones was "Swami," actor-surfer Billy Murphy was "Red" and stand-in Boyd Cabeen was "Tyrone." Tim Wallace was simply "Big Tim." Leading lady Jane Russell was "Hard John." They called Mitchum "The Goose" because of his chest-out strut. Calhoun was a B+ western star himself, having leading roles in *Powder River* (1953), *The Yellow Tomahawk* (1954) et al., and later starring in the TV series *The Texan* (1958–1960). Interviewed in *Conversations with Classic Film Stars,* Calhoun commented on Mitchum: "He's one of the greatest guys you'll ever meet in your whole life. I'm very fond of Bob. He's a hell of a guy. I guess we could have swapped roles, but he was right for that and I was right for what I was doing because I was more greasy, more slick."

Reviews for *River of No Return* were mixed with *Variety* noting, "Mitchum, Miss Monroe and Calhoun perform acceptably in roles that make no great demands." *The Los Angeles Times*: "Mitchum is at home as the rugged outdoors type who deadens most of his emotions."

The Hollywood Reporter raved, "Casting Robert Mitchum as the co-star of this outstanding Stanley Rubin production was pure inspiration. Mitchum gives throughout his finest performance to date as a laconic backwoods farmer, expressing more with eloquent silence than other actors do in paragraphs." *The New Yorker* singled out Mitchum's contribution, writing, "Seldom have I seen an actor maintain an air of aloofness in the face of proceedings like shooting rapids on a raft, fighting a mountain lion, and dodging the arrows of outraged red-men." According to *The Los Angeles Herald Examiner*,

> Robert Mitchum is superbly cast as the rough and gentle man of adventure with a hidden past and a determined outlook for him and his son's future. It is probably his best role to date. A strong characterization is given to him in the Frank Fenton screenplay, and Mitch knows what to do with it. He gives an amazing performance as a woodsman, a wonderfully kind father, as a fighter, and a fellow who can take or leave the charms of the hottest conquest since fire was discovered.

Among later notices, Phil Hardy opined, "Mitchum and Monroe are marvelous together," and *The Rough Guide to Westerns* declared, "Mitchum was a fine foil for Marilyn Monroe." Mitchum biographer John Belton called it "Mitchum's best performance of the period," and John Howard Reid in his book *Great Hollywood Westerns* noted, "Mitchum has the uncanny ability to dominate a scene even if he stands in the background." Lincoln Center's *Film Linc Daily* said, "Mitchum's effortless subtlety beautifully balances Monroe's broad strokes." One notable aspect of Mitchum's performance is how well he works with young Rettig, foreshadowing the patient and loving father-son relationship between Chuck Connors and Johnny Crawford that resonated with viewers on the long-running TV series *The Rifleman* (1957–1963).

Many think it is Mitchum singing the title song "River of No Return" over the opening credits. The baritone sounds like Mitchum's singing voice and the singer is not credited. It is, however, the well-known Tennessee Ernie Ford of "16 Tons" and "Peace in the Valley" fame singing the song, which Monroe later repeats as part of her saloon show. Newspaper reports from the time back up this fact. To further confuse matters, a singer named Tex Williams released a version of the song during the same time frame. To add another wrinkle, in 1953 Mitchum co-wrote a song with Dok Stanford entitled "Hey, Mr. Cotton Picker." Tennessee Ernie Ford and Tex Williams each recorded versions of the song, leading the movie star to briefly consider touring and recording.

Mitchum was good friends with rodeo cowboy turned western swing musician Ray Reed from Ruidoso Downs, New Mexico. The two met as teenagers jumping boxcars in El Paso, Texas, during their hobo days. In 1986, Reed told *The Albuquerque Journal*, "Mitchum's been a pal of mine for years. He's a hell of a drinkin' man and a storyteller."

Subbing for Jimmie Fidler, Mitchum discussed his love for authentic cowboy tunes in the pages of America's newspapers. "I like cowboy music," Mitchum wrote, and he went on:

> I like any kind of music that expresses the moods and customs of people…. The old-time cowboy, the original range rider, was a forlorn and lonesome guy. He spent a lot of time, sometimes weeks on end, with nothing but horses and cattle for company. And talking to a horse becomes a pretty discouraging pastime. It's so one-sided. When talking got tiresome the lonely cowboy sang. He sang all the songs he knew. And after a while this got tiresome, because he plumb ran out of songs. So, to while away the hours, he began making up his own tunes. He wasn't much at composing; his tunes were simple. He was short on book-learning, too, so his words were plain. But somehow, out of loneliness, monotony and the urge for expression came a quiet sort of music. It was plain, but it was eloquent. It sounded like a ballad, which in a way, it was.
>
> From such rough-hewn beginnings, cowboy music developed…. The cowpoke sang of people, places, shindigs, jamborees, shootin' matches, necktie parties, love. He paid tribute to the heroes of his time: Jesse James, Jim Fisk, Sam Bass and all the rest. He sang of towns like Laredo and Cheyenne. He sang of the plains and sky and the clouds. He sang about roundups, robberies and rustlers. He sang about everything in the frontier world. As the pattern took shape, cowboy songs grew sturdier, bolder and more colorful. They became a part of a country that was busting out at the seams, growing up, bulging its muscles. They became a part of legend and history set to music…. Try listening to Tennessee Ernie or Red Foley some evening. Take the trouble to discover some of the worthwhile albums done by the Sons of the Pioneers. They are what I mean by real cowboy music. You'll understand why I like cowboy music.

Mitchum earned $5000 a week for *River of No Return*, but he was not entirely happy. RKO was making considerably more from Fox for Mitchum's loan-out services. As Mitchum neared the end of his ten years with RKO, the faltering studio did not have his best interest in mind. Howard Hughes, whom Mitchum dubbed "The Phantom," had grown more reclusive and strange. Mitchum felt Hughes' underbosses were out to intentionally sabotage his career with his final assignment, the absurd B-western *Cattle Queen of Montana* (1954). RKO wanted him to play the secondary Indian character Colorados opposite Barbara Stanwyck and Ronald Reagan. Some sources do contend it was the Reagan leading man part Mitchum was offered. Mitchum promptly refused the assignment and announced he was going fishing while his agents haggled out the small print of his exit from the studio. Lance Fuller played the part of Colorados. The film was savaged by the critics.

Producer-director Dick Powell had plans to star Mitchum, John Wayne, Jane Russell and Arthur Hunnicutt in *The Long Wire*, a RKO film about stringing telegraph wire across the Old West, but Mitchum's subsequent suspension from the studio nixed that. Instead, Powell and Wayne went ahead with the Mongol western *The Conqueror* (1956), a film that columnist Sheilah Graham announced in 1953 that Howard Hughes originally intended as a star vehicle for Mitchum. Wayne was notoriously miscast as Genghis Khan opposite Susan Hayward. The critically maligned film shot in the radioactive red dust of St. George, Utah, near where nuclear tests had recently been performed. Many members of the cast and crew allegedly developed cancer. Mitchum apparently dodged a bullet.

With a new baby daughter named Petrine born in 1952, Mitchum was attempting to be more of a father and family man. In the family's backyard, he taught his sons the manly arts of archery and boxing. For Jim's Cub Scout troop, he converted an attic over the garage into a meeting place filled with cowboy and Indian artifacts from his western films. He now had at his disposal a live-in camper trailer installed on his one-ton flatbed Ford truck by loyal RKO crew members. At the time, the design was cutting edge. It had a refrigerator and a butane stove, and could sleep multiple people. When a film wrapped, he'd take his flannel-shirted boys Jim and Chris along with Tim Wallace on extended hunting and fishing treks that would start in the High Sierras and stretch across the western United States. Cowboy character actor Joe Haworth was a Mitchum hunting and fishing buddy, as was *Sky King* TV star Kirby Grant, America's Flying Cowboy. Legend has it that on one fishing trip, Grant placed Mitchum in touch with real southern bootleggers who became the inspiration for the development of Mitchum's film *Thunder Road* (1958).

The great wide open was Mitchum's calling. "I hate crowds," he told *The Los Angeles Times*. "At every opportunity, I head for the timber." One trip with the boys went from Idaho down through the Colorado Rockies and across Texas all the way to New Orleans where they met up with Dorothy. The family flew home while Wallace drove the truck back to Hollywood. Regarding his father's time for his boys during this period, son Chris told the *Mesquite Local News*, "He started acting around the time I was born, so I grew as his career was growing. He did the best he could, and when he was around we had fun." Brother Jim echoed those sentiments, telling Prescott, Arizona's *Daily Courier*, "It was a different world when I was growing up…. It was really a fun time."

Track of the Cat (Warner Bros., 1954)

Cast: Robert Mitchum (Curt Bridges); Teresa Wright (Grace Bridges); Diana Lynn (Gwen Williams); Tab Hunter (Harold Bridges); Beulah Bondi (Ma Bridges); Philip Tonge (Pa Bridges); William Hopper (Arthur Bridges); Carl Switzer (Joe Sam).

Crew: William Wellman (Director); John Wayne and Robert Fellows (Producers); A.I. Bezzerides (Screenplay); William H. Clothier (Photographer); Roy Webb (Music); Al Ybarra (Art Director); Fred MacDowell (Editor); Gwen Wakeling (Wardrobe); Andrew V. McLaglen (Assistant Director); Nate Edwards (Production Manager); Joseph La Bella (Property Master); Mel Koontz (Animal Trainer); Les Hilton (Horse Trainer); Arthur Riste, Thomas Riste (Wranglers); Tim Wallace (Stand-in and Stunt Double).

102 minutes; Released November 27, 1954

Adapted from Walter Van Tilburg Clark's 1949 novel, *Track of the Cat* was a transitional film for Mitchum. Despite being given star billing as 1890s Northern California rancher Curt Bridges, he is cast as the bullying antagonist. It's the first time he'd played an out-and-out bad guy since the Hoppy westerns. Others in the Bridges clan live in fear of his words and threat of physicality, even as his mother Beulah Bondi dotes on his take-charge nature while his father Philip Tonge drinks himself into a daily stupor. Cerebral older brother William Hopper avoids confrontation and is chided by Mitchum for his lack of action. Middle-aged sister Teresa Wright regrets staying with the isolated family when she could have gotten away years earlier through marriage. She encourages youngest brother Tab Hunter to get out of the family with visiting girlfriend Diana Lynn, whom the aggressive Mitchum threatens to wrest away.

Into their lives comes a mysterious black pan-

As **Curt Bridges** in *Track of the Cat* (1954).

ther that intensifies the family tensions. Director William A. Wellman intentionally keeps the panther as a ghostly unseen entity that arrives with the first snow of the winter and feasts on the family's cattle. To an old Indian named Joe Sam (a heavily made-up Carl "Alfalfa" Switzer), the big cat has taken on mythical proportions. Mitchum scoffs at Joe Sam. For Mitchum it's a personal battle as the panther killed his dogs the year before. In many ways, it represents his own dark side. He sets out into the snow to hunt the beast down, taking a reluctant Hopper with him. Separated from Mitchum, Hopper is killed by the panther. Mitchum makes a critical error when he prepares to send Hopper's body back to the ranch. Because the horse is skittish due to the smell of the cat on Hopper's coat, Mitchum switches jackets, but in doing so sends away the beef jerky stored in his pockets. Instead of life-sustaining food, he is left with Hopper's book of John Keats' poetry. As he takes refuge from a snowstorm in a cave, the audience thinks Keats' words might enlighten the solitary Mitchum. Instead he uses the book to start a fire that immediately goes out. Poetic justice. Eventually delirious and snow-blind, Mitchum heads after the sound of the panther only to walk off a cliff to his death. With Mitchum gone, the rest of the family finally rallies around Hunter's impending marriage.

The film is best known for Wellman's experimental indulgence in making a color film in black and white. Aided by the snow-covered land, Wellman and cinematographer William Clothier use monochromatic colors, overwhelmingly black and white and gray in every scene with the jarring exception of the bearded Mitchum's red mackinaw coat and Diana Lynn's yellow blouse. The contrast in the surroundings is striking every time Mitchum enters the frame.

As an actor, Mitchum controls his environment as the bullying Curt. Even his name describes his aura. There's an interesting moment when Lynn freezes in her tracks upon encountering Mitchum on the stairwell. A strong sexual tension exists, although she is promised to younger brother Hunter. Outside of the red mackinaw, the rest of Mitchum's wardrobe is impressively Alpha Male, including his black chaps and black hat. When he later switches to Hopper's black and white cowhide coat, it signifies the moment he begins to lose his own power in his hunt for the panther. Mitchum becomes the prey instead of the predator. He plays the change subtly and effectively.

While there was plenty about the making of *River of No Return* that could be described as physically grueling, Mitchum declared Wellman's *Track of the Cat* his single toughest film yet to endure. This was due to the bitterly cold location and the deep snow encountered while shooting at Mount Rainier National Park in Washington State. Mitchum is on horseback or wandering around the snow-covered wilderness. Every step caused him or his horse to sink deeply into the heavy snow. Publicity declared Mitchum narrowly avoided a small avalanche brought on by Wellman's use of a bullhorn to give direction to Mitchum a quarter of a mile up a mountain slope. From then on, they used hand signals to communicate. Mitchum's evening activities consisted of endless poker games and drinking with only a few hours of sleep. It's the way he was wired. At one point on the shoot, former Little Rascal Switzer threw a live raccoon into Mitchum's cabin as a practical joke. Switzer, who moonlighted as a professional hunter and guide, took Mitchum, Wellman and Hunter on a supervised bear hunt while on location.

Horses were provided to the production by the Arthur Riste family and their business Indian Creek Corrals. The impressive ebony horse Mitchum rides through the heavy snow was an American Saddlebred stallion that came from Hollywood and the Fat Jones Stables. This horse, Black Diamond, carried Lash LaRue through several B-westerns and appeared in *Black Horse Canyon* (1954) with Joel McCrea. Its trainer was Will Rogers' protégé Les Hilton, best known in Hollywood circles for training Francis the Talking Mule, the Arabian sorrel Flicka, and the famous TV horse Mr. Ed. A specialized rearing stunt horse named Ski from Fat Jones Stables was also used. Ski was prompted to rear in the corral by an unseen air hose to display its skittishness regarding the panther. Scenes at the family ranch were filmed on an expansive Warner Bros. soundstage with a combination of gypsum and bleached corn flakes substituting for real snow. These interior scenes were done in the middle of the San Fernando Valley summer with the actors bundled up in winter clothing.

Mitchum was now considered a fine western horseman by Hollywood standards and was able to do his own riding and rearing. On the DVD feature *Black Diamond,* Mitchum's daughter Petrine spoke of her dad and his horse in the film:

> I have to believe that Mr. Wellman deliberately wanted a black horse. It's incredibly striking against the snow with his beautiful arched neck and his prancing gait against the snow and my father's red and black jacket. It's quite a stunning image. Snow is difficult for horses to walk in because it has suction. It's one of the things that makes Black Diamond look especially good because it caused him to really lift his knees. So, his actions look particularly spectacular when he is trudging through the snow.
>
> My father's character, Curt Bridges, is a tempestuous man in the film. When he goes out to get Black Diamond, whose character in the film is called Kentuck, you see the horse in his stall, sort of flexing his beautiful neck and kicking around. The horse is matching him in spirit. Of course, he was a very tame horse and all of these behaviors were either cued by my father, who'd been taught by the trainer how to cue the horse to do the rear, or being cued off camera by the trainer, who was Les Hilton. Black Diamond was a rearing horse, so he was trained to rear on command and paw. If you watch the scene in the snow with my dad, he does quite a lot of pawing. And you can sort of watch his ears and from the directions his ears are going, we know where the trainer is standing. In a rearing scene, the horse will have been trained to rear on command. Just like Trigger was trained to rear for Roy Rogers, Black Diamond was trained to rear on command. It's really a matter of knowing when the horse is going to go up and keeping your balance on him. If it's a trained rear, it's not scary. If it's a horse rearing because it's misbehaving, then it's scary because a rearing horse could flip over backwards.

The man vs. nature film was produced by John Wayne and Robert Fellows for Batjac Productions. Future Mitchum director Andrew V. McLaglen served as the second unit director. Cinematographer William Clothier photographed *Fort Apache* (1948), *The Alamo* (1960) and *The Man Who Shot Liberty Valance* (1962). Clothier was awarded the Heritage Award from the Cowboy Hall of Fame. William Wellman helmed the western films *The Ox-Bow Incident* (1943), *Yellow Sky* (1948) and *Westward the Women* (1951), all considered to be interesting, unconventional near-classics. *Ox-Bow* was a film Mitchum professed a fondness for. Regarding his *Story of G.I. Joe* director Wellman, Mitchum commented in the book *Wild Bill Wellman*, "He didn't waste a lot of time on useless, silly sentimentality. You know, he wore no man's collar. I was very, very fond of him, and he tolerated me."

Wellman appreciated the sense of rugged reality Mitchum brought to his western and war films, though they would have a famous falling-out on the set of *Blood Alley* (1955). Here they were an effective team. Wellman said in publicity material: "When I first read the book, I knew that Bob was the one man in Hollywood who could handle the difficult part. At least he was the player I wanted, and he has more than delivered. This guy has got more unrecognized talent than a dozen so-called leading men, and this picture proves it." *Track of the Cat* was Wellman's final film with a western theme. Screenwriter A.I. "Buzz" Bezzerides, co-creator of the *Big Valley* (1965–1969) TV series, told Lee Server that Wellman fell in love with his first draft, which Bezzerides felt was overwritten and needed cleaning up. "Bob Mitchum was fantastic," Bezzerides said. "He carried scenes that needed to be polished, and his performance made some of it work."

Tab Hunter wrote in his autobiography:

> If you want to talk about a "man's man" start with Mitchum. He was the biggest star I'd ever worked with, which was a little bit intimidating when we tested. It worked to my advantage, as it mirrored the relationship between our characters. I got over my nervousness in a hurry. Mitchum was so easygoing, such a pleasure to be around. Compared to someone like Van Heflin, who had extensive theatrical training and radiated an actor's aura, Mitchum approached work like a day laborer delivering a truckload of rocks to your backyard. "What picture are we shooting today?" he'd crack on the drive to the location. Such coolness was actually made possible by a photographic memory—one glance at a script page,

Mitchum was one of the few leading men willing to play dark characters and villains like his anti-hero in *Track of the Cat* (1954).

said Mitchum gave "a superb performance," and *The BFI Companion to the Western* called him "marvelously edgy." Western historian Jim Hitt wrote, "Mitchum's brooding Curt is one of the actor's most underrated performances." Internet blogger Jeff Arnold noted, "Even when on auto-pilot, [Mitchum] was superb, and this time he seemed to spark and was even better. He provided the western grit to what otherwise might have been an overly talky theatrical piece." According to Mitchum biographer Damien Love,

> His wickedness here had unprecedented depth, confidence and vigor. He's plugged into sex and enjoys scaring the people around him, taunting them, laughing at their aspirations. He takes obvious, arrogant pleasure from his loathsome deviancy, almost swaggering, but cold to the bone—here, out among the snowy wastes of the edge of the world Mitchum broodingly drafted the blueprint for the unthinkable monsters he would build in *Cape Fear* and *The Night of the Hunter*.

and Mitch had his lines down cold. He was the quickest study I've ever seen.

Young actress Diana Lynn was surprised at Mitchum's dedication, telling Erskine Johnson in the *Tacoma Daily Ledger*, "I expected a good-time Charley, but he's one of the most professional actors I've ever worked with."

Reviews were mixed. Bosley Crowther of *The New York Times* took his usual shot at Mitchum: "The illusion of an interrelation is not helped by Robert Mitchum in the role of the hard-bitten, mother-driven brother, since Mr. Mitchum is one of those boys whose screen personality is stubborn and resistant to the subtleties of such a role." On the flip side, *Motion Picture Daily* called it "a striking character portrayal" and an "expert performance." *The Los Angeles Times* wrote, "Mitchum provides a genuine study in his role," while *The Hollywood Reporter* praised Beulah Bondi and added, "Mitchum is equally good as the casually sadistic brother." *Variety* concluded, "The performances are good in that they meet the demands for mood from direction and plot."

Among contemporary sources, Phil Hardy

Playing a heel was out of the ordinary for a leading western actor. Established cowboy heroes like Randolph Scott and Joel McCrea wouldn't dream of upsetting their fans or their established screen image by playing a bad guy. Mitchum didn't care. His fans favored him because he didn't toe the line and his screen characters reinforced his own dangerous bad boy behavior. He smoked dope. He drank. He got into fistfights. He was a womanizer. "Most leading men avoid depravity," he told Erskine Johnson in 1954. "I cultivate it." Mitchum preferred to play characters with some degree of complexity. His willingness to do so led to his giving what many consider one of his best performances, the switchblade-wielding country preacher Harry Powell in director Charles Laughton's *The Night of the Hunter* (1955); Powell is a man who has the words LOVE and HATE tattooed onto his bare knuckles as he menaces a pair of innocent children. Mitchum and his characters were metaphorically capable of traveling dark trails no self-respecting traditionally vanilla cowboy hero would ever dare tread. His words and actions could be shocking to the genre. "I think I can be most convincing as a heavy," he told Cork Millner regarding his acting range.

Wearing a string tie and bringing a western look to his devious West Virginia preacher Harry Powell in *The Night of the Hunter* (1955).

Mitchum tried to stay out of trouble in real life, but that wasn't easy. Sometimes it was forces outside of his control; occasionally it was his own doing, done for the sake of a bawdy chuckle. Scott Eyman's John Wayne bio attributes one notorious bit of Mitchum lore to this film's location, although in his own book John Mitchum pegs the tale as occurring in Colorado during the making of *One Minute to Zero* (1952). The story goes that a young female writing for her high school newspaper inquired if Mitchum was able to enjoy the local hunting and fishing. With a straight face, Mitchum replied that his favorite hunting was for the elusive "poontang," macho slang for the female genitalia. The innocent girl had never heard of this creature, so Mitchum elaborated in metaphorical detail, claiming that he had personally nearly decimated the breed. The girl continued to think he was referring to a small animal. Legend has it the story made it into print and the shocked studio quickly bought up every copy and had them destroyed. Stuntman Chuck Roberson later appropriated the tale and claimed it occurred in Tucson, Arizona, during the making of *El Dorado* (1967).

During filming in Washington, a local construction worker with a tough-guy reputation sought Mitchum out at the Gateway Inn where cast and crew were quartered. Mitchum thought he might have to fight the man, but the two ended up draining a bottle together in the man's car. The scenario was not unfamiliar to the star. He could never be certain if a situation would warrant sharing drinks or throwing hands. He was always ready for the latter as a last resort. Mike Tomkies quoted Mitchum discussing the dangers of western location shoots: "These cowboys are no cream puffs. If they take a dislike to you, they can make things pretty tough. If they find you speak their language and can take care of yourself with your fists or at the bar, then you're in."

While promoting *Track of the Cat* at the Cannes Film Festival, Mitchum was besieged by would-be starlet Simone Silva, who was trying to garner attention for herself. Mitchum agreed to a simple photo with the sea as a backdrop. To the shock of Mitchum (and his wife Dorothy), Silva dropped her top and pressed her bare bosom against Mitchum while a gaggle of photographers stumbled over themselves snapping photos. The *Durham Morning Herald* quoted Mitchum declaring the visit to Cannes would be his first and last: "It is chaos." In early 1955, the scandal mag *Confidential* printed an outlandish story claiming a nude Mitchum doused himself in catsup and arrived at a costume party claiming to be a hamburger. Mitchum sued the rag and won, but with the marijuana bust still fresh in everyone's mind, the bad boy image persisted.

Man with the Gun (Formosa Productions/United Artists, 1955)

Cast: Robert Mitchum (Clint Tollinger); Jan Sterling (Nelly Blaine); Karen Sharpe (Stella Atkins); Henry Hull (Marshal Lee Sims); Emile Meyer (Saul Atkins); John Lupton (Jeff Castle); Barbara Lawrence (Ann Wakefield); Ted De Corsia (Frenchy Lescaux); Leo Gordon (Ed Pinchot); James Westerfield (Mr. Zender); and Jay Adler, Claude Akins, Florenz Ames, Joe Barry, Jimmie Booth, Archie Butler, Norma Calderon, Neil Collins, Thom Conroy, Angie Dickinson, Herman Hack, Mara McAfee, Burt Mustin, Maidie Norman, Robert Osterloh, Maudie Prickett, Stafford Repp, John Rice, Buddy Roosevelt, Pat Sheehan, Amzie Strickland.

Crew: Richard Wilson (Director); Samuel Goldwyn, Jr. (Producer); N.B. Stone, Jr., and Richard Wilson (Screenplay); Lee Garmes (Photographer); Alex North (Music); Hilyard Brown (Art Director); Gene Milford (Editor); Frank Parmenter (Production Manager); Sid Sidman (Assistant Director); Lennie Geer, Chuck Roberson, Jimmie Booth, Archie Butler (Stunts); Tim Wallace (Stand-in); Lennie Geer (Wrangler).

83 minutes; Released November 5, 1955

Mitchum's *enfant terrible* public image was reinforced when he was relieved of his leading man duties in William Wellman's seabound actioner *Blood Alley* (1955) for what was termed "horseplay." The story leaked to the press was that a drunken Mitchum deposited transportation manager George Coleman in the San Francisco Bay after a disagreement, and Wellman had seen enough of his star's rowdy behavior. Wellman had reportedly lost a night's sleep due to Mitchum's all-night partying and roughhousing in a nearby suite. Mitchum and insiders like assistant director Andrew V. McLaglen denied this, claiming instead the money men behind the film saw the window of opportunity to cast John Wayne (whose Batjac was co-producing) in the lead role and needed a reason to dismiss their star. Mitchum had reported to the film location early to do second unit pick-up shots aboard a boat that could easily have been done by a stand-in or photo double. Mitchum was made the scapegoat. He took it all in stride.

The furor did kibosh one potentially promising western project for Mitchum. Wayne and his Batjac partner Robert Fellows had commissioned popular tough guy fiction writer Mickey Spillane of Mike Hammer fame to write a western script for them. Spillane's completed screenplay *The Saga of Cali York* (aka *The Legend of Caleb York*) was about a mysterious gunslinger riding into a New Mexico town to take on a crooked, power-hungry sheriff. Spillane wrote with an eye for Wayne to portray the lawman, with William Wellman directing. However, it is likely Wayne and Fellows as producers would have assigned the starring role of Caleb York to their current *Track of the Cat* leading man Robert Mitchum. The Mitchum-Wellman flare-up on *Blood Alley* and Wayne's total immersion into getting his beloved Alamo project to the screen resulted in a temporary end to Spillane's story seeing daylight. In his twilight years, Spillane handed over his Caleb York screenplay and notes to his collaborator Max Allan Collins, who resurrected the character in the western novels *The Legend of Caleb York*, *The Big Showdown* and *The Bloody Spur*. It's easy to read these and picture Mitchum as York.

Regarding Mickey Spillane, in 1954 *Variety* reported that producer-director Robert Aldrich offered Mitchum $500,000 in $25,000-a-year installments to portray Spillane's private eye character Mike Hammer in back-to-back films. Mitchum was intrigued by the offer but was busy filming *Not as a Stranger* (1955). Mitchum's agent eventually talked him out of accepting the deal, reasoning the heavy doses of sex and violence in Spillane's books was something that Mitchum should steer clear of; the actor sought to broaden his image from that of the morally challenged RKO tough. Aldrich ended up casting Ralph Meeker as Hammer in *Kiss Me Deadly* (1955), which became a cult classic. Aldrich finally made *The Angry Hills* (1959) with Mitchum. It was a "gorilla picture" neither cared for.

After his *Blood Alley* dismissal, Mitchum began looking for a quick rebound project.

One screenplay that intrigued him was a Burt Kennedy western called *Seven Men from Now* (1956). Writer Kennedy had been signed by Wayne's Batjac and was trying to develop projects for his boss. But when Mitchum showed interest in the screenplay, Wayne took another look at the story and decided to purchase it for himself. Taking on the lead in *Blood Alley*, Wayne's own filming docket remained full. With Mitchum temporarily out of favor, Wayne decided to give the leading role to the older cowboy star Randolph Scott. The Budd Boetticher–directed film proved to be one of Scott's best and sparked a series of Scott-Boetticher-Kennedy films (including *The Tall T* [1957] and *Ride Lonesome* [1959]) that are now highly regarded. Mitchum was correct in identifying the project's strengths and remained on the lookout for an appropriate western. He even expressed interest in writing his own oater as many good western scripts passed through Wayne first.

After being fired from *Blood Alley*, Mitchum was given his choice of projects that were ready to go. He liked a minor frontier justice western entitled *The Deadly Peacemaker* for neophyte producer Samuel Goldwyn, Jr., and first-time director Richard Wilson. It was filmed in Hollywood on the Sam Goldwyn's back lot and an unevenly graded 20th Century–Fox street set. Mitchum led the cast as a highly skilled town tamer named Clint Tollinger, a man who deals in lead. Goldwyn had no problems with leading man Mitchum's bad boy rep, telling columnist Erskine Johnson, "He's great. He's a magnificent actor, and we're ahead of schedule." That was important as the film was not afforded a large budget. The choice to film in black and white when many A-westerns were being made in color, the lack of geographic scope, and the absence of any big action scenes outside of a saloon burning makes this play like a TV episode along the lines of something seen on the high-quality *Zane Grey Theatre* series. The gruff, 6'5" Sterling Hayden made several 1950s westerns like *Top Gun* (1955) and *The Iron Sheriff* (1957) with this look and feel. While *Man with the Gun* is not top of the line, it remains an interesting companion piece to *Blood on the Moon* and a must-see for Mitchum fans.

The effective, stripped-down storyline benefits from solid characterizations and a fine Alex North score. Mitchum commands the screen with little wasted movement as the grim gunslinger who rides into Sheridan City, Wyoming, and is recruited by the town to take on a greedy land baron (Joe Barry) and his gunmen (Leo Gordon and Claude Akins). Premier heavy Gordon shoots a boy's dog to start the film, creating a tense and edgy mood that is sustained throughout. Mitchum has an agenda of his own. He's there to ask his estranged wife Jan Sterling, the local madam, the whereabouts of their young daughter. A deputized Mitchum goes about cleaning up the town in his own rough way, instituting a no-weapons policy and a curfew that rankles saloon owner Ted De Corsia. To show

As town tamer Clint Tollinger in *Man with the Gun* (1955).

he means business, Mitchum shoots down two resistant gunmen who unwisely test his mettle.

Mitchum brings several subtle touches to his gray-clad character, like wiping dust from ineffectual marshal Henry Hull's gun rack. He eventually reveals that his own father, a man who didn't believe in guns, was brutally killed by land grabbers. Mitchum has since lived his life by rule of the gun, and it's this fact that drove Sterling away. Mitchum is heroic and well-mannered enough for pretty townie Karen Sharpe to begin questioning the manly attributes of her fiancé John Lupton, but Mitchum admits that any chemistry between himself and Sharpe exists because she reminds him of a younger Sterling. Mitchum keeps after Sterling about their daughter until Sterling reveals that the little girl got sick and died their first winter away from Mitchum. Mitchum leaves in a frightening rage. He heads to the saloon to goad cocky subordinate villain De Corsia into a fight. De Corsia throws a Bowie knife at Mitchum, who shoots him down and then sets fire to the saloon. The fire threatens to burn down the town, but citizens get it under control. Mitchum watches from the shadows, one of the scariest and most disturbing actions ever undertaken by a western hero. Despite the shocking behavior, he rights himself for the climactic shootout with Gordon and the land baron. He is determined to remain until the job is finished, despite his own personal motto: "Never stay in one town too long."

The film contains noir-like moments, including the haunting image of the fire's shadows flickering across Mitchum's face. Mitchum's behavior throughout sets an appropriately dark tone. When he shoots a shifty Claude Akins off his horse, Mitchum says coldly to the others, "Get out of town and take your dead with you." Mitchum's behavior is surprisingly brutal, a 180-degree turn from his white-hat RKO heroes, but there are enough moments of western heroism to please traditional audiences. On two occasions before the climax, he stands up to the land baron's gunmen, proving himself adept with his firearms, positioning and savvy. It's hard to imagine any other actor taking on such a remote, solitary and disturbed character. Tollinger is human and flawed and one of the more intriguing gunslingers ever committed to film. He kills because it's his job, but also to right wrongs stretching back to his own childhood. He admits to his own sense of personal mystery and hiding out from "questions I can't answer."

Mitchum is at home in the 1870s western milieu and proves himself believable as the two-gun man (one Colt Navy holstered, another bone-handled Colt .45 stuck in his front belt). When Leo Gordon knocks a drawn gun out of Mitchum's hand during an early confrontation, Mitchum draws his waist gun on Gordon quickly to detain him. It's fast enough that the camera, the audience and most importantly Gordon aren't ready for it. Tough guy Gordon, a real ex-con, menaced John Wayne in *Hondo* (1953)

Cast in the shadows, preparing to throw a knife in *Man with the Gun* (1955).

and was making his name as one of the scariest bad guys in Hollywood. He and Mitchum got along swimmingly. In Lee Server's Mitchum biography, Gordon calls the star "a helluva guy, just as easygoing as can be." Mitchum bests Gordon in their showdown. In the final shootout, Mitchum intentionally hesitates, allowing Lupton to restore his manhood in Sharpe's eyes by taking the fatal shot at land baron Barry. For his hesitation, Mitchum receives a bullet in the shoulder. The film ends with somewhat false happiness as Mitchum, bleeding in the dirt, and Sterling vow to restart their life together. Given it was Mitchum, audiences wouldn't have been averse to him picking himself off the ground and riding out of town a forever lonely and haunted man. Or dying in the dust.

Mitchum lobbied director Wilson to carry a stuntman out of the burning building so they could acquire a good shot of Mitchum emerging from the flames. Their timing was slightly off and Mitchum stayed in longer than expected, emerging with singed clothing from the flames licking at his body. The scene was crucial for the low-budget film, and Mitchum did all he could to see it came off well. In *Ok, You Mugs,* author Dave Hickey transcribed a 1980s Mitchum TV interview in his essay "Mitchum Gets Out of Jail" where Mitchum describes his own method of bringing strength and reality to the screen, setting the pace and tempo for his western actions. On props, specifically guns, Mitchum said:

> Most actors handle guns on screen like they're cap pistols. A real gun is a very serious instrument. It has serious implications and terrible consequences, so you want to handle a gun like that. If you do this, your character gets real in a hurry—it steals the reality of the gun. That's movie acting, you steal the reality of the prop and control the pace of the pictures. Oh, also you have to say the lines, but that's purely secondary.

Western fast-draw was becoming the new fascination in Hollywood with gun experts Arvo Ojala and Rodd Redwing the preeminent experts on the subject. They trained many of the cowboy actors to make them appear faster on the draw. When an actor couldn't clear leather convincingly, the studios resorted to an edited insert of Ojala or Redwing drawing and shooting. It's Redwing subbing for Alan Ladd's famous gun work in *Shane* (1953). Mitchum proved himself a worthy student of the art and didn't require a gun coach on the film. "That guy can do anything," Goldwyn, Jr., marveled to the *Times-Picayune.* "But he won't let you know he can do it." Studio publicity released a series of time-lapse photographs with Mitchum clearing his holster to fire a level shot in under three-quarters of a second. Inset in each photograph is a stopwatch documenting Mitchum's speed at drawing his firearm from beginning to end. Some actors, including Hugh O'Brian (who claimed Mitchum was his cowboy hero), boasted about their fast-draw speed to the press, but Mitchum never acknowledged his speed outside of these photos. Many in Hollywood considered Glenn Ford and Audie Murphy the quickest when it came to actors who could draw in the blink of an eye.

Audiences believed Mitchum and his natural interactions on the screen. He displays a keen ability to listen and think on camera. Few actors could blend so easily into their surroundings; yet have the charisma and physical stature to stand out against the scenery while doing nothing. Mitchum was a consummate film actor, highly skilled in the "less is more" school of acting. Film critics weren't always so enamored with his laid-back style. It was in sharp contrast to the rat-a-tat, spit-out-the-dialogue fashion so prevalent in the 1930s and 1940s. Publications called him "flint-eyed" and "poker-faced" yet many seemed to agree that he gave a multi-layered, three-dimensional performance. *Variety* reported, "Mitchum portrays the character most effectively; capturing the flavor of an old time, Max Brand–type of western gunman hero." *The New York Times* remarked, "Mr. Mitchum convincingly enacts the role," while *The Los Angeles Times* concluded, "Mitchum's personal magnetism is a strong asset." *Commonweal*: "Certainly one of the best performances he has ever given." *Motion Picture Daily* added, "Mitchum effectively accentuates the coldness of the character without being able to do much with the few flashes of warmth."

Among contemporary reviews, Herb Fagen's *Encyclopedia of Westerns* said, "Mitchum is su-

On the clock with his fast draw in *Man with the Gun* (1955).

perb in this slow-moving film with a familiar and standardized theme," while Michael R. Pitts in *Western Movies* called it a "slow-moving and brooding drama with good work by Robert Mitchum as the gunfighter." According to *Renegade Westerns,* Mitchum "locates the menace beneath his character's conventionally taciturn exterior." *Cinema Retro*: "Mitchum looks terrific in the part, strutting about town ramrod straight and looking handsome even when embroiled in shootouts. Even this early in his career there was evidence of a superstar in the making…. It's Mitchum's show throughout—and he delivers the goods."

The film was released in the United Kingdom as *The Troubleshooter.* Publicity declared that Mitchum "has an unabashed liking for playing in films with a western locale." George Stevens, the director of *Shane,* reportedly wanted Mitchum to play Jett Rink in *Giant* (1956). Mitchum would have seemed better suited for Bick Benedict, the character Rock Hudson played in the modern-day Texas tale. Stevens is said to have considered him for that as well. Perhaps Mitchum should have aligned himself with the industry's great western directors like Stevens and John Ford when he had a

chance; but then, John Wayne always had first dibs on any Ford project. As good as Wayne was playing the dark, obsessive Ethan Edwards in *The Searchers* (1956), Mitchum could have risen to the occasion and been his equal. In *Man with the Gun,* he was working with first-time helmsman Richard Wilson, a protégé of Orson Welles, who does a solid job with the assignment but carried little in the way of industry clout or prestige. Wilson later revisited the basic story and themes of *Man with the Gun* in the Yul Brynner western *Invitation to a Gunfighter* (1964). The Edward Dmytryk western *Warlock* (1959) starring Henry Fonda shares strong storyline similarities and shot on the same 20th Century–Fox street. *Man with the Gun* screenwriter N.B. "Bo" Stone went on to pen the classic *Ride the High Country* (1962).

During filming on the Fox lot, Mitchum got into an altercation with his brother John Mitchum, whose fledgling acting career had not yet taken off despite bit parts in films like *Flying Leathernecks* (1951), *One Minute to Zero* (1952) and *Stalag 17* (1954). John showed up drunk to ask for a loan to cover medical bills. He was so ashamed that he needed a handout that he picked a fight with Mitchum's stand-in Tim Wallace while waiting for the star to get off camera. Mitchum arrived backstage, surveyed the trouble and hit John over the head to subdue him. He sent his brother home and called the man's wife to inquire about his behavior. Upon learning of John's looming medical crisis, he quickly sent the family an envelope of money to cover their debts.

In his book *Camera! Roll 'Em! Action!,* veteran western bad man Pierce Lyden shared the following memory of the Mitchum brothers and their movie misadventures. He remembers giving a green John Mitchum tips on how to stay on a western horse for the serial *Perils of the Wilderness* (1956). John was forever in Lyden's debt, in more ways than one. Lyden wrote:

> John Mitchum, Bob's kid brother, borrowed a "fifty" from me once, because his wife and child needed it.' He lost it in a poker game that night. Later, when we worked a serial together for Columbia, I followed him to the bank in Gower Gulch when we got our checks. I said, "John, to

me you're not the kid brother of Big Bob the Star. I knew him before he was in pictures, you know. And I'm not star-struck. You're just another actor, and I need my money." He laughed, paid me, and we remained friends, of course.

John eventually became a highly recognizable character actor, logging notable western credits in *Bandolero!* (1968), *Paint Your Wagon* (1969), *Chisum* (1970), *High Plains Drifter* (1973) and *The Outlaw Josey Wales* (1976). He made the rounds of all the classic TV westerns, including *Have Gun—Will Travel, Bonanza, Gunsmoke* and *The Virginian,* and he had regular assignments on *Riverboat* (1959–1960) and *F-Troop* (1965–1967). John was extremely popular with the casts and crews and entertained with his guitar regularly at his San Fernando Valley home. He even wrote cowboy poetry and folk songs, notably an entire album entitled *America, Why I Love Her* for John Wayne to record. John was nominated for a Grammy in 1973 for this title. He recorded a similar album in the 1960s with *Bonanza* TV star Dan Blocker and, with musician–western actor Jon Locke, went on publicity tours with *Virginian* star James Drury. A little shorter and heavier than Robert, John was every bit as tough and won a boxing championship while in the Army. In the late 1940s, the brothers had a fight that wrecked Bob's home and went down as the toughest either would ever endure.

Mitchum's generosity was not limited to immediate family members. He was more apt to give to the downtrodden and do so anonymously. While filming *Man with the Gun,* he gave his stunt double Lennie Geer the shirt off his back, deciding the wardrobe looked good on Geer. Mitchum kept the stuntman's shirt that was ruined by a squib shot. Geer provided the palomino Mitchum rode in the film, the same distinctively marked horse Geer had on the Disney TV series *The Adventures of Spin and Marty* (1955–1958). In real life, Mitchum consistently displayed a strong sense of cowboy ethics. He was a man of his word, tough but fair, placing the needs of others above his own. Young actress Karen Sharpe told biographer Lee Server that working with Mitchum on the film (and their subsequent publicity tour of New York City) was one of the great experiences of her life because he was so helpful and gentlemanly.

Despite his altruistic nature behind the scenes, there remained a sense of danger about Mitchum that came across thrillingly on the screen. He was believable in confrontational situations and that tight-lipped, no-nonsense toughness was a quality that audiences lapped up. They believed him as a bad man trying to do good, or as a decent man fighting the temptation to turn to the dark side. Only Robert Ryan could play rugged cowboy heroism and cutthroat villainy as well. Writing on Mitchum in a 2001 *Newsweek* piece, Malcolm Jones declared him "an anti-hero when that meant something." Dave Hickey called the actor "a switchblade on a plate of cupcakes" in relation to other 1950s western actors like James Stewart, Ronald Reagan and Henry Fonda. An actor the likes of Gregory Peck would never risk his stolid heroic image by treading into villainous territory. Ditto cowboy heroes Randolph Scott and Joel McCrea, whose fans would have been appalled. Charlton Heston, Burt Lancaster and Kirk Douglas would allow their characters to be arrogant and self-satisfied, but ultimately redeemed in the final reel. Glenn Ford successfully toyed with portraying a charismatic baddie in *3:10 to Yuma* (1957), but no other 1950s cowboy hero could nearly burn down a town and keep the audience in his corner. It was a rare quality that was adopted by actors like Clint Eastwood and Charles Bronson in the following decades.

Mitchum's pal George Fargo was a film extra and stand-in. He isn't credited with working on any Mitchum films but was likely behind the scenes on several. When he wasn't picking up film work, Fargo worked a contractor's job digging swimming pools. From that side job, Fargo made friends with the young actor Clint Eastwood. On occasion, Fargo and Eastwood met up with Mitchum for a beer. It's interesting for no other reason than the fact that Eastwood had the opportunity to observe Mitchum first hand during this period, perhaps informing his own laconic underplaying anti-heroic gunslinger screen image to a degree while he labored on the TV western *Rawhide* (1959–1965) as the character Rowdy Yates. Eastwood said in inter views that Mitchum was an actor he admired, though he amped up the steely determination and played down the vibe of reluctance for his own screen portrayals. In the 1960s, Eastwood's Man with No Name in Sergio Leone's Spaghetti Westerns *A Fistful of Dollars* (1964), *For a Few Dollars More* (1966) and *The Good, the Bad and the Ugly* (1966) became infamous for shooting unsavory men in the back. A John Wayne cowboy hero would never shoot a man in the back on screen. Nor would he burn down a town.

Bandido (United Artists, 1956)

Cast: Robert Mitchum (Richard Wilson); Ursula Thiess (Lisa Kennedy); Gilbert Roland (Colonel Jose Escobar); Zachary Scott (Kennedy); Rodolfo Acosta (Sebastian); Jose Torvay (Gonzalez); Henry Brandon (Gunther); Douglas Fowley (McGhee); and Fidel Castro, Jose Angel Espinosa "Ferusquilla," Miguel Inclan, Victor Junco, Margarita Lunco, Arturo Manrique, Dorothy Mitchum, Jose Munoz, Alberto Pedret, Antonio Sandoval, Manuel Sanchez Navarro, Alfonso Sanchez Tello.

Crew: Richard Fleischer (Director); Robert L. Jacks (Producer); Earl Felton (Screenplay); Ernest Laszlo (Photographer); Max Steiner (Music); Jack Martin Smith (Art Director); Robert Golden (Editor); Oscar Rodriguez (Wardrobe); Virgil Hart (Assistant Director); John Burch and Luis Sanchez Tello (Production Managers); Paul Stader, Tim Wallace (Stunts); Tim Wallace, Robert Polo (Stand-ins); Thomas Haas (Armorer); Rafael Munoz (Technical Advisor); Chema Hernandez (Livestock Coordinator).

92 minutes; Released September 1956

During the 1950s, Mitchum was guilty of walking through routine and forgettable films for the paycheck. The transitional western *Bandido* was one of them. Playing up his casually macho aura to the hilt, it was prototypical of what became Mitchum's established screen image: the forever laidback man of action who didn't sweat any situation, not even a firing squad. In this noisy motion picture, he is introduced sauntering through a Mexican village in a hail of gunfire. Bullets continue to whiz through his hotel room while he calmly sips whiskey from a broken bottle. Finally, he decides to lob a few grenades into the fray to affect the outcome of the battle between soldiers and revolutionaries. In the film's pressbook, Mitchum called these over-the-top pictures

Mitchum (left) and Gilbert Roland fight off Mexican soldiers in action-packed *Bandido* (1956).

"derelict adventurers." Self-mockery became a favored Mitchum defense mechanism regarding his film career.

The wrinkle here was that Mitchum had a hand in writing and producing this film, a picture whose importance to his career is customarily glossed over in books on the actor. Biographer Lee Server does recognize it as one of Mitchum's most personal films, once again presenting him as the ultimate swaggering, raffish, hard-drinking gringo. At one point he even planned to sing a title tune over the credits. The fast-paced *Bandido* was impressively shot in CinemaScope by director Richard Fleischer and cameraman Ernest Laszlo, but it played for years on TV in an inferior pan-and scan version. Not many people saw it in its original format as it was released on a double-bill with a then-unknown Stanley Kubrick's *The Killing* (1956). It's not a bad film—merely run-of-the-mill.

Mitchum headlines as the opportunistic Wilson, a soldier of fortune armed with an abundant supply of hand grenades to fend off the federal Mexican "Regulares" after he aligns himself with Gilbert Roland's revolutionaries (including Rodolfo Acosta and Jose Torvay). Set during the 1916 Mexican rebellion, the film is colorful and passably entertaining with Mitchum never far from center stage as he wrestles leading lady Ursula Thiess away from her gunrunner husband Zachary Scott. Given its time period, the movie is not a traditional western, but there's plenty of rifle-fire, horses and sweat-soaked sombreros for devotees of the genre. For a good portion of the film, Mitchum is dressed in an increasingly worn white suit with a wide-brimmed Panama hat. He eventually loses the jacket and the hat and by the latter third of the picture is clad in tan jeans and cowboy boots for a big shootout where he wields a Browning machine-gun while fighting alongside Roland (the Cisco Kid of 1940s B-westerns). In true Mitchum fashion, he makes the end credits with no money for his trouble, but the hint of a future north of the border with Thiess.

Co-produced with Mitchum's recently formed DRM Productions, the movie benefits greatly from being shot on location in Acapulco, Cuernavaca, Bavispe and Yaltapec. Interiors were shot at Mexico City's Churubusco Studios. The production was filming on actual Mexican battle sites with veterans of the 1916 fight cast as extras to provide authenticity and local flavor. Mitchum's character actor pal Douglas Fowley has a part, as does grim-faced Henry Brandon as a German heavy. Brandon famously appeared the same year as Chief Scar in *The Searchers* (1956). *Bandido* is full of battles and impressive stunt work courtesy of action coordinator Paul Stader; publicity claimed the movie production fired more rounds of ammunition than the revolution itself. Stunt ace Stader worked with Mitchum at RKO and told the *Times-Picayune* he regarded the star "highly as a performer as well as a gentleman." As one of the film's producers, Mitchum was involved in scouting locations and even collaborated to some degree on the drastically altered screenplay. He had originally signed Anthony Quinn to essay Gilbert Roland's part, but Quinn became unavailable. Roland is a fine substitute.

The film initially had higher aspirations than the straight south-of-the-border adventure it became, but Mitchum never blanched. He and Fleischer were intrigued by the original satiric pitch from screenwriter Earl Felton involving a Hollywood movie outfit filming a Pancho Villa movie in Mexico. Mitchum signed on and headed to Europe to make *Foreign Intrigue* (1956), only to encounter upon his return his drinking pal Felton's ongoing problems completing that script (originally known as *Horse Opera*). Felton had turned it into a convoluted B-action film and Fleischer and Mitchum had no alternative except to trek ahead with looming financial and location deadlines. For Fleischer, there was the threat of a lawsuit from producer Robert L. Jacks for reneging on his contract. Fleischer requested Felton's presence in Mexico, so they could all continue writing as the film progressed. They still managed to make a solid, slightly tongue-in-cheek picture, which fit snugly into Mitchum's established realm as the maverick too wild to tame. Mitchum was aware of his lot in the industry and what he was hired by producers and the studios to perform based upon his own past. "You don't get to do better," he told *People* in 1983. "You get to do more." He elaborated in a 1997 Carole Langer interview regarding his choice of roles and evaluation of scripts: "It was not my business to like it or not like it. I just looked through to see how many times I fell down, how many times I got hit, and how many short days or days I could get off."

Mitchum liked a few things about *Bandido*, including extensive time in Acapulco and the fact he saw parts of himself in the adventurous, devil-may-care character Wilson. In the *Bandido* publicity material, Mitchum said:

> I've always been one to speak my mind about a picture, even those I'm in. If I don't like a picture, I don't mortgage my tongue. Like *Bandido*, the picture I made in Mexico. I like it in more ways than just as entertainment. The main character, Wilson, whom the natives call Alachran—a deadly stinging serpent, reminds me of Robert Mitchum. I've always led a kind of soldier-of-fortune life. I've done the things I want to do…. *Bandido* began with a writer friend of mine, Earl Felton. He had always told me that he wanted to write a script about a soldier of fortune to fit me. I told him I needed no fitting.

The explosive story turned out to be physically arduous for Mitchum. He told the press, "It was the toughest picture by far that I have ever worked in." In addition to plenty of horseback riding, he had to jump off the Palo Bolero Falls and trudge through a murky mangrove swamp. A pictorial feature titled "Bandido Bob" in the fan magazine *Silver Screen* showed him holding a tarantula and snaring a snake in a lagoon. At one point in the film, he scraped skin off his leg when he fell through a roof. On another occasion, a series of complicated special effects squib shots failed to detonate for the camera, so Mitchum allowed real ammunition to be shot in the dirt near his feet to avoid further delay. Then there was the grappling love scene in the sand with leading lady Ursula Thiess. The actress, recently married to actor Robert Taylor, had reservations about working with Mitchum given his reputation as a romantic rogue. But once on location, she became convinced that Mitchum was nothing but a gentleman and that it was fanatic females who were constantly in pursuit of him. "He was wrongfully labeled," she told *Western Clippings*. "What I saw was a lover of women."

The production had a few hiccups. In Tepotzlan, Mitchum was given armed guards when machete-wielding locals showed up angry that filming was being done in a church. On another occasion, Mitchum's stand-in Tim Wallace got into a nasty bar brawl where a local woman was injured. Authorities thought that it was Mitchum himself causing the trouble. Once Mitchum had been cleared, Wallace was spirited out of the country. Mitchum's makeup man Layne "Shotgun" Britton also got into local trouble and had to leave the country. Near the end of shooting, Mitchum's company car was pulled over and local cops found a large amount of marijuana in the trunk. It was likely a set-up; United Artists paid $10,000 to extricate Mitchum from a potential jail sentence.

It wasn't all bad though. Mitchum helped a local girl after she was stung by a scorpion, carrying her on horseback to the nearest medical help. During the filming, he became lifelong friends with British actor Trevor Howard, who was making the movie *Run for the Sun* (1956) near Acapulco and was staying in the same El Mirador Hotel. They were on location for six weeks with Mitchum's wife Dorothy visiting near the end of filming. She even worked as an extra. Upon wrapping, Mitchum and his wife threw a huge party for the cast and crew.

Legend has it that Cuban revolutionary Fidel Castro, in exile in Mexico at the time, worked on the film. He was training his rebel soldiers at the time in Cuernavaca and reportedly organized and provided extras for the action scenes. While in Mexico, Mitchum also encountered an American mining engineer who had been living in Bolivia. The American pitched Mitchum a story based on western outlaws Butch Cassidy and the Sundance Kid hiding out in Central America in the early 1900s. Mitchum listened with interest but was focused on his next picture, the modern moonshining yarn *Thunder Road* (1958), which he was scripting, producing, casting and writing the music for in addition to starring. Mitchum turned down the opportunity to portray the legendary bank and train robber Butch Cassidy. More than a dozen years later, screenwriter William Goldman and director George Roy Hill turned the outlaw story into the western classic *Butch*

Mitchum saw a lot of himself in the soldier of fortune character Richard Wilson in *Bandido* (1956).

Cassidy and the Sundance Kid (1969) starring Paul Newman and Robert Redford.

Bandido used custom gunsmith Thomas Haas as an armorer and technical advisor, a capacity the firearm expert filled on the Gary Cooper-Burt Lancaster western adventure *Vera Cruz* (1954). Haas was a friend of Mexican general Enrico Guerra and was well-known south of the border for his interest in vintage weapons. Mitchum and Gilbert Roland used the same 1905 engraved, gold-powdered Smith & Wesson .38 M&P revolver in the film. The double-action pistol with 5" barrel had a distinctive red-eyed steer's head carved into a pearl grip. Roland retained the handgun and used it in several more films.

Ubiquitous livestock coordinator Chema Hernandez furnished horses and served as the ramrod (head horse wrangler). His responsibilities were to provide and care for the horses as well as match the cast with their equestrians. As the star of the film, Mitchum received the top steed, a black stallion with white blaze. Before filming, it is the responsibility of the wrangler and his crew to warm up and prep the individual horses, insuring that each horse is in an even mood and camera-ready. They must be accustomed to the sound of gunshots and not spook. A horse with too much spirit could make an inexperienced rider look foolish or even place an actor in danger. On the other hand, the best horses could come alive for the camera and make their rider look good. Western fans were well aware of Gene Autry's relationship with Champion and Roy Rogers' love for his golden palomino Trigger. James Stewart wouldn't ride any horse other than his chestnut-sorrel gelding Pie, and in his 1950s films John Wayne favored the dark bay Banner. In his later films, Wayne rode the chestnut-sorrel gelding Dollor. Mitchum worked closely with the wranglers on his film sets and absorbed their horse knowledge. Hernandez, who worked on 500 films including *The Magnificent Seven* (1960) and *The Wild Bunch* (1969), showed up again throughout the course of Mitchum's career on *The Wonderful Country* (1959), *5 Card Stud* (1968) and *The Wrath of God* (1972).

In the glut of 1950s westerns, *Bandido* barely registered any substantial reviews upon its release. *Variety* commented, "Robert Mitchum is a likable not always understandable sort of hero-heavy in the Earl Felton plot." *The Hollywood Reporter* praised "a fistful of good performances topped by Robert Mitchum and Gilbert Roland…. The story's only major flaw was a happy ending which was not necessary for a star with Mitchum's qualities or the kind of part he plays. Mitchum is without a peer in this kind of tough, sympathetic part and he is well-complimented by Roland, who manages to convey charm and menace in about the same instant." *The Los Angeles Times* opined, "Earl Felton's story gives Mitchum a combination hero-villain characterization which the star tosses over his shoulder in usual nonchalant fashion." *The Beverly Hills Citizen*: "Acting is top-drawer, with Mitchum, Thiess, Roland and Scott all delivering fine performances." The *Boston Herald* said, "Mr. Mitchum and Mr. Roland make good foils for one another and toss around some high-sounding tough talk very well indeed." The *San Francisco Chronicle* called the film "a happy combination of Mitchum's nonchalance and a great deal of good-natured vigor."

Among contemporary reviews, Herb Fagen's

Encyclopedia of Westerns said, "*Bandido* delivers an excellent performance by Mitchum as the American soldier of fortune," while Michael R. Pitts' *Western Movies* claimed, "Robert Mitchum and Zachary Scott as the foes and Gilbert Roland as the rebel leader make this a fast-moving and pleasant feature." Mitchum biographer John Belton declared, "The soldier-of-fortune role is an ideal part for Mitchum, meshing beautifully with his amoral image." At the website *Great Western Movies,* Nicholas Chennault commented, "Robert Mitchum's voice is excellent, and his performance in this convoluted plot is fine."

The Wonderful Country (United Artists/D.R.M. Productions, 1959)

Cast: Robert Mitchum (Martin Brady); Julie London (Helen Colton); Gary Merrill (Major Stark Colton); Albert Dekker (Capt. Rucker); Jack Oakie (Travis Hyte); Charles McGraw (Dr. Herbert J. Stovall); Satchel Paige (Sgt. Tobe Sutton); Anthony Caruso (Santiago Santos); Mike Kellin (Pancho Gil); Victor Mendoza (Gen. Marcos Castro); Jay Novello (Diego Casas); John Banner (Ben Sterner); Max Slaten (Ludwig "Chico" Sterner); Margarito Luna (Margeurito Luna); Joe Haworth (Stoker); Tom Lea (Mr. Peebles); Chuck Roberson (Barton); Pedro Armendariz (Cipriano Castro); and Claudio Brook, Leonard Brooks, Eldon Grier, Chester Hayes, Victoria Horne, Mike Luna, Alberto Mariscal, Judith Marsh, James Edgar McCullah, Hernando Name, Alberto Pedret, Salvador Godnez, Antonio Sandoval, Ignacio Villabazo, Jose Chavez Trowe.

Crew: Robert Parrish (Director); Chester Erskine and Robert Mitchum (Producers); Robert Ardrey (Screenplay); Floyd Crosby and Alex Phillips (Photographers); Alex North (Music); Michael Luciano (Editor); Reeder Boss (Wardrobe); R.J. Lannan (Production Manager); Henry Spitz and Harry Horner (Assistant Directors); Chuck Roberson, Jack N. Young, Pablo Agustin Aldama (Stunts); Chema Hernandez (Boss Wrangler); Chuck Roberson, Sam Acton (Livestock Providers).

98 minutes; Released October 21, 1959

Free of his RKO contract, Mitchum opted to take assignments around the world as an acting mercenary for hire. There was Europe for *Foreign Intrigue* (1956), the Caribbean for *Fire Down Below* (1957) and *Heaven Knows, Mr. Allison* (1957), Hawaii for *The Enemy Below* (1957), North Carolina for *Thunder Road* (1958), Greece for *The Angry Hills* (1959) and Ireland for *The Night Fighters* (aka *A Terrible Beauty,* 1959). "Anything to get out of the house," he told Joyce Persico of the *Trenton Evening Times.* "Just give me a script and an airplane ticket, and I'm your man." In addition to these varied films, there was an unrealized 1957 western project titled *Night Riders* that would have co-starred World War II's most decorated soldier Audie Murphy, then working at Universal in B+ westerns. Scheduling conflicts prevented this from occurring. *The Wonderful Country* (1959), produced by Mitchum himself, returned him to the familiar environs of Mexico shooting principally in Durango, Chihuahua and Sonora.

It had been over three years since Mitchum made a western. He teased the press that he'd become allergic to horses in the same way Lockheed made him allergic to metal. It was more smoke. TV screens were deluged with cowboy series featuring overly familiar and watered-down storylines. In addition, the radio dial and record stores grew full of the popular gunfighter ballads of Marty Robbins, Frankie Laine, Johnny Cash, Sheb Wooley and Johnny Western. Even kids had a fast-gun to look

Dressed as a Mexican in his portrayal of expatriate gunrunner Martin Brady in *The Wonderful Country* (1959).

up to in the form of cartoon character Quick Draw McGraw. Mitchum was smart to take a step back and try something different during this period of oversaturation, even if it meant turning down high-quality projects like John Sturges' *Gunfight at the O.K. Corral* (1957) and John Huston's *The Unforgiven* (1960).

The physical landscape was changing. The Old West was becoming increasingly difficult to film with any sense of accuracy. Cities and towns were growing, power transformers stretched the horizon, and jet vapors filled the sky. The logistics and cost of making westerns would eventually dampen Hollywood's enthusiasm for them. Mitchum had made his share, and a break from the genre seemed a sensible approach. "I've been in more westerns than there are horses in westerns," Mitchum sighed during his 1957 appearance on the game show *What's My Line?*

Mitchum's attraction to the film adaptation of Tom Lea's lyrical novel *The Wonderful Country* is understandable. Texan Lea gained notice for his 1949 novel *The Brave Bulls* that became a 1951 film with Mel Ferrer and Anthony Quinn. Former film editor Robert Parrish expressed interest in directing Lea's 1952 follow-up novel and set about attracting Henry Fonda or Gregory Peck to the project. When those efforts failed, Mitchum and his production company DRM came aboard. Parrish had directed Mitchum in *Fire Down Below* (1957) and the two got on well.

As a motion picture, *The Wonderful Country* is a slow-paced, elegiac 1870s western and absorbing character study with Mitchum cast as tough expatriate Martin Brady. This is a westerner that the perpetual outsider Mitchum felt a strong kinship to. He effectively underplays the central role as a pistolero operating on both sides of the border with divided loyalties (making it a fine companion piece to *Blood on the Moon*). Originally from Missouri, Mitchum's Brady fled to Mexico as a teenager after killing the man who murdered his father. The subsequent years have seen him working as a gunrunner for the powerful Castro brothers south of the border. His sole kinship is with his horse,

Mitchum and leading lady Julie London have a difference of opinion in *The Wonderful Country* (1959).

a magnificent black Andalusian named Lagrimas (Spanish for "Tears"). "It's the only thing I've got in the world," he says.

Mitchum dresses as a Mexican complete with short jacket, ringing spurs and a sombrero. He speaks with an accent. However, on a gunrunning assignment north of the border, Mitchum's horse falls and he breaks his leg in the tiny Texas town of Puerto. He spends the first portion of the film hobbling around on crutches as he convalesces under the care of local doctor Charles McGraw. His presence attracts the attention of Texas Ranger captain Albert Dekker and U.S. Cavalry major Gary Merrill. Dekker knows of Mitchum's reputation with a gun and has knowledge of details regarding the long-ago killing in Missouri. Dekker claims the man Mitchum shot was a menace and the killing was understandable. He'll vouch for Mitchum and swear him into the Rangers as a lawman. As Mitchum ponders this proposition, he flatly rebuffs Merrill's efforts to work with the Castro brothers to chase renegade Apaches into Mexico. However, in doing so he finds himself immediately attracted to Merrill's neglected wife Julie London. At a party where London is insulted by bullying cowboy Chuck Roberson for her formerly promiscuous ways, Mitchum comes to her defense. When Roberson goes for his gun, Mitchum is forced to shoot him down. He's on the run again, crossing the Rio Grande into Mexico to meet the Castro brothers, who have risen to the ranks of general and governor and are now at odds with one another. They hold Mitchum responsible for the lost guns.

The film is atmospheric and authentic, capturing rich colors as it opens with Mitchum riding across unspoiled but violent land. Windblown tumbleweeds fill his path and even unseat him from his horse. Mitchum is grimy, whiskered, sunburned, and quickly hobbled with a broken leg and a bloody nose. Self-contained and tantalizingly elusive, he makes for an unconventional and melancholy western lead. Mitchum was 41 years old during filming, but retained his robust leading man looks and renegade mystique. It was one of the last films where he portrayed a man younger than his actual age. Subsequent films began casting him appropriately as a father figure with adult children, but in *The Wonderful Country* he's still able to show off the good looks and sensitive tough guy persona that made young female viewers swoon.

Mitchum's world-weary, tight-lipped character is a man without a country, a rootless drifter with divided allegiances. Mexican governor Pedro Armendariz, a John Ford favorite in *Fort Apache* (1948) and *3 Godfathers* (1948), shouts at him "You belong nowhere!" As Mitchum travels back and forth across the Rio Grande, his Mexican accent changes depending on which side of the border he is on. Some critics took him to task for the wavering speech, not realizing it was director Parrish's instruction Mitchum was following to a tee. Among Parrish's other stylistic choices were tighter camera framing in the U.S. scenes and wide, free lensing in Mexico. Cinematographers Floyd Crosby and Alex Phillips did exceptional work presenting the harsh environment. Phillips had recently lensed the Jock Mahoney western *The Last of the Fast Guns* (1958) on similar Mexican locations. The film is backed by a fine Alex North score, appropriately grand and Mexican-flavored.

Mitchum's gunman brandishes an Old Colt SAA (Single Action Army), a shaved gun with a removed front sight. He is handy with the weapon but doesn't think of himself as a hired gun. He is largely passive until asked to be an assassin by Armendariz. Mitchum balks and takes it on the lam from Armendariz's other gunmen. Making his escape, he comes across a mortally wounded Merrill and his shot-up cavalry outfit. Mitchum helps them fight off Apaches even as the gunmen catch up to him. In the finale, Mitchum's beloved black stallion Lagrimas is shot out from under him. He kills the assassin Chester Hayes but realizes he needs to put his horse out of its misery. He calmly withdraws his pistol and does the deed, then places his gun beside the animal, doffs his sombrero and prepares to head across the river to the United States and the chance for a life with London. The sorrowful ending is ambiguous but fitting and poignant.

The sugarloaf sombrero Mitchum wears throughout the film was given to him by writer Tom Lea. The sombrero was a Lea family heir-

Caring for his fallen horse Lagrimas in *The Wonderful Country* (1959).

loom that Mitchum took a liking to. "He was always trying to crease it and bring the wings forward so it looked more like a cowboy hat," Lea told Lee Server. At one point in the film when he is recuperating in Puerto and becoming Americanized, Mitchum tries on a Stetson but quickly ditches it in favor of the pointed Mexican hat. Wearing his sombrero, Mitchum made a personal appearance for the Boomtown Benefit Party in Los Angeles on January 1, 1959. The annual western-themed party was for the Share, Inc., charity organization, and if he was in town, Mitchum always attended or participated in the festivities. Mitchum was so fond of the sombrero look that he agreed to dress up as a Mexican bandito for an on-air skit enacted by St. Louis TV host Charlotte Peters while on the film's publicity trail. He visited Pittsburgh, Detroit, Chicago, Denver and Los Angeles to trumpet the film. Mitchum's dedication resulted in decent box office returns.

Author-artist Tom Lea wasn't sure what to make of the film business or Mitchum and his colorfully profane language. Lea's own scripting of his story received a polished rewrite by screenwriter Robert Ardrey, who significantly built up leading lady Julie London's part. When the Hollywood lawyers were done, Lea's original handshake deal with Robert Parrish resulted in no screenplay credit and little to no money coming his way. Parrish and Mitchum gave Lea a small role as a barber to send something monetary his way. Mitchum also posed for sketches and a Lea painting. "Bob Mitchum was a tough bird," Lea said in *Tom Lea: An Oral History*. "He was awful on those sets sometimes. He'd talk bad, very, very obscene. But you know, there's something about Bob that was okay. When Sarah [Lea's wife] came down to San Miguel de Allende to see some of the filming, why, Bob was this perfect angel."

The Wonderful Country is a film that has grown better with age. Mitchum biographer Alvin H. Marill calls it "his best western role" and many now seem to agree. In *"A" Western Filmmakers,* Henryk Hoffman tagged the

Mitchum characterization "one of his best performances," and according to *The Rough Guide to Westerns*, "Mitchum excels in this strangely neglected gem." Biographer David Downing called it Mitchum's best western since *Pursued*, adding, "The extreme individualism of the Mitchum character, and the problems it tends to create for him, have rarely been better portrayed." Film historian Bruce Crowther said, "To *The Wonderful Country* he gave to what might well have otherwise been an ordinary western an extra dimension that allowed the storyline to match the scenic splendor of the movie's setting." In *100 Westerns,* Edward Buscombe called it "a minor miracle of a film, which fits Robert Mitchum's persona perfectly." Lincoln Center's *Film Linc Daily* contributed, "Mitchum's layered performance as a reluctantly violent man at a moral crossroads and caught between two national identities is the heart of Parrish's eclectic and cerebral western."

At the time of release, however, few reviewers were completely sold on the slowly paced film's merits. *The New York Times* did give the picture a glowing review ("Mr. Mitchum is ideally cast as the hard-bitten derelict hero") and *Variety* called it "a wonderful western" with "honest dialog and characterization." *The New York Journal-American* commented, "Mitchum gives an excellent performance as the harassed pistolero," while *Motion Picture Daily* opined, "Mitchum is satisfactorily menacing and heroic by turns." *The Los Angeles Times*: "Mitchum gives a realistic performance of the gunman hero, a moody individual who never is better than he's supposed to be in the story," and *Film Daily* called it a "superb portrayal." *The Los Angeles Herald Examiner* termed it "right up the Mitchum alley," adding that the star "gives a strong performance, holding together the plot threads that spread in several directions." *The New York World Telegram and Sun* added, "Mitchum is just such a compelling personality that he never drifts out of audience attention.… He is the actor who makes no apparent effort but always remains the man in close-up."

United Artists built a complete western town 20 miles outside of Durango, Mexico, for the film. As a movie location, Durango was appropriately primitive and fresh to the eyes, still possessing wide open spaces. The mining town is located 600 miles northwest of Mexico City, nestled between the picturesque Sierra Madre Occidental in rugged land Mitchum described in press releases as rough country. "Bad territory," Mitchum mused to author Lawrence Grobel. He continued:

> That's where the best pistoleros came from. Every time I worked there, we never once came back with a complete crew. Somebody always turned up missing. I once talked with a guy in the local Chamber of Commerce and he said, "I don't understand why we don't have more tourism in Durango; it's on the Pan-American highway, and the beginning of the big Sierra, we have hotels." And all the time he was talking, his conversation was punctuated by gunfire outside, they were blowing each other away.

The streets of Durango were little more than cobblestone and dirt, with the local commerce consisting of a host of cantinas and whorehouses. There was one dilapidated hotel, the Mexico Courts, which crew members described as having the odor of backed-up sewage. Mitchum generously awarded the best suite in the languid hotel to leading lady Julie London while claiming, with tongue in cheek, that he fought off giant cockroaches in his own room with an axe. Mitchum embraced the ambiance. Regarding the local water, Mitchum opted to drink mescal and tequila to quell Montezuma's Revenge, reasoning that the continuous flow of alcohol in his digestive tract would kill any germs that found their way into his food. Mitchum's choice of alcohol tended to fit the locale of any production he was working on. His favorite establishment for recreation was the La Cucaracha Cantina in nearby Sierra Miguel De Allende. Despite the less than four-star Durango accommodations, Mitchum told *Trail Dust Magazine,* "I used to love Mexico. The people have such a couldn't-care-less attitude."

Mitchum had shown his ability to take the reins of a film when he wrote, produced, starred in, and created the music for the moonshine picture *Thunder Road* (1958), a classic of its kind with Mitchum as the anti-heroic pedal-to-the-floor driver trying to outrun the feds. As producer, Mitchum showed an eye for discovering talent and tried to recruit rock'n'roll singing sensation Elvis Presley to appear in the film as his younger brother (a role eventually played by Mitchum's own son Jim). Presley, a Mitchum fan, expressed interest, but his manager Tom Parker wanted the singer to stick to making musicals. Mitchum did make two noteworthy discoveries scouting local actors while on the North Carolina location. He signed Mitch Ryan and Peter Breck for supporting parts in the film and later brought both men to Hollywood.

Mitchum introduced Breck to several influential figures, including Dick Powell, who signed him for his Four Star Productions western TV series *Black Saddle* (1958–1959). The rugged Breck later landed the iconic two-fisted TV cowboy role of Nick Barkley on *The Big Valley* (1965–1969). Breck felt he owed a lot to Mitchum for helping him obtain his first breaks. Breck recalled in the pages of *Wildest Westerns,*

> When I started out in show business, I had nothing but decision-makers around me. They were all rugged individualists, starting with my mentor, Robert Mitchum. Not only did Bob know when, where and how to make a decision; he wouldn't let people push him around.... I often thought to myself how fortunate I was that Robert Mitchum had seen my performance and enough liked what he had seen, to bestow his generosity in giving me my first break and becoming my mentor. I don't know why he did it. Perhaps he saw the opportunity to help out a young actor.... It was a very open relationship with Bob. Although he was a private man, he was not standoffish. You knew where you stood with Mitchum, and I respected him for that.

Square-jawed Mitch Ryan, then a 23-year-old Navy vet, told a similar story. Mitchum arranged for the two actors' brief scenes to be spaced out over the duration of the extended *Thunder Road* shoot so they could earn more money and gain experience by being on the set. When filming was complete, "Big Mitch" invited "Little Mitch" to drive back to Hollywood with him and Tim Wallace over the course of six memorable days. It was such a monumental experience to the young actor that Ryan later recalled on his website that he thought of writing a book about the trip. Ryan called Mitchum "Just short of being a god and at the height of his popularity." Ryan went on to play the pivotal role of the desperate cowboy Shorty Austin in the elegiac western classic *Monte Walsh* (1970) and he provided able support to Clint Eastwood in *High Plains Drifter* (1973). He became a friend and drinking consort of Lee Marvin and Mitchum, appearing with the latter again in *The Friends of Eddie Coyle* (1973) and *Midway* (1976). Ryan sometimes found himself the beneficiary of being cast in authoritarian military roles or heavies that Mitchum had originally been approached for. When he felt reluctant to work, Mitchum was happy to pass on jobs to his pal.

Mitchum's aid to Breck and Ryan's careers was not something new. Rugged leading man Richard Egan, star of the early 1960s TV westerns *Empire* and *Redigo,* appeared in a small role in Mitchum's Korean War film *One Minute to Zero* (1952) and befriended the star. Egan found himself the beneficiary of Mitchum's generosity, telling Hedda Hopper that Mitchum would talk to producers about Egan's qualifications as a leading man. Egan found himself starring opposite Jane Russell in *Underwater!* (1955) and played parts originally earmarked for Mitchum in *Untamed* (1955) and *Slaughter on 10th Avenue* (1957). "Bob Mitchum has been very helpful," Egan said. "He's a great fellow and a fine actor. He plays it down and hides behind a rock, but he knows. He introduced me to Jane Russell, and if it hadn't been for Jane I wouldn't have gotten the part in *Underwater!* Mitchum is the most generous man I've ever worked with."

As executive producer of *The Wonderful Country,* Mitchum cast several of his friends. Charles McGraw, Anthony Caruso, Joe Haworth and stuntman Chuck Roberson all show up. Mitchum was instrumental in getting baseball legend Leroy "Satchel" Paige cast as a soldier in a black cavalry regiment hunting the Apache into Mexico. At the time, there were not many strong roles for actors of color, and Mitchum was glad to initiate change. He disliked the racism and anti–Semitism that existed in Hollywood in the '40s and '50s. "There were so many hateful bastards," he told Garry Armstrong. "They were always disrespecting Negroes and Jews. They always thought I was with them. I had a few fights and dumped a few jobs because I couldn't stand the two-faced bastards."*

There has been gossipy speculation that Mitchum was racist based on his turning down the script to Stanley Kramer's chain gang drama *The Defiant Ones* (1958). The misinterpreted story, started by an offhand comment made by that film's eventual star Tony Curtis and repeated by Kirk Douglas, is that Mitchum refused to be chained to Sidney Poitier for the duration of the film. Mitchum maintained, having been in the segregated South on a chain gang during that period, that he doubted a white man and a black man would have been chained together in the first place. He personally liked Poitier and hated the idea of subjecting the actor to the script's inflammatory dialogue. Mitchum was prone to making provocative comments, especially if he wanted to offend someone, but he was not a racist. He frequented jazz joints and nightclubs of color, where one of his good friends was the black cowboy actor–singer Herb Jeffries. In his Ava Gardner bio, Lee Server quoted the Bronze Buckaroo Jeffries saying, "Bob was the greatest guy."

On the Durango set, Mitchum talked baseball with Paige and helped stunt ace Roberson teach the ageless athlete how to ride a horse. Everyone called Paige "Satch" except for Mitchum, who called him Leroy. Paige biographer Donald Spivey maintained that the ballplayer "got along exceedingly well with Robert Mitchum, who went out of his way to make sure that Paige and family were comfortable." Paige turned out to be a character, exactly the kind of eccentric personality Mitchum was attracted to. They bailed him out of a Florida jail for the film, and he carried a pistol with him throughout filming. When warned that he could get into trouble if caught carrying a handgun in Mexico, Paige opined that he could get into a lot more trouble without it. Mitchum was especially intrigued by the fact that Paige brought along his daughter's teenage babysitter—but no daughter. In the film's press materials, Paige called Mitchum "a great guy."

As far as Mitchum wielding his executive clout on the film, that was the extent. He preferred being the cowpuncher riding fence as opposed to the ranch foreman calling shots. Some in Mitchum's camp, however, saw to it that his presence was fully felt when the finished product hit the screen. During filming, Mitchum sang the praises of character actor Jack Oakie to Hedda Hopper, even finding a part for Oakie's actress wife Victoria Horne. However, when *The Wonderful Country* was released, Oakie found his role carefully edited, feeling it was due to his scene-stealing habit of talking over under-player Mitchum's lines. Leading lady Julie London was also dismayed that the size of her part was reduced and complained to the press. At the premiere, she logged her screen time and counted her close-ups, upset that Mitchum was given more camera time and reaction shots. She did feel it was his right as producer, though Mitchum dispelled any notion of him lobbying an editor for additional close-ups. Mitchum claimed his involvement as a producer was a tax write-off. He couldn't have cared less about his number of close-ups. *Billboard* magazine reported that Mitchum and London recorded a song for *The Wonderful Country,* but it failed to materialize in the finished project. Despite being angry, London told *The Milwaukee Journal* that the location shoot itself was one of the best times she'd ever had in her life.

"Life on location with Bob Mitchum was never dull," Chuck Roberson wrote in his autobiography *The Fall Guy*. Joe Haworth made his film debut opposite Mitchum in *Gung Ho!* (1943) before becoming a yeoman in the westerns *The Outcasts of Poker Flat* (1952), *Gun Belt* (1953) and *3:10 to Yuma* (1957). Veteran character actor and top screen heavy Anthony Caruso was a fixture in the films of his friend Alan Ladd, appearing in the Ladd westerns *The Iron Mistress* (1952), *Drum Beat* (1954), *Saskatchewan* (1954) and *The Big Land* (1957). He enjoyed a similar working relationship with Mitchum and echoed the sentiments of the others regarding the making of *The Wonderful Country*. "We had a great time in Durango," Caruso told *Wildest Westerns*. "Even though

---

*Garry Armstrong (e-mail correspondence, December 2018).

Bob liked to drink, he never got into trouble and it didn't affect his performance. Some actors are just like that. He had a hollow leg."

In addition to drinking buddy Charles McGraw (who had Tom Lea pour ice-cold water over Mitchum in the bathtub scene as a joke), Mitchum found a kindred spirit in Roberson. The native Texan had been serving as John Wayne's primary stunt double for the past decade in films such as *Hondo* (1953) and *The Searchers* (1956). Roberson was a capable actor, frequently cast as henchmen. Mitchum used him in *The Wonderful Country* as the man who insults London, takes a Mitchum punch to the jaw, then unwisely goes for his gun. The two originally bonded on the set of *The Lusty Men* when "Bad Chuck" lassoed a pretty female in a bar scene. In Durango, they spent off-hours carousing in the local cantinas until they saw one man shoot another in the head after a quarrel. The killing quickly sobered the actors up, and they chose to spend the remainder of the filming schedule sticking close to their motel.

During one break in the day when the crew were changing locations, the two rode off together to a shade tree where they drank fermented Pulque cactus juice offered by locals. They became plastered, and shooting had to cease for the day. That was one of the few occasions that Mitchum exerted his influence as executive producer in calling the day a wrap. An upset Parrish bowed to his friend Mitchum on that occasion, but it was a lesson learned on a generally smooth production. "He'll give a creative performance if he believes in what he's doing," Parrish said in his autobiography. "He's about the best movie star in the world." The Andalusian stallion Mitchum rode in the film was doubled in action scenes by Roberson's legendary stunt horse Cocaine, dyed jet black for the production. Cocaine was trained by Roberson to lie still for the horse's death scene. The magnificence of the Andalusian was played up by the film's publicity with the tagline describing Mitchum being a man "as proud as the mighty black stallion he rode."

The magnificent Andalusian was portrayed by Pancho, a black Morgan Stallion from Oklahoma that was not yet sufficiently trained for motion picture cameras. Mitchum recalled his first encounter with the horse for *The Detroit Times*:

> Sam Aston, the Choctaw Indian, assured me the stallion was gentle as a lamb. I took his word for it, since he owns the animal. But as soon as I had the Morgan saddled and he reared up, I knew there would be trouble. I soon found out the stallion, which is 18 hands high, had never been broke to riding. So, I had to break him before we could use him. The Morgan was rough to handle. Just as soon as Sam said he wouldn't bite, he nipped my shoulder. If I changed my weight from one foot to the other, he'd butt me. He made me nervous.

Roberson kept busy taking over chores as the film's second unit director. He trained local horsemen to do minor stunts and did many of the more dangerous gags himself, like the horse fall that breaks Mitchum's leg in the beginning. In the latter portions of the film, Mitchum did his own riding and shooting at full gallop in an impressive tracking shot. Roberson sent out a call for an American pal to come down for a few days to help with all the climactic stunts, including the assassin's death scene in the final shootout. Veteran western stuntman Jack Young doubled Chester Hayes for an impressive saddle fall and stirrup drag. Mitchum was the first to check on his well-being and help him to his feet. Young remembered, "After I hit the ground, they cut and rigged the saddle to come off the horse when I pulled a cord. I remember when Mitchum stood over me he just said, 'Shit!' and we both laughed."*

As a producer-star, Mitchum had proven himself a success. *Bandido*, although not what was intended, emerged as an entertaining action picture. *Thunder Road,* a script Mitchum had completed in 1952 when it was known as *The Rounder,* was a smash and became one of his signature films. *The Wonderful Country* was less commercial but a fine realization of a top western novel. Biographer John Belton declared that Mitchum "emerged alongside John Wayne as one of the most original of the actor-producers of the '50s." He still thought of himself as a

---

*Jack Young (e-mail correspondence, 2013).

lunch pail–carrying common man, telling the *Independent Star-News*:

> I became an actor because I needed a job. Nothing in me cried out artistic expression. Now I've got my own production company. I own what's left of my soul. I work all the time because I've got a wife and three kids to support and obligations to meet and taxes to pay. But I'm not much of an actor. The reason I'm in demand is that I work fast and I'm cheap. I don't waste the producer's money. I'm too middle class for that. I've got all the middle-class virtues. That's why I snicker when people call me a rebel. I'm no rebel. So, I once went to jail for 50 days on a marijuana rap. Ever since I've been so middle class it hurts. Also lucky. Just look at my record…. I'm the luckiest son of a gun ever born.

Mitchum was always on the look-out for interesting properties, especially in the western genre. In the early 1950s, he discovered an old Colorado miner named Smokey Smithlin and optioned the man's memoir for Howard Hughes to produce. Mitchum also developed a screenplay based on his own Norwegian grandfather Gustave Olaf Gunderson's seafaring adventures. Former B-western star Don "Red" Barry claimed to have written a script for Mitchum; Mitchum's level of interest in Barry's script is not known.

Actor Steve Hayes was a bit player with a high social profile in Hollywood. He was pals with Errol Flynn and dated Lana Turner, in addition to managing the popular Sunset Strip coffee shop Googies. Mitchum knew Hayes well enough to learn he wanted to be a screenwriter. Mitchum took an option on an early Hayes story, and the writer eventually broke through in the business. Hayes and actor Leo Gordon co-wrote the Victor Mature oater *Escort West* (1959), and Hayes became a staff writer on the long-running TV western *Gunsmoke*. He later became a prolific novelist, churning out several western stories.

In his autobiographical account of his career, Hayes recalled meeting Mitchum in the early 1950s while working a small part on an Alan Ladd film at Paramount:

> Bob Mitchum and Jane Russell, who were under contract to RKO, the adjoining studio, often came over to have lunch with Ladd. And though neither of them actually got me work in one of their films, years later Mitchum optioned one of my western screenplays for his production company, DRM. The option price was only a thousand dollars, and the picture never got made, but it was early in my writing career and I was grateful for the money and the warm encouragement Mitchum gave me. Years later when I got to know his son Chris well, he said that my experience with his dad wasn't unusual: Mitchum was a square-shooter who always tried to help the underdog.

Mitchum purchased the Weldon Hill novel *The Long Summer of George Adams* about an early 1950s railroader trying to save his small Oklahoma town as a water stop on the rail line as his employer converts from steam engines to diesel. Mitchum believed in the project, but Hollywood didn't think the folksy, homespun story was commercial enough. Mitchum eventually sold the property to James Garner, who saw it made as a TV movie in 1982. Mitchum expressed interest in producing and starring in a remake of the first big epic silent western, 1923's *The Covered Wagon*. Based on the Emerson Hough novel, it depicted the trek westward from Kansas to Oregon. That film never came to be. In the early 1960s, Mitchum optioned an unpublished Robert Ruark adventure novel titled *The Well at Ras Daga* and moved into pre-production with Sy Bartlett scripting and TV producer-director Charles Marquis Warren under consideration to direct. Mitchum had Claudia Cardinale set as his leading lady and attempted to hire Steve McQueen as co-star. McQueen was hot off a star-making turn in *The Magnificent Seven* (1960) and was finishing his western TV series *Wanted—Dead or Alive* (1958–1961). Mitchum could never get all the moving parts together and the film was dropped.

With the Mitchum family's move to the 300-acre Belmont Farms in Trappe, Maryland, Mitchum seemed to lose interest in steering his career in a definitive direction as producer-star. Some of his subsequent films carried the DRM or Talbot banner (named after Talbot County, where they lived on Maryland's Eastern Shore), but that was for tax purposes. "At heart I'm just a hired hand," he told the *Springfield Union* in 1981.

Home from the Hill (MGM, 1960)

Cast: Robert Mitchum (Capt. Wade Hunnicutt); Eleanor Parker (Hannah Hunnicutt); George Peppard (Rafe Copley); George Hamilton (Theron Hunnicutt); Everett Sloane (Albert Halstead); Luana Patten (Libby Halstead); Anne Seymour (Sarah Halstead); Constance Ford (Opal Bixby); Ken Renard (Chauncey); Ray Teal (Dr. Reuben Carson); and Charlie Briggs, Nora Bush, Gene Coogan, Oliver Cross, Duke Fishman, Bess Flowers, Tom Gilson, Duncan Gray, Jr., Chuck Hamilton, Hilda Haynes, Jack Henderson, Bill Hickman, Freda Jones, Ann Kunde, Burt Mustin, Denver Pyle, Stuart Randall, Ed Russell, Dan Sheridan, Orville Sherman, Stephen Soldi, Dub Taylor, Luree Wiese, Guinn "Big Boy" Williams.

Crew: Vincente Minnelli (Director); Edmund Grainger and Sol C. Siegel (Producers); Harriet Frank, Jr., and Irving Ravetch (Screenplay); Milton Krasner (Photographer); Bronislau Kaper (Music); Preston Ames and George W. Davis (Art Directors); Henry Grace and Robert Priestley (Set Decorators); Harold F. Kress (Editor); Walter Plunkett (Wardrobe); William McGarry (Assistant Director); Edward Woehler (Production Manager).

150 minutes; Released March 3, 1960

Mitchum won critical accolades bringing added dimension to his macho, lustful East Texas landowner in Vincente Minnelli's modern western *Home from the Hill* (1960). His constant handling of hunting rifles in the picture and his appearance in veteran costume designer Walter Plunkett's authentic Texas wardrobe contributed mightily to his contemporary western image.

Home from the Hill was taken from the popular William Humphrey novel. Many moviegoers found the melodrama absorbing if somewhat inferior to its famous West Texas counterpart *Giant* (1956). Mitchum let the role of Bick Benedict in *Giant* pass him by but wouldn't make the same mistake with *Home from the Hill*'s Capt. Wade Hunnicutt, a callous, womanizing middle-aged character that fits Mitchum superbly. Outfitted in a cowboy hat, Texas string tie and expensive boots, he looks the part of an authoritative cad with one ineffectual son who can't shoot or hunt (George Hamilton) and one

(From left) Cowboy hat-wearing Texans George Peppard, George Hamilton and Mitchum on a hunt in *Home from the Hill* (1960).

rough-hewn illegitimate son (George Peppard) who's a chip off the old block. Both young men seek recognition and acceptance from Mitchum's "Big Daddy," a man who is incredibly strong but deeply flawed.

Small town legend Mitchum and his wife Eleanor Parker co-exist in a complex, loveless marriage based on appearances. She dotes on young Hamilton, forbidding Mitchum to corrupt the boy with his vices. Mitchum has honored her request since the boy's birth. The unacknowledged bastard son Peppard lives on the property under the guise of being a handyman. Peppard could move on at any time but chooses to stay. He has a strong buddy relationship with Mitchum but seeks something deeper and familial. Mitchum is aware that Peppard is his son but attributes his involvement to youthful indiscretion—"sowing my wild oats on a haystack." Considering Peppard's long-departed mother a tramp, he can't bring himself to call the man his son. After Hamilton becomes a practical joke victim of local western types (Denver Pyle, Dub Taylor, "Big Boy" Williams), Mitchum becomes determined to toughen up the mama's boy. These townies hang on Mitchum's every word, even waiting to raise their guns when duck-hunting until Mitchum takes the first shot. It riles him to see his boy Hamilton the butt of their ribbing. With Peppard's help, he introduces his son to the manly pleasures of drinking, handling weaponry and hunting wild boar. Hamilton quickly takes to having a gun in his hand. It's in his blood.

For Mitchum's Hunnicutt, the hunt is a metaphor for manliness, and the action of performing it leads to a sense of entitlement. "It's my right to cross any man's fence when I'm hunting," Mitchum states. This extends both to game and women. He has cut a wide swath through the town when it comes to females. Yet he attempts to grow and reconcile with his wife, who can never forgive him for the pre-marriage dalliance with Peppard's late mother. They haven't made love since Hamilton's conception. She keeps her bedroom door locked while Mitchum broods over drinks in his masculine den, content in the fact he could have any other woman he wants.

The film is bookended by scenes of Mitchum being shot. The first shooting is due to a jealous husband; the second because of young beauty Luana Patten's distraught father Everett Sloane mistakenly thinking Mitchum has impregnated the girl (it was actually Hamilton). When Hamilton learns of his father's philandering ways and refusal to formally acknowledge Peppard, he announces his intention to escape the situation. Peppard steps in for his half-brother to marry Patten, whom he cares for. Mitchum shrugs off the bullet to his shoulder at the beginning of the picture, dulling the pain with whiskey and wisecracks. The wound is little more than an annoyance and is quickly forgotten. The second shooting in his lair near the film's end proves fatal. Servant Ken Renard stands over the bleeding Mitchum believing the Texan is too tough to die. Renard runs through a laundry list of times Mitchum has tempted fate in the woods. This time is different. Mitchum dies before having a chance to call Peppard his son.

Oscar-winning director Minnelli was accustomed to helming glossy MGM musicals and had never done a western. "I don't think I could do a western," Minnelli said honestly in Mark Griffin's *A Hundred or More Little Things*, "though lots of people think *Home from the Hill* is one." It was filmed on location in Oxford, Mississippi, and the bordering communities of Clarksville and Paris, Texas. It is highly debatable if *Home from the Hill* should be considered a western, although Michael R. Pitts includes an entry for the title in his comprehensive guide *Western Movies*. Pitts calls it "a powerful psychological drama with an excellent performance by Robert Mitchum as the landowner." To Garry Armstrong, Mitchum referred to the film as a "contemporary cowboy soap opera."*

The Texas filming location was approximately 100 miles northeast of the Dallas–Fort Worth area. Mitchum biographer David Downing and Minnelli biographer Emanuel Levy have drawn parallels between the film and the popular TV series *Dallas* with Mitchum effectively essaying an early version of the oil baron Jock Ewing that cowboy actor Jim Davis

---

*Garry Armstrong (e-mail correspondence, 2017).

made famous in the late 1970s. The film was scripted by the husband-and-wife team of Irving Ravetch and Harriet Frank, Jr., who went on to handle the writing chores on the Texas-set *Hud* (1963) with Paul Newman. They also wrote *Hombre* (1967) for Newman and *The Cowboys* (1972) for John Wayne. *Home from the Hill* hints at being Southern Gothic, and there's but a single scene of men on horses herding Mitchum's cattle. Some western flavor may have been excised, although there remains a big Texas barbecue scene. Minnelli's cut was originally a full three hours before MGM edited out 30 minutes prior to release. The picture is included here because Mitchum absolutely nails this portrayal of a proud, rich, larger-than-life Texan, and it would seem an oversight if it wasn't.

MGM invested heavily in promoting its young male leads George Peppard and George Hamilton (dubbed Dirty George and Clean George on the set by Minnelli), but the picture is carried by Mitchum's considerable testosterone. He was paid $200,000 and a percentage of the gross. The part was originally intended for Clark Gable, but when Mitchum came aboard he brought the charismatic character to life. Lee Server doubts the older Gable "would have been capable of anything like the violent, intimidating physical presence of Mitchum or the cruel arrogance of the actor's uncompromising characterization." In Griffin's book, George Hamilton explains Minnelli's total reliance on his leading man:

> He loved Mitchum for what he was. Mitchum was this Mount Rushmore and all Vincente wanted him to do was be in the middle of the action, do his lines, and then Minnelli could do the whole ballet around it. He loved that force of Mitchum. It was a power for which other things could vibrate. You can't create that. You couldn't have added menace or power to Mitchum. Mitchum was Mitchum. And Minnelli loved that about him.

Mitchum brings nuance to the man and his relationships. He's complicated, and some have

Mitchum as Capt. Wade Hunnicutt in his masculine western den with George Hamilton in *Home from the Hill* **(1960).**

noted that Wade Hunnicutt doesn't seem too far removed from Mitchum himself. Few of his characters ever do. In addition to Mitchum, the film has a rich production design with art directors Preston Ames and George Davis winning kudos for the layout of Mitchum's den. This too says a lot about the man. There's a brick fireplace, animal head trophies and fishing rods on the wall, a bearskin rug, bookshelves, liquor and gun cabinets, and a plush red leather chair where Mitchum enjoys his drinks and fixes his pipe tobacco, loyal hunting dogs resting at his feet. It's the kind of man cave where a Winchester Model 99 can be discharged into the fireplace and not cause too much of a ruckus in the home. Mitchum lights matches on the bricks, never failing to produce fire on his first strike. His dogs cease to bark at a single command. But this powerful, influential man can't connect with his wife, and his youngest son is close to an embarrassment. He maintains a considerable emotional distance from everyone.

Minnelli's visual skill as a filmmaker is showcased in the exciting wild boar hunt filmed outside Paris, Texas, along the Red River County and the Sulphur Flats. The quicksand-heavy swamp and Piney Woods area had to be wrangled first, with Mitchum telling Hedda Hopper the snake handlers removed nine copperheads, six water moccasins and two rattlers before they could begin filming. The wild boar used for filming in Texas did not survive being transported to California's MGM studio, necessitating that an unconvincing hog with fake tusks be used for close-ups. Mitchum joked to Emanuel Levy that the cultured Minnelli "shoots all his pictures in Paris."

Mitchum continually surprised his director. "I don't know why Bob puts on his act," said Minnelli. "Few actors I've worked with bring so much of themselves to a picture, and none do it with such little affectation as Bob does." When it came time for a high-stepping square dance sequence (eventually cut), Minnelli was shocked to find Mitchum already had the dance mastered with his partner Melissa Ten Eyck. In his autobiography *I Remember It Well,* Minnelli wrote, "Bob, who has an indolent image, could have walked through the picture but he didn't…. Throughout the filming, Bob helped the young people enormously, and me too. He spoke from the viewpoint of a veteran actor—and star—and the young people were impressed." Mitchum boiled it down to the simplest terms regarding his young co-stars, the two Georges: "They were impressed because I was very impressive," he said of the robust persona he adopted for his character and carried over into real life.

George Hamilton recalled in his autobiography *Don't Mind If I Do* that the charismatic Mitchum's behind-the-scenes boozing, doping and womanizing lasted around the clock. Mitchum's Alpha Male behavior was on full display as he casually lounged around his motel room in his boxers, cowboy hat and alligator boots. Even on the set, Mitchum dined on oranges that had been injected with vodka, an old Errol Flynn trick. "I never saw any star care less about being one," Hamilton says. "He was completely indifferent. He liked to get drunk and then sing songs, sea chanteys, cockney ditties, Australian football songs, anything. He had a perfect mimic's ear and never stopped." Hamilton claims that Mitchum knocked production manager Edward Woehler through a door when the man tried to curtail Mitchum's revelry. Mitchum's off-camera behavior was tolerated by MGM because he was acting the part perfectly in front of it. Hamilton became a gopher for the star, making liquor runs while otherwise standing in awe. In the *Los Angeles Times,* Hamilton remembered it being a surreal experience for a young man: "All of a sudden, I'm in a room, and movie stars are talking to me like a human being. It was like I had been thrown into a movie screen from a seat in a movie house and I couldn't quite believe it. I'm talking to Robert Mitchum and he's bigger than the guy on screen."

George Peppard told Hedda Hopper he was "pleasantly surprised" upon getting to know Mitchum. The brash, opinionated Peppard, a former Marine, was a strong proponent of the emerging Method acting popular with New York actors. He was initially dismissive of the carefree Mitchum and his simplistic old-school technique of saying lines as written and not bumping into the furniture. When Peppard said he followed the Stanislavsky method, Mitchum countered he favored the Smirnoff, as in vodka. However, Peppard soon realized Mitchum was living his part as realistically and effectively as any Method disciple. To Wanda Hale in the *New York Sunday News*, Peppard revealed that Mitchum gave "a perfect performance."

Peppard caused his own problems getting into character. He wanted to know his motivation for every scene to the consternation of Minnelli. With each delay, the budget began to balloon. Mitchum took Peppard aside and suggested the young man might never work again if he ran afoul of the powerful director and MGM. Peppard heeded Mitchum's advice and they soon became drinking associates behind the scenes. Peppard was a heavy drinker and competitive, but Mitchum easily outdistanced him as they indulged in all-night poker games. The star nursed Peppard through many a hangover and the younger actor took to calling him "Mother Mitchum" on the set. As a joke, Mitchum sent Peppard an annual Mother's Day card.

Peppard garnered superb notices and became a star. Mitchum received less critical praise but did win the Best Actor Award from the National Board of Review for his performance in this and *The Sundowners* (1960). *Variety* said, "Mitchum delivers his strongest performance in years." The *Saturday Review* echoed this sentiment: "[Mitchum] has not given a performance as good as this in years." *Film Bulletin* announced, "Mitchum turns in an exceptionally fine performance as the lusty landowner who lives by self-created laws," while *Commonweal* opined, "Robert Mitchum played the father's role very well, with just the right display of vitality, thoughtless conceit, and willful determination to have his own way." The *San Francisco Chronicle* stated, "[Mitchum] has never been in better form." According to the *New York Daily News*, "Robert Mitchum has never done a better job of acting than here," while the *New York Herald Tribune* noted, "Mitchum plays the father as a sturdy man's man who divides his time between guns, a pipe and other men's wives—he looks very much the part."

Minnelli biographer Emanuel Levy wrote, "Mitchum's acting was superb. As the lecherous patriarch, Mitchum conveys the character's masculine virtues, and a vague awareness of the heavy toll he has taken on his life and that of his family." Eleanor Parker's biographer Doug McClelland was equally impressed by Mitchum's portrayal of a Texan, calling it "one of his most skillful jobs. His drawling but forceful, almost practically rhythmic readings of the wholly accurate regional lines are faultless, and he manages to create sympathy for this hulking feudal lord, who beneath the swagger, dissolution and violence, does love his wife and sons—at least as Mitchum wisely delineates him."

Mitchum's biographers generally agree, with John Belton declaring it "the best performance of his career." Jerry Roberts called Mitchum's work "one of the cinema's great portraits of patriarchal machismo and arrogance." Damien Love wrote,

> Mitchum struts lazily around the place with utter, spiteful confidence, cocksure and duded-up in shining pointed boots, spotless big hats, and pristine menswear. Playing this son of a bitch patriarch he goes whoring and ties on a four-day drunk, he intimidates his family and lords it over all those around him without straining a muscle. What is so extraordinary about his performance, though, is that never once does he slip over into caricature.

With his move to the Maryland farm, Mitchum developed a new passion for horse breeding. *Tales of Wells Fargo* TV star Dale Robertson provided Mitchum with two mares and a stallion to get him going. Mitchum devoured books on breeding and became an expert on the subject, able to talk on par about thoroughbred bloodlines with Jim Goodhue of the American Quarter Horse Association. Mitchum raised speed racers of a championship caliber, working with noted trainers Merle Bourne, Nic Zemo and Mark Harrison. Stuntman Chuck Roberson wrote in his autobiography:

> Mitch and I both have a fondness for good race horses, and the guy's memory for pedigrees amazed me. We spent at least two hours talking horses, and he traced the leading thoroughbred's lines back to horses I had never known existed. Not only that, he had the ability to remember small bits of information he had read about breeding and about the genetic combinations in all the best horses.

Mitchum became a frequent visitor to the Triple R Ranch in Frankfort, Illinois, to check stock horses and made breeding trips around the country with his stud horse. On one occasion, a black mare escaped its trailer in Yukon, Oklahoma, and Mitchum and his ranch foreman C.B. "Bird Dog" Rogers had to lasso the wild horse on the highway. Mitchum's western image had been completely transferred to his own personal life now that he was a horse rancher.

On the Trappe, Maryland, property Mitchum farmed alfalfa, corn and oats, specifically to feed the horses. He eventually bought Hereford calves, so he could exercise his quarter horses. When scheduling permitted, the family continued to take annual vacations to the Remuda Dude Ranch on the Hassayampa River in scenic Wickenburg, Arizona. In the cowboy town, Mitchum visited the infamous Antler's Bar. Other favored destinations for the Mitchum brood were the Garden of the Gods Club and Resort near Pike's Peak and the Wildhorn Guest Ranch near Colorado Springs. They also visited the western-themed Hotel El Rancho in Las Vegas when the children were younger. Mostly Mitchum kept to himself on his new property alongside the Chesapeake Bay, content that he didn't have to keep up appearances in Hollywood. "My unsocial nature is well-known," he told Bob Thomas in 1960. "In Maryland I can be as unsocial as I want, and nobody gives a damn."

Talbot County Sheriff Bob Gerlock was quoted in *The Tidewater Times* regarding Mitchum and his Maryland farm:

> He was a nice guy. Treated everyone who worked for him right. Didn't have a lot of time for those ten-cent millionaires, though. He liked regular people, because even though he was rich and famous, he was a regular guy. You didn't want to cross him. When he was drinking, he did have a temper. But he loved animals. They ran quarter horses into that farm and started to breed 'em. "I'm a gentleman farmer," he'd say and laugh, but that's what he was. And he worked on the farm same as anyone else. Drove tractors, pitched hay, did whatever needed to be done. And you never saw him without animals. He loved dogs. Always had some dogs following him around. All kinds of famous people came out to the farm, but he never acted like he was anyone special.

In 1961, Mitchum showed up wearing a Stetson at the Timonium State Fair in Maryland with three horses ready for competition. *The Baltimore Sun* wrote, "Leaning against the wooden fence cowboy fashion with other spectators, he was obliging to all who recognized him and free and easy with his autograph." Mitchum entered the cutting competition as a rider. The newspaper explained, "To the city folk, this means Mitchum will mount his favorite quarter horse, race up to a herd of cattle, and separate a calf from the group. The quarter horse actually does all the work, but the Trappe cowboy will give the orders from the saddle." His son Chris began winning championships in reining and cutting competitions. In 1963, Mitchum brought a horse to perform at the Washington International Horse Show and presented the feature race award for friend Gene Hensley at Ruidoso Downs, New Mexico. He became so knowledgeable that he served as an NBC guest commentator for the Labor Day races at Ruidoso Downs in 1965. His own race horse Belmont Scare became a winner during the mid–1960s, validation to Mitchum's passion for the sport and the animals themselves.

Mitchum's daughter Petrine (aka Trina) developed a lifelong love for horses while living on the farm. Her fascination with equines manifested itself in the writing of the informative book *Hollywood Hoofbeats*. On the 2011 radio show *Horses and Friends,* she revealed another of her father's contradictions: "My dad's interest was mostly in breeding horses. He really didn't ride very much. He liked looking at the horses and he liked breeding the horses, but beyond his movie career I didn't really see him get on a horse much. He enjoyed owning them and watching them, but he really didn't ride all that much—which is kind of funny. My brother Christopher and I were the riders in the family."

The Sundowners (Warner Bros., 1960)

Cast: Deborah Kerr (Ida Camody); Robert Mitchum (Paddy Carmody); Peter Ustinov (Rupert Venneker); Glynis Johns (Mrs. Firth); Dina Merrill (Jean Halstead); Chips Rafferty (Quinlan); Michael Anderson, Jr. (Sean Carmody); Lola Brooks (Liz Brown); Wylie Watson (Herb Johnson); John Meillon (Bluey Brown); Ronald Fraser (Ocker); Gerry Duggan, Leonard Teale, Peter Carver, Dick Bentley

(Shearers); Mervyn Johns (Jack Patchogue); Molly Urquhart (Mrs. Bateman); Ewen Solon (Halstead); Max Osbiston (Farmer); Mercia Barden (Farmer's Wife); and Ray Barrett, Jon Cleary, Jack Cunningham, John Fegan, Lloyd Lamble, Bryan Pringle, Colin Tapley, Allister Williamson, Michael Segal, Jim Brady, Norman Fisher, Jack Sharp, Pat Hagan, Jack May, Jeff Silk, Colin McKenzie, Ron Whelan, Ed Lorke, Brian Schiller, Terry Gurney, Ron Bennier, Eric Garner, Ray Modystack.

Crew: Fred Zinnemann (Director); Gerry Blattner (Producer); Isobel Lennart (Screenplay); Jack Hildyard (Photographer); Dimitri Tiomkin (Music); Michael Stringer (Art Director); Jack Harris (Editor); Denis Blake, Harold Sanderson, Ray Austin, Jeff Silk, Tex Watson, Stan Simmons, Del Watson, Neville Sellwood, Rodney Turner, Cliff Clare (Stunts); Ware's Livery (Livestock Provider); Lionel Ware, Graham Ware, Jack Burraston (Wranglers).

133 minutes; Released December 8, 1960

Sometimes described as an Australian western, Fred Zinnemann's *The Sundowners* meets few of the traditional oater criteria. Based on Jon Cleary's 1952 novel, the story is set in the 1920s Outback and definite signs of mechanization exist, including a few trucks and motorcycles. But horseback is still the preferred mode of transportation with Mitchum's Ireland transplant Paddy Carmody and his wife

As Paddy Carmody in *The Sundowners* (1960).

Ida (Deborah Kerr) and son Sean (Michael Anderson, Jr.) traveling by wagon. They're an itinerant family, driven by beer-loving sheep drover Mitchum's wanderlust. With his wide-brimmed hat, Mitchum looks like a cowboy, absent a gun belt. His herding of the sheep by horseback could as easily have been cattle on the move in the American West. The family does have a rifle, but that's used for rabbit hunting. Mitchum drinks and brawls throughout the film but, when Ida and Sean indicate they're tired of the constant travel, he tries to go against his natural instincts and put down roots with a sheep-shearing outfit. Mitchum wins a promising thoroughbred racehorse they name Sundowner and his son serves as jockey, giving Kerr hope they can earn enough for their own farm. That's the conflict. No good guys and bad guys. Only human beings trying to get by in a tough land.

Warner Bros. proposed conveniently shooting the film on either a California studio set with a fake backdrop or in the Arizona desert with kangaroos bouncing around. Director Zinnemann (of *High Noon* fame) refused, feeling it would make the movie look like a cheap western. Instead they would shoot in the rugged Australian Outback with little pampering for the stars. It was tougher on him personally, but Mitchum felt the decision aided the film immensely. He recalled sitting on a horse surrounded by the red dust from Down Under, telling *The New York Times,* "There is no substitute for misery." To Hedda Hopper he commented, "You can't imagine how hot it was, how dry and dirty. I was only clean twice during the entire shooting." He elaborated further in his trademark beleaguered manner on the rough conditions to the *Evansville Courier and Press*:

> We started in the Snowy River Mountains. Then we worked our way down to Whyalla. Winds off the Victorian Desert raised temperatures to 116 degrees. We didn't have stuntmen, so they got an Irish expatriate off the docks, and he beat the tar out of me. Suddenly the director fainted from the heat. I gave him smelling salts, and he came around. The Irishman went back to pounding me. The director fainted again. It was a wrap.

The authentic location and dialects give the leisurely paced film style, and the lead per-

Mitchum throwing a punch in a brawl in the Outback on *The Sundowners* (1960).

formances are top-notch. Mitchum and Kerr worked together effectively in *Heaven Knows, Mr. Allison* (1957), and here they continue their on-screen chemistry as husband and wife. Each declared the other their favorite co-star. Mitchum fans are glad he agreed to take over for an ailing Gary Cooper in *The Sundowners*. As Paddy Carmody, he gives one of his best performances. Mitchum earned $200,000 for the intelligently made film, which shot in Cooma, Nimmitabel, Adaminaby, Jindabyne, Port Augusta and Iron Knob with the esteemed Jack Hildyard behind the camera. Mitchum took his share of physical abuse in the film. There's an especially effective bushfire scene with Mitchum braving the smoke and flames to save their sheep. Some interiors were filmed at Elstree in Borehamwood, England.

"He makes acting look as easy as falling off a log," Kerr wrote in the foreword of Alvin H. Marill's book *Robert Mitchum on the Screen*. Recalling their first meeting on the set of *Heaven Knows, Mr. Allison* in Tobago for *Photoplay*, she said, "I realized immediately that far from being like his image of a lazy kind of a character who doesn't seem to care about anything, he was in fact extremely intelligent and cared about so many things. He was such a surprise." The admiration was mutual. "It was an honor to feed her lines," Mitchum told the Australian press. Co-star Peter Ustinov does well in a showy supporting role in *The Sundowners* as a randy traveler who latches on as a drover and drinking mate for Mitchum. Ustinov recalled in his autobiography, "Robert Mitchum was superb in the role of an Australian, his usual distant look matched by an accent authentic beyond belief." Fred Zinnemann was fond of working with Mitchum. He told *The Saturday Evening Post*, "He's one of the finest instinctive actors in the business, almost in the same class as Spencer Tracy." He expounded in an interview with the *Australian Women's Weekly*: "Bob was quite a surprise to me. He's intelligent, quiet, cooperative, and completely professional. He picked up shearing know-how and the accent quickly."

Mitchum's film son is played by 16-year-old Michael Anderson, Jr., son of the English film director. The youngster went on to co-star in

Major Dundee (1965), *The Sons of Katie Elder* (1965), *The Glory Guys* (1965) and the TV western *The Monroes* (1966–1967). When Anderson's mother learned that Mitchum would be replacing Gary Cooper, she was aghast, frightened that her underage son would be exposed to all manner of Mitchum debauchery based upon his reputation. Years later, in an interview with Dick Dinman for WMPG Radio, Michael recalled that the film was pushed back three weeks upon his arrival in Australia. When Mitchum learned of the delay, he disappeared into the Outback, leaving the press and the production company to guess at his location. Anderson remembered, "There'd be a sighting of him in Willmot or some strange place where he'd gotten into a fight with some ranch hand and nobody could find him. So, his legend preceded him."

Anderson added, "When I met him, I was incredibly impressed with his stature. He was a big man. I think he was about 6'2" or 6'3", and he was handsome as the day is long. He was very, very male and had a deep voice. He was charming—absolutely, charming…. He had enormous power as an actor, and I loved his accent in the movie." On one occasion, Anderson observed Mitchum fishing in the Snowy River. Mitchum cast out several times from the bank, catching nothing. When Anderson commented it didn't look like Mitchum was having any luck, Mitchum asked Anderson if he wanted a trout for lunch. On Mitchum's next cast he reeled in a beautiful trout and gave it to an amazed Anderson. "There was a certain kind of magic to Bob," Anderson said. "I really, really admired him. We were very close, and he had a great sense of humor." Anderson fondly recalled the moment that Mitchum learned they shared the same birthday, although it was months away. "He just reaches down into his bag and passes out a record album to me," Anderson said. "Marty Robbins' *Gunfighter Ballads*. And he said, 'Happy Birthday.' He was a wonderful character. My mother didn't need to worry for a second about me being with Bob…. He was the consummate professional."

At first Mitchum did not take to the Aussie locals, slightly miffed by their intense curiosity and adoration. He wanted to blend in, not have his every move, swallow of vodka and tomato juice, or bite of steak tracked and accounted for by the all-access Australian press. He did not care for the flies, the lack of air conditioning, the constant smell of sheep, and the customary warm beer. The weather in Cooma was cold and rain-soaked, keeping a testy Mitchum largely indoors. When questioned by reporters regarding his disposition, Mitchum would respond he was "horrible" or "worse." In the warmer Port Augusta, he brightened, spending his idle hours on a boat in the harbor, shooing away females who would swim out attempting to climb aboard. What comes across on screen is a completely professional performance and a sign of a maturation in his screen image. He does loosen up to sing the drinking songs "The Wild Colonial Boy," "Moreton Bay," "Lime Juice Tab" and "Botany Bay," nicely complimenting Dimitri Tiomkin's jaunty Down Under score. A London recording company proposed an album of Mitchum singing Aussie songs, but he wasn't interested. Mitchum had his best time on the film shooting a mass brawl sequence between two groups of rival sheepshearers in the Outback. Many of the sheepshearers for this humorous sequence were portrayed by English stuntmen. Denis Blake and Harold Sanderson were on hand to double Mitchum, but the star performed his own screen fighting.

Mitchum did eventually make a great location friend, local horse wrangler Jack Burraston. The Carmody family's plow horse was named Sam; once anointed the Most Handsome Milk Horse in Sydney. The horse portraying Sundowner was a well-known racer by the name of Silver Phantom, a champion in the Australian Derby. The climactic horse race involving more than 20 professional horses and riders was coordinated by jockey Neville Sellwood, with Rodney Turner and Sellwood doubling Anderson. The young actor was atop the powerful Silver Phantom for close-ups when someone clacked a clapboard and the horse spooked. It took off on a dead sprint with a terrified Anderson holding on for dear life. He had learned to ride for the film, but this was far more horse than he could handle. A camera car went racing after him. There was nothing they could do. When the horse finally stopped

After the critical praise awarded *The Sundowners* (1960), Mitchum joked he was no longer limited to co-starring with horses.

six minutes later, Mitchum was the first person to Anderson, helping him off the horse and steadying his nerves.

Mitchum learned to shear sheep for a memorable and humorous sequences, a contest to see who can garner the greatest number of shaved animals in an allotted time. The robust Mitchum thinks he will have an easy go of it against his extremely aged competition Wylie Watson, but the calm veteran Watson puts the exhausted younger man to shame. Preparing for this scene was especially concerning to Mitchum. He worried he might injure the sheep. Half a dozen real sheepshearers were hired as atmosphere players under the supervision of shearing specialist F.A. Doecke. Shearer Brian Schiller spoke of Mitchum to the *Australian Women's Weekly*: "He's not a bad sort of joker. He hasn't any time for society life; he really seemed happiest when he was out in the bush."

Learning to shear a sheep was yet another skill Mitchum picked up through his work in making films around the globe. He proved himself once again to be one of the handiest of Hollywood's stars and at this point a veteran cowboy. Mitchum had been in the saddle for over 15 years and was now a solid horseman with a keen appreciation of the animals. Director Budd Boetticher, a trainer of Lusitano horses, praised his pal's equestrian abilities. Mitchum was comfortable in western wear, with his exposure to the milieu making him handy with guns, knives and ropes. His adaptability occasionally manifested itself in his afterhours recreation and contributed to his rowdy bad-boy image. In Ireland for *The Night Fighters*, he fashioned a noose, wrapped it around meddlesome producer Raymond Stross' ankles and hung him from a lamppost. "I do that to all my producers," Mitchum deadpanned to journalist pal James Bacon.

For his consummate performances in *Home from the Hill* and *The Sundowners,* Mitchum was named Best Actor by the National Film Board of Review. When it came to the Academy Awards, Deborah Kerr and the film were Oscar-nominated. So were supporting actress Glynis Johns, screenwriter Isobel Lennart and director Zinnemann. Mitchum was not. It seemed a glaring oversight. Mitchum's son Jim weighed in at the time, telling Bob Thomas, "He should have had the Oscar for *Heaven Knows, Mr. Allison,* but he wasn't even nominated. He should have had it for *The Sundowners* this year. They asked him if he wanted to campaign for it. You've got to spend money to get a nomination. He said to heck with it, so he wasn't nominated."

His reviews were superlative. *Variety* noted, "Mitchum's rugged masculinity is right for his part. His thespic range seems narrow, but that can be deceptive, for there are moments when he projects a great deal of feeling with what appears to be a minimum of effort. This may be the finest work he has done in films." *Film Bulletin* weighed in with, "Mitchum's delineation of an itchy-footed, tough-working, whiskey-drinking Irish-Australian shapes up as his best to date. He combines harshness with softness in a winning and creditable manner." *The Los Angeles Herald Examiner* opined, "Bob Mitchum, to my knowledge, has never been given the credit he merits on the screen. In his strength and masculinity, we are inclined to overlook the sensitive shadings beneath the surface. In *The Sundowners* these qualities cannot be overlooked."

Film Daily said, "Both Mitchum and Kerr give fine performances," while *Cue* claimed the leading roles were "excellently played." *The Hollywood Reporter* wrote, "Robert Mitchum gives an especially bright performance," and *The Los Angeles Times* found him in "rare good humor." *Box Office* added, "Mitchum has rarely been better." *Films in Review* remarked, "Robert Mitchum has grown as an actor, and in *The Sundowners* he projects a surprising variety of emotions, effortlessly. Mitchum deserves more critical attention than he has received." *Motion Picture Daily* noted, "Mitchum is weather-beaten and unshaven throughout, both of which qualities fit the role aptly."

Mitchum and Kerr co-starred again in *The Grass Is Greener* (1960) and the TV movie *Reunion at Fairborough* (1985). In 1961, there was talk of teaming them with Rod Taylor for a 20th Century–Fox adventure titled *The Jungle.* Their on-screen chemistry was so strong that western director Budd Boetticher wrote the screenplay *Two Mules for Sister Sara* as a project for Mitchum and Kerr in the early 1960s. Unfortunately, Boetticher fell out of favor in Hollywood as he labored for years on a bullfighting film about Carlos Arruza in Mexico. *Two Mules for Sister Sara* was finally made by Don Siegel in 1970 with Clint Eastwood and Shirley MacLaine in the starring roles. It is one of many westerns Mitchum had the chance to appear in. During this period, Mitchum was up for or vetoed *Gunfight at the O.K. Corral* (1957), *Rio Bravo* (1959), *The Alamo* (1960), *The Unforgiven* (1960), *North to Alaska* (1960), *Heller in Pink Tights* (1960), *The Misfits* (1961), *4 for Texas* (1963), *Cat Ballou* (1965), *The Professionals* (1966) and *The Ballad of Josie* (1967) for various reasons.

John Wayne produced, starred in and ultimately directed his personal epic *The Alamo,* about the 1836 siege on the Texas fort by Gen. Santa Anna's Mexican troops and the protection of the values of a Republic. Wayne's dream cast consisted of himself as Davy Crockett, William Holden as Col. William Travis and Robert Mitchum as knife fighter Jim Bowie. However, Holden wasn't free. United Artists already had Richard Widmark under contract and were pushing him for one of the top roles. Wayne decided Widmark could play Travis, but Widmark preferred playing Bowie. Wayne felt Widmark was too short for Bowie and the role demanded an actor the stature of Mitchum. Stressed due to looming deadlines and financial pressures, Wayne gave in on Widmark as Bowie. Laurence Harvey moved into the Travis role. It was not what Wayne wanted for his pet project. Mitchum didn't care one way or the other.

Dick Powell wanted to produce a $5 million epic, *Big River, Big Man,* from Thomas W. Duncan's novel, with Wayne and Mitchum as rival pioneers settling the west, but a union strike delayed the filming at 20th Century–Fox. Mitchum was under consideration to co-star with Wayne later that year in *North to Alaska* (1960), a two-fisted logging picture rushed into production as Wayne tried to recoup the money he sunk into *The Alamo*. *North to Alaska* didn't even have a completed script, causing original director Richard Fleischer to pass. When he left, so did Mitchum. Stewart Granger took over the brawling Mitchum role as director Henry Hathaway was brought aboard to shoot on the fly. Mitchum didn't sweat the loss of these roles opposite Wayne, although appearing in them would have enhanced his western résumé. Having missed out on these and *Rio Bravo*, Mitchum and Wayne finally co-starred in *El Dorado* (1967) to critical and audience acclaim.

While making *Heaven Knows, Mr. Allison*, director John Huston had Mitchum swimming in coral reefs and being pulled around Tobago on the back of sea turtles. In one scene, Mitchum was bloodied doing a belly crawl through stinging nettles. It was a tough shoot, but Mitchum manned-up to every action Huston requested. "He is one of the finest actors I've ever had anything to do with," Huston wrote in his autobiography. When Huston called Mitchum with an offer to play "the last of the cowboys" in *The Misfits,* Mitchum looked at the sketchy Arthur Miller script and saw he'd be dragged around the desert by horses. Mitchum turned the film down. He was beginning to sour on getting beaten up for film productions. Huston got him a quick rewrite on his way to Australia, but by that time Clark Gable had agreed to the role. Mitchum was offered the dual lead of falling-down-drunk Kid Shelleen and nasty gunman Strawn in *Cat Ballou*. The role was ultimately played by Lee Marvin, whose seriocomic performance won him a Best Actor Oscar. In 1964, Columbia purchased the rights to the Frank O'Rourke western novel *A Mule for the Marquesa* with hopes of turning it into an adventure starring Frank Sinatra, Gregory Peck and Mitchum. The film became the iconic action classic *The Professionals*, with Burt Lancaster, Lee Marvin and Robert Ryan joining Woody Strode in Nevada's Valley of Fire as the men of the title.

Mitchum signed to star in his biggest western project in June 1964: producer David Weisbart's epic tale of the Battle of Little Big Horn, *The Day Custer Fell*. Mitchum was to be cast as Capt. Frederick Benteen, the pensive sub-commander who did not come to the megalomaniac Custer's rescue when the general severely underestimated his Native American foes. Fred Zinnemann was slated to direct an all-star cast, with Charlton Heston courted to portray Custer. Others in the proposed cast included Jack Palance, George C. Scott, Cliff Robertson, Robert Shaw, Stuart Whitman and Toshiro Mifune as Sitting Bull. Weisbart hoped to film on actual battle sites in Hardin, Montana, or in South Dakota with 6000 horses and 10,000 Indian extras filling the screen. Weisbart even had designs on coordinating the largest mass horse-fall in screen history as 65 riders and their horses would simultaneously hit the ground for the camera. The oft-delayed picture kept growing until the budget approached $18 million. 20th Century–Fox, still reeling from the financial losses of 1963's *Cleopatra*, finally pulled the plug in the summer of 1965. Weisbart used his notes and preproduction work to turn the epic film into the TV series *Legend of Custer* (1967–1968) with Wayne Maunder cast as the general. Robert Shaw went on to play the title character in the Spanish-lensed *Custer of the West* (1967). Jeffrey Hunter played Benteen in the Shaw film with Peter Adams taking on the part in the Weisbart TV series.

During his absence from the cowboy film genre, Mitchum's now adult son Jim launched an acting career. The spitting image of his father, he debuted as his dad's younger brother on screen in *Thunder Road* (1958) and appeared in several films after that. He starred in the westerns *Young Guns of Texas* (1962), *Grand Canyon Massacre* (1964) and *The Tramplers* (1965), the latter two made in Europe for the Spaghetti Western audience. *Young Guns* was made at Old Tucson and co-starred cowboy star Joel McCrea's son Jody. Jim also appeared on episodes of the TV westerns *Have Gun—Will Travel* and *The High Chaparral*. Robert neither encouraged or discouraged a film career for his son. Jim was left to find his own way. That's how the Mitchum men did it. "I only hope I can be half the actor and half the man he is," Jim told the *Independent Star-News*. "Not because he's my father, but you can ask anyone and they'll tell you the truth. Bob Mitchum is one helluva nice guy."

Having purchased property in Maryland to escape Hollywood, Robert Mitchum was not seen in another western for seven years. He did step in for recently deceased TV host Dick Powell to introduce the 1963 *Dick Powell Theatre* episode "The Losers." This was directed by Sam Peckinpah and starred Lee Marvin and Keenan Wynn as Dave Blassingame and Burgundy Smith, characters first introduced in Peckinpah's great but short-lived TV series *The Westerner* (1960). Powell died of cancer a week before the episode aired. Powell had hoped to pair Mitchum and John Wayne in the western adventure *Big River, Big Man* at the time of his diagnosis. Warner Bros. announced Mitchum and Ty Hardin would star in *The Missourian*, based on the Brad Ward novel, but the film was never produced. Mitchum appeared in the pages of a 1964 *Esquire* feature in a Carl Fischer nature photo wearing a cowboy hat with cigarette dangling from his lips, an image inviting comparison to the popular Marlboro Man ad campaign. The shot was taken on his Talbot property.

Mitchum's films during this time consisted of a mixed bag of titles that are not well-remembered in his personal canon, save for his chilling villain performance as the rattlesnake mean Max Cady in the suspense drama *Cape Fear* (1962). Cady is one of the most realistically scary villains ever seen on the big screen, and Mitchum plays him to the hilt. *The Longest Day* (1962) was an all-star World War II film about the D-Day Invasion with Mitchum, John Wayne, Robert Ryan and Henry Fonda showing up in extended cameos. *Rampage* (1963) was a routine jungle adventure filmed in Hawaii. The military courtroom drama *Man in the Middle* (aka *The Winston Affair*) called for high-grade emoting. The serious roles were welcome for Mitchum, who told columnist Erskine Johnson in 1963: "At one time I was permitted to act with horses only. Then they decided I might be acceptable company for girls. Now I'm even offered roles that require acting."

The Last Time I Saw Archie (1961) was a military comedy misfire with Mitchum playing the real-life South Dakota cowboy turned B-movie stuntman Arch Hall. *The List of Adrian Messenger* (1963) was a gimmicky mystery thriller by John Huston with major stars Mitchum, Kirk Douglas, Burt Lancaster, Frank Sinatra and Tony Curtis appearing in supporting cameos under heavy makeup before revealing themselves in the final credits. Kirk Douglas let actor Jan Merlin portray him in the makeup throughout the film rather than take the time to have it applied. Lancaster and Sinatra also used doubles. Mitchum went the full nine yards himself playing an Irish character. In the breezy comedy *What a Way to Go* (1964), Mitchum had fun as a jet-setting playboy businessman with hopes to settle on a ranch opposite Shirley MacLaine (also his leading lady in 1962's *Two for the Seesaw*). *Mr. Moses* (1965) was a *Maverick Goes to Africa* with Mitchum trading in his horse for an elephant as a con man whom a Kenyan tribe mistakes as a holy man meant to lead them to the Promised Land.

According to columnist Mike Connolly, in late 1964 Mitchum expressed interest in starring in *The Loners*, a 90-minute western TV pilot written by Larry Cohen. Then Cohen moved forward as the creator of the Chuck Connors western series *Branded* (1965–1966) and was unable to devote sufficient time to Mitchum. Mitchum's TV debut would have to wait.

Mitchum nearly returned to Australia a few years after *The Sundowners* for another modern western: *Last Bus to Banjo Creek,* an *African Queen* in the desert that was intended to co-star Shirley MacLaine. Rod Taylor picked up the option on the story in the late 1960s and tried making it for nearly a decade. Twenty years after *The Sundowners,* Mitchum was asked to return to Australia to make the 1880s period western *The Man from Snowy River* (1982). He would have starred as one of a pair of rival brothers (with Burt Lancaster as the sibling). At that time, Mitchum wasn't interested in returning to Oz or working with Lancaster, whom he felt was a little too arrogant and controlling on set for his tastes. Kirk Douglas ended up playing both brothers in the well-received film. (In 1962, Douglas took on another western role Mitchum would have been ideally suited for: the modern horseman in *Lonely Are the Brave.*)

The Sundowners is one of Mitchum's most

delightfully enjoyable films. He's engagingly low-key and understated throughout, but soulful and complex as the vagabond with a need to roam close to his own heart. "That's one movie I'll admit to being proud of," he told Pierre O'Rourke. "It's a keeper."

El Dorado (Paramount, 1967)

Cast: John Wayne (Cole Thornton); Robert Mitchum (Sheriff J.P. Harrah); James Caan (Mississippi); Charlene Holt (Maudie); Paul Fix (Dr. Miller); Arthur Hunnicutt (Bull); Michele Carey (Josephine MacDonald); R.G. Armstrong (Kevin MacDonald); Ed Asner (Bart Jason); Christopher George (Nelse McLeod); Marina Ghane (Maria); Robert Donner (Milt); John Gabriel (Pedro); Johnny Crawford (Luke MacDonald); Robert Rothwell (Saul MacDonald); Adam Roarke (Matt MacDonald); Victoria George (Jared's Wife); Jim Davis (Jim Purvis); Anne Newman (Saul's Wife); Diane Strom (Matt's Wife); Olaf Wieghorst (Swede Larsen); and Richard Andrade, Danny Borzage, Charlita, Don Collier, Enrique Contreras, Chuck Courtney, Linda Dangcil, Nacho Galindo, Joe Garcio, Betty Jane Graham, Robert "Buzz" Henry, William Henry, Lars Hensen, Riley Hill, Chuck Horne, Rodolfo Hoyos, Jr., Bonnie Charyl Josephson, Joe King, Mike Letz, Frank Leyva, Myra McMurray, John Mitchum, Ruben Moreno, Deen Pettinger, Lee Powell, Chuck Roberson, Anthony Rogers, Danny Sands, Robert Shelton, Dean Smith, John Strachen, Neil Summers, Rosa Turich, Ralph Volkie, Christopher West.

Crew: Howard Hawks (Director); Howard Hawks and Paul Helmick (Producers); Leigh Brackett (Screenplay); Harold Rosson (Photographer); Nelson Riddle (Music); Carl Anderson and Hal Pereira (Art Directors); John Woodcock (Editor); Edith Head (Wardrobe); Andrew J. Durkus (Assistant Director); Earl Olin (Prop Master); Robert "Buzz" Henry (Stunt Coordinator); Polly Burson, Joe Canutt, Gary Combs, Chuck Courtney, Jim Feazell, Chuck Hayward, Chuck Henson, Bill Hickman, Walt LaRue, Terry Leonard, Kimo Owens, Bill Raymond, Chuck Roberson, Danny Sands, Alex Sharp, Dean Smith, Kenneth "Blackie" Stephens, Bud Stout, Neil Summers, Tom Sutton, Bobby West, George P. Wilbur, Jack N. Young (Stunts); Gordon G. Jones, Tom Sutton, Ben Ward, Bud Stout, Gerry Searle, Ron Searle, Chuck Henson (Wranglers).

126 minutes; Released June 7, 1967

"The westerner is the last gentleman, and the movies which over and over again tell his story are probably the last art form in which the concept of honor retains its strength," wrote Robert Warshow in his motion picture treatise *The Immediate Experience.*

In 1965, Mitchum was lured back to the western genre by a phone call from veteran director Howard Hawks, who was gauging the actor's interest in co-starring opposite John Wayne in a film called *El Dorado*. Mitchum was immediately interested. The title town is a nod to a legendary city of gold, but it might as well have been referring to the golden years of two long-in-the-tooth gunslingers played by the 58-year-old Wayne and the 48-year-old Mitchum. The younger star was familiar with Hawks from the time the famous director wanted him to play a frontiersman in *The Big Sky* (1952). Mitchum's name had been bandied about by the producers as a potential co-star for Wayne in *Rio Bravo* (1959), but that role went to Dean Martin. On a 1980 *Tonight Show* appearance, Mitchum related that when he asked Hawks about a story for *El Dorado*, the director replied, "No story, Bob. Just characters." The character Hawks wanted Mitchum to play was a jowly, drunken sheriff who is an old range-riding cohort of Wayne's gun for hire. Mitchum agreed over the phone to be, as Lee Server noted Mitchum joked, "John Wayne's leading lady."

There was a script written by Western Spur

As Sheriff J.P. Harrah in *El Dorado* (1967).

Award-winning novelist Leigh Brackett (*Follow the Free Wind*); she based it on Harry Brown's book *The Stars in Their Courses*. Brackett's script was serious and downbeat in nature, dealing with advancing age and mortality, but once on location Hawks began implementing levity and basic elements from his and Brackett's previous Wayne western classic *Rio Bravo* (1959). This lifting of plot points was followed down to the drunken, pride-shaken lawman Dean Martin portrayed in the earlier film, this time essayed by Mitchum. Taking stock of Mitchum's condition, Wayne memorably announces, "I'm lookin' at a tin star with a drunk pinned on it."

Early in the production conferences, Wayne proposed switching the leading parts so he'd play the drunk and Mitchum the hired gunman, but Hawks stuck with the roles the audience expected them to play. Paramount advertising called the film "The Big One with the Big Two!" Rejected by a female, Mitchum intended to play the drunken sheriff dramatically, but Hawks wanted it done with a light touch and plenty of physical business including back and forth banter with Wayne. Whiskered, sweating profusely, and covered in weeks of dirt, Mitchum and his tearing-at-the-seams wardrobe are a sight to behold. He gets the film's biggest laughs without saying a word. *Los Angeles Times* film critic Kevin Thomas termed it "the loveliest hangover sequence on record," while Pauline Kael of *The New Yorker* noted that Mitchum was "an actor who wore a gut as a badge of honor." The tried-and-true formula Hawks advocated works as this middle-aged western is immensely enjoyable, and at times poignant. It was also a lot of fun to make.

The picture was shot at Old Tucson, Arizona, located 12 miles west of the city of Tucson through the mountainous Gates Pass. The rocky Sonoran Desert area is peppered by saguaro cactus and remains wonderfully photogenic with Golden Gate Mountain serving as background for the western film set. Wayne loved the location, declaring to Dick Kleiner that Old Tucson had "the best western street there is." The area is noted for its clear blue skies, but Hawks opted to shoot a great deal of *El Dorado* on the streets of Old Tucson's western town at night. For this, there was no one better to hire as director of photography than 70-year-old Harold Rosson, who had lensed the western classic *Duel in the Sun* (1946) in some of the same southern Arizona locations two decades earlier. Rosson made the darkly lit Tucson streets vividly come alive like a Frederick Remington painting of the Old West. The filming pace was languid and relaxed, with Hawks waiting interminably for the

A drunk Mitchum and John Wayne effectively played their fight scene in *El Dorado* (1967) for laughs.

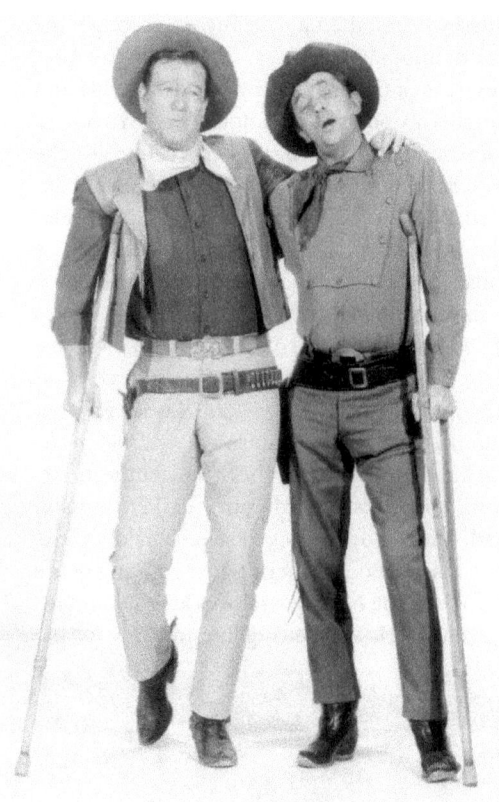

John Wayne and Mitchum mug it up for the camera on crutches in *El Dorado* (1967).

camera to capture the perfect sunset and twilight. Elaborate dinners of steak, shrimp and lobster were served with regularity on white linen and crystal for the entire crew. There was a lot of down time. Mitchum befriended a young University of Arizona coed during filming and introduced her to cast and crew as his "acting coach." No one batted an eye. The film went 24 days over schedule, shooting from October 1965 to February 1966.

James Caan was a rising star in more ways than one: The 5'10" actor wore three-inch lifts in his boots so as not to be dwarfed by larger actors Mitchum and Wayne. Mitchum good-naturedly accused the 6'4" Wayne of wearing lifts himself to stand even taller than the rest of the cast. Mitchum got a kick out of seeing Wayne's personal station wagon, whose roof was modified to accommodate the cowboy icon wearing an oversized Stetson. Wayne was up for matching Mitchum's sense of fun, filling a bucket of water with ice cubes before dousing Mitchum in a scene. The two older stars made Caan earn his paycheck in offstage razzing and practical jokes. Rookie Caan got along well with the veterans, though he once got into a heated exchange with Wayne concerning chess pieces mysteriously moving on the board of a game in progress behind scenes. Mitchum stepped in between the two men to calm Caan's fiery temper down. Wayne was cheating at the game to test Caan's reaction.

On screen, Caan wore a pained smile throughout his scenes in reaction to Wayne's exaggerated line readings, which Mitchum was quick to pick up on. On several occasions, the strong-minded Wayne gave Caan direction opposite of what Hawks wanted the young actor to do. Wayne expressed interest in directing Mitchum in a film one day, to which Mitchum replied that an oblivious Wayne had already been directing him this entire picture. Mitchum took to calling Caan "Jiminy Crickett," referencing the Walt Disney cartoon character, because of the riverboat hat Caan wore during the film playing Mississippi (aka Alan Bourdillion Trehearne). It was a happy and cordial set, with Mitchum and character actor Arthur Hunnicutt holding court and telling hilarious stories. Mitchum's brother John has a role as the bartender Elmer, memorably getting shards of the bar top blown into his hand when he reaches for a gun to take on his brother. Hawks surprised John by setting off the squib on the count of one rather than the expected three, obtaining a genuine shocked reaction. The name Elmer was an ad-lib by Robert, referencing the Mitchum brothers' mutual Long Beach friend Elmer Jones. "We met by pure accident on the set of *El Dorado*," John told *The San Francisco Chronicle*. "We were surprised as hell to see each other…. Bob and I, we get along good, but we're men and we each have to have our own way. We accept each other and that's why there's never any trouble. We have the same temperament. We're from the same stock."

James Caan, born and raised in the Bronx, had recently finished making the western *The Glory Guys* (1965). He so readily embraced the cowboy culture exhibited in *El Dorado* that he later became a member of the Professional

Cowboys Rodeo Association where he acquired the nickname "The Jewish Cowboy." On the other hand, fellow East Coaster Ed Asner was dismissively referred to throughout filming by Wayne as "that New York actor." On the film's DVD commentary, Asner recalled Mitchum being more open. "He was a great storyteller," Asner said of Mitchum. "He'd buddy down with us the whole time." During filming, tough guy Caan was particularly taken with Mitchum, whom he talked about in a Q&A session for the National Board of Boiler and Presser Inspectors in 2015. Caan called Mitchum "the greatest guy that ever was. He was a rounder, man. When we would go out somewhere, he'd drink and fight. Not that it's a wonderful thing to fight, but he'd back you up, God forbid. He was just a great guy." Server's biography describes Mitchum encountering a convention of boisterous German pilots in the Tucson hotel bar and calmly returning with one of the pilots in a headlock to engage in a game of poker with the wranglers and stuntmen.

In addition to Caan, Mitchum was helpful in his own way to young actors on the film like Christopher George, Robert Donner, Johnny Crawford and Adam Roarke, giving them career advice and pointers about how to deal with the business. Nineteen-year-old Crawford, best known as Chuck Connors' son on *The Rifleman,* recalled Mitchum for the Turner Classic website as "a real down-to-earth friendly guy" who "came on set when he wasn't needed, just to hang out." Western character player Robert Donner told Lee Server, "Mitch was really a nifty guy…. Wayne was always ready to tell you what to do, grab you by the shoulders and put you where he wanted you, tell you how to say a line…. Mitchum was a lot more easygoing. You could play around with Mitch and didn't have to worry you had overstepped your bounds. He was very generous with other actors."

Christopher George was a U.S. Marine, private investigator, and bar bouncer who gained prominence appearing in a shaving cream commercial. *El Dorado* was his first major acting role. "What I learned from Duke Wayne and Bob Mitchum you couldn't learn in five years of acting classes," George told *The Chicago Tribune.* When it came time to film George's death scene, Mitchum offered to read the off-camera lines for an under-the-weather Wayne so George had something he could react to. This is unusual. Stars of Wayne and Mitchum's magnitude are seldom expected to read off-camera lines, typically letting production assistants handle that work. George was even more surprised to see Wayne had rallied and was now standing beside Mitchum. Wayne declared he'd read his own lines, not wanting to let the young actor down in his big scene. George, excellent as the scarred gunslinger, won further parts in the Wayne westerns *Chisum* (1970) and *The Train Robbers* (1973).

Mitchum and Wayne created many humorous pieces of business on the film, from eye-rolling punch-takes to the embarrassment Mitchum shows when female lead Charlene Holt walks in on him taking a bath. Cowboy humor, or horsing around, was a real and largely untapped entity in Hollywood's view of the Old West. The daily interplay of good-natured ribbing between friends is welcome, and something Wayne and Mitchum proved wonderfully adept at for the camera. In real life, Mitchum was a sharp wit with a fine sense of comic timing. Self-amusement was a daily quest for Mitchum, and co-star Wayne enjoyed a good hearty laugh. Even through the biting humor, the two stars dig deeper to show moments of loyalty between the gunmen. One of the best silent bits between the actors occurs when Wayne helps the struggling Mitchum by loading his gun for him. The story is, after all, about their friendship and the professional courtesy men of this ilk share.

Western artist Olaf Wieghorst created the title cards and plays the gunsmith. His painting "Fighting Stallions" is symbolic of the stars. The anticipated fight scene between the screen titans was kept short in the final edit and played for laughs. Set visitor Army Archerd wrote that Mitchum and Wayne's punches were coming so close to one another, it made the professional stuntmen on the set wince. Yet the two pros never connected. Hawks filmed more than a dozen takes of a spittoon clobbering Mitchum before he got the glassy-eyed take he wanted. Mitchum recalled, "Duke and I were pretty well lubricated for those scenes. We could've done a hundred takes."* It's effective comedy, but fans of the actors would have preferred a more serious fistic display between the men based on their well-established cinematic tough guy personas. The brief exchange of haymakers still merits a spot in the book *Classic Movie Fight Scenes*.

Perhaps the most memorable ongoing business is the nauseating physical discomfort Mitchum's character feels from ingesting Caan's homemade concoction of cayenne pepper, hot mustard powder, ipecac, asafoetida, croton oil and gunpowder. The emetic, spice and purgative combination is intended to react violently at the introduction of alcohol, which Mitchum is initially tempted to consume. Throughout the film, Mitchum garners laughs by asking off-handedly who Caan is and how he joined them for the fight against villainous rancher Asner's gunmen. Another humorous bit has Mitchum continuously switch which leg he was using a crutch for after being shot in the right leg. Mitchum claimed he was aware of the continuity problem, but Hawks told him to use the crutch on his left side to keep his gun hand free. Hawks didn't think the audience would notice. Screen veteran Wayne quickly spotted the gaffe and with Mitchum's help they improvised a line that made the final cut. By the end of the film, both stars are on crutches and switching injured legs. A scene with Mitchum singing at a piano was cut when Hawks' son told him during an early viewing of the picture that a tough sheriff shouldn't sing.

El Dorado premiered for motion picture exhibitors in November 1966 and ran shortly after that in Japan, but the film was not released theatrically in the U.S. until the summer of 1967. This delay was largely because Paramount was selling the studio and wanted to spread their already existing product out. They had the Steve McQueen western *Nevada Smith* (1966) already slated for release and didn't want to be in competition with themselves. *El Dorado* was released at the same time as another John Wayne western, *The War Wagon* (1967). Wayne wasn't happy about this, but each film did robust business. *El Dorado* took in over $12 million at the box office.

The two stars make a great team in *El Dorado*, working together effortlessly as they needle one another while capably handling the action requirements. Hawks explained to Michael Munn: "Robert Mitchum was one of the few actors who can work with Wayne without Wayne blowing him off the screen. But I don't think Mitchum has the power Wayne has. He can't carry a picture as well as Wayne can, and Wayne knows this, which is why I gave people like Dean Martin and Robert Mitchum the more interesting characters." He elaborated in a *Cashiers du Cinema* interview:

> Mitchum and Wayne hit it off together very well. They liked each other: it was easy for them to work together, there was mutual respect and they never tried to steal each other's scenes…. It was the first time I'd worked with Mitchum and he's a very, very good actor. He's got no limitations—he can do almost anything. I've always thought he was droll, that he'd be good in a comic role. And he proved it to me in this film without trying to be.

Filmmaker Peter Bogdanovich was a set visitor and he revealed on the film's DVD featurette *Ride, Boldy, Ride*: "Mitchum is the kind of actor who pretended he didn't work at it, pretended he didn't care, and was just sort of phoning it in, and Howard called him out on it. 'You're a lying son of a bitch because you pretend like you don't care, but you work very hard.' And Mitchum said, 'Don't tell anybody.'" Hawks biographer Todd McCarthy revealed on the same featurette, "I think Hawks admired Mitchum for that because he made no big deal out of it, but he was an incredibly hard worker and always there and always delivered the goods…. I think it's a shame that Mitchum didn't make a whole lot more films with Hawks because the cadence, the kind of sly, humorous, kind of sarcastic attitude is perfect."

Film critic Richard Schickel also weighed in on the DVD:

> Mitchum, as everybody who ever worked with him would testify, was one of the hardest working actors on a set that you'll ever find. He was physically strong. He was able to do take after take of difficult action sequences. He really cared.

---

*Garry Armstrong (e-mail correspondence, August 2017).

What he didn't care about was showing you he cared.... I think the pairing of him and John Wayne is a clever one because they're kind of dissimilar. Mitchum is the kind of actor that kind of lies in the reeds a little bit. He's not a man who's going to make an overt statement with his character. He's going to let it kind of emerge as the picture goes along.

Critic Molly Haskell commented, "There's something kind of surly about Mitchum, and he's a little more frightening because he has been a force of power. When he loses it, you really feel that something's dangerous and awry in the world."

John Mitchum commented on the pairing of the stars when interviewed by Tim Lilley for the John Wayne retrospective *Campfire Conversations*: "That was a gem as far as I was concerned when [Wayne] worked on *El Dorado* with my brother, Bob. Of course, the two of them were marvelous together. They had a complete and total respect for each other. The picture went smoothly because the two of them just fit so well together; there were just no big problems. It was kind of fun being on that show, though I didn't have much to do with it. But I did get a chance to observe them all through it." Chris Mitchum said in *Campfire Conversations*, "I think it showed a wonderful ability of my dad to do comedy."

On the set, professional photographer John Hamilton hoped to capture a good, intimate promotional photo of the stars. Wayne and Mitchum sidled up to one another and stared into Hamilton's camera. Hamilton wasn't satisfied and asked them to get a little closer in frame. The stars obliged. Hamilton still wasn't satisfied. He asked if they could inch together even tighter. The stars were nearly on top of one another. Mitchum finally broke everyone on the set up into hysterics when he loudly and ribaldly asked Hamilton if the photographer wanted him to get risqué with Wayne for his camera. When the laughter from the crew died down, Hamilton got the iconic shot of the two stars in tight frame that he had been hoping for. His pictures appear in the fine western movie photo book *Thunder in the Dust*. The stars also posed for publicity photos with their respective mothers Molly and Ann!

Regarding character nuance, a point rarely delved into is Mitchum's reason for descending into drunkenness between Wayne's visits to El Dorado. A few references are made to a no-good saloon girl Mitchum has briefly fallen for—"a wandering petticoat"—who has broken his heart. Charlene Holt mentions that she hasn't seen Mitchum in the few months since Wayne left. He'd stop by occasionally, but she says he seemed quiet and lonely. At the film's beginning, it is established that Holt has had a romantic history with both Mitchum and Wayne. When the latter shows up after many years, she rekindles her fire with Wayne, who plants a big kiss on her lips before leaving again. Mitchum realizes he's lost her. It is highly likely Mitchum is secretly pining for her and soon begins drowning his sorrow in booze. He cares more for Holt than he is willing to let on but respects her decision to align with Wayne. The Mitchum-Holt association has been too casual and non-com-

A grimy Mitchum cleans up in *El Dorado* (1967).

mittal, and Mitchum realizes she has slipped away. He's lost her to his friend. The wandering petticoat is a shield to mask his own unspoken feelings for Holt. Hawks and Mitchum opted to keep this hidden in the subtext, and the film and Mitchum's performance is stronger for it.

Like Wayne in the film (and Chuck Connors on TV's *The Rifleman*), Mitchum used a Winchester 92 rifle with a modified lever. The modification is mentioned in the film. The Winchester has been referred to as "the rifle that won the west," and Mitchum and Wayne contribute to that reputation in *El Dorado*. There's an especially good nighttime action sequence at the Old Mission church with a gunman in the bell tower. During filming, Mitchum trained at his handgun fast draw with noted studio gun coach Rodd Redwing. A bothersome thumb injury led him to holster a SAA Colt Peacemaker throughout the film but use a Colt New Service double action revolver with a dummy ejector rod during action scenes. This switch in firearms allowed him to fire off more shots in a quicker manner for dramatic effect, a deceit that was quite common in films and TV. In one memorable sequence, after the heavies have laughed at his sweat-soaked drunken degradation, Mitchum uses the rifle's butt to jab henchman Jim Davis in the belly. "Laugh now," he taunts, regaining some of his old toughness.

Old Tucson's owner Bob Shelton had a small part in *El Dorado* as one of the outlaws and got to know Mitchum on the film, later renting a piece of local property to the actor. During filming, Mitchum hosted a barbecue party for the cast and crew at his adobe-style house. Interviewed in the *Tucson Citizen,* Shelton remembered Mitchum as a "very professional" actor who behaved like an ordinary guy on the *El Dorado* set: "He was extremely friendly and very professional in his work. He was considerate of people around him. He was a guy who liked to hang out with the other guys, the wranglers in the corral, rather than be with the bigwigs. He was one of the guys I worked with over the years that I really admired. He was a man's man. But the ladies liked him, too, to say the least." Shelton last saw Mitchum in the late 1970s in the lobby of the Beverly Hills Hotel. "I walked over to him and stuck out my hand and said, 'I'm Bob Shelton from Tucson.' He said, 'I know who the hell you are. You don't have to say that.' He was very gracious. Most everybody I know who'd spent any time around him would say that…. I hope everyone understands what a nice man he was. Because he was."

Stuntman turned Arizona location manager Jack Young agrees. "Black Jack" Young doubled Clark Gable and Robert Taylor on several westerns and was a friend of Wayne and Mitchum's stunt double Chuck Roberson. He remembers Mitchum as

> a genuine fellow. A little quiet when you first meet him, but he soon opened up. When we did *El Dorado,* he kept looking at me like he recognized me but wouldn't say anything. I finally mentioned that I worked with him on [*The Wonderful Country*] and he sat back and roared with laughter. I asked what was funny, and he said, "I just realized you are that guy that I stood over and said, 'Shit.'" We had a big laugh. When I was set to double Jimmy Caan getting run over by horses during second unit shooting, he came out to watch. I was very proud of that, because he told Buzz [Henry], the coordinator, "That fucker used to be great. Made my day."*

Stunt coordinator Henry had been a horseback riding child star in films such as *Buzzy Rides the Range* (1940). In *El Dorado,* he appears as the outlaw that Mitchum shoots hiding behind the piano. Chuck Roberson doubled Wayne on the film and appeared as one of Asner's gunmen. Stuntman Dean Smith is the Chris George cohort whose gun can't beat Caan's thrown knife. The film's head wrangler was Gordon Graham Jones, a veteran horse handler who had worked with Wayne and John Ford on *Stagecoach* (1939), *She Wore a Yellow Ribbon* (1949) and *The Searchers* (1956). Jones worked with Hawks and Wayne on *Red River* (1948). Wayne was so fond of Jones' abilities and horse sense that he had him signed to a permanent contract with his Batjac production company. Many of the *El Dorado* wranglers were local hires from the surrounding ranches.

Old Tucson employees like street show gunfighter Kimo Owens worked on *El Dorado*

---

*Jack Young (e-mail correspondence, 2013).

as security, background, stand-ins or filling in for utility stunts. "My dad did a little bit of everything on those John Wayne and Robert Mitchum pictures," Owens' son Cliff says. "He was out there at Old Tucson for 12 or 13 years and was the stunt coordinator for quite a few shows."* Kimo Owens passed away in 1979 after a nighttime motorcycle accident near the Desert Museum, not far from Old Tucson. His funeral was held at the western town, the lone time that's ever been done. In addition to Mitchum's *Young Billy Young* (1969), Kimo's credits include *McLintock!* (1963), *Rio Lobo* (1970), *The Life and Times of Judge Roy Bean* (1972), *The Last Hard Men* (1976), *The Sacketts* (1979) and *Tom Horn* (1980). He also did episodes of *The High Chaparral, Gunsmoke, How the West Was Won* and several of Don Collier's Hubba Bubba gum-fighter commercials.

Howard Hawks gave Wayne an impressive though undersized Appaloosa, Zip Cochise, to ride. Mitchum does not appear on horseback in the finished film, but he did ride a horse during the making of the picture. It belonged to a local stuntman and wrangler named Chuck Henson, a former football player for the University of Arizona who competed in rodeo events at the college in the mid-1950s. Henson eventually became a legend in the rodeo arena for his work as a red-wigged clown distracting bulls for downed cowboys. He was in great demand at rodeos around the country, and by the late 1960s was the go-to man in Hollywood when it came to Brahman and Mexican bulls. The Professional Rodeo Cowboys Association Hall of Famer is best known in Hollywood circles for doubling James Coburn and Slim Pickens in the rodeo film *The Honkers* (1972). He worked primarily in Arizona, doing stunt work and wrangling on such films as *Monte Walsh* (1970), *Rio Lobo* (1970), *The Life and Times of Judge Roy Bean* (1972), *Tom Horn* (1980) and *The Quick and the Dead* (1995). According to Henson,

> Mitchum rode my horse Ironsides in *El Dorado*. Old Ironsides was a really good horse, a champion halter back at the Houston Fat Stock Show. A great horse that originally belonged to my father-in-law. He could do anything. Mitchum really liked that horse of mine. So did Howard Hawks. Hawks hauled him back to Hollywood, and I had a devil of a time getting him back. I got my SAG card on *El Dorado*, and it started a good time for me in the business between rodeos. I worked on *The High Chaparral* and lots of other things at Old Tucson—*Little House on the Prairie, Father Murphy, The Young Riders*. On *El Dorado*, I did some riding with runaways down the middle of the street and a little doubling for a few of the guys. I worked with Mitchum again later in Old Tucson with Angie Dickinson.
>
> Bob was really a nice guy, a great person to work with. He'd hang around the set when he wasn't on camera, holding a horse or whatever or just sitting down to joke and BS with the wranglers and stunt guys. He could ride and was a good hand with horses. He got in trouble a few times with Hawks for talking when they were trying to shoot. When we weren't shooting, we stayed at a hotel in downtown Tucson on that; all the wranglers and stunt guys. We'd hang out at the bar at night and Bob would come in and pick up the tab for everybody, sit down and talk with us. He was really a nice guy—a common, good man—besides being a good actor.†

John Wayne's bodyguard on location for *El Dorado* was John Gammons, the former police chief of Tombstone, Arizona. Gammons served in a similar security capacity for Wayne at Old Tucson on *Rio Bravo* (1959) and *McLintock!* (1963). On the *El Dorado* set, Gammons was assisted by his teenage son Jay. The younger Gammons remembers,

> John Wayne was tough to work with, but he was fair. Robert Mitchum and John Wayne got along fine. There were no problems. Mitchum played the drunken sheriff. There's a scene when he goes to the bar to pick up his nightly bottle. His clothes are a mess. He looks terrible. Ed Asner and Jim Davis, the bad guys, are there and they say, "There's the sheriff, come to get his bottle." Mitchum hangs his head down and walks back out to the street. John Wayne sees him there, and says, "What are you doing in the middle of the street?" Mitchum puts his head down again and goes into the sheriff's office. Now, Mitchum had a hat on in the film that was horrible, all beat up. Well, nobody on the film caught it, but he wore three different hats in that scene. One in the bar,

---

*Cliff "Erik" Owens (phone conversation, April 2018).
†Chuck Henson (phone conversation, August 2017).

one on the street, and one when he entered the sheriff's office. Three different hats that didn't look alike. I asked him about it. I said, "Why did you wear three different hats?" And he said, "'I did it for a joke. Nobody will notice.' And he was right. Nobody noticed!"*

El Dorado reviews were positive with *The Los Angeles Times* opining, "Mitchum has rarely if ever given such an uproarious comic performance." *The Hollywood Reporter* added, "Mitchum is excellent as the drunken sheriff," while *Variety* found him "especially good." *The New York Times* wrote, "Mr. Mitchum is simply wonderful as the whiskey-sodden sheriff.," and *Time* concurred: "As the liquor-laden lawman, Mitchum is a perfect foil for Wayne.... With crutches as swagger sticks, they limp triumphantly past the camera, two old pros demonstrating that they are better on one good leg apiece than most of the younger stars are on two." *Motion Picture Daily* said, "Under Hawks' direction, Wayne and Mitchum play so well together they look like a veteran team," while *The Monthly Film Bulletin* found them "all at the top of their form." *The Hollywood Citizen News* added, "There can be little wrong with a film that features two pros the likes of John Wayne and Robert Mitchum bucking each other from start to finish." According to *Box Office*, "John Wayne and Robert Mitchum are at their professional peak, which is hard to top in or out of a western."

The *Times-Picayune* noted,

> The saddle now fits Wayne like a second skin. Laconic, lazy-eyed Mitchum is much more at home in old Arizona than he is in any modern environment Hollywood digs up for him. As a couple of old cronies who reunite from opposite sides of the law to set things straight in El Dorado, the two are irresistibly appealing.... The combination of John Wayne and Robert Mitchum is lagniappe. James Bond does it now with technology. The Hollywood veterans do it with pistols and personality.

The *Plain Dealer* focused on Mitchum:

> [He] could make millions playing only westerns, as he has that same look and touch for the oat-burners as Wayne. It was once said that Mitchum could look the part of a saddle tramp better than anyone in movies and few would deny it. Once he gets that sleepy-eyed look going and starts rubbing a stubble and beard and yawning and scratching, Mitchum's hard to beat.

Cowboys & Indians places the film in their top 100 westerns: "Wayne, Robert Mitchum and James Caan play the familiar material with a wink to each other and to the audience that is irresistible." Among contemporary sources, Herb Fagen's *Encyclopedia of Westerns* notes, "The real joy is watching Wayne and Mitchum work together."

Howard Hawks was especially impressed by the professionalism of his stars on location and talked up the veteran duo upon the film's release, telling the *Hollywood Citizen-News*, "Duke and Mitch are twice as old as the young he-men today, but they're ten times the men the kids are. And it isn't the age that does it. They're both good actors. They're both real men. They've got authority. Give me the Waynes and the Mitchums every time. They're about the last of the tough guys."

During the making of *El Dorado*, Mitchum shared several belts of liquor with the hard-drinking Wayne, who as a total professional was known as an after-hours drinker. Even following late nights, Wayne was habitually the first man on the set come morning. When filming of *El Dorado* was completed, Wayne and Mitchum continued their association as drinking buddies, getting together occasionally to down a bottle or two of Wild Turkey bourbon or Sauza Conmemorativo Tequila. "I was happy to be with my pal Duke Wayne," Mitchum told the nostalgic magazine *Memories*. At a party one evening at Olive Carey's, they impressed director John Ford when they matched one another to the tune of 22 martinis apiece. At Frank Sinatra's Palm Springs compound, they drank until the morning sun with William Holden and Glenn Ford. Mitchum recalled being in a saloon when the 6'4", 245-pound Duke lost his balance and fell into a cowboy line-up, knocking over everyone like a row of dominos. Another time, they crashed a lavish black-tie party at producer Ray

---

*Jay Gammons (phone conversation, August 2017).

Stark's home, given for Barbra Streisand upon the release of her film *Funny Girl* (1968). In his autobiography, assistant director Paul Helmick recalls meeting them at the door, asking incredulously, "What are you two *cowboys* doing here?"

Wayne told biographer Michael Munn, "In recent years, I've worked in partnership with only three actors who I could honestly say I had a chemistry with. One was Dean Martin. One was Mitchum. The third was Kirk [Douglas]." There was talk of originally pairing Wayne and Mitchum in *Rio Bravo* (1959), *The Alamo* (1960) and the rollicking *North to Alaska* (1960), but those match-ups fell through, as did other potentialities. The eventual on-screen teaming of Wayne and Mitchum in *El Dorado* was deemed so successful that Hawks called on Mitchum a few years later to appear with Wayne in the western *Rio Lobo* (1970). But Mitchum was tied up in Ireland making *Ryan's Daughter* (1970) for David Lean. Hawks subsequently retooled Mitchum's *Rio Lobo* character into the one portrayed by Mexican action star Jorge Rivero. "It didn't help a bit not having Mitchum," Hawks told Peter Bogdanovich. "It's definitely a story built for two strong characters and we didn't have them, so we couldn't do it."

The idea of pairing Wayne and Mitchum for the elegiac western *Monte Walsh* (1970) was under consideration before Lee Marvin and Jack Palance signed on as the aging cowpokes. For several years, mutual friend Budd Boetticher had in development a script titled *When There's Sumpthin' to Do*, that was to have starred Wayne and Mitchum as American adventurers south of the border during the Mexican Revolution.

But the two stars never reteamed, a genuine disappointment considering Mitchum told Michael Munn, "We had the time of our lives working together." Interestingly, Mitchum and Wayne each claimed they wanted to be remembered by the Spanish phrase "Feo, fuerte, y formal": "He was ugly, strong, and had dignity." In the spring of 1979, with the Duke in ill health, Barry Goldwater sponsored a bill for Wayne to receive a special Congressional Gold Medal of Honor. Among those contributing words on behalf of Wayne to the Subcommittee of Consumer Affairs were cowboy stars Randolph Scott, James Stewart, Ronald Reagan, Gregory Peck, Glenn Ford, William Holden, Kirk Douglas, Ben Johnson, Forrest Tucker and Robert Mitchum.

Mitchum wrote of Wayne's sterling character:

> In a nation so young as ours we are blessed with far more globally popular heroes than ogres. Our mighty oak of state grows with the names of those who have defined for history the value of principle in a humane society. As these principles are tested and adopted, we broaden understanding of ourselves. As an advocate in the field of understanding, John Wayne is unique. His gifted projection of the virtues of justice and equality, purpose and determination and forthright honesty have affected the American image all over the world. His living testimony to his spoken beliefs contributes respect to that image. Under the magnifying lens of mass scrutiny, he has unfailingly delivered as promised. Without hesitation or exception, he loyally defends his reasons with reason and example. He has helped stamp the American brand on goods and custom universally welcomed. With strength to inspire, he shares charity with the weak. As an institution he represents the rock-solid faith of our founders, in the American dream. As a man, he has achieved his place with dignity. A sturdy bough indeed, the Duke, so stands our mighty oak.

The Way West (United Artists, 1967)

Cast: Kirk Douglas (Senator William J. Tadlock); Robert Mitchum (Dick Summers); Richard Widmark (Lije Evans); Lola Albright (Rebecca Evans); Sally Field (Mercy McBee); Katherine Justice (Amanda Mack); Jack Elam (Preacher Weatherby); Stubby Kaye (Sam Fairman); Michael McGreevey (Brownie Evans); Harry Carey, Jr. (Mr. McBee); Connie Sawyer (Mrs. McBee); Michael Witney (Johnnie Mack); William Lundigan (Michael Moynihan); Elizabeth Fraser (Mrs. Fairman); John Mitchum (Little Henry); Patric Knowles (Capt. Grant); Hal Lynch (Big Henry); Timothy Scott (Middle Henry); Roy Glenn (Saunders); Paul Lukather (Mr. Turley); Stefan Arngrim (William J. Tadlock, Jr.); Roy Barcroft (Mr. Masters); Eve McVeagh (Mrs. Masters); Peggy Stewart (Mrs. Turley); Anne Barton (Mrs. Moynihan); Nick Cravat (Calvelli); Michael Keep (Indian Brave); Michael Lane (Sioux Chief); and Jack Coffer, Everett Creach, Mike Dilley, Sam Elliott, Clarke Gordon, John Harris, Hollis Hill, Jonathan Hoffman, Alma Massey Humbird, William "Smokey" Humbird, Mike Letz, Dawn Little Sky, Eddie Little Sky, Tom Mills, Gary Morris, Ken Murray, Mitchell

Scholars, Hector Smith, Rex Trailer, Arlie Troupe, Lorie Troupe, Paul Wexler.

Crew: Andrew V. McLaglen (Director); Harold Hecht (Producer); Ben Maddow and Mitchell Lindemann (Screenplay); William H. Clothier (Photographer); Bronislau Kaper (Music); Edward S. Haworth (Art Director); Otho S. Lovering (Editor); Gordon T. Dawson and Edna Taylor (Wardrobe); Terry Morse, Jr. (Assistant Director); Tom Coleman (Prop Master); May Boss, Jim Burk, Roydon Clark, Jack Coffer, Nick Cravat, Everett Creach, Gary McLarty, Hal Needham, Eual Whiteman (Stunts); William B. "Billy" Jones (Livestock Coordinator); John Treadwell, Wayne Cutlip (Wranglers).

122 minutes; Released May 24, 1967

"Between movies, I try hard to avoid the next one," Mitchum told *The New York Daily News*. It was true that he valued the pay and the creative filmmaking process, but the idea of committing to anything except an interesting locale was beyond the ingrained nature of his being. He was a rover, and many scripts he read provoked no excitement. Even the prospect of headlining George Roy Hill's epic *Hawaii* (1966), cameoing as General George S. Patton in the World War II comedy *Is Paris Burning?* (1966) or co-starring with Paul Newman in a project as high-quality as *Cool Hand Luke* (1967) couldn't get him to sign on. In 1966 alone, there was a proposed MGM remake of *Red Dust* (1932) opposite Ann-Margret; a Boer War flick with Rod Taylor, *The War Horses*, and a John D. MacDonald–scribed adventure titled *Bimini Gal* that was transported to Hawaii and became the unmemorable *Kona Coast* (1968). Richard Boone took the latter role after Mitchum declined. Mitchum had earlier backed out of Frank Sinatra's directorial debut in the World War II film *None but the Brave* (1965) and was replaced by *Cheyenne* TV star Clint Walker. John Huston wanted him to star opposite Richard Burton in *The Man Who Would Be King* and producer Joel Freeman sought him for a musical version of *Tom Sawyer*. Mitchum couldn't get enthused about any of it.

Upon completing the principal filming of *El Dorado*, Mitchum traveled to Vietnam to visit soldiers in the jungle fighting the spread of Communism. It was the first of two such goodwill trips he made. Traveling to a controversial war zone was apparently preferable in his mind to anything Hollywood had to offer. Not seeming to give a damn regarding his own safety, he'd be transported in open Jeeps or fly around in Huey helicopters. He slung a rifle over his shoulder and fired off an M-79 grenade launcher with the 101st Airborne in Tuy Hoa. Mitchum dropped into the hottest areas for the chance to commiserate with the men. Sharing beer and cigarettes with the grunts, he'd write down names and phone numbers, then contact the young men's parents. It gave him plenty of new life experience to draw from and created more tall tales for gullible journalists. He'd tell reporters he was on CIA missions. Anything to hide his real reasons for being there.

Marine Corps veteran Ron Irwin recalled Mitchum in his memoir *Live Die Live Again*:

> Unlike any other celebrity who visited Vietnam during the war, Bob Mitchum was not there for publicity. He was not surrounded by photographers, lackeys or even military protection. Bob Mitchum had come to Vietnam just to see how us troops were doing and greet as many as he could man to man. His true character has stayed with me and has often inspired me throughout my life. Whatever else Bob Mitchum did or did not do in his Hollywood career, in Vietnam he was a genuine man and he brought significant happiness to a whole lot of America's fighting men.

Senior military advisor H.N. Benham backed up Irwin's assertion. Benham shared a bottle of Scotch with Mitchum in a bivouac tent in Vietnam and told *The Mesa Tribune*: "He was there visiting the troops trying to boost morale. He had a fabulous memory. He asked me for my wife's phone number. When he got back to the States, he called her to say I was okay. Later on I found out he did the same thing for lots of the men he met. He paid for the calls himself. What can I say but that Robert Mitchum was a helluva guy." Marine artillery officer Earl J. Gorman also encountered Mitchum and shared his memory in *Fire Mission: The World of Nam*: "As a great actor and true celebrity, Mr. Mitchum's visit provided some excitement. Impressed by his icon status and his down-to-earth demeanor, the guys couldn't get enough of him. Friendly with the Marines, he slid onto a barstool to drink a beer with the group clus-

On location in Oregon as trail scout Dick Summers in *The Way West* (1967).

tered at the bar and shared upbeat stories that entertained us. The hissing sound of popping open a beer can united our small fraternity for a movie moment."

Before leaving for Asia, Mitchum and Dorothy discussed the ongoing costs of maintaining the Maryland homestead. Having been permanently 86ed from his favorite bar at the Tidewater Inn, he blithely told her she could sell the farm if she was that concerned about the everyday costs of spraying crops and feeding livestock. He was beginning to think a ranch in Arizona or New Mexico suited him better anyway. Upon landing in Hawaii and phoning home, he was surprised to learn that Dorothy sold Belmont Farm and they were moving back to California to reside in Bel Air. The expensive horses would need to be moved and stabled. Mitchum, in a state of semi-retirement, decided he needed to go back to work to raise some money for this endeavor. He checked in with Reva Frederick and agent-manager George "Bullets" Durgom for any potential script properties ready to go. They informed him that producer Harold Hecht was moving forward on *The Way West*, an adaptation of A.B. Guthrie's Pulitzer Prize–winning frontier-spirit novel that Burt Lancaster had optioned for years. Mitchum was more than familiar with the story. It was one of his favorite books, and "Bud" Guthrie happened to be a friend. In 1951, Mitchum was set to star as two-fisted trapper Jim Deakins in Howard Hawks' filmization of Guthrie's novel *The Big Sky*. Mitchum respect fully pulled out of the project when Guthrie expressed concern over the screenplay deviating from his novel.

Mitchum went to lunch with Hecht, learning that his own *Out of the Past* (1947) co-star Kirk Douglas was set to star in the film alongside Richard Widmark. The three-star combo would provide plenty of box office clout. Douglas, who coincidentally took on the part Mitchum would have played in *The Big Sky*, would play megalomaniacal Senator William Tadlock, originator of the 1843 Great Migration push west over 2170 rough miles from Independence, Missouri, to Oregon City, Oregon, documented in Guthrie's story. The other two leading parts were that of a veteran trail scout with failing eyesight and a married farmer enticed by the promise of fertile land and uncut timber, who begins challenging Douglas for leadership. Hecht asked Mitchum which role he wanted to play, and the star casually said he didn't care. Hecht was incredulous. He had never come across an actor who disregarded screen time or his number of lines. When prodded, Mitchum opted for the part of trail scout Dick Summers. Fewer lines to learn, he reasoned, and more time outdoors. Less interaction with the egotistical and competitive Douglas. He'd let Richard Widmark deal with that. The unencumbered Mitchum would offer a few sage words of wisdom, then wander off to the nearest river between takes to cast his fishing line. The part of the seasoned pathfinder was a natural fit. Guthrie's own words describe Summers as possessing "an easy slouch in the saddle" and a "half-sad smile that showed just a little of what he might be thinking."

Under the helm of director Andrew V. McLaglen, the movie was set to film on location with the cast and crew vividly recreating the epic struggle of the early settlers' journey over grasslands, desert and mountains from the Great Plains to the Rockies. Veteran cinematographer William H. Clothier stood behind the lens, guaranteeing that the vast land was captured in all its splendor. The beautiful state of Oregon stood in for several points along the Oregon Trail. The meeting between Mitchum and the Indians was filmed in Central Oregon at the natural 265-foot tall monolith called Fort Rock. The film's major river crossing took place on the banks of the Willamette. The buffalo herd encounter occurred at the Ponderosa Ranch 35 miles east of Burns. The desert scenes were at Shifting Sands, and the daunting mountain crossing took place at the 7700-foot-tall crest of Mount Bachelor. Some of these locations were only accessible via ski lift or helicopter. There would be filming at the Crooked River Gorge and the Deschutes River, with the production headquartered in the cities of Eugene in the Willamette Valley and Bend in the Deschutes National Forest.

McLaglen spent years working as an assistant under John Ford, William Wellman and Budd Boetticher, eventually sharpening his directorial skills on dozens of episodes of TV's *Gunsmoke* and *Have Gun—Will Travel*. He directed John Wayne in *McLintock!* (1963) and James Stewart in *Shenandoah* (1965) and *The Rare Breed* (1966). McLaglen was well-liked and economical, and the big stars didn't have a problem working with him. But McLaglen lacked the scope and artistic vision of his mentors. His films are genuinely rugged adventures with colorful casts, but nothing on his résumé is deemed a classic. Interestingly, McLaglen did not have an affinity for filming westerns. It was simply the way his career worked out.

The Way West starts off well but quickly becomes a meandering and disappointing misfire. The scenery is impressive, as is the dangerous attempts to cross and film it in continuity. Most of the cast, Mitchum included, are lowered down the face of a mountain in a sling. Even some of the livestock are lowered. When they filmed this sequence, one of the animals began defecating in midair, and the crowd assembled below scrambled for cover! Some serious mishaps occurred. An assistant cameraman was injured and trapped on a rocky ledge, and stunt ace Hal Needham had to rappel down to rescue him. Actress Lola Albright was knocked unconscious when her wagon overturned crossing the river, and she spent a night in the hospital. Mitchum accumulated his usual quota of bumps and bruises along the way.

There are solid moments here and there, courtesy of the steely contributions of Widmark and Mitchum, but overall, it's not a good

In buckskin and domed Indian hat in *The Way West* (1967).

film. The sprawling picture is weighed down by poor supporting acting and extraneous subplots. Kirk Douglas gives a grating central performance as the opportunistic visionary obsessed with making it across the land as quickly as possible even at the cost of lives. Douglas was best when he could smile and milk charm on screen to balance his own penchant for scene-stealing histrionics. Here he's in full teeth-clenching mode from the get-go, which turns to self-hatred midway through the story when his pushiness causes the death of his own son Stefan Arngrim. It's the type of self-loathing character Charlton Heston specialized in playing. (Heston was attached to the role before Douglas came on board.)

In the film's opening, Douglas convinces Mitchum's scout to join him by reasoning even more lives will be lost without Mitchum's experience leading the way. Mitchum is reluctant, but eventually gives in for the sake of the many families hoping for a better life. Director McLaglen complained about the studio demanding over 20 minutes of the rambling film's beginning be cut, taking out valuable character motivation, but his poor handling of the crowd scenes and soap opera subplots suggests tighter editing might have benefited the story's labored pacing. It simply needs more action, and after several seasons of TV's *Wagon Train* (1957–1965) the basic storyline of settlers moving west had become clichéd. During filming, cast and crew thought they were turning out a classic. Ever the wise cynic, Mitchum knew better. The script had problems with the myriad subplots, but it wasn't his place to offer change. He'd do the job he was contracted for. "I'd like to just get it done and get away," he told Richard Schickel for *Sound on Film*. "I suppose I just sharpen it up and do it as quickly as I can and as well as I can. But, I am inclined to overlook things."

Photogenically, the Mitchum visage was holding up, as was the physique. The horseback riding and farm work kept him in reasonable shape, but co-stars such as Polly Bergen from *Cape Fear* remembered Mitchum exercising constantly when not on camera. "The studios pay me a lot of money," he wrote in the *Desert Sun*. "So, I preserve the figure." Mitchum's character is a widower after the death of his Indian wife. He looks the part of a man of the wilderness clad in a worn green shirt, buckskin pants, moccasins and Indian necklace. The buckskin wardrobe recalls his *Rachel and the Stranger* character plus 20 years of hard trail. This film's costumer Gordon Dawson was a veteran of Sam Peckinpah's *Major Dundee* (1965) and two years away from expertly dressing *The Wild Bunch* (1969). Some of this film's western costumes were found and recycled from what was available in the various studio vaults or Western Costume in North Hollywood. Mitchum shared a story with Garry Armstrong involving his tight, itchy wardrobe from *The Way West* and supporting player William Lundigan's association with another western released in 1939:

> I wasn't thrilled with buckskin at this point in my life. The stuff chafed and scratched in the worst places. The first buckskin outfit they gave me was way too small and smelled funny. It was dry-cleaned, I think, but still stunk to me. I got the wardrobe guy and he apologized. Told me he'd get me another buckskin outfit.... Then Lundy walks into my trailer grinnin' like a cheetah. What the fuck now, I wondered? "Mitch, I know that buck

skin," he said. "I know it. It's old, very old, man." Anyway, I'm staring Lundy down. He's laughing his ass off. He reminds me he was in *Dodge City* with Mr. Errol Flynn a thousand years ago. "So, big deal, Lundy. I know you worked with *Mr.* Flynn. So, what?" It hits me. They'd given me goddamn *Mr.* Errol Flynn's buckskin from *Dodge City*. I kind of doped out what the stains and smells were.

Upon examination, Mitchum found the initials E.F. stenciled into the buckskin's crotch.*

Mitchum wears an unbecoming domed hat throughout the picture, in contrast to his co-stars whose Stetsons are carefully creased and wrinkled for the camera. The high crown Mitchum sports was at least functional, as it served to keep the head cool. It should be noted that Mitchum displayed a curious affinity for unusual headwear in his westerns. Randolph Scott wore the same shapely Stetson in two dozen features, as did James Stewart and Audie Murphy for their westerns. Glenn Ford wore a turned-up Jaxonbilt, while John Wayne favored an anachronistic Resistol with a pinched-front. Mitchum, on the other hand, wore everything under the sun. He donned the Panama Hat in *Bandido* (1956), the Mexican sombrero in *The Wonderful Country* (1959) and a dirty, battered Stetson in *El Dorado* (1967). In *Pursued* (1947), *River of No Return* (1954) and *Villa Rides* (1968), he rarely bothered wearing a hat to keep the glare out of his eyes. Mitchum's contemporary Lee Marvin always remarked that he found his own characters through the wardrobe, and it seems that Mitchum might have cottoned to that idea.

The saddle that Mitchum used in the film was the property of stunt coordinator Hal Needham and was originally designed at San Fernando Valley Saddlery by leather makers Cliff Ketchum and Art Hugenberger. When Needham moved into directing, he stored the special stunt saddle with removable horn at Stevie Myers' Picture Barn before it was passed down to a new generation. Wrangler-stuntman Darwin Mitchell and stunt artist Joe Pepper used the well-worn Needham saddle in *Wild Wild West* (1999), *Hidalgo* (2004) and *The Far Side of Jericho* (2006). Pepper took great delight in spotting his saddle being used by Mitchum in *The Way West* and by John Wayne in *The Undefeated* (1969) and *Rio Lobo* (1970). "That saddle is worth more to me than diamonds or gold," he told *Shop Talk*. "It gives me goose bumps to see the saddle in a film with those guys."

Mitchum's character Dick Summers has a solitary but ideal existence living outdoors by the river in Missouri, his fishing pole constantly in the water as he ruminates on his increasing age and failing vision. Prodded out of his self-imposed hibernation, he proves that he's still capable of crossing the rugged land on his buckskin quarter horse and negotiating with combative Indian tribes. The horse was Mitchum's Cap-Gun, beginning a late 1960s trend where he provided his own familiar mount. Mitchum's personal horses would be used in *Young Billy Young* (1969) and *The Good Guys and the Bad Guys* (1969).

In *The Way West*, Mitchum speaks several lines in the Sioux language. He picked up the dialogue from co-star Eddie Little Sky, a real-life Oglala Lakota cast in the film as an Indian brave and retained as a technical advisor. Little Sky's wife Dawn also worked on the production. In the early 1970s, Mitchum was invited to speak on the Sioux tribe's behalf at Wounded Knee, but he felt his celebrity would detract from the message. "If I'd been anonymous, I might have gone," he told Roderick Mann in 1973.

One observation that can be gleaned from Mitchum's overall western output is that in his choice of material, he was largely sympathetic to the American Indian. Perhaps due to his own Blackfoot lineage, he rarely opposed savage Indians on screen. The bad guys in his westerns, when they weren't Mitchum himself, were largely Caucasian outlaws or Mexican ool diers. He was inducted into the Shoshone tribe by Chief Owanahea in the late 1940s as part of RKO's publicity machine. In *The Way West*, his character has been married to a Blackfoot Indian and justifies why the Sioux will make war on the wagon train after a young native boy is

---

*Garry Armstrong (e-mail correspondence, November 2018).

needlessly killed by foolhardy settler Michael Witney. Mitchum does what needs to be done to save the wagon train, using his experience to outsmart the natives, but he doesn't suddenly draw out his rifle and begin picking them off their horses. The Indians here are presented in a manner that attempts to understand their society and culture, likely a reason Mitchum was attracted to the project. Outside of *Rachel and the Stranger* and *River of No Return,* Mitchum's films do not present Native Americans as a stereotypically faceless enemy meant to be mowed down in mass carnage.

Interviewer William Wolf managed to get Mitchum to reveal some of his feelings regarding his Native American ancestors in a syndicated 1972 piece:

> We shouldn't treat Indians as a minority group. After all, they own the joint. It was their country and they're the ones who were rooted up and plundered, with everyone taking a crack at it—the Dutch, the French, the Spanish, you name them.... Indians have no great power. They are proud people, simple in their worldliness. They're not degenerates, they are not subversives. But they are treated as if they were. Indians should administer themselves and not be subjected to the vast bureaucracy that outnumber them. They should determine their own future and take charge of their own lives. The Bureau of Indian Affairs should inform the public of the true character of the Indians, and the Bureau should be run by the Indians.

As befits his on-screen character, Mitchum seems a largely reluctant contributor to the film's action, save for a silly chase scene where he and Widmark wear identical clothing to confuse the Indians chasing them in circles. He has a brief fight with stuntman Jim Burk after his double Roydon Clark executes a saddle fall. Near the film's end, Mitchum takes several healthy swings with an axe to bring down a tree to create a raft. But mostly he is ruggedly sedentary, sitting astride his horse and staring into the distance. Witness an early fistfight with cattlemen in the river where Mitchum is the last fighter to join the fray. He had two buckskin costumes courtesy of wardrobe and took turns hanging them out to dry between takes. The Willamette River was a chilly 50 degrees, but Mitchum spent more than an hour in the water doing the fight for the cameras (he was wearing wetsuit bottoms under his buckskin trousers to keep from becoming hypothermic). Later, when Douglas and Widmark's characters come to blows, Mitchum is slow to intervene. He is the group's real leader as the trail scout, but at the same time an observer of few words who doesn't buck Douglas' authoritarian rule. He leaves that to Widmark's farmer, who towards the end of the picture takes over the role of vocal leader from Douglas. The contradiction is worthy of Mitchum's by now well-established screen image. The ending is pure Mitchum. The wagon train arrives at its destination, and he turns around to ride off alone the other way to live out his last dim years.

Looking increasingly leathery and sunbaked, Mitchum remains a stalwart, broad-shouldered Rock of Gibraltar. He brings a sly sense of humor to the part. He takes on stowaway preacher Jack Elam as his legal mate, justifying Elam's spot on the wagon train's roster. Mitchum and Elam swear their oaths on a Bible in perfunctory fashion. This was one of the first roles that helped soften Elam's image from vicious screen heavy of *Rawhide* (1951) and *Gunfight at the O.K. Corral* (1957) to the comic character type that stole the show in *Support Your Local Sheriff* (1969) and *Rio Lobo* (1970). Elam told the *Augusta Chronicle* that early in his career, he drew parallels between himself and Mitchum. "When I did *Rawhide,* I was under contract to Fox Studios," Elam said. "I thought, like Mitchum, I'd go from tough guys to leading men." Elam became so fond of the Oregon scenery that he retired to Eugene when his career wound down. Douglas and Widmark stayed in rented homes during filming, but Mitchum chose to bunk with the wranglers and the stuntmen in a more primitive setting.

Between scenes, Mitchum could be found walking around shirtless, cigarette dangling from his lips, and sunglasses covering his eyes. The epitome of laidback cool. Young actress Sally Field was on her first film location and recalls Mitchum's mysterious loner quality in her autobiography. "I was crazy about Bob Mitchum," she writes, "even though I could barely understand a word he said." Mitchum would sidle up to Field, lean down and mumble in low conspiratorial tones what she understood to be career encouragement. Once he made her a sandwich slathered in mustard and presented it to her. Then he stood in apparently approving silence watching her eat. Twenty years later, when Field won a People's Choice Award as Best Actress, Mitchum approached her table and said simply, "Told you so." At least that's what Field thinks he said.

John Hinterberger of *The Seattle Daily Times* was a set visitor who observed the curious contrast between the professional Mitchum and his public image as the mythical bad man

Shirtless and wearing sunglasses, watching co-star Sally Field skip rope on location in this publicity photograph from *The Way West* (1967).

of ill temperament. "Mitchum is not the kind of actor who trades on his star status," Hinterberger wrote. "He gives no trouble on the set. There are no fits of temper. When he has finished a scene, he usually stays around to socialize with the actors, extras and technicians. In fact, the easiest way to find Mitchum is to look for the biggest gathering of people. He is generally in the middle of the group. The group is generally smiling."

Mitchum's brother John portrayed one of the settlers. Other buddies like Harry Carey, Jr., and Roy Barcroft were also on the picture. On a few evenings, the Mitchums played their guitars and sang folk tunes. Robert led all-night revelries and poker fests among the cast and crew staying at the Maverick Motel. Columnist Dick Kleiner attended one such night, taking notes on soggy napkins regarding Mitchum's wide-ranging discourse on esoteric worldly facts. Cast member Ken Murray shot 16mm home movies of Mitchum. The footage found its way into *Ken Murray's Shooting Stars* (1979), a compilation of behind-the-scenes encounters from Murray's long career. Some of the crew teased Mitchum about his long hair, likening him to the Dick Tracy comic strip character Gravel Gertie. Mitchum took it in good humor.

In stark contrast to Mitchum's *laissez-faire* on-screen attitude, Kirk Douglas dominates the film with his histrionics. Various sources contend that he was a force to be reckoned with on the set, constantly attempting to change dialogue to his favor and at one point even grabbing Widmark by the arm while trying to direct him in a scene. Widmark nearly punched Douglas, but Mitchum stepped in to tell a long-winded parable about actors who overstepped their bounds in thinking they were directors. Mitchum's story defused the situation, as Douglas was wary around his larger, more dangerous-by-reputation co-star. Mitchum reckoned it would take one blow "between the horns" to silence Douglas and end his cocky strutting.

Everything was a competition with Douglas vying to come off best, even if it meant having crew members build a ramp for him to stand on, so that he could look taller co-stars in the eye. He tried pulling that with John Wayne in *The War Wagon* (1967). Twenty years earlier he had attempted to underplay Mitchum when they were sending smoke signals back and forth on the screen as opponents in *Out of the Past*. Douglas was still at it, and Mitchum couldn't have cared less. He didn't need a bagful of actor's tricks to be interesting on screen. When Mitchum was presented with any Douglas script changes, he'd calmly wad them up and discard them, reasoning he could have pulled the same shenanigans. On more than one occasion when Mitchum was joking with crew members, he overheard Douglas preaching from a distance there would be no levity on the set. When Mitchum turned his eye to Douglas, he'd see his co-star smiling a cocksure grin. Mitchum finally asked the stuntmen which crew member was putting up with the Douglas crap. They informed him that it was Mitchum whom Douglas was speaking to from afar. Mitchum had a laugh at that and the levity continued. Reporter Alex Freeman picked up on the animosity between the stars, writing: "Mitchum gets credit for being the first person to calm the fiery Kirk's famed temper without a shouting match. Mitch simply froze Kirk with a look that wasn't guaranteed to see them part pals but would certainly reduce Kirk's raving demands to a whimper from the second he saw the threat in Mitch's eyes."

Interviewed in *The Westerners*, Andrew V. McLaglen commented on directing the three stars:

> It happened to be easy for me. Widmark is a terrific guy; he's a friend of mine. Mitchum was Mitchum. Everything was okay with Bob. My main concern at the beginning of that picture was working with Kirk, because with *Spartacus* and all that, his tough reputation preceded him. But on *Way West* he couldn't have been easier. I felt a little bit of tension, but Bob didn't let it out too much, between Mitchum and Douglas, but Douglas never gave me any big guff at all.

On handling a director's cues, Mitchum told the *Eugene Register-Guard,* "I'm just like a horse. They point you in a direction and tell you what to say and what to do, and I go." Douglas diplomatically told the wire services, "Bob was a very talented actor with a unique style."

Co-star Widmark talked to *Film Comment* regarding Mitchum, saying, "He was a good actor, and he'd never admit it. A complex guy." Widmark was a longtime acquaintance from Mandeville Canyon with whom Mitchum would share a drink or food on location when the mood dictated. Even then, Widmark recalled what a loner Mitchum could be. For an entire week, both men stayed in an old motel near a remote location, so they wouldn't need to be helicoptered in and out daily. In the evening they dined in a small restaurant. Mitchum would enter, say hello to Widmark, then sit in the corner to eat by himself. On their final night, Mitchum knocked on Widmark's door and invited him to dinner. They had an enjoyable evening together. "Who knew why Bob did anything?" Widmark told *The Advocate*. Despite their collective A-list status, the stars did not require tux and tail dining establishments for their after-hours socializing. Mitchum recalled, "Dick Widmark and I practiced our fight scenes at a little hole in the wall place that smelled like urine."*

The film took three months to shoot (June to September 1966). In addition to buffalo, cattle and oxen, the production included 100 horses, 50 Conestoga wagons and 200 Indian extras from the Warm Springs Reservation. An Oregon local by the name of Sam Elliott worked on the film as an extra. The experience convinced the rangy young man to journey to Hollywood where he joined this film's Michael Witney to portray popular cowboy pitchmen for Falstaff Beer in the early 1970s. Elliott became one of the last great western actors in TV films like *The Sacketts* (1979), *Wild Times* (1980) and *Conagher* (1991), as well as the feature *Tombstone* (1993).

Two other locals of note were the husband-and-wife team of William "Smokey" Humbird and his wife Alma Massey. "Smokey" was known as Oregon's Man of the Past, producing period reenactments and gunfight shows in front of the Barlow Saloon in the small western town Frontier Village in Damascus. The TV series *Have Gun—Will Travel* filmed episodes in Oregon, and star Richard Boone took a liking to "Smokey" and his handlebar mustache, ensuring that he was cast in more than one segment. The Humbirds were hired for the duration of the *Way West* shoot as a pioneer couple. During breaks in filming, they had the opportunity to mingle and take photos with the stars. Of the three main actors, Mitchum proved the friendliest and most accessible, posing for pictures and signing autographs for the Humbirds. Mitchum sat with the pair at lunch and invited Alma to ride with him in his pickup truck to the top of the Crooked River Gorge, saving her a long uphill walk. Alma wrote in her memoir *The Humbird's Reel Stories*:

> Robert Mitchum was a very nice person. Smokey and I got along very well with him. He enjoyed talking about fishing and all the beautiful scenery. One day while he was fishing between shots, Smokey and I stopped by for a brief visit with him. He showed us the fish he had already caught and said he would bring us some fish to eat the next day. Sure enough, he did bring us the fish…. He asked how Smokey and I liked being on location. I told him we both enjoyed it very much. He then said, "I watch you and Smokey whenever action is called, and you two sure do look and act like real pioneers. I also enjoy the way you two always hold hands whenever you're on the move."

One complicated scene would have turned out disastrously for Alma were it not for Mitchum's presence. In her book, she related:

> When action was called, we pioneers were dancing out in the fort yard, while Kirk Douglas and the Scotchman stood talking in front of the camera. The next shot was of a flaming arrow as it shot through the air. Then a shot of all the people running in all directions to their wagons. I started out running in one direction but got turned around because of a pair of horses coming right at me, causing me to run in a different direction. By this time, I really didn't know where I was running. This is where I ran into Robert Mitchum. "We meet again, Alma," he laughed…. He then headed me in the right direction. At that time, I don't know what I would have done if he hadn't helped me out. This was a dangerous scene as horses, oxen, mules and people were all running in the darkness, not really seeing where they were going. No one cared for any retakes. Thank goodness it was a take.

In Oregon, Mitchum made a surprise appearance at the Christmas Valley Lodge to present trophies to reigning rodeo queens

---

*Garry Armstrong (e-mail correspondence, August 2017).

Sandy Dollarhide and Linda Kittredge. The cast and crew put on a Cancer Fund charity benefit in Bend. Kirk Douglas met and interacted with fans on the golf course, while Mitchum and the stuntmen created a wild west show featuring a multitude of stunt falls and fights. Mitchum wasn't always so giving, especially to the press. A surviving video interview from local TV station KGW shows him reticent and less than forthcoming in answering questions about the film. After all, he was intercepted on his way to the latrine. When Londoner William Hall of BBC Radio asked him on set if westerns had changed since the Hopalong Cassidy films, a deadpan Mitchum's reply was, "Guess not. Horses still shit the same end." Mitchum then attracted attention by loudly suggesting Hall had propositioned him. A flummoxed Hall finally realized that Mitchum was pulling his leg. That evening, the star treated the Brit to dinner at the Maverick restaurant and gave him an in-depth interview for being a good sport.

Locals in Eugene were still talking about the hell-raising that Mitchum and William Holden did 20 years earlier during the making of *Rachel and the Stranger*, but *The Way West* proceeded largely without incident. There was an altercation with a local cowboy in Bend whose female friend propositioned Mitchum as he was having a steak dinner at the Copper Room. When Mitchum declined her ribald invite, the cowboy intervened, demanding an apology for the perceived slight to her honor. The cowboy followed Mitchum to the parking lot and stood defiantly in front of the actor's truck talking up a storm. Mitchum measured the man as all hat and no cattle and neutralized him with a single blow. Brother John knew city attorney Bill Holmes from his time spent in Bend making episodes of *Have Gun—Will Travel*, and the belligerent local was persuaded to drop his threat of pressing charges against Bob. Whenever he entered a new town, Mitchum recommended the first order of business should be meeting the local chief of police. "Brother Robert is a paradox," John Mitchum wrote in *Them Ornery Mitchum Boys*. "He is as tender as a buttercup with children, old people and the needy; but he is hard as steel with those he feels are power-hungry or callous toward others."

The Way West began a solid if unspectacular string of films for Mitchum, several of them westerns. His 1960s output was defined largely by mediocrity, but he didn't seem to care as the New Hollywood was more about making business deals. He was in his early 50s now, well past the age of relevance for his Hollywood ilk. Interestingly, he was being discovered by the younger generation same as the 1950s youth attached themselves to Humphrey Bogart's cynical cool. *Arizona Republic* writer Bob Fenster termed Mitchum "Humphrey Bogart with muscles." Author Carrie Richey referred to him as "a hipster John Wayne." By the end of the decade, he was still consuming an abundant quantity of booze and cannabis. Westerns kept him grounded in this turbulent era, a fresh-air safe haven from middle age craziness. His strong constitution and physical capacity for alcohol remained. He'd been in the saddle for close to 25 years. Westerns provided a sanctuary, a feeling of comfort for a man who was increasingly pondering permanent retirement. He figured he might as well go out the way he had come in, on a horse.

Reviews for *The Way West* were harsh. *The New York Times* remarked, "Robert Mitchum, droopy-eyed and surly, as though peeved at having to wear that Indian hat, views the whole silly business with contempt." *Variety* commented, "Mitchum, evidently aware of the script vapidity, didn't try too hard." *The Los Angeles Times* praised Douglas' energy: "It is the force of Douglas' personality that keeps the picture from falling apart. Mitchum and Widmark do the best they can with the limits of their severely proscribed parts." According to *The Hollywood Reporter*, "Of the trio of above-the-title stars, Mitchum fares best, aided by a more sympathetic role and the humanity and humor with which he invests it." *The Saturday Review* noted that Mitchum was "the most convincing of all the players," while Roger Ebert of *The Chicago Sun Times* contributed, "Widmark and Mitchum are excellent in roles unusual for them, and Douglas, as always, is a seasoned old hand." *Films and Filming* called it "Mitchum's return to the saddle; his laconic playing only serving to emphasize his lack of engagement with the material." *The Oregonian* commented,

"Robert Mitchum has some good moments as a beat scout," but the *Fort Worth Star-Telegram* said, "[Mitchum] appears to close his eyes to it all and just rock along in the saddle until his next picture."

Mitchum biographer Mike Tomkies had a soft spot for the film, calling it "one of the best westerns made in recent years." Regarding Mitchum's performance, he wrote, "He added subtle innuendos of compassionate humanity and humor." Prolific western novelist Brian Garfield wrote in his entertainingly opinionated tome *Western Films*, "Mitchum comes off best but his role is relatively small." Jenni Calder in *There Must Be a Lone Ranger* opined, "Although the movie is carelessly undisciplined it is one of Mitchum's finest western roles; with dry restraint he conveys the character of a man who is profoundly asocial." McLaglen biographer Stephen B. Armstrong focused on the film's commercial disappointment: "Despite William H. Clothier's sterling photography and strong performances from Mitchum, Douglas and Widmark, *The Way West* floundered at the box office." The highly anticipated film was ultimately deemed less than successful, but the process of making it on location in Oregon proved memorable. "I went on the set with my dad a lot," says John Mitchum's daughter Cindy Azbill. "I was 14 years old during *The Way West* and spent the summer on that set with my dad and Uncle Bob. It was an amazing experience."*

Villa Rides (Paramount, 1968)

Cast: Yul Brynner (Pancho Villa); Robert Mitchum (Lee Arnold); Grazia Buccella (Fina); Charles Bronson (Rodolfo Fierro); Herbert Lom (Gen. Huerta); Robert Viharo (Urbina); Frank Wolff (Ramirez); Alexander Knox (President Madero); Robert Carricart (Don Luis); Andres Monreal (Capt. Herrera); Fernando Rey (Fuentes); Julio Pena (General); Jose Maria Prada (Major); Regina de Julian (Lupita); Antonio Ruiz (Juan); Jill Ireland (Girl in Restaurant), John Ireland (Man in Barbershop); Diana Lorys (Emilita); and Francisco Arduras, Xan das Bolas, Rock Brynner, Jose Canalejas, Raoul Castro, Jose Luis Chinchilla, John Clark, Miguel de la Riva, Antonio Jiminez Escribano, Fernando Hilbeck, Jose Luis Lazalde, Nazzareno Natale, Miguel Pedregosa, Jose Riesgo, Enrique Santiago, Seyyal Taner.

Crew: Buzz Kulik (Director); Ted Richmond (Producer); Robert Towne and Sam Peckinpah (Screenplay); Jack Hildyard (Photographer); Maurice Jarre (Music); Jose Alguero (Art Director); David Bretherton (Editor); Ted Haworth (Production Designer); Eric Seelig (Wardrobe); Sam Gordon (Property Master); Chuck Hayward, Jose Luis Chinchilla,,Miguel Pedregosa (Stunts); Francisco "Paco" Ardura (Livestock Coordinator).

125 minutes; Released July 17, 1968

This uneven actioner, bolstered by a flavorful Maurice Jarre score, fits firmly into the Mitchum Mexico subgenre. He's cast as Lee Arnold, a gun-running American biplane pilot who reluctantly joins up with Pancho Villa during the Mexican Revolution. Initially he works with the Federales, but a damaged plane wheel lands him in a local village where he becomes sympathetic to the people and their fight for independence. The Federale soldiers brutally raid the village, hanging several men and raping the blacksmith's daughter (Grazia Buccella) whom Mitchum has taken a liking to. Villa (Yul Brynner) and his men (led by Charles Bronson and Robert Viharo) surprise-attack the soldiers. Gringo Mitchum is earmarked for execution for helping the Federales, but Brynner realizes that his skills as a pilot might prove to be worthy for tactical purposes. Soldier of fortune Mitchum is persuaded by the lure of money to fly low enough to drop homemade bombs onto a train full of soldiers. The protagonists prove every bit as sadistic as the antagonists, though they have the fight for freedom as their goal. It's a long way from the white hat-black hat days of Hopalong Cassidy.

The vibrant large-scale battle scenes feature huge explosions and excellent stunt work spearheaded by American action coordinator Chuck Hayward. But the film is too long and loses its way throughout. A miscast Brynner (with hairpiece) and a clearly uninterested Mitchum are largely to blame. Mitchum carries the film's early scenes, but once Brynner and Bronson are introduced, Mitchum steps aside and becomes little more than an observer of the seriocomic action. He had all the best lines in *The Way West*, but here there's nothing wry for him to contribute. Sometimes he

---

*Cindy Azbill Mitchum (phone conversation, August 2017).

Publicity photograph of Mitchum being met by swimsuit models upon his arrival in Madrid to film *Villa Rides* (1968).

stands before the camera like a wooden cigar store Indian.

The film was originally written by Sam Peckinpah, who intended to direct, but Brynner wanted to take the hard edge off Villa and make him more of a "Robin Hood of the people" character. Robert Towne was brought in to rewrite and television veteran Buzz Kulik was assigned the directing chores. It was a "play or pay" deal, meaning the stars were contracted to be paid whether the film was produced or not. Towne continued rewriting on the Spanish location for the duration of the 14-week shoot, never a good sign. Mitchum's superfluous character seems largely an afterthought, a familiar Caucasian presence for the American audience to identify with. Puffy-eyed and burnt out, a disengaged Mitchum doesn't add a lot beyond his sturdy physical presence. He simply says the lines assigned to him and hits the deck any time he's clubbed with a gun, slapped with a money belt or kicked in the belly by Bronson. In one sequence, he regains consciousness amongst a pile of dead bodies, shrugging off the death surrounding him like a layer of trail dust. Joyce Haber wrote in *The Los Angeles Times*, "He is the kind of matinee idol who appeals to the kind of woman who wants to help a fellow get up off the ground."

Mitchum's clothes (white shirt, tan pants, boots) recall his wardrobe throughout the last half of *Bandido*. He adds a leather bomber jacket, short-brimmed hat and a zebra-handled Colt revolver (which he never uses), showing he is still able to dress the part of the romantic leading man despite his sleepy, hangdog look.

"I've made more crap than anybody in this lousy business," he told *True Magazine,* a brutally honest assessment of his career. Mitchum had grown accustomed to repetition and monotony when it came to moviemaking. Unless prodded to do more, he was content to offer less. "Paint eyes on my eyelids, and I'll walk through any part," he told Mike Tomkies with tongue in cheek. Reciting his lines and hitting his marks was money in the bank. Mitchum had been in the game long enough that it was inevitable he'd begin to recycle himself either wittingly or unwittingly. It didn't matter. He saw himself as a commodity that fit a formula, and when a producer valued professional experience to draw off, Mitchum was their man. "In most cases, most experiences, I've been there," he told *The New York Times*.

Perhaps if Peckinpah had remained, he would have made more of Mitchum's conflicted character, explored a thirst for vengeance over the rape of his girlfriend and the murder of her kindly father. Mitchum didn't press for motivation or better lines. He took what words they gave him and let co-stars Brynner and Bronson take center stage. Mitchum had no need for the myriad of scene-stealing tricks Steve McQueen attempted opposite Brynner during the making of *The Magnificent Seven* (1960). If all Buzz Kulik wanted him to do was stand in front of the camera while sharing the frame with Brynner, then that was fine with Mitchum. He was a natural reactor who would never be caught overacting on film. "There's no mystery about acting," Mitchum explained to Harlan Kennedy for *American Film*. "But you've got to have the basics. It's a matter of timing, talent, and mimicry. Some pictures you get to use all these to the full. Others, the best you can do is speak the lines believably. I've been accused of 'coasting' through movies. But there are some parts you cannot do anything else. There is literally nothing to do but to be there."

Top-billed Brynner was appreciative of Mitchum's on-screen generosity and made him a frequent guest at his elaborately decked-out on-set trailer and shaded caravan. For Mitchum, the spacious air-conditioned unit was a nice place to take a recuperative siesta, and Brynner was happy to share his abundant liquor supply. Mitchum welcomed the opportunity to hide, complaining to the press that tourists were being led through his motel room at the Castellana Hilton. The quiet coolness was welcome. They were filming in 100-degree heat, necessitating up to six different changes a day of Mitchum's undershirt due to sweating inside his bomber jacket. Mitchum still wasn't convinced the life of a movie star was all that difficult. "This is not a tough job," he told Larry King for *USA Today*. "You read a script. If you like the part and the money is okay, you do it. Then you remember your lines. You show up on time. You do what the director tells you to do. When you finish, you rest, then you go on to the next part. That's it."

When not working on *Villa Rides,* Mitchum enjoyed the abundant Spanish nightlife, occasionally with a pair of twin blonde bookends. On one occasion he escorted leading lady Maria Grazia Buccella, a former Miss Italy contestant, to Madrid's world-renowned bullring Plaza de Toros de Las Ventos. Mitchum even purchased a Spanish vineyard that produced a wine he liked. He was 50 but, true to his movie star persona, he could carry on until dawn like a man half his age. The only matinee idol that burned so brightly was Errol Flynn, who became a shell of himself the final ten years of his life and was dead at 50. At the same age, Mitchum remained tan, robust and otherwise bored with the professional material handed to him. In the annals of outlaw-rebel adoration, his name had grown synonymous with such real-life legends from the Old West as Johnny Ringo and John Wesley Hardin. He was now the full-fledged notorious living legend Big Bad Bob.

Charles Bronson as Fierro walks away with the film, casually shooting dozens of Federales without a second thought. Bronson's sly smile and witty line readings make him an engaging and welcome presence in the violent film. The veteran character actor, one of Brynner's *Magnificent Seven* co-stars, was on the verge of hitting it big in Europe as the star of Sergio Leone's *Once Upon a Time in the West* (1969) and shows his commanding screen potential here. In real life, the muscular Bronson was an extremely quiet loner who preferred to spend time with his wife Jill Ireland (who makes a cameo in this film) rather than intermingle or make small talk with his co-stars. Between takes, he'd shed his shirt to soak in the sun's rays and perform freehand exercises to keep his physique taut. Some accounts place Bronson and Mitchum at odds during filming due to their contrasting personalities. Other references have them friendly to one another. When asked by biographer W.A. Harbinson about the crevice-faced, legendarily surly Bronson, Mitchum offered, "He pointed a pistol quite well."

John Mitchum worked with Bronson on the western *Breakheart Pass* (1976) and nearly came to blows with the by-then superstar. This occurred when Bronson criticized how Brother John was delivering a pulled slap for the camera. Both actors were moved to take on a fighting stance before clearer heads prevailed and the slap was delivered perfectly for the camera. Having grown up working in the Pennsylvania coal mines, Bronson climbed hard through the character actor ranks for 20 years before his hardened charisma was rewarded with the money befitting an A-list star. Tight-lipped and guarded, he had a chip on his shoulder for all his years of struggle. In contrast, Robert Mitchum was anointed a stardom he couldn't have cared less about within his first two years of working in Hollywood. That had to have rubbed Bronson the wrong way. Interviewed in *White Hats and Silver Spurs,* John Mitchum attempted to attribute a reason for Bronson's testiness, noting: "My brother talked with him at great length and Bob is very perceptive. He said that Charlie is really a street guy and carried that Depression Era attitude with him. He's hard to reach."

Villa Rides was a U.S. co-production made with a largely Spanish crew attempting to cash in on the growing popularity of the European western genre. The Sergio Leone–directed Clint Eastwood films *A Fistful of Dollars* (1964) and *For a Few Dollars More* (1967) had been tremendous international successes and were followed in short order by their third collaboration *The Good, the Bad and the Ugly* (1966). Leone was approached to direct *Villa Rides* when Peckinpah was cast aside but wisely declined. Several rugged American actors were brought to Spain and Italy to star in copycat Spaghetti Westerns. One such actor was Mitchum's old pal John Ireland, Cherry Valance in *Red River* (1948). Ireland cameos in *Villa Rides* near the conclusion. The landscape around Madrid and Almería could effectively stand in for Mexico and the American Southwest, and films were made on the cheap there with the foreign crews. Italian Spaghetti Western director Sergio Corbucci of *Django* (1966) and *The Great Silence* (1968) fame publicly declared Mitchum to be one of his favorite actors. When he couldn't attract Mitchum to his projects, he cast the next best thing in Mitchum's lookalike son Jim for *The Grand Canyon Massacre* (1964). During this period the senior Mitchum turned down the script to a Romanian western. He had recently made the Italian-lensed World War II film *Anzio* (1968) and was ready to head home.

U.S. actor Thomas Hunter, star of *The Hills Run Red* (1966), had a supporting role with Mitchum in *Anzio* (1968). He recalls Mitchum in his autobiography *Memoirs of a Spaghetti Cowboy*:

As soldier of fortune Lee Arnold, Mitchum spent much of *Villa Rides* (1968) being knocked to the ground in action scenes.

Big, bad Robert Mitchum—you couldn't help but admire the guy. At age 50 he could still heft up his belly and puff out his chest like a drill instructor. Bob was half Norwegian, half Native American. His trademark look, very distinct and almost impossible to copy, started with his triangular-shaped head tilted back halfway to his shoulders. The triangle contained squinty gray eyes, hooded and cold-blooded, yet somehow sympathetic. The nose had been broken a few times. It meandered down to a sensual mouth that didn't smile much. A muscular neck gave you a hint that he could still handle himself.... Bob's droopy, stoned eyelids had dropped even more as he passed 50, causing his head to tilt back farther and farther, far enough back to get a look at your face when you stood by the camera for his close-ups. Mitchum was a poster boy for the late '60s and early '70s, very relaxed, very cool, somewhat mystical, with a superhuman tolerance for smoking and drinking. But his memory was up to it; I never saw him blow a line of dialogue.

A Paramount publicity photograph of Mitchum taking a break on the set of *Villa Rides* (1968).

Actor Robert Viharo, star of the low-budget tough guy favorite *Bare Knuckles* (1977) and a guest on the TV westerns *Cimarron Strip, The High Chaparral* and *Gunsmoke*, made his film debut in *Villa Rides*. He said:

Mitch and I got along real well and actually did some hanging out. He was a kick in the ass to be around on and off the set. A major very funny and intelligent man who abstained from all "star" pretentiousness and bullshit. This was my first film and having a warm and engaging relationship with him was really the highlight of the movie for me.... Mitch is one of the very few star actors I have worked with who is more engagingly human than pompous celebrity.

Regarding *Villa Rides*, Viharo reminisced:

Many gypsies worked on the film as extras and in minor roles. Also, there were Mexican mariachis hired for several scenes or background. I had a son born in Madrid during filming. It is or was a gypsy tradition that when a son is born to a family, a huge party of only men is provided to celebrate the birth of the son. I guess I was considered family as was Mitchum, who to my observation was always warm and friendly to extras and smaller role players. The gypsies asked for and provided a party in the apartment complex where we were staying while filming. The large room was packed with celebrators and mariachi music when Mitchum arrived with a huge pot of his homemade chili recipe. It was definitely "his" homemade recipe made especially by him personally as his offering. He generously included in the most delicious chili a generous portion of North African Kife, a much, much stronger plant than marijuana. It did not take long for the "main ingredient" to take effect on the happy crowd of well-wishers, and all I remember of the rest is laughing and singing and dancing. My wife who has just given birth and our maid danced with everyone and sang with everyone—their highlight being dancing with Mitchum. The music and singing and dancing lasted past dawn.... And the next day was a filming day. Unequivocally, it was the greatest party I have ever been a part of. Ever. Mitchum became more a star in the eyes of the gypsies and mariachis and me at that occasion than he ever was in any movie, and even the one we were doing and he was starring in.

My memory of him is he was a very engaging and funny and intelligent and generous man with no pretensions. He had a photographic memory and only skimmed through a script once and remembered verbatim every line of his and everyone else's without looking at the script again. He wrote in large letters on the margin of his scenes "NAR" which he disclosed was "No Acting Required." Now, this may be true of his other movies also. He wrote a letter to the producer of his next movie, also a western, that he would like me cast as a certain character in the movie. Turns out a "name" actor was already cast in the role, but the producer flew me out to meet with him anyway as he was impressed with the letter…. Stuntmen and wranglers loved him, man. He was the best. Never anyone like him nor likely to be ever again…. I have a more lasting fondness for Mitchum than any actor I have ever worked with. I do not share this with many people.

Regarding Bronson, Charlie was initially diffident and surly on the set. Especially with me, as I was the new kid on the block and I had scenes with him. Also, I had decided to have my character be somewhat expressive and expansive…. Bronson always played everything close to the vest, except for his first couple of movies where he kind of opened up as an actor. He wisely realized this was not the way for him to go. Charlie kind of gave me a quite rough time initially, but then one day I went to him and said, "Charlie, you come off as a tough guy but at heart I think you are just a sweet boy looking for love." I took a chance saying it, I know. But he responded with a smile and said, "You think so, huh?" From that moment on, he was so open to me and invited me to ride back to Madrid with him in his car with him. When Sergio Leone came on the set to talk to him about *Once Upon a Time in the West,* Charlie called me over to introduce me and asked Sergio if there was a part in the movie for me. If you saw the movie, a great one, you could see there wasn't. When I bumped into Charlie when in L.A., he was always very outgoing and friendly toward me.

As regards Mitchum: My impression is Charlie took stock of Mitchum as no one to fuck with, as Mitch had a "don't give a shit" air about him. In one scene, Mitch had a line that cracked up Charlie's usual stoic demeanor. Other than that, Mitch only said to me once that Charlie was "overly developed." They really didn't have much to do with one another on the set or in the film, but I heard from others how difficult Charlie could be…. Come to think of it, I loved both Mitchum and Bronson in memory and still do. Although the *Villa Rides* movie was conventional claptrap and not very good, Charlie told me the original script by Sam Peckinpah was far better as were his and my written parts. In fact, Charlie was going to pull out of the film when he first got to Madrid. Paramount wanted him badly as he was getting hot and they brought Robert Towne in to do rewrites for Bronson which greatly enhanced his part. He took Towne out to dinner every night to make sure his part was enhanced, and it was…. I had a great time doing the movie.*

There was a valid reason for filming in Spain: Pancho Villa was still too politically touchy a subject to film in Mexico. The cost of extras was also significantly less. However, all the western props had to be shipped from America, and *Villa Rides* ran 14 days over schedule, meaning the cheap extras cost more in the long run. Hollywood termed these expatriate films as "runaway productions." They unfortunately forced a great deal of American technical crews and background actors out of work. The noisy, sprawling *Villa Rides* plays loose with the facts but contains some interesting historical tidbits like Villa's penchant for multiple marriages.

Mitchum was met by swimsuit models wearing sombreros when he got off the plane in Spain, but it wasn't all fun and games. A stunt pilot took his place for the flying scenes in the Curtis Jenny (a De Havilland Tiger Moth was used) while Mitchum sat in the cockpit in front of a blue screen for close-ups. On the ground, Mitchum rode a donkey and took his own stunt falls. During one fight sequence, a Spanish stuntman hit him with a rifle, bloodying his nose and cutting his eye. Mitchum bled profusely and was taken to a Madrid hospital, where a press release from the film's publicist noted he was "in good spirits." Mitchum received a few welcome days off from the film, and all he had to do was get clobbered over the head.

"Seldom have we watched Robert Mitchum get knocked down so often with so little effort," wrote the *New York Magazine* reviewer. "He's reached the point of seemingly counting to ten before talking, but considering the lines allotted him, a hundred would be a wiser figure." Few of the major review outlets were impressed by the film, though *The Hollywood Citizen News* remarked, "Robert Mitchum gets across one of his better jobs…. The laconic charm of Mitchum's

---

*Robert Viharo (e-mail correspondence, August 2017).

work was seldom better seen than here matched against the affable simplicity of the Mexican native." *The Los Angeles Times* said perceptively, "The most notable thing about *Villa Rides* is the contrast between the ways in which [Brynner and Mitchum] approach their work. Mitchum, easily the most talented of the two, seems to walk his way through a role that wasn't much to begin with. Brynner, on the other hand, hasn't as much to give, but he gives it his all." According to *The Hollywood Reporter,* Brynner was "particularly strong in some of his humorous exchanges with Mitchum, whose reactions are expert in their comic suggestion and laconic grace." *Film TV Daily* concurred: "Both Brynner and Mitchum go through the drama with easy command of their roles." *Variety* wrote, "Mitchum, still a gutsy actor who commands attention just by being seen, takes the curse off of the script by reacting in bewilderment to events." *The New York Times* said, "Neither the imperturbable Mr. Mitchum, nor Mr. Brynner…try to dig beneath the surface of the characters involved." Finally, *The Chicago Sun Times* complained, "Even Robert Mitchum seems defeated by the great weight of *Villa Rides.*"

5 Card Stud (Paramount, 1968)

Cast: Dean Martin (Van Morgan); Robert Mitchum (Reverend Jonathan Rudd); Inger Stevens (Lily Langford); Roddy McDowall (Nick Evers); Katherine Justice (Nora Evers); John Anderson (Marshal Dana); Ruth Springford (Mama Malone); Yaphet Kotto (Little George); Denver Pyle (Sig Evers); Bill Fletcher (Joe Hurley); Whit Bissell (Dr. Cooper); Ted De Corsia (Eldon Bates); Don Collier (Rowan); Roy Jenson (Mace Jones); and Jerry Gatlin, Joe Gray, Chuck Hayward, Robert Hauser, Robert F. Hoy, Merle Kilgore, Louise Lorimer, Boyd "Red" Morgan, Bob Orrison, George Robotham, Hope Summers, Jose Trinidad Villa, Henry Hathaway.

Crew: Henry Hathaway (Director); Hal B. Wallis (Producer); Marguerite Roberts (Screenplay); Daniel L. Fapp (Photographer); Maurice Jarre (Music); Warren Low (Editor); Jerry Gatlin, Joe Gray, Chuck Hayward, Billy Hughes, Boyd "Red" Morgan, Bob Orrison, George Robotham, Tom Sutton (Stunts); Chema Hernandez, Tom Sutton (Wranglers).

103 minutes; Released July 10, 1968

One of Mitchum's enduring roles is the part of the demented preacher Harry Powell in Charles Laughton's *The Night of the Hunter* (1955). It makes sense that he was immediately thought of to play the part of a vengeance-seeking man of the cloth in the mid-budget Henry Hathaway western *5 Card Stud.* Sufficient motivation is provided for Mitchum's Jonathan Rudd to kill off the men from a poker game who lynched his brother, and for a good portion of the film the killer's identity is not revealed.

Mitchum arrives in Rincon City, Colorado to bring religion to the area, although his true motives remain a secret even if the audience has strong suspicions. They catch on a lot quicker than honest gambler Dean Martin, who works with Mitchum to find the killer as the suspects themselves dwindle via strangulation, suffocation, hanging and gunshot. The fire-and-brimstone preacher's handy with a firearm and claims he is backed by "God and Mr. Colt." The best scenes feature the two stars testing one another. Mitchum is a crafty villain, using a derringer hidden in a hollowed-out Bible as his secret back-up. He and Martin make worthy adversaries.

Adapted from the Ray Gaulden novel *Glory Gulch* by *True Grit* screenwriter Marguerite Roberts, the atypical western whodunit is a loose remake of the noir film *Dark City* (1950). It's a decent picture, featuring a solid cast of old pros (John Anderson, Denver Pyle, Ted De Corsia) and a forceful, knowing portrayal by an animated Mitchum. Dean Martin is a familiar and welcome western presence, although he looks as tired here as Mitchum is often accused of being. Roddy McDowall is given a great character to play, a manipulative weasel out for himself, but the slight English actor is woefully miscast in the crucial role. A more physical cowboy performer like Richard Jaeckel or Jeremy Slate would have made far better casting. Burt Reynolds met with producer Hal Wallis about the part. Two female leads pining over Martin (Inger Stevens as a madam and Katherine Justice as McDowall's sister) bog the film down. Stevens' character could easily have been dropped altogether. The film boasts an odd, overactive Maurice Jarre score. Its uniqueness does make it memorable.

5 Card Stud is set in 1880s Colorado but was filmed in the village of Chupaderos in Durango, Mexico. The high pines and picturesque Sierra

Madre are well-captured by Daniel Fapp's camera. Interiors were filmed at Churubusco Studios in Mexico City. Pancho Villa's son Jose Trinidad Villa appeared in the film as a featured extra. The young Villa worked on several of John Wayne's Durango-lensed films. The intriguing teaming of Mitchum and Dean Martin was the film's selling point. Mitchum had recently played opposite Kirk Douglas, John Wayne and now Dean Martin. "They always got the girl," Mitchum humorously complained to the press. "I got the horse." Mitchum and Martin were nearly teamed once in the past: Before Frank Sinatra was brought into *4 for Texas* (1963) as producer-star, there was talk of pairing Mitchum with Martin in that comedy-western from director Robert Aldrich.

Stylized scenes filmed in the cloak of darkness stand out as a spry Mitchum moves specter-like through a firelit night dodging Martin's gunfire. For these scenes, Mitchum is dressed like Johnny Cash in gunfighter-black. Coincidentally, this film's bit player Merle Kilgore wrote Cash's hit song "Ring of Fire." Scenes involving the female leads are executed routinely, and Hathaway has an odd, mildly distracting habit of using the same stunt actors throughout the film in various guises. Jerry Gatlin, Chuck Hayward and George Robotham show up as different characters distinguished by droopy mustaches or beards. They might be killed in one scene only to pop up again later as another featured extra. At one point, Hathaway himself can be seen looking through a window. Mitchum's *River of No Return* double Roy Jenson plays one of the gamblers, but Robotham doubled Mitchum on this film. A poorly motivated and ill-conceived shootout with local miners led by Don Collier makes little sense dramatically but provides an action moment. Mitchum strides down the middle of the street firing his gun during the shootout as if protected by God himself.

Bullets are correctly referred to as cartridges in the scene with Martin and Mitchum target shooting at a windmill's blades. This is one of the more memorable moments as the men test one another's skill. Knowledgeable western viewers will note that each actor uses a New Service Single Action Army conversion but carries a SAA during non-shooting scenes. The conversions allow them to fire off multiple rounds in quick succession without having to cock the hammer back for every shot. Mitchum hits the windmill blades six out of six times. Martin is impressed and congratulatory when he rings only five out of six blades. In typical fashion, Mitchum shrugs the victory off. "My shooting was way off," he says. "I was aiming at the spaces in between."

The darkness of character that Mitchum exhibited in *Man with the Gun* is on display again in *5 Card Stud*. These were the violent resources Mitchum could tap into to explore such frightening aspects of humanity as *Night*

Mitchum, as Reverend Jonathan Rudd, gets the drop on Roddy McDowall with his hidden derringer in *5 Card Stud* (1968).

of the Hunter's Harry Powell and *Cape Fear's* Max Cady, two of the greatest villainous portrayals in screen history. These dangerous aspects of Mitchum's own personality were sense memory he could convey, having been cultivated in the hobo jungles of the Great Depression where one sometimes needed to fight to survive. They were further crafted in boxing rings and barrooms. With age and years of prolonged alcohol use, these facets were perhaps closer to the surface than the laidback Mitchum liked to admit. He was a nice guy by overwhelming account, but he had a capacity for violence few could comprehend or relate to. In *5 Card Stud*, there's a tense struggle with bartender Big George (Yaphet Kotto) which results in Mitchum firing his pistol at close range into Kotto's belly. Mitchum then gathers and composes himself in front of a mirror, casually smoothing his hair upon completing an act of murder. It's an interesting moment and scary as hell. Writer Mike Tomkies, author of the biographies *Duke: The Story of John Wayne* and *The Robert Mitchum Story: It Sure Beats Working*, was visiting the set to interview Martin and Mitchum. Tomkies later referred to Mitchum as "the most enigmatic, iconoclastic, charismatic, witty, poetic and possibly physically powerful movie star I ever met."

Mitchum's western skill set and on-set professionalism extended to the rank and file members of Hollywood cowboys. Members of the cast and crew were impressed. Stunt actor Robert Hoy and Don Collier, both of TV's *The High Chaparral* (1967–1971), were brought in to play small parts during the street shootout. Hoy also worked with Mitchum on *River of No Return*, *Thunder Road* and the TV movie *Promises to Keep* (1985). At western fan events like the 2007 Wild Western Festival at Pioneer Village in Phoenix, Arizona, Hoy told the humorous story of Mitchum and Henry Hathaway introducing themselves to one another in the early 1950s. Hathaway warned he would yell and curse at actors during filming but didn't mean anything by it. Mitchum replied that he punched out directors who yelled and cursed at actors, but that he also didn't mean anything by it.*

Don Collier, Sam Butler on *Chaparral*, had a real cowboy background and was a handy actor who could do his own riding and fighting, making him popular with producers and directors. Collier had small parts in *El Dorado* and *Tombstone* (1993) and worked with Mitchum on the mini-series *The Winds of War* (1983) and *War and Remembrance* (1989). His western career stretched all the way back to extra work on John Ford's *Fort Apache* (1948) and supporting roles opposite "The Duke" in *The War Wagon* (1967) and *The Undefeated* (1969). Collier starred in *Outlaws* (1960–1962) and made guest appearances on TV's *Death Valley Days*, *The Virginian*, *Wagon Train*, *Bonanza*, *Branded*, *Hondo*, *Gunsmoke* and *How the West Was Won* in addition to the telefilms *The Last Ride of the Dalton Gang* (1979), *Mr. Horn* (1979) and *The Sacketts* (1979). He spent the latter portion of his career in Tucson and played a regular character part on the series *The Young Riders* (1989–1992). In 1993, he hosted the Old Tucson Studios promotional film *Hollywood in the Desert*. Collier was extremely popular at western festivals and had a one-man stage show entitled *Confessions of an Acting Cowboy* where he shared stories of working with legends Mitchum, John Wayne and Elvis Presley. Regarding *5 Card Stud*, Collier said,

> I killed Bobby Hoy on that show. Bobby was a good stuntman and a good actor.... The stunt guys liked working for Henry Hathaway because he'd have them do a bunch of things. They were always working on three or four different contracts. Henry was an asshole and could be hard on them, but his pictures were always good for the stunt guys. They made a lot of money on them. Henry liked me and extended my contract on that. He took me down to Mexico City with them after we finished in Durango. So, I got another three weeks on that show. Henry and the producer Hal Wallis wanted to give me a part on *True Grit*, but Bill Claxton wouldn't let me out of *High Chaparral* for that one. He did let me out to work on *The Undefeated* with Duke and *Flap* with Anthony Quinn. But not *True Grit*.
>
> I worked with Robert Mitchum three times, *5 Card Stud*, *The Winds of War* and *War and Remembrance*. [He] was a great actor and an interesting guy. He was a good guy, friendly. He'd say hello to you when you walked past in

---

*Robert Hoy (western festival appearance, September 2007).

Dean Martin (left) and Mitchum on location outside Durango, Mexico, at Sierra de Organos, engage in shooting action for *5 Card Stud* (1968).

the morning. I had coffee with him. He was nice to work with, but he kind of kept to himself on that show. He didn't get out amongst the others. A loner. He was a pretty good boozer, but not with the rest of us on that film. He'd go off and drink alone. He always had a driver who had to sit in the car while Bob went in and drank. When we finished in Durango, Bob didn't want to fly to Mexico City. He wanted to drive. I remember his driver said, "Oh, no…" He knew that to drive Mitchum all the way from Durango to Mexico City would take two or three days.*

On co-star Yaphet Kotto's Facebook page, the actor shares an extensive and incredible story about the making of *5 Card Stud*. When the cast and crew were moving from Durango to Mexico City, many preferred to fly. Mitchum opted to travel by road with his studio-provided limo driver Jorge Javier. He invited the young actor Kotto to ride with him and the two bonded on the road. As they made their way through Zacatecas, they entered a more decrepit area of old Mexico and came across an empty American limo. Stopping to investigate, Mitchum and Kotto found an ailing American actor in a small hotel room who claimed he was near death. Mitchum determined the American had been drinking powerful agave Pulque and would ultimately recover. He sent Javier to find the American's driver in the local cantina while lifting the drunken man from the floor. Mitchum had Kotto carry the American to his car while he investigated a woman's scream from across the hall. The woman was giving birth and it was a difficult labor. The baby was born blue and lifeless and after some work, the local doctor declared the baby dead. Mitchum wasn't so convinced.

Taking control of the situation, he sent Javier for the Courvoisier in his car and requested

---

*Don Collier (phone conversation, May 2018).

a tub of warm water and a tub of cold water. Mitchum began working to heal the baby with his hands. Kotto stared in disbelief as a heavily perspiring Mitchum labored feverishly over the child for the next two hours, all the while singing songs in Spanish in front of a roomful of hotel staff and onlookers. Against all reason, the baby finally showed signs of life and began to cry. Healer Mitchum placed the child with the mother, turned to Kotto and said simply, "How about that shit?" As they walked to their limo, Kotto asked if the near-death American actor they sent to the hospital was Jason Robards, Jr. Mitchum replied that he'd never seen Robards in Mexico and that Kotto hadn't either. Kotto understood the implied code of silence that existed between men like Mitchum and Robards and was high fived. "Bob was totally cool," declares Kotto.

Mitchum enjoyed his castmates on this film and shared his remembrance of the back room struggle with the 6'4" Yaphet Kotto to Garry Armstrong in 2012. "Mr. Kotto was a very strong gent and deceptively fast on his feet. He also had a terrific sense of humor. He didn't make it easy for me in the master shot where I killed him. We had to do three or four takes because Yap held on hard. I wound up owing him two or three rounds of the good stuff. Very good guy. Stand-up guy." Regarding his equally famous co-star Dean Martin, Mitchum told Armstrong, "[He was a] lovely gent. So professional. He didn't go near the booze 'til we were done with the day's shoot. He even fed me some lines in scenes he wasn't on camera. He listened to lines and made it so easy to tone your work. Enjoyed the hell out of working with Mr. Martin."*

Several parallels run between the careers of Mitchum and Dean Martin. Each took on the drunken lawman role in Howard Hawks' *Rio Bravo* (1959) and *El Dorado* (1967), and both had strong real-life associations as heavy drinkers who sometimes preferred the company of no one except themselves. However, popular crooner Martin's drinking reputation, while well-earned, was by the time of filming *5 Card Stud* played up for the press and fans who thought he was a humorous lush. The ever-present glass of diluted "whiskey" that he sipped between takes was nothing more than iced tea. Martin was instead a workaholic, a tireless professional who made several films a year, recorded albums, gave concerts, golfed daily and even managed to host and perform in the weekly variety program *The Dean Martin Show* (1965–1974). He enjoyed a drink, but it didn't rule his life and he was well-liked by film crews. Like Mitchum, Martin was comfortable in westerns and took every opportunity to make one. His performances were natural, relaxed, and as effortless in execution as his charismatic co-star.

Following *Rio Bravo,* Martin reteamed with John Wayne in Henry Hathaway's *The Sons of Katie Elder* (1965), a case of curious casting for audiences to accept the two disparate men as brothers. Martin, born Dino Crocetti, was Italian with thick dark hair and was several inches shorter than Wayne. More appropriate casting for the co-starring part of Wayne's brother in *Katie Elder* would have been Mitchum himself, who carried the same hefty swagger and bulk and descended from similar Scotch-Irish stock. Martin was similarly miscast as the outlaw brother of anti-hero James Stewart in Andrew McLaglen's *Bandolero* (1968), another role that Mitchum would have been physically better suited for.

Mitchum's role as *5 Card Stud*'s vengeful preacher contains echoes of his crazed Appalachian preacher Harry Powell in *Night of the Hunter,* a film that boasted original quirks that make Hathaway's shooting of *5 Card Stud* pale in comparison. *5 Card Stud* is a routine western for Mitchum, enjoyable to watch, but one that would never be considered for the canon of great cowboy films. Dave Ferrier in *Wildest Westerns* does count Mitchum's Reverend Rudd as one of the ten greatest western villains in screen history. It would have been interesting if Martin and Mitchum had switched parts. To be fair, Martin's heroic cowboy character is bland and even less of a challenge for Mitchum to tackle. It's doubtful if this switch was considered because Martin recently played a ruthless western villain in *Rough Night in Jericho* (1967)

---

*Garry Armstrong (e-mail correspondence, November 2018).

and sought to balance out his portrayals for his fans. The stars play the parts they are expected to, successfully carrying out the required dramatics by-the-numbers.

Mitchum got on well with Martin, an old acquaintance he felt was funny but serious about his work. Mitchum would readily appear on subsequent TV specials with Martin when asked. If people were expecting nightly fireworks from the two on location, they were disappointed. Each man did their job as professionals, even though Mitchum predicted to the columnist Bob Thomas it might be "the drunkest set in town." On a 1975 appearance on Martin's TV special *Dean's Place,* the two stars poked fun at their bad boy images over a game of gin. "Hey, this is kind of like that picture we did together," remarks Dean while dealing the cards. "Remember *5 Card Stud*?" Mitchum doesn't miss a beat in his response. "Yeah, that was a wild one. We had a fight in the street, broke up the saloon, and burned down the town." Martin is even quicker with his comic retort: "And that was before the picture started…. Boy, you sure had me fooled. I didn't know you were such a hard drinker." "I'm not," replies Mitchum. "That's the easiest thing I do." Martin then proposes, "Let's do another picture together." "I don't think so," says Mitchum. "Haven't got the stomach for it?" asks Martin. "I haven't got the liver for it," replies Mitchum.

Despite appearing fit and athletically leaping from his horse, Mitchum used a portable oxygen tank to aid his breathing in the high altitude's action scenes. John Wayne, with one lung, began using oxygen in Durango during *The Sons of Katie Elder*. Mitchum had two lungs but had been smoking for close to 40 years. The turbulent Sierra Madre winds proved troublesome, upending a camera platform and nearly causing a heavy camera to plummet onto Mitchum's head. Mitchum casually stepped out of the way of the falling equipment. Regarding drinking hard liquor on location, Mitchum told Roger Ebert: "At high altitudes, this stuff can kill you. Drinking in a place like Durango is serious business. You got an altitude of five, six thousand feet, you can get drunk by accident. Get sick. Of course, that's one of the best ways to lose weight, getting sick."

A homesick Martin didn't care for the Durango location or the swirling dust, saying it was so dirty he wanted to take 20 showers when he got home. He missed his wife and kids throughout the shoot. "If the world ended tomorrow," the *Kansas City Star* quoted him saying, "Durango would have a week to go." Martin and Mitchum both put their hand and boot imprints into the cement outside of Durango's movie house. Other motion picture cowboys whose imprints rested beside theirs included John Wayne, Robert Ryan, Burt Lancaster and Jason Robards, Jr.

As for local accommodations, loner Mitchum asked for the bungalow furthest away from the rest. That happened to be the bungalow with a faulty heater, leading to a physical encumbrance for Mitchum to endure and ultimately grouse about without ever resorting to "star tantrum" demands. The situation did give him sufficient ammo for the press to voice his self-deprecating humor: He told *The Evening Capital,*

> What I wanted was privacy. And what did I get? A freeze-out. Why didn't somebody tell me the boiler was weak? Everybody else was cold as well but not as cold as I was. And all I could get was one blanket. I put my overcoat on the bed and piled in with my socks on, and all night I'd shiver. One night, Hathaway came in and said, "Great Scott, it's cold in here!" I said, "Henry, that's what I keep telling you," and showed him my pitcher of drinking water—frozen solid. So, then he got after them about the boiler. But they couldn't help the shower water. By the time it got to me, it was frigid.

Mitchum complained he couldn't retire from the film business because of the debt he incurred taking on the 300-acre Belmont Farm for his horses. "Years ago we bought that little farm in Maryland," he told the *Evening Capital*.

> All we wanted was a nice, quiet, little joint where we could go and rest. But my wife Dottie kept inviting guests and they'd say, "Got anything to ride?" We didn't. So, after a little prodding I went to Dale Robertson, figuring he was a man who knew about horses. You know what he sent me? Two mares, a stallion, and a bill for $10,000. When I screamed, he said, "Good quarter horses don't come cheap. But quit squawking. Just breed 'em a little and you'll make money." So, I get all the books and a couple of hands to help me and

With co-star Dean Martin (right) on horseback in Durango, Mexico, for *5 Card Stud* (1968).

begin to "breed 'em a little." I also began going to horse shows and buying a few more critters, because you know, a thing like breeding quarter horses can get into your blood—especially when you also race them a little—and I was doing that.

Mitchum explained that by selling the Maryland farm, he now needed to house the expensive herd and his staff in Atascadero, California, while he toiled on movies in Italy, Spain and Mexico. He had 26 horses stabled on his 76-acre property. Some of his horses were quartered at the Whispering Winds ranch near Creston, California, others at the 6-B Ranch on the Tackett Stock Farm in Grass Valley, California. "It's like having 40 daughters at Vassar," Mitchum said of the exorbitant costs. He considered horse-breeding a business venture. The IRS insisted it was a hobby that he couldn't deduct expenses on. Mitchum simply shrugged his shoulders and kept making movies. "I've gotta keep working because of those horses," Lee Server quoted him saying. "My whole acting career adds up to a million dollars worth of horse shit."

5 Card Stud supporting player Denver Pyle, an instantly recognizable veteran of dozens of TV westerns and films, revealed to syndicated writer Bob Rose that many actors didn't really like horses, "except maybe Bob Mitchum, and he's crazy." In California, Mitchum enjoyed the quiet isolation of being on the road between Bel Air and Atascadero, frequently making the 200-mile one-way drive alone to visit his beloved animals. He had a genuine connection with them. As western trail-herder Andy Adams wrote in his 1903 book *The Log of a Cowboy*: "No better word can be spoken of a man than that he is careful of his horses." Mitchum's favorite horse was his stallion Cap-Gun. Mitchum proudly told Harold Heffernan, "Believe me, that horse has a personality. And smart? At a show I'll say, 'Go on out there, Cap-Gun, and show 'em what you can do.' He goes out all by himself and performs. Then he comes charging at me like he's going to run me down and stops dead with his eyeballs three inches from mine. No wonder he has fan clubs, he's a ham."

Henry Hathaway helmed several early 1930s Zane Grey stories starring Randolph Scott and later directed a segment of *How the West Was Won* (1962) as well as the Steve McQueen western *Nevada Smith* (1966). Mitchum had worked with Hathaway on *White Witch Doctor* (1953); *5 Card Stud* was their first western collaboration. It was on the subpar Congo adventure that the two had the infamous exchange stuntman Robert Hoy was still talking about 40 years later. The bullying Hathaway got the message and never pushed too hard with his leading man. Mitchum commented on Hathaway's reputation as a tough director in co-star McDowall's photographic book *Double Exposure 2*: "Off the set he wore the white hat of compassion, geniality and true, honest generosity. The moment he walked on the set, chewing his cigar, breathing fire, he donned the black hat of Simon Legree, lashing out at incompetence, inattention, and rigidly intolerant of any effort which fell short of his own total dedication."

Mitchum pranked the director during *White Witch Doctor*, feigning ignorance about a scene, then rattling off several pages of dialogue letter-perfect. According to Mike Tomkies, Hathaway is credited with begrudgingly saying of Mitchum, "This sonuvabitch is the most phenomenal actor I've ever seen."

Mitchum and Hathaway nearly worked with one another on other occasions, including the John Wayne adventure *North to Alaska* (1960). Mitchum was offered the Wayne role in Hathaway's *The Sons of Katie Elder* when the producers feared that Wayne's cancer surgery would keep him out of the part. Mitchum spoke to Wayne first, who assured him he'd be able to complete the role. Mitchum turned the producers down to give Wayne every chance to keep the part. Hathaway considered Mitchum as an option for the top role in *True Grit* (1969) before Wayne was inked. While doing a cameo in *Secret Ceremony* (1968), Mitchum famously warned Mia Farrow of Hathaway's bullying style, causing her to back out of the leading role Kim Darby took in *Grit*. Five years later, Mitchum was sent the script for the sequel *Rooster Cogburn* (1975) when it was again feared that Wayne's faltering health would not allow him to reprise his Oscar-winning role. Wayne toughed it out. Mitchum was glad he did.

Mitchum seemed to have the market cornered on homicidal preachers, though Glenn Ford did play a gun-toting man of the cloth in the following year's *Heaven with a Gun* (1969). The western filmed at Old Tucson Studios immediately before Mitchum's own arrival in Arizona to make *Young Billy Young*. Mitchum trumped Ford by playing yet another mercenary masquerading as a Catholic priest in the south-of-the-border action film *The Wrath of God* (1972).

In his personal life, Mitchum was non-religious. He had been baptized in a Methodist church and was later married in the kitchen of a Methodist minister, but he followed no organized religion. Sister Julie described the entire Mitchum family as skeptical agnostics, though she and their mother eventually became followers of the independent modern faith Baha'i. *The Cowboy Encyclopedia* describes range riders of the Old West as indifferent to religion. They had their own sense of morality, the Cowboy Code. This was a belief system Mitchum more readily understood.

5 Card Stud reviews were favorable. *Variety* said, "Mitchum's character at times seems contrived but he handles himself well nonetheless." *The Hollywood Reporter* remarked, "While neither is apportioned the degree of humor that might spur them to more memorable performances, Martin and Mitchum underplay for maximum conviction and strength." *The Hollywood Citizen News* said the stars gave "colorful and exciting performances…. Mitchum just gets better as he keeps rolling the roles to his size. You may like him best of all as the hellfire-and-damnation preacher here." *The New York Times* noted, "Robert Mitchum is tough, laconic and quite good as the fire-and-brimstone preacher," while *The Monthly Film Bulletin* wrote, "The initial pleasure of seeing Mitchum repeat what might have been another *Night of the Hunter* quickly palls when we find that this hunter carries no wicked conviction, but, as they say, just models for it." *The Los Angeles Times* complained, "Hathaway has Mitchum and McDowall play it so cool they turn characterless." *The Chicago Sun Times* added, "Mitchum eventually has to carry the picture, as he has carried so many before, and his scenes work even when they shouldn't."

Young Billy Young (United Artists, 1969)

Cast: Robert Mitchum (Deputy Ben Kane); Angie Dickinson (Lily Beloit); Robert Walker, Jr. (Billy Young); David Carradine (Jesse Boone); Jack Kelly (John Behan); John Anderson (Boone); Paul Fix (Charlie); Willis Bouchey (Doc Cushman); Parley Baer (Bell); Bob Anderson (Gambler); Rodolfo Acosta (Mexican Officer); Deana Martin (Evvie); and Christopher Mitchum, Rusty Lee Stockwell, Billy Murphy, Jay Gammons, Alex Jacome, Jr., Alberto Pina Moore, Gilbert Romero, Frank Soto.

Crew: Burt Kennedy (Screenwriter-Director); Max E. Youngstein (Producer); Harry Stradling, Jr. (Photographer); Shelly Manne (Music); Stan Jolley (Art Director); Jerry Alpert (Wardrobe); Otho Lovering (Editor); Jerry Gatlin, Dave Cass, Steve "Bunker" DeFrance, Buddy Anderson, Neil Summers, Stacy Newton, Bud Stout, Kimo Owens, Chuck Henson, Gerry Searle (Stunts); Allen Lee, Chuck Henson, Gayle Bell (Wranglers); Kenneth "Kenny" Lee (Livestock Coordinator).

89 minutes; Released September 17, 1969

"Every time the same damned role," Mitchum complained to writer Tim Tyler. "I'm wearing the same hat and boots I wore in *5 Card Stud*." The over-familiarity didn't end there when it came to the routine western *Young Billy Young*. The mid-budget film shot at the same Old Tucson location as *El Dorado*, and Mitchum was riding his own buckskin horse Bull's Eye Bee. He couldn't gripe too much, as this late 1960s $2 million dust-and-crust story was being co-produced by his own Talbot Company with Mitchum earning $200,000 and 20 percent of the gross to enact six-gun law. "My agent said, 'Do it,' so, why not?" explained Mitchum to the *Los Angeles Herald Examiner*. He claimed to Tyler he only worked now to be around "the wranglers and the stagehands, the simple folk."

A fictional retelling of the relationship between Wyatt Earp and Billy Clanton in Tombstone, Arizona, before the events of the infamous O.K. Corral, the story was based on Will Henry's 1955 novel *Who Rides with Wyatt?* Prolific western writer Henry (a pseudonym) was perhaps better known to cowboy fans as Clay Fisher or Heck Allen. The Spur Award winner's real name was Henry Wilson Allen.

Western movie writer-director Burt Kennedy adapted the screenplay for John Wayne before it ended up with Mitchum. Kennedy changed the names of the lead characters to freshen the story and provide further dramatic allowances, with Mitchum taking the leading part of Marshal Ben Kane. During production, the film was known as *Who Rides with Kane?*, but it was released under the inferior title *Young Billy Young*. Trying to relate to youthful audiences, the title change drew emphasis away from Mitchum's older lawman to co-star Robert Walker Jr.'s neophyte outlaw character Billy Young. It is, however, clearly a Robert Mitchum western, and another aging gunman role that he plays ably and interestingly.

The film lensed in Arizona during the hot summer months of July and August 1968, taking full advantage of the blue skies and abundant saguaro filling the mountainous Sonoran Desert landscape. However, this was the period of the summer monsoons, with thunder and lightning moving in late in the 110-degree day. Kennedy countered the weather by starting each work day at six a.m. and wrapping by 3:30 in the afternoon so his cast and crew could have a cooling swim and enjoy the evening Happy Hour margaritas. Mitchum favored the Kon Tiki Lounge, the popular cowboy steakhouses Palomino and Li'l Abner's, and the Mexican restaurant La Fuente in Tucson's popular Miracle Mile. The crew took to calling the experience a location-vacation.

Harry Stradling Jr.'s open sky cinematography is as impressive as any western shot on that southern Arizona desert location. *Who Rides with Kane?—Young Billy Young* was notable as the first film to use Old Tucson's new 13,000–square foot soundstage and the newly built Kansas Street movie set which represented the film's fictional town Lordsburg. The older Main Street was the setting for the climactic shootout while the more southwestern style Front Street represented Bisbee earlier in the film. This meant no extra footage had to be shot in Hollywood. It was 100 percent Arizona. Old Tucson is a great location, but by this film's 1969 release

With Robert Walker, Jr. (right), on horseback in the desert outside Tucson, Arizona, in *Young Billy Young* **(1969).**

it had lost some of its uniqueness due to its own popularity. Old Tucson was seen weekly on the TV western *The High Chaparral* (1967–1971), which was headquartered there among the cholla, ocotillo, organ pipe and prickly pear. In addition to Old Tucson and Starr Pass Trail, some *Young Billy Young* desert scenes were shot at the nearby Knagge Ranch property and the White Stallion Ranch near Sombrero Peak and Rattlesnake Pass.

Despite a devastating fire that destroyed a significant section of the historic cowboy town in 1995, Old Tucson still functions as a viable production location and popular tourist destination for nostalgic western fans. John Wayne made four films at Old Tucson beginning with *Rio Bravo* (1959) and concluding with *Rio Lobo* (1970). He remains the most popular subject and top selling point for the studio. Mitchum was never the western archetype that Wayne became, but he has not been forgotten at the studio. Posters for *El Dorado* and *Young Billy Young* are prominently displayed in the studio's memorabilia museum.

Regarding Old Tucson, Mitchum commented in the press releases, "I love that location."

Old Tucson Studios tour guide Marty Freese said:

> Working as a movie historian for the last 18 years at Old Tucson Studios, I've often been asked about Robert Mitchum. He co-starred with John Wayne in *El Dorado* in 1965 and Angie Dickinson in *Young Billy Young* in 1968 at the studio. Bob Shelton, who owned Old Tucson Studios for 25 years, said Robert Mitchum was the ultimate professional. Bob Shelton's wife Jane Lowe, whose family owned Lowe's Theaters, observed that Robert Mitchum and Duke Wayne worked well together, and Mitchum was always accessible to everyone on the set. Fellow actor Don Collier had high praise for Mitchum, as did the stuntmen who worked on both movies. Bob Mitchum starred in some of the finest westerns of all time, and it's been my privilege to show folks where some of those were filmed.*

Several elements in the film recall *Rio Bravo* including the exact same buildings and sets, and plot-wise the final siege on the lawman's jail.

---

*Marty Freese (e-mail correspondence, March 2018).

Leading lady Angie Dickinson is cast in a similar role to the one she played in *Rio Bravo* as a dance hall girl who catches Mitchum's eye. A secondary role is played by young Deana Martin, daughter of Dean Martin (Dean played the drunken deputy in *Rio Bravo*). Veteran western actor Paul Fix, who played Micah on the TV series *The Rifleman* (1958–1963), plays a stage driver and all but does a Walter Brennan impersonation. Brennan played Wayne's second deputy in *Rio Bravo*. While the Wayne–Howard Hawks film is considered a western classic, *Young Billy Young* is not. It's a tired retread. But that doesn't make it a bad picture.

Mitchum's Kane is motivated by revenge, but the part of the central bad guy John Anderson (*Ride the High Country* and a dozen episodes of TV's *Gunsmoke*) as a craggy-faced rancher responsible for Mitchum's son's death is underdeveloped. One wonders why Mitchum hasn't gone after him sooner. The denouement where the two finally face off is over quickly and a disappointment. Anderson is a fine western actor, but here he's given too little to do. He replaced actor Wendell Corey during production, perhaps accounting for the shortchanged part. Corey died a few months later at the age of 54 from cirrhosis of the liver. Poor editing and continuity errors abound despite the utilization of veteran 75-year-old film cutter Otho Lovering, who also died months after this film's completion. Perhaps Lovering's shaky work on the film reflected his deteriorating condition.

Taking a cue from recent co-star Dean Martin's warbling of "5 Card Stud," Mitchum sings the film's so-so opening theme song "Young Billy Young." The score by unlikely jazz musician Shelly Manne gets some mileage out of repeating the song's simple but catchy chord progression. But in the latter half of the film, the theme is jettisoned for a generic western guitar-tinged score. Overall, the music is a weakness.

What the film does have going for it are some fine performances. The hard-bitten Mitchum works especially well with his castmates, par-

Paul Fix (left) and Mitchum riding shotgun on a stagecoach in Old Tucson for *Young Billy Young* (1969).

ticularly Robert Walker, Jr., and Dickinson. Rising young actor David Carradine has a solid role as Walker's no-good saddle partner, the son of Anderson whom Mitchum jails as bait.

The film is laced with humor, a staple in Kennedy's agreeable approach. Mitchum gets off a few wry lines as Walker's wily mentor, explaining that he's left Kansas for Arizona seeking "a climate with less lead in the air." One of the better comic moments sees Mitchum fix Walker's jammed gun after Walker has drawn it on the lawman. Mitchum gives it back to the nonplussed Walker. Another has Mitchum warn the impetuous Walker about trying to take a burro across a creek. Mitchum remains nonchalant as the foolish Walker and the burro sink in the center. Flashbacks reveal some of the violent happenings that influence Mitchum's behavior, but they are nowhere near as effective as those seen in *Pursued* some 20 years earlier. *Young Billy Young* starts well but eventually reveals itself as one of Mitchum's weakest westerns. Several shootouts and fistfights occur, but none are staged in a memorable fashion. Robert Walker Jr.'s stunt doubles Bunker DeFrance and Jerry Gatlin are painfully apparent throughout the film in riding and fighting scenes. Mitchum's double Dave Cass, less evident, was present for such tricky maneuvers as jumping onto a moving stagecoach.

Cass, 6'4" and 220 pounds, got his professional start in Old Tucson's gunfight and stunt shows for Bob Shelton and Jack Young in the early 1960s. His work on the film *McLintock!* (1963) garnered him an introduction to John Wayne, who helped Cass get started in Hollywood on the TV shows *Gunsmoke* and *Hondo*. Doubling Mitchum was his first big assignment and led to a regular TV gig as stuntman for series star Robert Brown on the Pacific Northwest–set 1860s logging show *Here Come the Brides* (1968–1970). Cass doubled Kenny Rogers in the 1980s *Gambler* TV movies and became a highly respected stunt coordinator and first unit director, helming western telefilms for the Hallmark Channel. Cass recalled Mitchum:

> After a discharge (honorable) from the Army, I was back in town (Tucson) watching over my mother and working on shows that came in like *The High Chaparral*. I was hired to stunt double Robert Mitchum on *Young Billy Young*. It was a wonderful experience. Mitch never thought of himself as any better than anyone else on the crew. The assistant director would say, "It's time

Contemplating his coffee cup while Robert Walker, Jr., struggles with a burro in the pond in *Young Billy Young* (1969).

to go to work." Mitch would bellow out, "Work? This isn't work! I have worked for a living. This is fun time!" The crew loved him because he identified with them. He was a good horseman and would ride if he had to.*

It was true that Mitchum could still handle his riding and screen fighting. It's simply cost-effective in the picture business to have a second unit out on their own shooting long-range riding scenes with doubles while Burt Kennedy's first unit handled the dialogue scenes. In action, the 51-year-old Mitchum moves with the athletic grace and assurance of a man far younger. Witness Mitchum swing himself into the front seat of Fix's stagecoach. He still throws one of the most realistic punches in the business, here flattening Jack Kelly and Carradine for the camera. Mitchum beats up crooked town boss Kelly easily and often for his mistreatment of Dickinson, making former *Maverick* TV co-star Kelly more an annoyance than a threat. Mitchum revealed that the script called for him to hit an actor in the face with the butt of his gun, relying on his timing and experience to pull up an inch short of connecting. Mitchum performed this action so convincingly his fellow actor's bowels loosened out of fear.

Mitchum's years working in westerns have made him a pro at bits of cowboy business. He readies his horse's saddle and washes out his coffee tin like he's been doing these actions his entire life. Despite his star status and nightly revelry, Mitchum was the first person to report to the set in the morning. He'd share his dry humor and hearty laugh with cast and crew at whatever he deemed amusing. Reporters were surprised to see him drinking a root beer float instead of something harder served at the studio's Red Dog Saloon. Mitchum tolerated the hundreds of tourists who were barely off camera, and sometimes interrupted him for autograph requests on his way to the bathroom. On occasion, onlookers heard Mitchum let loose a string of creative profanity when a scene didn't come off as planned. On one occasion, Mitchum wandered out of his trailer clad only in a shower towel to the shock of the crowd of spectators.

It was a fun set with Mitchum holding court for the young cast as they sat around in their chairs on the streets of Old Tucson waiting for the camera set-ups. The crew even threw a cake and champagne birthday party for the hip older guy who kept marijuana cigarettes between his script pages as bookmarks. The younger actors affectionately called him "Momma Mitch." Twenty-year-old Deana Martin revealed in her memoir that she fell hard for the charismatic older actor. After her part was finished, she returned to L.A. but soon called asking if she could return to Tucson for the final week of filming. According to Deana,

> Robert was a wonderful guy and we had a remarkable and fun week together. He was intelligent and articulate. He liked to read, go out to dinner, and play cards until late in the evening. Everyone felt comfortable around him and came to him with their problems. Young and impressionable, I was momentarily smitten at being in the company of such a cool screen legend. I knew it couldn't last, but I enjoyed every minute and am grateful to this day for the brief time I had with him. Goodness knows what Dad would have thought if he'd known about the two of us. He and Mitch had just worked together on *5 Card Stud* and were the same age.

The film's climax has Mitchum rambling into the Gaslight Saloon and throwing leading lady Angie Dickinson over his shoulder, a virtual recreation of the final scene of *River of No Return* with Marilyn Monroe. Dickinson let the film's director Kennedy know she was uncomfortable with nudity and riding a horse. Kennedy assured her she wouldn't have to do the two actions at the same time. Mitchum helped put her at ease during her mildly revealing bathtub scene, and Dickinson appreciated his thoughtfulness. "He has a fabulous sense of humor about himself and about the whole world," she said in a *Variety* interview. "He acts like he's just had one drink all the time where he's always just a little bit devilish, a little bit risqué, a little bit confident, but never arrogant.... He was a very sensitive and very fascinating man."

Dickinson was a good sport on the set. She was married to musician Burt Bacharach. As

---

*Dave Cass (written correspondence, March 2018).

a joke Mitchum and director Kennedy had the Old Tucson period paper print a headline claiming "Bacharach—Wanted Dead or Alive." Dickinson first appeared with Mitchum in a small role in *Man with the Gun* and she was his leading lady again on a TV film shot in Reno, Nevada, in 1982. In 1994 she presented him with his Golden Boot Award, one of the highest honors bestowed on a Hollywood cowboy. Dickinson elaborated on their developing friendship in an interview with the western movie publication *Trail Dust*: "When you work together, especially on location, you get a chance to know each other. We did a non-western TV movie, *One Shoe Makes It Murder,* and we really got to pal around. You can't do that in town—only when you're away somewhere. You breakfast together, eat dinner together, and generally spend 'set' time with each other."

In his book of movie memories *Hollywood Trail Boss*, director Kennedy called Mitchum "very professional and one of the finest actors I have worked with. I did two pictures in a row with him. He's amazing in that if you listen to him you think he's a little crazy, but he's not at all. He is one of the brightest guys I know." The two worked together again in *The Good Guys and the Bad Guys* (1969), and the partnership was one Mitchum enjoyed. Kennedy's best known western comedies are *Support Your Local Sheriff* (1969) and *Support Your Local Gunfighter* (1971) with James Garner. Those "charming rogue" roles seem tailor-made for Garner, but it would not have been out of the realm of possibility for Mitchum to glide through those amiable films. In the late 1980s, Kennedy helmed nostalgic western TV movies with casts that included Richard Widmark, Stuart Whitman, Chuck Connors, Harry Carey, Jr., Gene Evans, Jack Elam, Don Collier, Angie Dickinson *et al.* Had Mitchum not been wrapped up in his epic World War II mini-series, he likely would have appeared in at least one of Kennedy's TV oaters.

After working security with his dad on *El Dorado,* Jay Gammons continued to find employment at Old Tucson Studios as a celebrity bodyguard and actor. He appeared as part of Old Tucson's gunfight show staged for tourists, playing undertaker character Digger O'Dell. As a youngster, Gammons appeared as a featured extra in *Rio Bravo* (1959) and *McLintock!* He was the boy with a drum in the former and appeared in a single shot over character actor Jack Kruschen's shoulder in the latter. On *Young Billy Young,* Gammons was once again hired as an atmosphere player. He recalled:

> You can see me on camera in *Young Billy Young* if you look real close. There's a bunch of guys in the saloon at the end of the picture. I'm the only one with a black hat and a Marsh Wheeling cigar. When Mitchum throws Angie Dickinson over his shoulder and leaves the bar, I take off my hat and hold it in the air and wave the cigar around.
>
> I got to talk with [Mitchum] a little bit. He wasn't a bad guy. He seemed nice. I worked on *The Life and Times of Judge Roy Bean,* and Paul Newman was nice too. I was the bodyguard for Ava Gardner on that, and she was very nice. I can't say that about all the Hollywood stars I worked with, but Robert Mitchum was a good guy. He was kind of a loner. Quiet. Sat off in the corner by himself. I had a picture taken with him, but unfortunately I don't have it any more. I do have a picture of him visiting the set of *Rio Lobo* that his son Chris worked on. It's a group shot. Robert Mitchum is standing there reading the script with sunglasses on. He really stands out in the picture. It's with the photos on my memorabilia wall.*

Gammons is now the proprietor of the western film set Gammons Gulch. All the cowboy films he worked on helped him realize a lifelong dream of building his own western town, and in the early 1970s Gammons found the perfect parcel of land in Cochise County, Arizona. He began collecting authentic buildings and artifacts from the 1860 to 1930 era and erected a living, functioning western set complete with saloon and grand motel. Jay and his wife Joanne live in the motel and host private tours for interested parties; Jay explains the history of his authentic western antiques, among them the badge Dean Martin wore in *Rio Bravo* that was given to his dad. He'll gladly tell stories of the many celebrities he knew or worked with, including John Wayne and Mitchum. Gammons Gulch has served as a location for several

---

*Jay Gammons (phone conversation, August 2017).

recent western-themed movies (including *The Gundown* [2011] and *Ambush at Dark Canyon* [2012]), music videos and commercials.

New Mexico–born Steve "Bunker" DeFrance entered films chasing Paul Newman on horseback in the Tucson-made *The Outrage* (1964). On the Arizona-lensed *Hombre* (1967), *Pocket Money* (1972) and *The Life and Times of Judge Roy Bean* (1972), he was Newman's stand-in. In the '60s, DeFrance began to follow the work, nomadically traveling Arizona, New Mexico and Utah wherever there was a western being made. He worked on *The Hallelujah Trail* (1965) in Gallup and *Duel at Diablo* (1966) in Kanab, in addition to episodes of *Death Valley Days* at Apache Junction. He worked on 52 episodes of *The High Chaparral* at Old Tucson. "I spent 30 years in the business getting paid to play cowboys and Indians," DeFrance recalled fondly.

> I started out doing horse work. I was hired as the stand-in for Robert Walker, Jr., on *Young Billy Young*. I was his riding double and did some stunts on the show. I doubled him in the shootout at the end and was one of the ranch hands and a Mexican soldier. I also stood in for Willis Bouchey and even put a frock on and doubled for the actress Deana Martin during the stagecoach chase. Jerry Gatlin doubled Walker for the fight in the saloon with David Carradine. I think Buddy Anderson from Old Tucson might have doubled Carradine for the fight. Most of the stunt guys were from Hollywood. Dave Cass doubled Mitchum. Old Tucson was reluctant to let their guys work on the film because it would take them away from doing their gunfight shows for the tourists. The Old Tucson guys were good at doing fights, but they were not really horsemen.
>
> Mitchum starred in some of the best westerns ever made. *The Wonderful Country* and *Blood on the Moon* are two of my favorite films. He was a very impressive man; imposing in some ways not only because of his physical stature but because of his stardom. To me, he was what people think of when they think of a star. He'd been around a long time as a leading man and was always prepared. He was a tremendously funny man, a world-class raconteur as far as telling stories. I was always like a fly on the wall in those situations. I loved being around that kind of guy. Guys like Mitchum told stories at a different level. I think part of it goes with being a good actor and knowing how to milk a story a little bit.*

After debuting as a teenage stunt extra in the mud-pit fight in *McLintock!*, Arizona-raised Neil Summers and his cowboy pals made their way around the southwest picking up work as riding extras on films: *The Rounders* (1965), *Duel at Diablo* (1966), *Rough Night in Jericho* (1967). Summers' first stunt was a stair-fall on the Audie Murphy western *Arizona Raiders* (1965). By the late 1960s, he was working regularly as one of Henry Wills' stunt troupe on *The High Chaparral*. According to Summers,

> Whenever director Burt Kennedy did a western in Arizona, he had us do a lot of the dangerous riding scenes like chasing the stagecoach in *Young Billy Young*. Stacy Newton and Bud Stout both worked as wranglers and stuntmen-extras and were part of the elite group of riders, as were Bunker DeFrance and myself. We had about a dozen guys that always rode their hearts out. We did dozens of films and TV shows all over the southwest until I moved to Hollywood and was elected for membership into the prestigious Stuntmen's Association. Henry Wills sponsored my membership, and I went to so-called professional stuntman status. I did *El Dorado* and *Young Billy Young* with Mitchum but had no extended interplay with him. He knew who I was and always spoke in a friendly greeting. I was supposed to work on *The Good Guys and the Bad Guys*, but I was working on *Gunsmoke*, I believe, and missed it.†

Mitchum's personal generosity was evident on the set of *Young Billy Young*. Dave Cass related:

> During this show, my mother died. The production company rushed me to the hospital, still wearing my double clothes. I missed her by ten minutes.… Insight to Mitch. The funeral was over, and flowers filled the funeral parlor from the production company. A week or so later I still had not paid the funeral bill. I called and was told that the bill was paid in full by Talbot Productions, Mitch's company. I thanked him. His response was, "Get out there in front of

---

*Steve "Bunker" DeFrance (phone conversation, August 2017).
†Neil Summers (written correspondence, May 2018).

the camera and make my ass look good!" As he turned and walked away, he said, "We only get one mother. You must have had a good one." A month or so later, I received a card from City of Hope, telling me $5000 had been donated in my mother's name. You guessed it—Talbot Productions. That was a lot of bucks back then. On the inside of that tough exterior was a very good spirit. However, he did not suffer fools.*

Billy Murphy was a muscular actor whose career went all the way back with Mitchum to *The Story of G.I. Joe* (1945). He is best known for playing the brawling brother of Richard Jaeckel opposite John Wayne in the World War II classic *Sands of Iwo Jima* (1949). A Malibu surfer, Murphy was one of Mitchum's friends and a true character who by many accounts went off the deep end in his behavior. In the late 1950s, Murphy dressed in gunfighter black and walked down Hollywood Boulevard trying to garner interest in a script for a film about Billy the Kid. Murphy hung around with Elvis Presley but eventually his flaky, occasionally threatening presence made him persona non grata among Hollywood producers and casting directors. Murphy showed up out of the blue in Arizona in the summer of 1968 and Mitchum gave him work on *Young Billy Young*. Presley did the same thing for Murphy on his Apache Junction–lensed western *Charro* (1969).

While Mitchum would extend a hand to an older, down-on-his-luck actor, he was also known to help promising young actors like Richard Egan, Mitch Ryan and Peter Breck get started in the business. One thing Mitchum loathed to do was show nepotism when it came to his own sons. He had mixed feelings about getting Jim started in the business in *Thunder Road* (1958). By the late 1960s, he wasn't about to hand out money or high-profile acting jobs to either Jim or Chris. He wanted them to find their own way as men. Jim was doing so, forging ahead in an up and down acting career that saw highlights like the World War II films *The Victors* (1963), *In Harm's Way* (1965) and *Ambush Bay* (1966) balanced out by exploitation titles like *The Beat Generation* (1959), *Girls Town* (1959) and *Ride the Wild Surf* (1964). Chris was attending the University of Arizona studying English Literature and occasionally worked as an extra at Old Tucson for $13 a day. The blond-haired Chris appears in a *Young Billy Young* flashback playing his father's on-screen son.

Former movie stuntman turned Old Tucson program director and Arizona location manager Jack Young related:

> In early 1968, I was advertising for a new stuntman to join my cast of actors doing the street shows at Old Tucson. My secretary brought me a résumé to peruse. Didn't pay much attention to the name but liked everything else I read. When she brought the young man in, I looked up into the eyes of one Christopher Mitchum.... Robert Mitchum's son. I asked what he was doing here. He said he was enrolled at the University of Arizona and needed a part-time job. Then I asked why he didn't work in movies and he said he didn't want to tread on the heels of his dad— rather do it himself. I turned him down as an Old Tucson stunt performer and explained to him this: "You have a famous father. Use it and everything else in your power to open all the doors you can. Once in, you and you alone will be responsible to keep the doors open." I sent him away. At the end of that year, we were preparing to shoot *Young Billy Young* when my secretary said there was someone to see me. When she brought that person in, it was Chris Mitchum. He grabbed me and gave me a big bear hug, then he said, "I took your advice, went back to Hollywood and opened some doors. I'm here because I have a part in this movie and it's all thanks to you. I must say I was pretty proud of myself for that."†

The first professional acting credit for Chris came in Los Angeles when production executive Sam Manners hired him to portray a corpse on an episode of the TV western *Dundee and the Culhane*. Chris' presence on *Young Billy Young* as a production assistant and small-part actor was also facilitated by Robert Mitchum, who knew that Chris wanted to write screenplays and work behind the scenes. To that end, Chris applied himself vigorously to the job. On-set reporters took note of the lack of emotion exhibited between father and son. The elder Mitchum was rarely seen to offer more than a half-smirk in his son's direction at a job well

---

*Dave Cass (written correspondence, March 2018).
†Jack Young (e-mail correspondence, 2013).

done, although he would praise the young man's performance to others in private. Chris, whose screen time in the film proved brief, was soon being asked by the press about the nature of their relationship. His reply was that his dad's strong sense of stoicism was simply the way the older Mitchum had always been. Robert Mitchum was never one to bare his feelings for anyone to see, even his own sons. All the Mitchum men were independent and made their own way in life. Chris would never ask his dad for money or a job and didn't expect one to be handed to him.

Chris had another blink-and-you-miss-him part in his dad's next western *The Good Guys and the Bad Guys* and took on the leading part of a young biker in the low-budget *Bigfoot* (1969) featuring his Uncle John Mitchum and veteran character actor John Carradine. Chris had a small assignment in John Wayne's western *Chisum* (1970) as a friend of Geoffrey Deuel's Billy the Kid. On location in Durango, Mexico, Wayne suggested that Chris should have been playing the Kid. Chris won an important second lead opposite Wayne in Howard Hawks' *Rio Lobo* (1970). Wayne took a shine to the young Mitchum and gave him another prominent part playing his son in the western *Big Jake* (1971). *The New York Times* ran a profile on the promising acting careers of Chris and Patrick Wayne (John Wayne's son), who also had a part in the film.

Chris was still being asked to publicly probe his relationship with his father, although he was now leery of reporters trying to create friction out of space between the men. He revealed in this story that he remained at odds with the reptilian-cold public image of Robert Mitchum, a man for whom sentimentality revealed weakness and distance suggested strength. Any praise for his sons came in the way of intricate parables they had to dissect for clues to life's lessons. Chris was dismayed to see his dad putting up the macho cowboy façade 24/7. "People are always talking about him as the living paradox and all that bull," Chris said. "You always hear about his fights and his drinking. But I think he is really a kind, warm, generous, poetic type of person. He writes poetry, you know, but he sees himself as the violent, son of a bitch, don't-give-a-damn actor who's riding the rails at 13 and was locked in a Georgia chain gang at 17. But he's not really the way he thinks he is. He himself doesn't know that he really isn't that way."

The early identification with Wayne's films and that bigger-than-life star's patriotic hard-right politics regarding the Vietnam War kept the younger Mitchum from winning roles in the increasingly counter-culture atmosphere of early 1970s Hollywood. This came despite his being named by *Photoplay* as Most Promising Male Newcomer in 1972. Needing to support his own growing family, Chris went to Spain and Asia to star in several low-budget martial arts action films that featured his Kenpo karate skills. His most notable Hollywood title is the Andrew McLaglen western *The Last Hard Men* (1976). In the States, he found the Mitchum name worked for and against him. Big-budget producers didn't want to be accused of nepotism, and Chris was passed over in favor of Jan-Michael Vincent for the role of his own dad's son in the mini-series *The Winds of War* (1983). Oftentimes Chris was offered a low-budget picture only to have the producers press for him to involve his father in some capacity. Some of these B-films involved full-contact fight scenes, non-existent or bounced paychecks, and even death threats. It was a wild and woolly existence. Titles run the exploitation gamut from *Ricco* (aka *The Mean Machine*) (1973) and *Cosa Nostra Asia* (1974) to *The Executioner Part II* (1984) and *American Commandos* (1986).

Chris' brother Jim's career was on a bumpy trail during this period. In 1967, Jim married stuntwoman turned actress Wende Wagner. His work consisted of undistinguished actioners like the Iranian-made *The Invincible Six* (1970) opposite Stuart Whitman. There was a significant stretch where he didn't act at all after playing a cowboy in Dennis Hopper's Peruvian-made misfire *The Last Movie* (1971). In the mid–1970s, Jim managed a couple of starring roles in the drive-in picture *Moonrunners* (1974) and *Trackdown* (1976), where he played a modern-day Montana cattle rancher punching his way through the seedy underbelly of Hollywood in search of his missing

As Marshal Ben Kane, Mitchum prepares for the final shootout at Old Tucson in *Young Billy Young* (1969).

sister. Many critics earmarked any success on his part on the fact that producers viewed him as a cheap surrogate for his lookalike father. However, critic Mick Martin of *The Express* did compare Jim favorably to Clint Eastwood, John Wayne and Gary Cooper. "The western has never been the same," wrote Martin. "Perhaps now that a young actor has taken up the torch, we can anticipate new classics in the genre. Jim Mitchum is a natural, but it took years to perfect this style."

In late 1974, Jim attempted to take control of his own career, producing and starring in the western *King of the Mountain* on location in Las Cruces, New Mexico. Esteemed professionals Slim Pickens, Arthur Hunnicutt, and John Mitchum were part of the cast, but the film ran into financial problems midway through principal photography and was forced to shut down. A grumbling Robert Mitchum had to reluctantly ride to the rescue to pay off local vendors, but the film itself was never resumed. In 1977, *Return to Thunder Road* was announced as going into pre-production in Bristol, Tennessee, with Jim Mitchum, Ben Johnson and Slim Pickens leading the cast. It too went nowhere. For these reasons, Robert Mitchum groused to the press that he wished his sons would have never entered the film business. By the end of the decade, Jim was starring with John Carradine in a cheap and embarrassing south-of-the-border horror-adventure, *Monstroid* (1980).

"My dad's a pretty fair man, actually," daughter Petrine Mitchum told *Rolling Stone* in 1973. She continued:

Difficult to understand, but he's a pretty fair man. He really is. When I was growing up, he wasn't around too much, so I had a lot of freedom. When I was between eight and fourteen, we had a farm, and I spent a lot of time there. I ran around a lot and did whatever I wanted. There were no big rules or anything—no strict church training or any regimentation like that. The only thing Dad would get upset about was if one of us did something stupid. Then he got mad. Dad has a very low tolerance for stupidity. But that's worked out for my benefit, really. My mother's much the same way. She's a great lady. Don't ask me how she puts up with Dad—I don't know. I don't know if I could put up with him for 30-some years. She's a very strong lady, though. She's stood by him through everything, and I guess she's put up with a lot and suffered a lot, but she keeps on going. She's a beautiful lady, very stable, very steadfast. My mother's always been there—for me, too, and very steady. I haven't just been tossed around like a lot of Hollywood brats.

Young Billy Young reviews were on the weak side, though many found the elder Mitchum fine in the lead role of yet another rugged individualist adopting faraway gazes and sideways glances. *The Motion Picture Herald* remarked,

> Robert Mitchum is due for the belated critical recognition accorded John Wayne. Mitchum, like Wayne, has reached the point where he can humorously burlesque his own image. *Young Billy Young* extends the actor's celebrated laconicism to quiet-parodic arrogance. Mitchum mocks himself in the role of the roving, moralistic gunman without the least bit of self-consciousness. This quality gives *Billy Young* a good deal of its charm—which like *True Grit* manipulates its star's presence for nostalgic dividends.

The Motion Picture Exhibitor offered a similar assessment: "The acting is surprisingly effective. Robert Mitchum gives another of his easygoing performances that are low on exhibitionism and high in professionalism. Like John Wayne, he plays one role over and over again, but he is always fun to watch, having developed a stereotype that is in some ways more interesting and effective than 'The Duke's.'"

Most critics didn't dig so deep into the film's appeal. *Variety* wrote, "Mitchum is quietly effective as the hunter, fast with a gun and accustomed to taking on great odds," while *The New York Times* called his work a "casually expert performance…. Even in a walk-through set-up, Mitchum can do laconic wonders with a good wisecrack, such as the devastating one that closes the picture." *The New York Post* added, "Mitchum has never been more loftily, contemptuously confident. The whole show runs off like the 99th printing from the same stencil, but it's amazing how much of it Mitchum can make you believe anyway." *The Los Angeles Times* found it to be "a rather mechanical performance," while *The Hollywood Citizen News* commented, "Mitchum attempts a profound portrayal but the banal script clouds his efforts." *The Hollywood Reporter* wrote, "Mitchum, almost asleep, is good enough," while *The Los Angeles Herald Examiner* noted, "Mitchum is slow and easy as usual, hitting people with great regularity and muttering, 'It depends on how you look at it,' whenever anyone questions him about it."

According to the *Dallas Morning News*, "Mitchum is smooth and entirely proficient as the aging gunman," while the *San Francisco Chronicle* stated simply, "Mitchum is Mitchum and is good." The *Boston Herald*, not so easily swayed, remarked, "Robert Mitchum is still pushing his tired, bulging carcass through countless assembly-line westerns that are slapped together to cash in on his box-office clout among action-adventure fans. A Mitchum western can be bearable if it's competently made, but his newest is as silly and uninspired as its title."

The contemporary publication *Cinema Retro* found the film enjoyable enough: "Somehow it all works very well, thanks mostly to Robert Mitchum's stalwart presence. With his trademark ramrod stiff walk and cool persona, Mitchum tosses off *bon mots* like a frontier version of 007…. He has considerable chemistry with Dickinson."

Mitchum remained a movie star, one of the few in his age range, but the promise that he opened the decade with in *The Sundowners* (1960) and *Home from the Hill* (1960) had descended into mediocrity. He was comfortable in westerns and knew audiences liked him in that period, so that's why he made them. However, his selection of scripts was more suspect. He turned down Sam Peckinpah's highly regarded, exceedingly violent *The Wild Bunch* (1969) to make the far less demanding *5 Card Stud*. William Holden played Pike Bishop instead. Mitchum reasoned they were both westerns and the Henry Hathaway picture would provide better accommodations and not be as strenuous to make. "What do I need with crazy Sam Peckinpah?" he asked the *Pittsburgh Post-Gazette*. "I was down in Durango the same time he was. I was doing *5 Card Stud* with Dean Martin, and we lived much better. Peckinpah's company was living in tents in the desert, with reptiles and spiders and cheap whores crawling around. Who needs that?"

The Good Guys and the Bad Guys (Warner Bros., 1969)

Cast: Robert Mitchum (James Flagg); George Kennedy (McKay); Martin Balsam (Mayor Wilker); David Carradine (Waco); Tina Louise (Carmel); Douglas V. Fowley (Grundy); Lois Nettleton (Mary); John Davis Chandler (Deuce); John Carradine (Ticker); Marie Windsor (Polly); Dick Peabody (Boyle); Kathleen Freeman (Mrs. Stone); Jimmy Murphy (Buckshot); Garrett Lewis (Hawkins); Bobby Riha (Billy); Jackie Joseph (Doris); Howard Storm (Harry); George Dunn (Engineer #1); Nick Dennis (Engineer #2); Phil Vandervort (Simms); and Dorothy Adams, Robert Anderson, Jimmie Booth, Nick Borgani, Danny Borzage, Paul Bradley, Thordis Brandt, David Cargo, Dee Carroll, David Cass, Noble "Kid" Chissell, Willis Clark, John Fritz, Bobby Gilbert, Angela Greene, Buddy Hackett, Darby Hinton, Irene Kelly, Kenner G. Kemp, Allen Lee, Stuart Lee, Paul Lees, Stephen Liss, Randy Meyer, Christopher Mitchum, Ernesto Molinari, Mike Morelli, Art Passarella, Hank Robinson, Robert Robinson, Danny Sands, Jeffrey Sayre, Russell Schulman, Phil Schumacher, Cap Somers, Arthur Tovey, George Tracy, Mike Wagner, John Wheeler, Bob Whitney, Chalky Williams.

Crew: Burt Kennedy (Director); Robert Goldstein (Executive Producer); Ronald M. Cohen and Dennis Shryack (Screenplay); Harry Stradling, Jr. (Photographer); William Lava (Music); Stan Jolley (Production Designer); Bill Finnegan (Production Manager); Red Turner (Prop Master); Howard Deane (Editor); Richard Bennett (Assistant Director); Stan Barrett, Jimmie Booth, May Boss, Dick Bullock, Billy Burton, Joe Canutt, Tap Canutt, Dave Cass, Everett Creach, Steve "Bunker" DeFrance, Tony Epper, Richard Farnsworth, Joe Finnegan, Jerry Gatlin, Alan Gibbs, Jerry Hardy, Kent Hays, Chuck Hayward, Clyde Hudkins, Jr., Dick Hudkins, Loren Janes, Leroy Johnson, Max Kleven, Walt LaRue, Allen Lee, Gary McLarty, Jack Perkins, Glenn Randall, Jr., Danny Sands, Walter Scott, Fred Stromsoe, Bob Terhune, Glenn R. Wilder, Jack Williams (Stunts); Kenny Lee (Ramrod); Allen Lee (Wrangler); Fargo Graham (Livestock Coordinator).

91 minutes; Released October 1969

Upon finishing *Young Billy Young* in Arizona, Mitchum was quick to saddle up for another western in the fall of 1968. Burt Kennedy was once again the helmsman, bringing his patented humor and charm to the genre for *The Good Guys and the Bad Guys*. The script was originally attached to Kirk Douglas in 1967 when it was known as *The Old Breed*. Mitchum's co-star George Kennedy was fresh off an Oscar win for Best Supporting Actor in *Cool Hand Luke* (1967), in which he played the role of the prison yard bully originally pegged for Mitchum. It was a winning combination, but Mitchum was growing tired from his non-stop string of pictures and openly contemplating retirement. For the *Los Angeles Herald Examiner*, Mitchum added the burly George Kennedy to the list of "beautiful dames" the likes of John Wayne and Dean Martin he was paired with on screen. Adopting a shield of grumpiness, he humorously complained he kept reading he was going to make this film in the trades but that when he got the script, he put it away with all the other screenplays gathering dust. He claimed he woke up one Monday morning on location in New Mexico, unaware how he ended up in the film. His story must be taken with a large grain of salt. There's plenty to like in *The Good Guys and the Bad Guys*, including Mitchum's finely tuned performance.

The plot sees aging Marshal James Flagg (Mitchum) lobbying the mayor of Progress (Martin Balsam) to form a posse to go after his arch-foe Big Jim McKay (George Kennedy), a notorious bank robber who terrorized the country in the 1880s (but now, the turn of the century, is barely remembered). Balsam is appalled by the idea of forming an old-fashioned posse in the age of mechanization. Instead, he opts to retire Mitchum and give him a gold watch for his many years of service. Mitchum is concerned that Kennedy and his gang are going to rob a large money shipment headed for the Progress bank, but when he catches up to the gang in the high country he is dismayed to find that Kennedy is being bossed around by younger outlaw David Carradine. After some soul-searching reminiscences and the realization that all their old cohorts are dead and gone, the two men unite to stop Carradine's gang by using all their wits and experience.

The film was shot on picturesque locations in

On his horse Bulls-Eye Bee, sharing the screen with Douglas Fowley in *The Good Guys and the Bad Guys* (1969).

Chama, New Mexico, and Silverton, Colorado, during the changing seasons, symbolic of its two aging stars. It's beautiful to view as filmed by veteran cameraman Harry Stradling, Jr., in Aspen-heavy elevations that reached 11,000 feet in the San Juan Mountains. In Chama (population: 1500), most of the cast and crew members were quartered at the Elkhorn Lodge while Mitchum stayed alone in a remote hunting lodge 15 miles from the set (seven miles of it gravel road). He cooked his own meals and referred to himself in press releases as "a part-time hermit." When not filming, Mitchum toured the area as a passenger in the company helicopter, on the lookout for personal ranch property.

New Mexico Governor David Cargo claimed Mitchum was looking at a home in Santa Fe and a horse ranch in Socorro, but Mitchum opted to stay quartered in California. Cargo was instrumental in luring Mitchum and the production to his home state to kick-start the local film industry after meeting with the star in Hollywood. *The Good Guys and the Bad Guys* was originally going to be filmed in Mexico, but Mitchum took a liking to Cargo's sales pitch and the untapped location. Cargo was given a small part in the film. Mitchum returned often to New Mexico, always staying at the Governor's Mansion at the politician's invitation. Cargo and Mitchum were friendly and would discuss world politics into the wee hours. Cargo let Mitchum use his home phone and fondly recalls Mitchum joking with people on the other line that he was staying with the governor. "He got a kick out of that," Cargo told the *Albuquerque Tribune*.

In the well-done, large-scale climax, the stars board the train Carradine's gang is attempting to rob. This was shot using the Cumbres & Toltec Scenic Railroad along the Cumbres Pass. The train scenes were slow to film and a logistical nightmare for Burt Kennedy. Significant time was spent traveling back and forth along the rails to match exterior backgrounds filmed on the train. Stuntmen on horseback chased the train repeatedly for two weeks. The press reported that a bored Mitchum suggested they simply quit and try another movie. No one knew if he was joking. A town façade was built in Chama to replicate the Warner Bros. studio, with the famed back lot Laramie Street in ample use when the film was in Hollywood. The star's firearms were handcrafted and imported from Spain and Italy. As was becoming his habit, Mitchum rode his own three-year-old buckskin Bull's Eye Bee in the film. The horse was the son of his beloved quarter horse Cap-Gun. Cap-Gun was the son of King's Pistol, a champion cutter. Mitchum's son Chris worked as a production assistant and briefly appears on screen.

A comic highlight is a one-minute fistfight between the two aging actors after the 6'4", 235-pound Kennedy is dismissed by Carradine and ordered to kill Mitchum. The one-minute fight, included in the book *Classic Movie Fight Scenes,* resembles Mitchum's fistic exchange with John Wayne in *El Dorado* and is largely played for laughs as the men punch away at one another in the Chama River. The long shots and falls off the rocks are taken by stunt doubles Tap Canutt and Bob Terhune. Canutt was the oldest son of rodeo champ turned legendary stuntman Yakima Canutt. The two actors quickly run out of slugging energy after falling into the water, and by fight's end old-timer Douglas Fowley is tying the drenched, exhausted men into their saddles for a trip back to Progress. Once in town, they grow to like one another, with Kennedy turning Mitchum on to the charms of local boarding house owner Lois Nettleton. Consumed with his work, Mitchum has never married. Kennedy reveals he lost his wife to illness. They begin to long for their lost youth. The Mitchum-Kennedy dialogue exchanges are rich and well-played, gaining audience sympathy for these men who have spent the entirety of their lives living by the gun. Veteran western writer Joe Millard turned out the tie-in novelization to the film, and it is a page-turner.

The crew was filled with talented veterans of the western genre. Ramrod Kenneth Lee's career stretched back to the 1940s where he exercised the movie horse Steel on Mitchum's RKO films under his head wrangler dad Allen Lee. Cinematographer Stradling worked regularly on TV's *Gunsmoke* and *Cimarron Strip* (1967–1968) and shot *Little Big Man* (1970) the following year. Screenwriter Dennis Shryack later co-wrote the Clint Eastwood western *Pale Rider* (1985). Co-writer Ronald M. Cohen won a Western Heritage Award for adapting the Elmore Leonard story *Last Stand at Saber River* (1997) into a TV movie starring Tom Selleck. Costumers Bob Richards and Dominic Di Bona worked throughout the 1950s and 1960s on the TV series *Death Valley Days*. Veteran editor Otho Lovering of *Stagecoach* (1939) fame died at the start of *Good Guys* production and was replaced by Howard Deane. Cast member John Davis Chandler, playing a dangerous Carradine gun, was a Sam Peckinpah regular who suited up for *Ride the High Country* (1962) and *Major Dundee* (1965). Carradine's character actor father John Carradine shows up as a railroad conductor. Former western stuntman Chick Hannan worked as a representative for the American Humane Association. Folk singer Glenn Yarbrough sang "The Ballad of Marshall Flagg" throughout. Seven Arts announced plans to make a sequel, hoping Mitchum and Kennedy would become a recurring team. But Mitchum spent the next year in Ireland making *Ryan's Daughter* (1970) and talk quickly faded like smoke in the wind.

Kennedy, popular western villain from films like *Lonely Are the Brave* (1962) and *The Sons of Katie Elder* (1965), said of Mitchum in his autobiography: "This man was the best-read actor I ever met. ... I loved every second [of *Good Guys and the Bad Guys*], and never ceased to marvel at the way his mind worked." Mitchum was equally fond of his big co-star, telling Garry Armstrong, "George Kennedy was a blast to work with. The man could hold his hooch."* At one point during filming, Mitchum received a pound of Beluga caviar sent from Iran by his son Jim. Mitchum shared the delicacy on horseback with co-star Kennedy. Director Kennedy told western writer C. Courtney Joyner in *The Westerners* that Mitchum was "a wonderful

---

*Garry Armstrong (e mail correspondence, August 2017).

actor. He has great ideas. I found it very easy to work with Mitchum." David Carradine from the TV series *Shane* (1966) said in his own autobiography, "Mitchum was an interesting man and was as tough and uncompromising as they come."

Stuntman Dave Cass, playing a David Carradine gang member named Tuber, was happy to work on another Mitchum film after doubling him on *Young Billy Young*. Cass recalled:

> Within a year after [*Young Billy Young*], I was back in Hollywood. I get a call from Burt Kennedy about *The Good Guys and the Bad Guys*. Burt was a great, old-school filmmaker. Mitch wanted to make sure I would be on it. Another chance to double Mitch. I was excited. Burt said no double work, that Tap Canutt would do that. Mitch wanted me to do a part, so I would have a run of the show and make more money. There was a catch. Mitch always drove to location work. Tim Wallace had been his stand-in for years. Tim drove with him, but Tim had retired so I was asked to drive with Mitch. Of course, I said yes, so he picked me up in Sherman Oaks, California, and off we headed to Chama, New Mexico. That trip alone would fill the pages of a book. Of course, when we were done on location, Mitch flew home and I drove the car back.
>
> Mitch did a lot of horseback riding on that show. He would ride into a scene, do dialogue, ride out a short distance, and stop. Burt Kennedy would call out for Tap Canutt to mount up. Tap would do the fast ride away. Tap Canutt did a great transfer from horse to moving train. Mitch was a very good horseman but always wanted to make sure everyone earned their keep. Wranglers and crew loved working with him. He always covered their backs. During an interview for that show on the set, he was asked what it was like being a movie star. He replied, "Lassie is a movie star." I heard him say that more than once.... Careers went on. From time to time I would get a call from Mitch. "Just checking on you." We would always chat for a short time about nothing special. He would always remind me that all we're doing is chasing rainbows.... He had a great caring nature when it came to stuntmen. He knew us all on a first name basis.*

Steve "Bunker" DeFrance, another *Young Billy Young* stuntman who found work on *Good Guys*, recalls:

> I was hired as a riding double for one of the actors doing second unit work before the principles arrived in Chama. I'm 5'8½" and the actor I doubled was about 5'7". I also worked as a stand-in on that. I always stayed close to the camera, so they'd use me a lot. I even stood in for George Kennedy, who is almost 6'5", and Mitchum, who is about 6'2". In those cases, I'd stand on an apple box or a half box when they set up the shot.
>
> My favorite memory of Mitchum on *The Good Guys and the Bad Guys* involved David Carradine's dad John Carradine, who came up for a small part on the film as the train conductor. Whenever we were done filming, there'd be about 20 to 30 of us who would gather around Mitchum to listen to him sit and tell stories. His stories were really like a performance. But on this occasion, I remember Mitchum sitting back to listen to John Carradine, who was one of the great Hollywood storytellers. He could talk for hours, and Mitchum became one of us.†

Former stuntman turned Arizona location manager Jack Young found himself on the New Mexico location with Mitchum. Young said:

> I left Old Tucson and went to Santa Fe to work for the governor (David Cargo) and helped build the film industry there. He gave me the old Armory located on Old Pecos Trail to turn into a film center. I was having a sound stage built in one of the buildings when he called and said he had a small part in the movie they were shooting in Chama and did I want to go with him? We drove up there in this big limousine. When we got to the set, the director was Burt Kennedy and the actors were Robert Mitchum and George Kennedy. We hung out with them for a couple days until Cargo did his line. He was a reporter at the end of the movie. However, his voice was so bad, they dubbed it with another. I had worked with all those guys before and most of the crew. It was a great time to be had.‡

Veteran horse wrangler Fargo Graham recalls, "I only worked with Robert Mitchum the one time up in Chama north of Santa Fe on 'The Good Guys and the Bad Guys.' I provided all the livestock on that... He was al-

---

*Dave Cass (written correspondence, March 2018).
†Steve "Bunker" DeFrance (phone conversation, August 2017).
‡Jack Young (e-mail correspondence, 2013).

Taking a punch from George Kennedy and falling into the Chama River in *The Good Guys and the Bad Guys* (1969).

ways doing something else than what I was. He'd be in Mexico, and I'd be up in Colorado or someplace. I worked all over on location in Old Tucson, Mescal, Colorado, Santa Fe, even down in Mexico. Always somewhere else than Mitchum… He was a good man, and he was a good horseman. And I'll tell you, he didn't take shit from no one."*

Dave Cass recalls Mitchum's distaste for fools:

> On that show, we had a couple of young producers. They shall go nameless. One of those ground on Mitch's nerves. It had snowed heavy one day. Mitch and I were in his dressing room when the two came knocking on the door. He told me to let them in. I did. The grinding one started going off about the weather, getting behind shooting and such. He stopped and looked at Mitch. "Mitch, are you hearing me?" Mitch calmly sipped the drink in his hand. He set the drink down and said, "Some people call me Robert, some call me Bob, friends call me Mitch. You can call me *Mr. Mitchum*." The producer smiled and said, "Oh, now, Mitch, lighten up." In a flash, Mitch was on his feet, grabbing the man and spinning him around and yelling at me, "Dave! Open the door!" I did, and Mitch threw the fellow out into three feet of snow. Mitch turned to the other producer. The man almost jumped out the door. Mitch smiled at me and said, "Dave, would you please close the door." I did.†

There's a fitting sadness to Mitchum in the film, as he and his character knew the end of the trail was coming soon. It's a companion performance to Mitchum's Jeff McCloud in *The Lusty Men*, another aging cowpoke who has outlived his usefulness. The film had a joint world premiere held in Albuquerque and

---

*Fargo Graham (phone conversation, August 2017).
†Dave Cass (written correspondence, March 2018)

Santa Fe to promote the film business in New Mexico. The critical reception was mixed, although Mitchum received positive notices. *The Hollywood Reporter* raved, "Mitchum delivers one of his liveliest and best performances in a long time. His reactions in the public ceremony, which is his firing, are eloquent, his too infrequently exploited gift for comedy ever on beat." "A fine piece of acting by Mitchum," hailed *Films and Filming*. "Mitchum and Kennedy are steamroller actors," said *The New York Daily News*. "At times, it seems like they don't play a part so much as crush it. Yet they both have an easy-sell, genial quality that keeps you liking them all the while."

The Los Angeles Times said Mitchum and Kennedy "perform handsomely," while *The Los Angeles Herald Examiner* offered, "George Kennedy and Mitchum are suitably wry about being obsolete." *Variety* chimed in: "Both Mitchum and Kennedy imbue their roles with sound values, Kennedy probably faring better because of lines and business handed him." *The Motion Picture Herald* added, "Mitchum creates a strong audience sympathy, which gives strong satisfaction when the growing-old hero outmaneuvers the crass young gang members." *The Motion Picture Exhibitor* praised "the warmly human performances" of the star duo. *The Miami Herald* wrote, "Mitchum and Kennedy bounce off each other beautifully, both literally and figuratively. It's a great team and fun from two real pros."

Among contemporary reviews, Michael R. Pitts' *Western Movies* called it a "fanciful western comedy with fine work by Robert Mitchum and George Kennedy," while Herb Fagen's *Encyclopedia of Westerns* said, "Burt Kennedy got his money's worth by teaming the sardonic Mitchum with the burly Kennedy and an energetic supporting cast." Mitchum biographer Mike Tomkies called it "one of the liveliest and best performances he had given for a while," while Bruce Crowther wrote that the film allowed Mitchum "to express a feeling for times past which matched the nostalgic recollections of many who had never in fact experienced the changing times the film displayed."

Mitchum had worked three straight years with little rest and continued to talk of retirement, mirroring his character in *The Good Guys and the Bad Guys*. Writer Burt Prelutsky asked him what he'd do instead. "Goof off," replied Mitchum. "Fool with the horses. I don't think I'd miss the movies. Most of them stink, and, for my part, stardom is meaningless." When *Good Guys* wrapped in late 1968, Mitchum got out of Dodge, climbing into his car to drive aimlessly across the countryside to the back of beyond. His tendency to drift the land was an effort to reconnect with the rambling railroad adventures of his wild boy youth. This escape was akin to Mitchum's fellow Hollywood iconoclast Sterling Hayden's desire to hit the open sea after filming. Both actors despised Hollywood yet relied on the industry to fund their love of horses, boats and drink. Hayden turned his adventurous follies, including spiriting his children away from his ex-wife for a voyage to Tahiti, into the highly acclaimed and literate book *Wanderer*. Mitchum remained reluctant to commit his own wanderings to the page, hesitant to reveal that sensitive side of his personality to the masses. So he drank, and he roamed.

"I just float off like I used to when I was a kid," he told the *Daily Mail*. "Dorothy? She understands." One of Mitchum's favorite escape destinations: the area known as Gringo Gulch in Puerto Vallarta, Mexico, and its open-air seaside bar The Oceana. He also liked the uncrowded beaches near the sleepy village of Mazatlan and the Playa Hotel where he'd charter boats for deep sea fishing. Once he spent several days with a Louisiana family who had no idea who he was. Mitchum liked it that way. The smaller the burg, the better for this carefree bum. "I'd come riding into town like the Lone Ranger," Mitchum told *Photoplay*. "And sure enough, someone would come up to me and ask, 'Ain't you that feller who plays in them westerns?' 'Yep,' I'd say, and like as not he'd ask me to join his family for supper, and I'd spend the whole night just talking to them."

Fine character-driven westerns were made during this period like *Will Penny* (1968) and *Monte Walsh* (1970); even a solid action pic in *The Stalking Moon* (1969) starring Gregory Peck. Sam Peckinpah turned out the enjoyably offbeat *The Ballad of Cable Hogue* (1970) with

Jason Robards, Jr. However, Mitchum didn't lobby for the best scripts and made his work choices without regret. Location and days off were prime motivating factors. "My inflexible and inviolable rule—the least effort for the greatest return," he told *Time Out*. Charlton Heston starred in *Will Penny* as the aging title character, arguably his best role, while Lee Marvin headlined in the bittersweet *Monte Walsh*. Mitchum had been under consideration to star in the latter. Both films dealt with a changing west and the symbolic death of the aging cowboy and his rugged dignity. *The Good Guys and the Bad Guys* tackled this theme in a more lighthearted fashion. For fans of the western genre, it's a completely enjoyable experience and ranks in the upper third of Mitchum's oaters thanks to the reliable lead performers and pristine western scenery.

The Wrath of God (MGM, 1972)

Cast: Robert Mitchum (Oliver Van Horne); Frank Langella (Thomas De La Plata); Rita Hayworth (Senora De La Plata); John Colicos (Col. Santilla); Victor Buono (Jennings); Ken Hutchison (Emmet Keogh); Paula Pritchett (Chela); Gregory Sierra (Jurado); Frank Ramirez (Carlos Moreno); Enrique Lucero (Nacho); Jorge Russek (Cordona); Chano Urueta (Antonio); Jose Luis Parades (Pablito); Aurora Clavel (Senora Moreno); Victor Eberg (Delgado); Pancho Cordova (Tacho); Guillermo Hernandez (Diaz); and Ralph Nelson.

Crew: Peter Katz (Producer); Ralph Nelson (Director); James Graham (aka Jack Higgins) (Screenplay); Alex Phillips, Jr. (Photographer); Lalo Schifrin (Music); Ted Parvin (Wardrobe); Robert Watts (Production Manager); Richard Bracken, J. Terry Williams, Albert Wilson (Editors); Everett Creach, Terry Leonard, Bennie Dobbins, Greg Walker, Rock A. Walker (Stunts); Chema Hernandez (Livestock Coordinator).

111 minutes; Released July 14, 1972

An offbeat 1920s pseudo-western concerning a Latin American revolution, *The Wrath of God* starts well but becomes increasingly inane and convoluted despite its vigor. Mitchum once again appears in the guise of a priest, this time toting a machine-gun, a knife hidden in a cross and, in a nod to *5 Card Stud*, a derringer in his hollowed-out Bible. Mitchum's Father Oliver Van Horne, a bank robber hiding out south of the border, is spared from a firing squad when military leader John Colicos sees an opportunity to team him with gunrunner Victor Buono and Irish mercenary Ken Hutchison to assassinate powerful local despot Frank Langella. The rub is that Langella hates Catholic priests, a fact that is exploited by Colicos in the form of Mitchum. The star becomes caught up in his priestly duties for the small town, winning an admirer in Langella's own mother Rita Hayworth. "All is not quite what it seems," Mitchum announces during the film's more whimsical opening moments. He has over $50,000 hidden in his suitcase and a devil-may-care attitude. We're never sure if he is or was a priest.

The shaded character was no stretch for Mitchum, combining elements of *The Night of the Hunter, Bandido, Villa Rides* and *5 Card Stud* to routine effect. Old Sleepy Eyes stands his ground admirably, chewing on a cigar while firing his Thompson Tommy Gun and knocking back whiskey after his dialogue. It's hard to picture any other actor outside of Lee Marvin excelling in this broad character lead as Mitchum does, although Mitchum claimed Clint Eastwood, Burt Lancaster and Burt Reynolds were offered the part before director Ralph Nelson talked him into doing it over drinks at the Beverly Hills Polo Lounge. The early scenes

As Father Oliver Van Horne in *The Wrath of God* (1972).

establish a nice tongue-in-cheek attitude but that gives way to mindless action even as Mitchum rebuilds the small town's church and perhaps his own inner psyche. There's enough mystery to the Mitchum character to keep it interesting, and Buono and Hutchison, his partners in "the unholy trinity," are fine in their colorful parts. Hutchison has the romantic lead opposite beautiful Indian girl Paula Pritchett, while Mitchum takes on the experienced "father figure" assignment. Mitchum does have a shirtless scene while drinking in his skivvies. The fact he was in his middle 50s and becoming increasingly jowly didn't stop him from parading around his thickening, weather-beaten beefcake.

Director Nelson made the western *Duel at Diablo* (1966), but *The Wrath of God* falls short of that film's professional polish despite good moments. "Ralph would get all hung up making the movie looking for meanings and validities," Mitchum told the *Dallas Morning News*. "I would say, hell, it's three clowns robbing their way." In one action scene, Mitchum is behind the wheel of an open Lincoln Touring Car being chased by soldiers on horseback with Hutchison firing the machine-gun. Plenty of bodies and horses hit the dirt to seriocomic effect in the many violent shootouts. It was reported that the film was targeted for animal abuse by the American Humane Association, but the truth is the Werner Herzog film *Aguirre, the Wrath of God* (1972) was the culprit. It's hard to believe horse-lover Mitchum would stand by idly while any horses were injured in his vicinity. The horses in Mitchum's film were stunt horses safely trained to fall.

The ending is an epic shootout with a wounded Mitchum a martyr wrapped in barbed wire and tied to a cross that he improbably topples onto Langella, apparently ending their lives. Mitchum allowed his double Terry Leonard to handle that stunt. Mitchum's knee was bothering him, and he kept aggravating it tripping over his flowing cassock robes during action scenes. The film has a certain goofy charm, and it looks as if Mitchum had some fun making it even if the material wasn't too taxing. "This business has robbed me of my initiative," Mitchum told columnist Hal Boyle.

"It's so easy to do. There are only two hard things about it—wiping off the makeup at the end of the day and putting on and pulling off your boots while you're making a western."

Based on a novel by James Graham (aka Jack Higgins), *The Wrath of God* was shot in Cuernavaca, Sonora, and Mexico City, Mexico. A primary location was the ghost town of La Luz in the Sierra Madres. It featured an intact Catholic church and a hacienda façade which the film company restored. The setting is, however, an unnamed Central American country. It seems an odd assignment to accept considering Mitchum's self-confessed semi-retirement. Coming off Oscar buzz for *Ryan's Daughter* (1970), he had recently turned down prime starring assignments in the critically heralded commercial films *Patton* (1970), *Dirty Harry* (1971) and *The French Connection* (1971). "In development" was an intriguing mystery from a novel by Tucker Coe (aka Donald Westlake and Richard Stark), *Kinds of Love, Kinds of Death*. In it, Mitchum would have played gloomy private eye Mitch Tobin, but that project went into turnaround. Orson Welles wanted Mitchum to star with Jack Nicholson in the spy drama *Midnight Plus One*, but that too went unrealized. So Mitchum signed on the dotted line for something utterly familiar in *The Wrath of God*. "You're sitting on a rock, and suddenly you realize, 'What the hell am I doing here?'" Mitchum told the *San Antonio Express and News* regarding his involvement in the picture. At the presser, he derisively referred to the film as *The Mild Bunch* in mock reference to Sam Peckinpah's *The Wild Bunch*.

The Wrath of God was a troubled production, mostly due to the cast members drinking and experimenting with mind-altering drugs, a reflection of filmmaking in the 1970s. At the film's contentious press conference, Mitchum was quoted saying that during the film's making, he was, "stoned as usual. We all were." Producer William S. Gilmore, Jr., maintained that Mitchum was not the problem. It was everyone else trying to emulate him. Co-star Ken Hutchison badly cut his arm on a pane of glass in his motel room, and production shut down for several weeks while he recovered. Dorothy Mitchum heard Hutchison scream and fashioned a tourniquet to save his life. At first there was talk of recasting his role and re-shooting his existing footage. Hollywood veteran Rita Hayworth, Mitchum's leading lady in *Fire Down Below* (1957), was drinking during filming and couldn't remember her lines. She wouldn't travel to location in a vehicle going faster than ten miles per hour. Her problems during filming are now attributed to the early onset of Alzheimer's Disease. Mitchum lobbied for her involvement, unaware of her worsening condition. He was seething at MGM head James Aubrey for severely cutting and dumping his last film *Going Home* (1971) after a week in the theaters. Mitchum had taken less pay on that father-son drama for a piece of the box office, which was nil. To get back at Aubrey, known in the business as "The Smiling Cobra," Mitchum ingeniously chose to work for him again—yet be at his most gruff and cantankerous. Whenever cameras were ready to roll on *The Wrath of God,* Mitchum would announce he needed to use the bathroom in his trailer. The longer this took, the better to stick it to Aubrey and MGM's budget.

Mitchum was content to be drinking on location once again in Mexico, although at one point he suggested recasting his part to the *San Francisco Chronicle*. He'd rather "go to the beach." Alcohol flowed freely as it did on many macho Hollywood productions, and Mitchum reveled in the loco digs. The agave-based Mescal was his drink of choice on this film. "Mescal keeps me regular," he told his friend Robert Parrish. "Scotch keeps me drunk." Trying to rein in Mitchum, director Nelson paid a local cantina owner to close his business. Mitchum paid the man more money to reopen and be at his beck and call at all hours. Mitchum partied the nights away, yet still displayed the ability to perform all day. Work hard, play hard. Nobody could keep up with his round-the-clock revelry.

A cigar-chomping Mitchum fires off his Thompson machine-gun in MGM's *The Wrath of God* (1972).

Always generous to a fault, Mitchum footed the bill for his compadres' bar tabs and paid for a catered meal for the crew that was flown in from Chasen's in Hollywood. He told the *San Francisco Chronicle* he was tired of the production serving "rabbit and a hot dog." Mitchum grilled steaks on an open barbecue in his motel room at the Real de las Minas, to the consternation of the establishment and the local fire department. Mitchum also brewed his own booze from the local flora and baked a batch of special brownies to hand out to those willing to indulge. He confessed to the *Morning Star* that the marijuana-laced brownies "wiped out everybody."

The cast and crew generally enjoyed Mitchum's veteran presence, even if his behavior directed at studio head Aubrey was growing surlier and his verbal tirades more unhinged. "He's really a very nice man," Rita Hayworth told the *San Francisco Chronicle* in a lucid moment. "A few little old ladies might get shocked by his four-letter words, but that's Bob. It doesn't worry me." Producer Gilmore bore the brunt of a profane verbal assault on at least one occasion, although he told Lee Server that Mitchum was "the ultimate professional.... I can't say enough positive things about him." Assistant director Jerry Zeismer chose to remember Mitchum's biting sense of humor, recalling in his book *Ready When You Are*:

> Robert Mitchum was one of the best storytellers I have ever heard. Each morning that he'd film in La Luz, I'd ride out with him in his car, and he would tell me stories from his life and famous people he knew, that type of thing. Most mornings he'd have me laughing so hard I'd be falling on the floor of the car before we left Guanajuato. Ken Hutchison, a young actor from Ireland, would ride with us. Ken was a bit of a wild man, or so he hoped. He tried to keep up with Robert Mitchum in all vices, and he couldn't. I looked upon it like Mitchum had been in the big leagues for 40 years and Ken was just a rookie.

Hutchison was nearly comatose from drink before one important scene. Mitchum and Zeismer carried him onto the set and propped him into position while the crew set up the lighting for a scene in a church pew. Mitchum used his own time-worn tricks to revive the young actor for the cameras. When director Nelson called for action, Hutchison rallied with a moving soliloquy before collapsing in exhaustion. "Emotionally draining," explained Mitchum as he and Zeismer hauled Hutchison back to his room. Unit publicist Tom Miller had worked with Mitchum on *Ryan's Daughter* and considered him his all-time favorite personality. "The man was outrageous," Miller wrote in his memoir (using the pen name Tom Canford). "He was continually breaking me up.... To have known and worked with him was a real treat."

New York actor Frank Langella, playing the eye-popping, over-the-top bad guy, got off to a rough start with Mitchum due to his inexperience with horses and handling guns. Langella felt Mitchum was testing him, seeing if he could control his horse in the scene and still successfully deliver his line while pointing his weapon convincingly. After several attempts during rehearsal, a shaky Langella finally got his horse up a set of steps and managed to get the line out while awkwardly brandishing his firearm. Mitchum intentionally blew his own line with an off-color remark. Each successive line delivered by Mitchum in response to Langella's was another wittily profane rejoinder. Langella remained in character until Mitchum decided to run the scene for real and performed his dialogue flawlessly. The ice was broken. "From that day on, I adored every minute I spent around Robert Mitchum," Langella wrote in his book of remembrances *Dropped Names*.

Reviews were negative. *The Los Angeles Times* declared the film "trash," but added, "Mitchum, Buono, and Hutchison have been given colorful parts to play and come through with robust though extremely broad performances. Mitchum's portrayal of a renegade who may have actually been the priest he pretends to be has both ambiguity and strength, an alternating reverence and scorn, that in itself suggests what the picture might have been." *The New York Times* called it "junk" but once again admitted that Mitchum was "most excellent." *Variety* said, "Very few players can project the necessary toughness/tenderness which Mitchum herein has been able to do.... While he's one of the few remaining established male stars to have the guts to essay a broad spectrum of roles—not always successfully—in his long career, the casting here is relatively close to his primary image among audiences of all ages [and] his presence is felt throughout." *The Hollywood Reporter* wrote, "Mitchum is really splendid as the equivocal man of God," while *Cue* remarked, "Mitchum gives his customary sincere performance."

The Los Angeles Herald Examiner was impressed by the film's star:

> Mitchum leads the ranks as a devil-may-care priest with an on-again, off-again habit and a machine-gun to prop up his conscience. His offhand delivery and lazy charm, disguising powerful individuality, are perfectly suited to the role. He strides unselfconsciously over any quagmires of sentimentality which could have been created by the priest's friendship with a young urchin and sidesteps the boundaries of cliché with perverse humor. He's marvelous.

Films and Filming was impressed, calling Mitchum "probably the best non-actor in the business.... He does wonders in a film whose supporting cast suffers chronically from an excess of 'acting.'" Many reviews fell in line with *The New York Daily News*, which wrote, "Mitchum, as usual, shows his boredom. Delivering lines with all the emotion of a punch-drunk fighter, he makes you aware he considers the whole thing beneath him."

Today *Wrath of God* is seen as one of Mitchum's lesser films, especially among his westerns. There's no horseback riding for the star; no hat, no boots, no Colt hanging on his hip. Only the setting is familiar to the genre. Yet the picture remains entertaining for those interested in Mitchum or films set during the transitional period of the Mexican Revolution. Contemporary writer Michael R. Pitts' *Western Movies* noted, "Robert Mitchum is a delight as the priest," while Herb Fagen's *Encyclopedia of Westerns* said, "While Robert Mitchum's work is strong, the film loses its balance and symmetry." Mitchum biographer Damien Love wrote of Mitchum, "For his part, he seemed to be enjoying himself but after this he quit the West, steering clear of the territory for over 20 years."

Off the Trail

Mitchum's reasons for leaving the western are twofold. As explored in my coverage of *The Good Guys and the Bad Guys,* the genre had run its course in Hollywood. Cheaply made Spaghetti Westerns were flooding the international market with inferior product. At the same time, Sam Peckinpah's *The Wild Bunch* (1969) ushered in a new era of realistic, glorified violence and forever killed the notion of white hats and black hats. Ford, Hawks, Hathaway, Wellman and Walsh, masters of the genre, were long gone or retired. Any new Hollywood westerns were revisionist in nature, with young filmmakers casting long-haired hippie actors while drawing parallels between the Old West and current events like Vietnam. Sometimes they had no idea how to shoot a western or work with livestock. John Wayne, Dean Martin, Kirk Douglas, Burt Lancaster and Gregory Peck still churned out oaters during this period, but Mitchum opted to keep his distance from the changing genre. Climbing on and off a horse, in take after take, no longer appealed to him. "I'm not retiring," Mitchum told the *San Antonio Express and News*. "Just more time in between. I'm really in no hurry to do anything."

Had Mitchum been more actively seeking work in the early 1970s, he was well-suited for a few westerns that his contemporaries grabbed. Lee Marvin took on a whimsical role opposite Paul Newman as a down-on-his-luck modern-day cattle and horse trader in *Pocket Money* (1972), based on J.P.S. Brown's novel *Jim Kane*. It was Marvin again as a grizzled Old West bank robber mentoring a trio of teenagers to his criminal ways in Richard Fleischer's *The Spikes Gang* (1974). Lee Van Cleef headlined *The Magnificent Seven Ride* (1972) and Richard Widmark portrayed a rodeo cowboy turned drunk in *When the Legends Die* (1972). Mitchum was approached to star in Blake Edwards' *Wild Rovers* (1971), about an old hand and a young saddle partner (Ryan O'Neal), but turned it down, revealing to the *Pittsburgh Press,* "It sounded like Blake Edwards wrote it as a compilation of old *Street and Smith* western magazines." William Holden played the older cowboy part in what has become regarded as a fine film. Mitchum was even asked to play the part of the drunken Waco Kid in Mel Brooks' western spoof *Blazing Saddles* (1974) but quickly shot the offer down.

The Rebel Outlaw: Josey Wales, a blindly submitted paperback western sent to Mitchum by writer Forrest Carter, gathered dust or was lost and ignored by the increasingly unenthusiastic star. The post–Civil War story was about a notorious pistol-man from Missouri wielding his Colts 44s with lightning speed against unscrupulous bounty hunters and Comancheros as he collects a ragtag troupe of castaways in his slow escape to Mexico. Carter also sent a copy of the book to Clint Eastwood, who quickly bit: It become one of his most popular western films, *The Outlaw Josey Wales* (1976). A reader can see why Carter was moved to send the book to the hard-edged actors in hopes they would portray the wanted man.

Sam Peckinpah made overtures to Mitchum to play the title lawman in *Pat Garrett and Billy the Kid* (1973), but Mitchum had no interest in going to Durango, Mexico, with the erratic, demanding, combative director. What's more, the film was for James Aubrey and MGM. James Coburn (who once lived in the infamous Laurel Canyon home where Mitchum was busted for pot) accepted the role and starred opposite actor-singer-songwriter Kris Kristofferson as Billy. Even though Aubrey butchered the movie, it has found admirers in a variety of reissues. When it came to the studio suits in Hollywood, Mitchum claimed he had met a better class of people on freight trains. He was tired of dealing with them.

A Kristofferson-Mitchum pairing would have been interesting given the wild reputations of the two hard-drinking intellectual cowboys. Mitchum had seen the drawling Texas-born Rhodes Scholar turned Vietnam-era chopper pilot Kristofferson play at The Troubadour in West Hollywood and liked his literate outlaw country music, especially the hangover song "Sunday Morning Coming Down." Kristofferson, who went on to headline the range war western *Heaven's Gate* (1980) and the TV movie remake of *Stagecoach* (1986), took pride in the fact that the iconoclast Mitchum liked his music. "That was Sam Peckinpah's favorite song," Kristofferson said in *More Songwriters on Songwriting*. "And Robert Mitchum liked it…. I tried to figure out what we all had in common. And I think it was the drinking."

Mitchum had that charismatic effect on young rebels. It was little surprise Ken Hutchison ill-advisedly tried to emulate Mitchum's behavior during the making of *The Wrath of God*. Mitchum's drinking reputation preceded him, and there were always "young guns" ready to try taking down the man whose bar tabs around the world were the stuff of legend. Over the years, many of these tyros like Richard Harris, Stanley Baker and George Peppard were carried off, their toes pointing to the sky. "I used to astonish people with my capacity," Mitchum admitted to Jerry Roberts regarding his drinking ability. Mitchum's *River of No Return* stunt double Roy Jenson told Lee Server that when Mitchum felt the urge to let loose, his pals had to drink in shifts to keep up with the star. "Mitchum was incredible," Jenson said. "The guy could drink two or three quarts of gin and not even show it." While three buddies were at play, a fourth would retire to recoup, returning after sufficient rest to replace the next member of the Mitchum revelers. This routine could go on for days until Mitchum finally called an end to the revelry. There was no one in the business who could drink him under the table. Mitchum worked and drank with "big guns" Duke Wayne, Robert Ryan, Jack Palance, Lee Marvin, Richard Boone, Oliver Reed and Trevor Howard. His ability to set the bar (so to speak) was never in question.

With no westerns on his docket, drinking heavier, and as tired as ever of the Hollywood marketing and publicity machine, Mitchum surprisingly strung together a trio of what are considered some of his best films. He was a small-time Boston criminal providing guns to gangsters in Peter Yates' spot-on *The Friends of Eddie Coyle* (1973), a still tough World War II vet helping old friend Brian Keith (a modern cowboy) fight Japanese mobsters in *The Yakuza* (1975), and an aged and weary Philip Marlowe in Dick Richards' *Farewell, My Lovely* (1975). *The Yakuza* has some interesting parallels of East meets West with Mitchum toting a pistol and a shotgun against sword-wielding killers in the exciting climax. Mitchum's performances in all are aged tough guy perfection.

It was an autumnal hot streak he could not maintain, largely in part due to his continued choice of inferior material, laziness and his own vices. Even these three solid films were under-the-radar titles. Old reliables Charlton Heston and Gregory Peck were getting the biggest studio features. They were safe choices who didn't fill their off-hours with booze, broads and brawls. There were not many good parts out there for a hardboiled 60-year-old cowboy except John Wayne's own swan song to the genre, Don Siegel's *The Shootist* (1976). *The Last Hard Men* (1976), an interesting Tucson-set western made from the Brian Garfield novel *Gundown*, featured an aging, retired lawman going against a half-breed nemesis. The latter has escaped a Yuma prison and kidnapped the lawman's daughter as an act of revenge. A reader could see Mitchum vividly essaying either part based on Garfield's detailed writing. Charlton Heston played the good guy and James Coburn the villain. The Andrew McLaglen–directed western died at the box office.

Mitchum was instead saddled with such routine actioners as *The Amsterdam Kill* (1977) for martial arts director Robert Clouse and *The Am-*

bassador (1984) for Golan-Globus. His Philip Marlowe follow-up *The Big Sleep* (1978), lensed in London by Michael Winner, was described as exactly that by critics. Mitchum afforded far more care to the selection of horses in his stable than the films on his résumé. The critics sharpened their knives. Mitchum should have been mining Oscar gold, but he found himself shoveling out more horse crap for the money. While making the spottily released thriller *Agency* (1979) in Canada, a nervous Valerie Perrine declared she'd never made a movie with guns and shooting. Mitchum countered he'd never made one without. "Send for Mitchum; he'll do anything," Mitchum told Bob Thomas in 1985.

There were missed opportunities and chances at quality. Mitchum turned down Stephen Spielberg's *Jaws* (1975), William Friedkin's South American–set thriller *Sorcerer* (1977) and Ted Post's *Go Tell the Spartans* (1978), the latter concerning the beginnings of the Vietnam War. He backed out of Dick Richards' ambitious French Foreign Legion picture *March or Die* (1977) and allowed himself to be talked out of Walter Hill's "disguised western" *The Driver* (1978). Mitchum also pulled out of a solidly robust actioner, Andrew McLaglen's *The Wild Geese* (1978), about a team of mercenaries in Africa, co-starring Richard Burton and Roger Moore. Robert Shaw assumed the career-defining part of Quint in the popular shark picture, Roy Scheider starred in the critically acclaimed *Sorcerer*, Burt Lancaster headlined the solid, thought-provoking *Spartans*, Gene Hackman starred in *March or Die*, Bruce Dern played the lawman in *The Driver*, and Richard Harris took over for Mitchum in the well-regarded McLaglen adventure film.

Mitchum was considered for what became the William Holden part in Sidney Lumet's Oscar-nominated *Network* (1976) and turned down Louis Malle's *Atlantic City* (1980), a film for which Burt Lancaster received a Best Actor Academy Award nomination. A straightforward early script for Walter Hill's *48 Hrs.* (1982) paired Mitchum as the cop with Clint Eastwood as the criminal before radically changing into the popular action-comedy starring Nick Nolte and Eddie Murphy. The sci-fi classic *Blade Runner* (1982) was written by Hampton Fancher with Mitchum in mind to portray the future detective Deckard.

They wanted him to play the tyrannical sheriff in *First Blood* (1982), and pal John Huston was after him for years about starring in *White Hunter, Black Heart* (Clint Eastwood finally played the part in 1990). Instead of tackling any of these memorable, challenging assignments, Mitchum did a cameo on his back in a sick bed for the disappointing World War II blockbuster *Midway* (1976), took a supporting role as a sportswriter opposite a boxing kangaroo in the maligned *Matilda* (1978), and special guested with fellow aging stars Richard Burton and Rod Steiger in the World War II box office dud *Breakthrough* (1979). He called *Midway* his new favorite film due to its lack of physical demands.

Mitchum endured plenty of bad press. In 1974, financing fell through on the high-profile *Jackpot* after Mitchum refused to report to the Rome location, and Mitchum walked out or was fired from the disastrous Otto Preminger thriller *Rosebud* (1975). He claimed legitimate reasons in both cases, but the newspapers had a field day when Preminger charged that Mitchum was drunk in the morning. Mitchum denied this. Preminger hired the hard-drinking Peter O'Toole to replace Mitchum. O'Toole allegedly spilled more alcohol in a day than Mitchum consumed. Mitchum declared it was like replacing Helen Keller with Ray Charles. Deserved or not, the cowboy from a different era was branded by the new studio heads as difficult and headache-inducing. He could be.

While making *The Friends of Eddie Coyle* in Boston, Mitchum had fit right in with real members of the infamous Winter Hill Gang, spending nights drinking with them while he absorbed their culture. They immediately accepted him as a bona fide tough guy, with real-life hit man Johnny Martorano recalling for Howie Carr, "Mitchum was a John Wayne type, a two-fisted drinking cowboy." Character actors Peter Boyle, Alex Rocco and Richard Jordan backed up that assertion in an explicit Grover Lewis *Rolling Stone* article ("The Last Celluloid Desperado") that portrays a poetic, tired Mitchum downing an endless supply of Budweiser beer between takes on the set. The fellow actors are amazed at Mitchum's acting ability, presence and pace of self-destruction. Words like "inhuman" are bandied about.

(From left) Guy Madison, Mitchum and Bill Williams down shots of alcohol in RKO's *Till the End of Time* (1946). Heavy drinking remained a strong part of Mitchum's screen image.

Richard Jordan made *Eddie Coyle* and *The Yakuza* back to back with Mitchum and termed him "the elemental male…. The sexy reactions Mitchum gets from women are just incredible."

At this point, Mitchum's drinking was growing more troublesome. Alcohol revealed the dual characteristics of Mitchum's personality, morphing the quiet intellectual into a loud, fist-slinging cowpuncher who could release enough steam to power a train across the country. After a hard day on the trail, cowboys relaxed and unwound in saloons and cantinas, washing down the dust in their throats with warm beer or rotgut whiskey. Some ranch hands saved up their month's wages for a boisterous town rollick filled with women, gambling and imbibing that often led to trouble. Mitchum had this trait of spree-drinking in common with his western ancestors. In his noteworthy autobiography *A Texas Cow Boy,* the infamous Old West figure Charles A. Siringo noted that whiskey was "the greatest curse ever known to mankind."

Drinking was a pastime Mitchum enjoyed, chasing the feeling of relaxation and gentle numbness the alcohol produced in his body while transforming him into a verbose raconteur whose charisma made fellow males want to buddy up to him and the opposite sex bed down next to him. He once told the *Boston Herald,* "Give me a few drinks and some friends to provide some laughs, and I'll smile my way through to the next sunrise." Because he was a physical man with a healthy musculature and superior genetic framework, his metabolism worked efficiently to burn the alcohol off. For years Mitchum was a functioning alcoholic, one who manages his daily work schedule without interruption and can withstand the physical detriments associated with consuming large amounts of alcohol until later in life. As he entered his 50s, the alcohol created subtle changes in his mental and physical state, occasionally elicited by slips in judgment and words. Depending on what he was drinking and how much sleep he'd missed, Mitchum could become "a mean drunk" as a night or a bender wore on. Loaded, he was the good, the bad and the ugly rolled into one.

Burdened by celebrity, Mitchum became ensnared in a psychological trap. He was living up to the legend of his own prowess either for the benefit of others or his own need to prove himself physically. The face was noticeably more lined, the chin less hard-edged, and the eyes barely at half-mast, but his aging muscles still had the consistency of granite. When he sucked in his gut and puffed out his 48" chest, females half his age became weak in the knees. However, the sex symbol movie star image became a box canyon with little chance of escape. Mitchum was at the forefront of Hollywood's legendary hell-raisers for the better part of 25 years, even if he had astutely stepped away from the bright lights for the solitude of the Maryland farm. That move toned down his drinking without ending it. The return to a busy film schedule in the late 1960s and his elevation to legend status accelerated the level of consumption as he became a rebellious symbol for the younger generation to idolize and encourage into recklessness. Always a private man, Mitchum began to pay less attention to the chronicling of his life as *Penthouse* and *Rolling Stone* followed him around to detail his adventures. Mitchum felt these writers had their own agenda. They were determined to print the legend, so he played the part of Big Bad Bob Mitchum for them: drink constantly in hand, a cloud of crazy weed coming from his trailer, young would-be starlets at the ready, and his fists always clenched as part of his overall threatening aura. *Penthouse* writer Brad Darrach was constantly on his heels, feeling at times Mitchum was ready to take a swing at him during their extended interview. *Rolling Stone* scribe Robert Ward was nearly head-butted as a tequila-swigging Mitchum demonstrated his bar-fighting tough guy credentials, pulling up a fraction of an inch shy of Ward's face. Life became the legend and vice versa.

Some members of the press received the strong, silent treatment, saddled with mumbled one-word answers to their mundane questions. "Yup. No. Don't know." TV host Michael Parkinson was frustrated by Mitchum's unwillingness to expound on anything, while Larry King considered a clearly uninterested Mitchum his worst interview ever. Turner Classics host Robert Osborne was dismayed to find Mitchum talkative off camera and shut down in front of it. *San Francisco Chronicle* reporter William Otterburn-Hall found himself dodging feigned punches between questions. He wrote, "Any meeting with the heavy-lidded giant who breaks horses for a hobby is an alarmingly unpredictable affair." Columnist Earl Wilson labeled Mitchum his most difficult interview, saying, "Mitchum's conversations are thrilling with unexpected allusions to geography, literature and fights he's been in—but you come away with sea legs as though you've been through a storm." Paul Hendrickson of *The Washington Post* writes, "The trouble with trying to figure out Robert Mitchum is that Robert Mitchum isn't going to help any." Biographer George Eells wasn't even granted access to Mitchum for an interview, finally deciding, "He is a man about whom one could say almost anything and at some point, be correct."

Yet Mitchum displayed fondness for a few writers and reporters. If he felt like talking, he displayed a fascinating wealth of knowledge garnered from his years of voracious reading and world travel. A well-prepared Dick Cavett got a particularly good Mitchum TV interview, and the star made multiple appearances on *The Tonight Show* with Johnny Carson through the years without incident. If no cameras were present, Mitchum was apt to reveal a bit of his outlaw image to the press if they dared to keep up. Long-time syndicated columnist James Bacon was a drinking buddy who shared Bloody Marys and Moscow Mules (ginger beer and vodka) out of copper mugs with Mitchum at the Cock 'n' Bull. "Mitchum is a two-fisted drinker," Bacon wrote in his book *Made in Hollywood*. "You can sometimes get into trouble with him." Dick Lochte shared Mitchum's vodka during a marathon interview session for the *L.A. Daily News*, marveling at the star's alcohol capacity while gaining a wealth of material as Mitchum took stock of a changing Hollywood as the western and the studio system faded into the sunset. Adventurous biographer Mike Tomkies, interviewing Mitchum for the fourth time in the early 1970s, was shocked when Mitchum casually pulled out a joint and offered him a toke. Tomkies wrote that Mitchum was "the most baffling, complicated and charismatic star I'd ever met."

Cliff Harrington interviewed Mitchum over a hefty liquid lunch in Japan, amazed the rock-steady star could then bound down a narrow stairwell with athletic grace and recite all his dialogue perfectly in the second half of the shooting day. Harrington called him "perhaps the most unusual star that I met." In 1973, Mitchum casually offered the use of his Bel Air home and swimming pool to London-based journalist Roderick Mann, who had interviewed him several times dating back to the 1950s. "A character he started out, a character he remains," Mann wrote in the *Los Angeles Times*. British interviewer Clive James got the effusive Mitchum for an early 1970s taped TV interview, noting that the star lit up after he imbibed a monstrous drink. "He liked it that I knew about the off-trail movies as well as the mainstream ones," James revealed of the secret to his interview's success. "It went so well that we asked him if we could keep rolling long enough to turn the footage into two programs instead of one. He agreed on the spot. It was as if he didn't want to go home. I didn't either. Finally, the electricians pulled the plugs, Mitchum wandered off into the gathering dusk."

Garry Armstrong of Boston TV's Channel 7 News had a similar experience with the veteran cowboy actor. He wrapped a particularly quick and tidy interview, asking not about Mitchum's current film *The Friends of Eddie Coyle* but about lesser known westerns which intrigued the star. Mitchum asked western film maven Armstrong where a good place for food was and the actor and the newsman found an off-the-trail Beantown pub where over the course of several hours they ate lunch, shared drinks, talked about a variety of subjects, and dueted on Johnny Horton B-sides from the jukebox. Mitchum led the conversation and invited Armstrong to call him Mitch. Armstrong fondly recalls Mitchum as "an affable and literate man who didn't take himself seriously.... Mitch, at times, rambled a bit in our afternoon into evening gabfest. I let him ramble. It wasn't booze. He was on a run with stories."*

Pulitzer Prize–winning *Chicago Sun-Times* film critic Roger Ebert interviewed Mitchum several times from the late 1960s into the 1990s, meetings where the actor is especially casual and witty. "Robert Mitchum is a great interview," Ebert wrote, "as long as you do not ask a question and expect him to answer it." Ed Masley of *The Pittsburgh Post-Gazette* agreed: "You don't conduct an interview with Robert Mitchum. You ride it out. Like a sea squall or a bucking bronco." Mitchum told witty anecdotes laced with humor at his own expense and peppered his stories with four-letter words. If the setting was relaxed and over drinks, he was comfortable. If he was forced to feel like a freak on display being asked about character motivation or artistic aspirations, he clammed up or spoke out to end the situation.

Mitchum hated the interview tours. "You see 40 people in a day and each one wants to have a drink with you," he complained to Bob Thomas. "That sort of adds up." As the decade wore on, an increasingly cranky Mitchum occasionally exhibited outrageous behavior during the never-ending, contractually required publicity parade, saying or doing anything when the mood struck. Sometimes, the crazier the situation, the better in his mind for its shock or entertainment value when he felt too pressed upon. He was the Mustang too wild to be tamed; Hollywood could build a fence around him, but he'd be damned if they were going to ride him too. Mitchum's speech became increasingly complex and rambling the longer he drank. Colleagues noted his moods could change with the wind. It was the same protective shield he'd built up for years, but it was growing darker and edgier. His temper

---

*Garry Armstrong (e-mail correspondence, August 2017).

was easier to trigger, even during the extended periods when he swore off the booze. By the 1970s, he felt harassed from several angles and was especially ticked off that he still had to work so hard in the motion picture game. Yet once on a film set, he settled in and enjoyed his time with the crew if the producers didn't try to take too great an advantage of him and stretch his workday into overtime. He'd keep his eye on the clock and was quick to point out to a director when quitting time approached.

New York newspaperman Pete Hamill, scriptwriter of the western *Doc* (1971) and author of the celebrated memoir *A Drinking Life*, managed to quit drinking and reorganize his life to enhance his work, his health and his personal relationships. Interviewed for *The Harder They Fall*, a book on alcohol and professionalism, he reflected on the chemical effect that years of drink had not only on his own brain, but that of his acquaintance Mitchum. Ultimately, alcohol had the potential to turn a good-humored Will Rogers into a dastardly Black Bart. "I remember I met Robert Mitchum a couple of times," Hamill says, "and liked him very much. He was intelligent, self-deprecating, and had a real sense of irony. But if you stayed with him to the point at which he became drunk, he became a nasty piece of work. So that even in the movies, the directors knew that they could only get a performance out of him in the morning. After lunch it was impossible."

Director Michael Winner penned a *Daily Mail* article on the difficulties of working with actors who drink, writing:

> There was one bizarre night when I was directing *The Big Sleep* in 1978. At the end there was a gunfight between Robert Mitchum and fellow thespian Richard Boone. Richard was normally the quiet drunk. He'd arrive with two bottles of Scotch and drink throughout the day but was always in perfect control. Mitchum drank during the day on occasions, but at night it was another story. We shot until dawn. Mitchum and Boone were both plastered. Guns were going off at the wrong time. They lurched. They staggered. It was terrifying. "It's the Gunfight at Alcoholics Anonymous," I thought. Somehow or other it was all cleaned up in the editing.

It is with great irony during this period that Mitchum, sounding stone cold sober, provided the narration to the 1970 counterculture drug documentary *The Distant Drummer* and the 1973 short public service film *Alcoholism: America on the Rocks*. In his professional narrative, Mitchum declared that drinking can provide "a shield of armor in social situations," but he warned that society needs to be aware of the dangers of going to extremes. Mitchum was acutely aware of his personal situation; and yet he repeatedly tested his own boundaries and borders of consumption. Why? Only Mitchum had the true answers, and he wasn't about to drop his armor for anyone. Mitchum's drinking mate Richard Harris, star of *A Man Called Horse* (1970), attempted to explain his (and Mitchum's) drinking compulsion, saying of Mitchum, "His response to the stresses of the business was exactly mine. The creative tension overspills and one is blamed for bad behavior—but show me an artist, any real artist that you can call a perfect gentleman. It does not, cannot, exist."

Mitchum still exhibited his wry sense of humor. Gillette Razors offered him a huge sum to spend one minute shaving on camera for a commercial. He turned them down, explaining he was worried he might cut himself. Mitchum talked about easy money but considered hawking product in this manner selling out. Charles Bronson could advertise Mandom cologne in Japan, but Mitchum would have none of it. It was beneath his cowboy dignity. He'd earn his keep the hard way. Old aches and pains from all his westerns and action roles were taking longer to heal and creating physical discomfort. Mitchum had gone through all *The Wrath of God* with a shoulder injury that was constantly barking at him, and he banged up a leg on *The Yakuza*. He'd freely grouse about those maladies to anyone within earshot, but private thoughts and concerns were seldom revealed even with long-time friends. He was loath to express himself emotionally, but as a travelling companion and trail buddy he remained unparalleled when it came to fun and adventure. Las Vegas became a favored destination for letting off steam. He'd take in boxing matches and hook up with old pal Frank Sinatra for crazy nights on the town.

Mitchum's trips to Vegas often involved reunions with a soldier he had met in Vietnam, Butch Huff. Huff remembered:

> Having met Bob in Vietnam, it didn't take me long to realize what a remarkable guy he was. I don't know how many guys he met there, but he left with God knows how many slips of paper with names of wives, mothers and girlfriends. And he called them all, including my mom! We stayed in touch over the years and became quite close. We would meet up in Vegas or on some film location and whoop it up whenever we could. Bob had a phone that would accommodate conference calls, so he, his brother John and I would talk frequently and swap lies. What I learned over those 30-odd years of friendship was that Bob really enjoyed genuine camaraderie of all kinds. The honest kind, not the kind propagated by some Hollywood hot shot. As reticent as he was to speak seriously about his career, one could discern that he was proud of his professionalism, and of doing his job well.
>
> When he began his career in the Hopalong Cassidy series, I'm quite sure he felt like he'd hit the lottery. In his words, he got to play cowboys and Indians, got a free lunch, and actually got paid for it! I believe that because of the way he'd grown up, he enjoyed immensely the communal atmosphere of a film set and the crews he worked with. In the seven Hopalongs that he made, the actors were mostly the same, as was the crew. This contributed to a familial atmosphere that had previously been denied him in his youth. This really appealed to Bob. He really enjoyed palling around with the grips, the juicers (electricians), and some of the actors. Very early on, he gained an intense dislike of shows of ego and prima donna behavior. And as anyone who worked with him will tell you, this remained true through the rest of his career. Because the western is where Bob got his start, I believe there remained a special place in his heart of hearts for the genre. He gave some wonderful performances in them too, and we should all be grateful for that.*

Character actor Steve Moriarty, veteran of over 180 films and 300 TV shows including the westerns *Joe Kidd* (1972), *Blazing Saddles* (1974) and *Silverado* (1985), knew Robert and his brother John from the mid–1970s on. He reminisced:

> John and Mitch were two of the best friends I ever had. I did *Breakheart Pass* with John up in Idaho in 1975 where we were up to our buns in snow. I worked with Mitch on both the mini-series *The Winds of War* and *War and Remembrance*. I played his naval aide. I was also sort of his designated driver on that. The director Dan Curtis knew that I didn't drink and that I'd get Mitch where he needed to be. We spent more time ducking over to the Stagedoor Bar across from Paramount on that than we did at home! I did get drunk one time because my wife got a false positive test on breast cancer. Believe it or not, Robert Mitchum got me home. So, I like to say that for that one time, Robert Mitchum was my designated driver! I worked with the Mitchums, I worked with Eastwood, I worked with John Wayne on *McQ*. Those guys were the end of the Golden Age of Hollywood. The young actors today don't compare.†

In addition to being a loyal friend, Mitchum always had his buddies' backs when it came to any dangerous situation. He didn't care for troublemakers and stood up against all odds. Forever the tough guy, Mitchum was still apt to get into fistfights if a brassy brawler targeted either him or a pal. His reputation as a drinker and fighter preceded him wherever he went. Mitchum was legendary in Hollywood circles for breaking heavyweight contender Bernie Reynolds' jaw at the Alamo Inn, single-handedly besting three Marines in the Caribbean, and cleaning out a Dublin pub with Richard Harris. Even approaching 60 years of age, he remained fearless and defiant. willing to take on all comers no matter the odds. "Never back down," he told Garry Armstrong. "Don't take any crap."‡

In his autobiography, Burt Reynolds recalled Mitchum being badgered by a would-be bruiser in The Keys, a bar near Universal. Before the man could get off a punch, Mitchum grasped him by the back of the neck and slammed his head into the bar top. "This man has fainted," Mitchum dead-panned as his unconscious harasser collapsed to the floor in a heap. Actor Michael Parks of *The Last Hard Men* (1976) and *The Return of Josey Wales* (1986), another

---

*Butch Huff (e-mail correspondence, September 2017).
†Steve Moriarty (phone conversation, September 2017).
‡Garry Armstrong (e-mail correspondence, December 2018).

Throwing a punch at John Wayne in *El Dorado* (1967). Mitchum's tough guy image on and off screen equaled his drinking legend.

drinking buddy, recalled Mitchum was constantly provoked on location and was once prepared to take on eight men in a German bar during the making of the World War II film *Breakthrough* (1979). "Bob was an extraordinary cat," Parks told *Worldly Remains*. "Didn't give a shit about anything. And he could back it up. Not just the menace.... He could really fight."

Mitchum's long-standing friend Budd Boetticher, a former boxer and bullfighter turned western film director, backed up this assertion of Mitchum's legendary toughness. Boetticher palled around with tough guys John Wayne, John Ford, John Huston and Audie Murphy. In his biography *When in Disgrace,* Boetticher named Mitchum, Robert Ryan, Jack Palance, Victor Jory and TV *Tarzan* Ron Ely as men in Hollywood he knew could fight from his own firsthand knowledge. "Mitchum was the toughest," Boetticher told Lee Server. The director of *The Tall T* (1957) and *Ride Lonesome* (1959) was no slouch himself. For the *Los Angeles Times,* Mitchum recalled a memorable night on the town in Tijuana, Mexico, where he and Boetticher got into a fistfight with "three of the toughest tequilaed-up yokels you've ever seen." Mitchum and Boetticher easily overcame the toughs.

"I never start a fight," Mitchum once said via an RKO press release. "But I can assure you I can always finish one if there's no other way out." To the *Los Angeles Times* in 1957: "Every now and then, some hooligan swaggers up to me in a bar and says: 'No so-and-so of an actor can outfight me.' When they're too persistent, you have to show 'em." Mitchum could show them with his fists, and was not immune to breaking fingers, gouging eyes or delivering a well-placed kick to insure an opponent stayed down. Mitchum didn't mind having the reputation of a dirty fighter if it meant he was the one still standing when the dust settled. Real fights seldom resembled choreographed reel fights and could get ugly fast. Regarding his brawling reputation, Mitchum expounded to syndicated columnist Vernon Scott in 1965: "I don't like to get hit, and I don't especially get a charge out of clouting some loudmouth in public either. The last thing I want is trouble. But if someone is looking for it, I'm not gonna let him push me around."

John Mitchum revealed in Herb Fagen's *White Hats and Silver Spurs* that when a Mitchum was involved in a fight, losing was not an option. It all went back to their tough childhood and history of riding the rails. "We were over at my brother's house one night," John says, "And Bob had a little too much to drink. My wife Bonnie had never seen him this way. At one point he had tears in his eyes and told Bonnie that we Mitchum boys had to fight for everything we had. We don't fight to show off or to be tough. We fight to survive. So, if we get into a fight we are going to win it, no matter how the hell we are going to do it. He was so intense about it that it made you back off a little bit." In his own book, John revealed, "I've fought a lot and won a lot but must confess that I want no part of Brother Robert in a free-for-all. I can attest personally to the fact that it ain't too much fun to get involved with him. Nobody wins when it's just the two of us."

Actor William Smith, muscular star of TV's *Laredo* (1965–1967), knew many of the same stuntmen and big-screen cowboys as Mitchum. The 6'2", 210-pound Smith had been an undefeated boxer in the Air Force and trained with Ed Parker in Kenpo karate. His toughness was legitimate. At Universal on the western *Laredo*, Smith was called upon to handle co-star Neville Brand when the highly decorated World War II veteran's notorious drinking got out of control. Smith said,

> I really liked Robert Mitchum. He was a tough guy. I drank with him. But Lee Marvin and Neville Brand couldn't fight their way out of a wet paper bag when they were drunk. They used to get into fights at this bar on the [Pacific Coast Highway], and Roy Jenson and I always had to step in and finish them. Leo Gordon and Roy Jenson were the two toughest men in Hollywood.

Roy Jenson didn't take shit from anybody. On *Gun Fury*, Raoul Walsh told Neville and Lee not to pull their punches in a fight with Leo. When Leo realized what they were doing, he wiped the walls with them for real.*

Due to his celebrity, Mitchum needed to be careful where he ventured. He generally avoided the limelight, once comparing large crowds in a Barbara Walters interview to "potential lynch mobs." The best way to stay out of trouble was wrapped up in a good book at his own residence, but he would soon develop an itch that needed to be scratched. It was his nature to see the world. He had a quaint second home in the small western style saloon The Old Place owned by former stuntman Thomas Runyon. The country canyon hideout bar, made of weathered wood with an antler display over the entry, is located near Malibu in the Agoura Hills on Mulholland Drive. It features bat-wing doors and a long bar top imported from a real Virginia City saloon. One could step outside to toss horseshoes and remain in relative seclusion. The bar served two items: oak grilled Black Angus steak and clams. It was frequented by veteran cowboy stuntmen, Hells Angels, surfers, Steve McQueen, Bob Dylan, Sam Peckinpah, Jason Robards and Nick Nolte.

Bullfighting novelist turned Barbary Coast barman Barnaby Conrad drank with Mitchum beneath a bull's head at his swank saloon El Matador in San Francisco. In his memoir *Name Dropping*, Conrad called Mitchum: "one of the most humorous—and intelligent—men I know. He is a great storyteller, telling fantastic tales complete with a variety of different voices and accents only he can do." Mitchum signed Conrad's saloon guest book with the cryptic message "When all the broken crockery of desperate communion is swept from under our understanding heels may we find on that clear expanse of floor the true and irrevocable target of infinite thrust." Mitchum claimed he had left poetry and similar esoteric messages on the walls of men's rooms around the world. "Half the time I don't know what he's talking about," his agent Bullets Durgom told columnist Earl Wilson.

---

*William Smith (personal meeting, July 1997).

Other places Mitchum was likely to show for a drink were the River Bottom near Warner Brothers, the Sportsmen's Lodge in Studio City, the Palomino Club in North Hollywood, the Pine Street Saloon in Paso Robles, the Formosa Café in Hollywood, Turk's Tavern in Sunset Beach, Chez Jay and Dan Tana's in Santa Monica, and the infamous cowboy saloon the Backstage Bar outside of CBS Studios (formerly the old Republic lot), where Brother John and pal Charlie McGraw were regulars. Jack Elam, Harry Carey, Jr., L.Q. Jones, Strother Martin, Morgan Woodward, Jim Davis and Forrest Tucker frequented the bar, as did the casts and crew of *Gunsmoke, The Big Valley, Cimarron Strip* and *The Wild Wild West*. Fights occurred on a semi-regular basis among the stuntmen and cowboy character actor clientele. Names like Big Bill Smith, Tony Epper and Bob "Terrible" Terhune were legendary for their toughness. "It was like walking into the middle of a western movie," wrote screenwriter–western novelist Stephen Lodge. "All your favorite cowboys were right there looking just like they did on screen."

Mitchum wasn't always a two-fisted wild man. Depending on the venue, Mitchum could handle himself with dignity and class when the situation warranted. He was equally in his element drinking martinis at the Polo Lounge in Beverly Hills as he was pounding beers in a backwoods dive with sawdust on the floor. As Mitchum aged, so did the saddle-tough cowboys and stuntmen working around him. Men in the new Hollywood were less inclined to throw punches at one another in their off-hours, and old-fashioned bar fights became a thing of the past. The big "John Wayne" roundhouse punch permanently disappeared. Bruce Lee, Chuck Norris and flashy black belt karate was the new thing in big-screen toughness. The entire era was changing.

The Hollywood western continued its slow death of the past decade, affecting many of its venerable players. In 1971, *The Virginian* completed its ninth and final TV season. It was followed in 1972 by *Bonanza* ending a 14-season run. In 1975, *Gunsmoke* filmed its final brawl at the Long Branch Saloon after 20 high-quality years. When these shows ended, many western character players, wranglers and stuntmen were out of business. The actors who regularly guested on these classic TV westerns saw a significant drop-off in their acting output and living wage. A generation of new producers and casting directors were suddenly unfamiliar with their work. The older players felt insulted by this lack of knowledge regarding their lengthy careers. Mitchum's friend Hal Baylor told *Trail Dust,* "I was at Universal one day and a punk behind a desk looked at me and said, 'What have you done?' And I replied, 'About what?'" The young man had no idea Baylor once dominated the airwaves exchanging punches with Clint Walker, Richard Boone and Chuck Connors on *Cheyenne, Have Gun—Will Travel* and *The Rifleman*. Baylor, a veteran of more than 50 films and 150 TV shows, retired on the spot.

Jim Davis, a cowboy reliable, was flummoxed by his inability to sell a quality western TV pilot entitled *Law of the Land* in 1976. "You can't make westerns like they used to," Davis told the *Times-Picayune*. "You can't be chasing Indians any more. You can't have the white hat-black hat business and savagery is out. You need a new, fresh approach." John Mitchum felt similarly slighted, elaborating on the new era of political correctness in *White Hats and Silver Spurs*: "Even to be on a commercial today is a real experience.... They are actually 'cattle calls.' They bring in eight people for maybe one 20-second spot and ask asinine things from everybody." In C. Courtney Joyner's *The Westerners*, top-of-the-line heavy Jack Elam, who logged more than 100 films and 200 television episodes, explained, "Hollywood's a different story now. They think you have to come down there and talk to them if you're going to do a picture, and I say bullshit. After all these pictures, if they don't know that they want me, then forget it." Veteran cowboy player Slim Pickens took a semi-regular gig on the country music TV show *Hee Haw* because of the lack of oaters being filmed, but he was hopeful the western would return. "They're not making many right now," he told the *Times-Picayune*. "But all it takes is just one good one and they'll come back like gangbusters."

As a marquee movie name, Robert Mitchum

wasn't faced with the unemployment line, but his choice of projects was growing more limited, especially within the western genre. So Mitchum hung up his spurs and donated his motion picture boots to Temple University's Shoe Museum. Keepsakes and mementos were never a big thing for him, and it seemed that cowboy flicks were now a thing of the past.

One ingeniously edited western project surfaced during this period: Trans America Films' *The Wild West* (1977). Producers Laurence Lee Joachim and Barbara Holden made a compilation of star-laden film clips with cowboy poet narrator Ray Owens telling the history of the Old West over the images. It was released overseas before a stateside video release a decade later. The poster art for the film heavily promoted the presence of Charles Bronson, Clint Eastwood and John Wayne. Appearing via film clips were Mitchum, Gene Autry, Ernest Borgnine, William Boyd, Rod Cameron, Buster Crabbe, Angie Dickinson, Wild Bill Elliott, Henry Fonda, Glenn Ford, Sterling Hayden, William Holden, Ben Johnson, Lash LaRue, Tim McCoy, Joel McCrea, Steve McQueen, Maureen O'Hara, Gregory Peck, Roy Rogers, Randolph Scott, Barbara Stanwyck, Lee Van Cleef and Richard Widmark, among others. The nostalgic film is now so obscure, there's little record to suggest from what titles Mitchum's clips originate.

The physical landscape surrounding Hollywood was changing. Western movie sets Corriganville, Ingram Ranch and Iverson Ranch were overtaken by growing subdivisions, apartment complexes and shopping plazas. Many of the studios replaced once bustling western streets with growing office space and pavement. Pierce Lyden lamented the lost locations in *Camera! Roll 'Em! Action!*: "They're all gone now. The beautiful green valleys, hills and mountains in and around Hollywood are now covered with high-rise condos, telephone poles and electric wires. The scrub brush and winding dirt trails have been replaced with the concrete ribbon. It's all a part of the passing parade." In *Company of Heroes,* Harry Carey, Jr., wrote about the Simi Valley where he'd filmed so many TV westerns: "It's all houses now." Carey was hard-pressed to find landmarks that

In Durango, Mexico, for *5 Card Stud* (1968). Durango was one of the few western locations that hadn't changed with the passage of time.

"haven't been knocked down, plowed under or covered with asphalt."

Mitchum was no longer making westerns, but he continued to live the life of a California rancher. He wore cowboy boots, bolo-string tie, monogrammed leather belt and brim hat in public while driving his pickup truck around his new Santa Barbara digs near San Ysidro Ranch and the chaparral-scrubbed horse country of the Santa Ynez Valley. To the west was the Pacific Ocean; to the east, Montecito Mountain. Other former screen cowboys (Richard Widmark, John Ireland, Stuart Whitman, Fess Parker, Robert Preston, Monte Hale and Jack Elam) lived nearby, as did Olive Carey and Mitchum's former leading lady Jane Russell. Many a lazy morning was spent shooting the breeze over coffee with his friends at the Café del Sol or enjoying barbecues in Jane Russell's backyard. Mitchum even had a seldom-employed swimming pool at his modest ranch home that he'd now gaze upon the same way he did the Pacific Ocean. For a cowboy heading west, this was the end of the line.

Mitchum's home featured personalized horse paintings by western artist-cattleman Darol Dickinson. On his website *Texas Longhorn,* the artist recalled, "The Mitchums were very kind, took me out to dinner, and Robert always wrote a nice letter of appreciation of the detail on the paintings." When Mitchum wanted to make a significant western impression for formal events, he was outfitted by designer Manuel Cuevas, the renowned tailor who clothed Johnny Cash in black. Cuevas was the son-in-law of famous western clothier Nudie Cohn. Mitchum's current movie scripts featured special leather covers designed by "cowboy artist to the stars" Al Shelton, a renowned saddler and maker of premium belt buckles.

Mitchum remained well known in the professional horse community, having grown into an accomplished breeder and owner of champion sprint racers. His 1960s winner Belmont Scare was replaced in the 1970s by Don Guerro and the palomino Golden Oldie. Mitchum worked with top trainers Earl Holmes and Don Francisco and established jockeys Ronnie Banks, Charlie Smith and Bobby Adair. In 1974, Don Guerro, who had the blood of the famous Man o' War in his veins, won the Golden State Derby at Bay Meadows and the prestigious Champion of Champions Tournament at Los Alamitos in Cypress, California. Don Guerro was crowned Quarter Horse of the Year by the California Racing Hall of Fame, making Mitchum one proud cowboy. In the *Arizona Republic,* Jim Murray likened the versatile quarter horse to Mitchum himself: "These are the hobo horses who can cut cows, chase rustlers, pony mail, circle wagons, catch buffalo, stop rattlers or buck cowboys. There's a lot of the barroom brawler in there, too."

Politically, the common association with modern cowboys is they are conservative flag-wavers who vehemently support the National Rifle Association and their constitutional right to bear arms. Despite being handy with them, Mitchum was never in love with guns, figuring correctly that his fists and reputation offered all the self-defense he needed. During this period, Mitchum made appearances in support of long-time acquaintance Ronald Reagan, who was running for the country's highest office while playing up his history as a star and host of westerns like TV's *Death Valley Days.* Reagan won a surprising victory in the 1980 presidential race and became a figurehead for the conservative movement and old-fashioned Hollywood cowboys. Mitchum is seen as a Republican in the eyes of the public because of this association. However, Mitchum considered himself apolitical and was never behind any issue to a great degree. He correctly assumed that bureaucratic meddling and pork barrel politics would muddy anything of his concern. He strongly supported the fighting men of the country's military, but his political leanings were across the map. In the case of Reagan, the independent-minded Mitchum simply felt obliged to offer support to the cowboy president because he was asked to do so, not because he agreed with the Republican doctrine. He had offered support for conservative Arizona Senator Barry Goldwater in the 1960s, but again only because he liked the firebrand man personally. When questioned about his political leanings by *Penthouse,* long-time establishment outsider Mitchum labeled himself with the contradictory tags of "a revolutionary conservative" and "a Republican radical."

As far as cuisine, Mitchum consumed such cowboy staples as western omelets, Texas beef and beans. Chili was his favorite, the spicier the better. He felt it staved off illness. Mitchum liked to flavor his food with Tabasco sauce and wash it down with cold beer. He knew his way around a kitchen and a chuck wagon, and his own recipes for Chili Wonder, Beef Mole and Border Hash Picadillo were shared with the public. As far back as the making of *The Wonderful Country* (1959), he began every shooting day with a chili breakfast. Mitchum was a connoisseur of the food and participated regularly in the popular Thousand Oaks Chili Cookoff. He served alongside fellow chili buffs Ben Johnson, Dale Robertson and Ernest Borgnine as a championship judge for the International Chili Society at the Tropico Gold Mine in the Mojave Desert near Vasquez Rocks from 1975 to 1979. In 1980, the event was held at the Paramount Ranch western town in Agoura Hills. Mitchum was also a celebrity judge at the 1979 Mexican National Championship Chili

Cookoff at the Posada Hotel near Guadalajara, Mexico. He took on the International capacity again in 1992 when the cook-off was held in Scottsdale, Arizona's Rawhide western town.

In 1979, Mitchum attended the Hollywood Stuntmen's Hall of Fame induction ceremony for his friend Chuck Roberson at the Antelope Valley Inn in Lancaster, California. One thing he did not do was appear for autograph signings at nostalgic western film festivals. Sitting behind a table all day on display for lines of gawkers was not his style. If someone wanted a Mitchum autograph, they merely had to write to him with a request. He often personalized replies and absorbed the postage cost of mailing off these photos. Mitchum banked with Wells Fargo; his personal checks displaying a stagecoach racing across the desert floor. He still appeared regularly in cowboy regalia at the annual Los Angeles Boomtown Benefit western party for the Share Organization charity in addition to his myriad of horse races and horse shows around the country. So, even if he wasn't making western films, he was keeping up the cowboy image and the overall Spirit of the West.

In his film career, Mitchum began mixing in supporting roles in theatrical features like *The Last Tycoon* (1976), *That Championship Season* (1982) and *Maria's Lovers* (1984). He was top-billed as a business suit heavy using subliminal messaging in advertisements in the minor modern thriller *Agency* (1979), co-starring Lee Majors of the TV western *The Big Valley* (1965–1969). Mitchum was paid $500,000 for the $5 million film, which stretched every cent in Canada utilizing Montreal locations as an unconvincing substitute for New York City. Leading man Majors decided to play a practical joke on Mitchum upon his arrival at the Mirabel Airport. He donned a chauffeur's outfit and hijacked the company limo. Keeping himself incognito, he drove Mitchum to the seediest part of town and dropped him off at a cheap motel before revealing it was a gag. The joke produced a good chuckle from Mitchum.

During this period, Mitchum wrote songs with Paul Williams and tinkered on a screen-

Eric Stoltz (left) and Lance Kerwin (right) portray the sons of murderous Mitchum in the TV movie *A Killer in the Family* (1983).

play with burly animal trainer Dan Haggerty, star of the western TV series *Grizzly Adams*. Their script was set in a Barbary Coast bordello in the early 1900s. Then Haggerty endured a well-publicized cocaine bust in the early 1980s and fell out of favor in Hollywood. It was a sign of the times. The old Hollywood cowboys drank and smoked but rarely let it interfere with their work. The new Hollywood celebrity was all about pedal-to-the-metal sports cars, expensive white powder and life in the fast lane. The bordello film was never made.

Adapting to the times, Mitchum ventured into the television medium, having previously turned down the pilot to the popular *Police Story* anthology in 1973 and the Revolutionary War mini-series *The Seekers* in 1979. Twice producers wanted Mitchum to portray President Lyndon Johnson, first in the TV movie *King* (1978) and later in an unrealized bio on the Texas politician. In 1980, producer Dirk Summers announced that Mitchum was going to portray legendary skyjacker D.B. Cooper in a TV movie. It never came to be. His actual TV debut was unintentional. To begin the new decade, he portrayed a modern-day Arizona investigator probing a murder in the thriller *Nightkill* (1980) starring Jaclyn Smith. He wore a cowboy hat and ostrich-skin boots for his sleuthing. The German producers sold the film to television. Mitchum originally thought it was a feature, telling the *Richmond Times Dispatch*: "I figured we'd spend three weeks in Arizona. It wouldn't tie me up for too long. They'd pay me by the hour." The die was cast, and film star contemporaries Charlton Heston and Gregory Peck soon followed trailblazer Mitchum onto the small screen.

More modern westerns for TV followed: *A Killer in the Family* (1983) and *Thompson's Last Run* (1986). The former was based on a real case involving Gary Tison (Mitchum) being broken out of Arizona State prison by his sons, then going on a murder spree in the desert. Mitchum was highly effective in the part, twisting his sons' emotions to fit his own needs. Although the film was set around Casa Grande, Arizona, it was shot in the popular western film site of Kanab, Utah, in the St. George area, "Mr. Mitchum gives a powerful performance," crowed *The New York Times*. "As the evil of the Tison character slowly becomes more apparent, Mr. Mitchum handles the transition with an ominous calm that is truly chilling." *Thompson's Last Run* was filmed in Dallas, with Mitchum cast as an aging outlaw with lawman Wilford Brimley in pursuit. Distinctive character actor Brimley shod horses for film companies in the 1960s and worked his way into riding-extra work on the television series *Gunsmoke* and *Bonanza*. Regarding Mitchum and his refreshingly down-to-earth humility, the walrus-mustached Brimley told the *Plain Dealer*, "I'd work with him if the script was written on the outhouse wall."

Thompson's Last Run could have easily been set on horseback in the Old West, but at this juncture the traditional western was becoming cost prohibitive. Hollywood no longer had the luxury of stables of movie horses near the studios. The days of Fat Jones and the Hudkins Brothers Ranch furnishing livestock were long gone. *Gunsmoke* had been off the air for a decade. Western TV reboots like *Wildside* (1985) with William Smith and *Outlaws* (1986–87) with Rod Taylor managed a handful of episodes before being cancelled due to poor ratings and high production costs. Teenage comedies and science fiction extravaganzas were in vogue. However, the real working cowboy remained in existence on ranches throughout the west, turning grass into beef. "Media disinterest might kill myths," writes J.P.S. Brown in the intro to a reissue of his authentic 1971 buckaroo book *The Outfit: A Cowboy's Primer*, "but not a cowboy's work."

So Mitchum kept working. A great deal of the 1980s were taken up with Mitchum headlining as career Navy man Pug Henry in the epic World War II mini-series *The Winds of War* (1983) and its sequel *War and Remembrance* (1989). These comprised some 41 total hours of television with a stalwart Mitchum carrying the load throughout. Each mini-series took a year to complete and were filmed around the world. "It's a little disconcerting to find that after shooting Scene 36 you're doing Scene 684," he told Cecil Smith of the *San Francisco Chronicle*. "You can get a double hernia just checking the script." The prestigious and lucrative productions extracted a great deal out of Mitchum physically and mentally. On the former, he worked through pneumonia in the bitter cold of Yugoslavia, telling *People*, "I spent most of my time falling on my ass in the snow and eating barley mush you could stand a telephone pole up in. I ate a helluva lot better in prison, and at cheaper prices."

A bone-tired Mitchum groused throughout *The Winds of War* but soldiered on for the demanding producer-director Dan Curtis. His weariness was his calling card. At one point, a feverish, sweat-soaked Mitchum told Curtis he was dying. Curtis simply told Mitchum where to stand in front of the camera. Mitchum did the scene. Production publicist James Butler noted of the star's constant seriocomic quipping for *People*: "Robert Mitchum has a good time with his hard times." Realizing the energy demand he was asking of his senior citizen star, Curtis occasionally attempted to soften the hefty workload. In his autobiography, character actor Barry Morse recalled Curtis once ordering production assistants to provide two mats for his star to sit on. "What the hell do I need two mats for?" Mitchum asked. "I've only got one ass."

The modern cowboy poses with (clockwise from top) Bentley Mitchum, Chris Mitchum, Tess Harper and Claire Bloom in the TV movie *Promises to Keep* (1985).

The heavy workload created a crack in the Mitchum armor. His years of heavy drinking finally caught up to him, and he was forced to make significant life changes after a free-wheeling 1983 *Esquire* interview in which a loose-tongued Mitchum lapsed into an anti–Semitic diatribe he later attributed to his character in *That Championship Season*. In the spring of 1984, Mitchum entered the Betty Ford Clinic in Rancho Mirage after he fell off a ladder at the Share Party. "I and the people around me were concerned I was getting out of control," Mitchum told columnist Bob Thomas. The experience was tough and embarrassing. When he got out of Betty Ford, his Santa Barbara neighbor Stuart Whitman asked what he learned from his time at the alcohol rehab center. "More ice," Mitchum answered, retaining his glib sense of humor. Going against the established rules for a rehabbing alcoholic, he'd still drink but do so in moderation. It was a start. Mitchum now swore off alcohol until a picture's wrap. His durability and reputation were his pride. He'd sometimes fall off the wagon. Everyone thought it best to keep him busy.

His son Chris wrote, co-produced and acted in the 1985 TV movie *Promises to Keep* starring his father as an aging present-day California cowboy who returns to his abandoned family after many years on the road. His character's reasons are selfish. He has been diagnosed with terminal cancer and wishes to make amends before dying. Filmed in Santa Barbara, the drama featured Chris' son Bentley and received mixed reviews. Terry Clifford of the *Chicago Tribune* wrote, "With his lead-lidded eyes, Texas-cowboy gait and Alabama-sheriff girth, Mitchum has given new meaning to the word languid, bringing a studied slouchiness to the screen.... Still, there is no denying his appealing professionalism not to mention his staying power."

Professionally there were less options, even with TV in the equation. *Blood Hunt* with Rod Taylor and Ernest Borgnine never got out of the chute. Ditto for *Out of Retirement*, a cop story about brothers that would have paired Mitchum with pal Frank Sinatra. John Mitchum tried getting a screenplay he'd written for his brother produced but couldn't find a taker. Bob himself didn't get excited about too many things. At his age, he wasn't about to sink his own money into a vanity project. Mitchum did play Col. Patrick Flynn, an Irish Army surgeon, in the Civil War mini-series *North and South* (1985) opposite Patrick Swayze, Elizabeth Taylor, David Carradine and Johnny Cash. It was a supporting role that demanded little of him in a star-studded cast. In typical Mitchum fashion, he delivered as little as was asked.

Despite entering his porch-sitting years, Mitchum retained a thirst for knowledge and adventure worthy of a youthful pioneer spirit as evidenced by a 1986 trip he and Dorothy took to New Zealand to promote tourism there. As part of his contractual requirements, Mitchum was expected to endure the same familiar press junkets he always had to sit through on such trips but leapt at the opportunity to accompany professional hunters Steve Collins and Rusty Phillips on a helicopter hunt of red deer in the wild bush country. Brief introductions were made as Mitchum climbed into the cockpit of a Hughes 500 with his guides to swoop down on stags and hind from the sky. Pilot Collins was totally unaware of Mitchum's movie star status and was prepared for the worst fame could offer. He was pleasantly surprised at Mitchum's deep interest in his profession and overall gentlemanly behavior. Mitchum went with the men on multiple excursions to escape the media circus and later invited the guides for dinner at the Rangitikei Pub with him and Dorothy.

Steve Collins recalled Mitchum in the pages of *Rod & Rifle* magazine:

> He was very unassuming, had a good firm handshake and looked you in the eye when he spoke to you. I liked him immediately. He was very interested and asked all about the net guns and what rifles we used, how long we'd each been doing our jobs, how we got involved in the industry.... He was a very cool guy, genuinely interested and thirsty for knowledge. He told us he was amazed with what he'd seen us do and offered us both jobs in Hollywood: Rusty as a stuntman, me as a stunt pilot and aerial cameraman. Robert Mitchum was old school, what you saw was what you got, and I appreciated our time with him.

One of Mitchum's favorite getaways remained relatively close to his Santa Barbara home; visiting his thoroughbred horses in Grass Valley at the 6-B Ranch (later the JL Ranch), run by ranch foreman Dale Tackett. In 1987, Mitchum rushed into action to get the horses to safety when a forest fire threatened them. On the TV doc *Hollywood Greats,* Tackett remembered Mitchum's initial trip and how he didn't want to be an imposition:

> The first time, he came up by himself and looked at the horses. As the day grew on, he said, "Can you get me a room at a motel?" and I said, "Sure. No problem. But you're welcome to stay here with us." He said, "Well, I don't know. I might get up in the middle of the night or something and piss in your refrigerator." And I said, "Well, that's all right. I never had Robert Mitchum piss in my refrigerator before!" From that time on, any time they came up, they stayed with us.

In the fall of 1987, Mitchum hosted the long-running late-night TV comedy *Saturday Night Live.* The best skit was a spoof of his noir films entitled "Death Be Not Deadly" with Mitchum's private eye confusing the sketch's other characters by breaking into bourbon-soaked voiceover narration. The show also intended to spoof Mitchum's western image, casting him as a broken-down cowboy stuntman confined to a retirement home. Run through in rehearsals, the cowboy sketch was ultimately cut prior to going before the live audience. In 1988, CBS approached him about a TV remake of the classic western *Red River,* but Mitchum was tied up with *War and Remembrance* and declined. James Arness of TV's long-running *Gunsmoke* series played the leading part John Wayne essayed in 1948. It was announced in 1989 that Mitchum would go to Canada for the Jack London Klondike adventure *Smoke Bellew.* He would have played Snass (aka Whiskers), a half-crazed Scotsman acting as chief of a tribe of wild Alaskan Indians. This promising project fizzled out. By this time, few westerns were in production, and fewer would have a role appropriate for a 70-year-old Robert Mitchum.

Veteran writer-producer Andrew J. Fenady, best known for creating the TV westerns *The Rebel, Branded* and *Hondo,* as well as John Wayne's feature *Chisum* (1970), approached Mitchum with a project that would dust off his trenchcoat and honor the star's long association with the private detective genre. It was an adaptation of the L.A. Morse novel *The Old Dick* which became the tongue-in-cheek TV film *Jake Spanner, Private Eye* (1989). Ernest Borgnine, John Mitchum, Jim Mitchum and Stella Stevens joined the laconic star in paying homage to his tough guy image in the entertaining film. It was Mitchum's last starring role. The producer and star were unable to find a complimentary western project to collaborate on despite Fenady turning out several sagebrush novels. Fenady had always wanted to work with Mitchum and came away impressed by his cool professionalism. On the next to last day of filming, Mitchum badly sprained his ankle. Fenady feared they would have to shut down production and strain their budget. Mitchum told him not to worry and toughed it out, hobbling through the final day and a half of filming. Fenady took to calling the ultra-cool Mitchum "The Ice Man."

Fenady discussed Mitchum's acting reputation with John Wayne biographer Scott Eyman:

> You never knew which Mitchum was going to show up. If Mitchum was with people that didn't know what they were doing, or weren't pros, he'd say, "Okay, I'll hit the marks and say the lines." If he was working for someone he thought had depth and character and knowhow and cared about what they were doing, he'd give a performance. Mitchum was a mirror; he reflected what was around him. He was highly intelligent, wrote poetry, and was a fine writer as well. He could discourse on almost any subject, from cattle to Communism. He was an interested party as long as you didn't bore the shit out of him.

But old guns like Mitchum were retiring or dying. William Boyd died in 1972 at the age of 77 from heart failure. Robert Ryan passed from lung cancer in 1973 at the age of 63. John Wayne succumbed to cancer in 1979 at 72. Charles McGraw perished at 66 in a grisly alcohol-related accident in 1980. William Holden likewise died in a drinking-related fall in 1981 at 63. Throat cancer claimed Richard Boone at 63 in 1981. Professional film extra George Fargo passed from a stroke in 1981 at 51, and notorious stand-in Boyd Cabeen died in 1984. Sterling

Hayden, the hard-drinking, hash-smoking, ocean-sailing renaissance man who subsisted on Mitchum's rejected western scripts throughout the 1950s, died from prostate cancer at 70 in 1986. Long-time Mitchum pals Richard Egan and Robert Preston died from cancer in 1987 at 65 and 68. Lee Marvin also died in 1987 at age 63, suffering a heart attack following abdominal surgery. John Huston passed at 81 that same year from pneumonia and emphysema. Cowboy double Chuck Roberson died from cancer in 1988 at 69, and Lennie Geer went in 1989 at age 74. Rodeo legend Casey Tibbs died from bone and lung cancer at 60 in 1990. Steve Brodie died in 1992 at 72, while John Ireland went in 1992 from leukemia at the age of 78. Dean Martin succumbed to emphysema and lung cancer at 78 in 1995. Ben Johnson had a fatal heart attack in 1996 at age 77. Through it all, Mitchum defied the odds by outliving everyone while still working in film after film. The legend lived on.

The Films: 1990s

Tombstone (Cinergi/Buena Vista, 1993)
Cast: Kurt Russell (Wyatt Earp); Val Kilmer (Doc Holliday); Sam Elliott (Virgil Earp); Bill Paxton (Morgan Earp); Powers Boothe (Curly Bill Brocius); Michael Biehn (Johnny Ringo); Charlton Heston (Henry Hooker); Jason Priestley (Billy Breckinridge); Jon Tenney (Behan); Stephen Lang (Ike Clanton); Thomas Haden Church (Billy Clanton); Dana Delaney (Josephine Marcus); Paula Malcomson (Allie Earp); Lisa Collins (Louisa Earp); Dana Wheeler-Nicholson (Mattie Earp); Joanna Pacula (Kate); Michael Rooker (Sherman McMasters); Harry Carey, Jr. (Marshal Fred White); Billy Bob Thornton (Johnny Tyler); Tomas Arana (Frank Stillwell); Pat Brady (Milt Joyce); Paul Ben-Victor (Florentino); John Philbin (Tom McLaury); Robert Burke (Frank McLaury); Billy Zane (Mr. Fabian); Wyatt Earp (Billy Claiborne); John Corbett (Barnes); W.R. Bo Gray (Wes Fuller); Forrie J. Smith (Pony Deal); Peter Sherayko (Texas Jack Vermillion); Buck Taylor (Turkey Creek Jack Johnson); Terry O'Quinn (Mayor John Clum); Charles Schneider (Prof. Gillman); Gary Clarke (Crawley Dake); Billy Joe Patton (Deputy); Frank Stallone (Ed Bailey); Bobby Joe McFadden (First Gambler); Pedro Armendariz, Jr. (Priest); Michael N. Garcia (Rurale Captain/Groom); Grant Wheeler (Drunk); Jim Dunham (Miner); Stephen Foster (Hank Swilling); Grant James (Dr. Goodfellow); Don Collier (High Roller); Cecil Hoffman (Lucinda Hobbs); Charlie Ward (First Cowboy); Clark Ray (Second Cowboy); Chris Mitchum (Ranch Hand); Sandy Gibbons (Father Feeney); Evan Osborne (Piano Player); Shane McCabe (Audience Member); Robert Mitchum (Narrator); and Bruce Andre, Anthony Auriemma, Michelle Beauchamp, Jemison Beshears, Hunter Brown, Jerry Brown, Reggie Byrum, Frank P. Costanza, Jerry Crandall, Arthur Crofutt, Jeff Dolan, Sam Dolan, Jim Flowers, Glen Gold, Heath Evan Hammond, Bruce Hampton, Cindy Hundt, John Jackinson, Gary Laramore, Chaz Lee, Lee McKechnie, Jonathan Mincks, Buck Montgomery, John Peel, Nikki Pelley, Eddie Perez, Chris Ramirez, Terry Rick, Garrett W. Roberts, Jan Robinson, Cynthia Shope, J. Nathan Simmons, Dickie Stanley, Curt Stokes, Christopher Shawn Swinney, George Swinney, Jerry Tarantino, Thadd Turner, Rene Van Alstine, Bob Vincent, Charlie Ward, Paul Ward, Tom Ward, Jerry Whittington, Michael Wise, Larry Zeug.
Crew: George P. Cosmatos (Director); Sean Daniel, Buzz Feitshans, Andrew G. Vajna (Producers); Kevin Jarre (Screenplay); William A. Fraker (Photographer); Bruce Broughton (Music); Chris Gorak, Kim Hix, Mark Worthington (Art Directors); Harvey Rosenstock, Roberto Silvi, Frank J. Urioste (Editors); Peter Sherayko (Buckaroo Coordinator); Thell Reed (Armorer); Terry Leonard (Stunt Coordinator–Second Unit Director); Perry Barndt, Michael Barnett, Tony Lee Boggs, Chris Branham, Hal Burton, Danny Costa, Richard L. Duran, Kip Farnsworth, Evelyn Finley, Teri Garland, J.B. Getzwiller, John Hock, Cody Lee, Malosi Leonard, Matt Leonard, Terry Leonard, Bob Lester, Clint Lilley, Lee McKechnie, Bobby McLaughlin, Cliff McLaughlin, Ben Miller, Jimmy Ortega, Jeff Ramsey, Tommy Rosales, Ben Scott, Russell Solberg, Chris Swinney, Matthew Taylor, R.L. Tolbert, Mark Warrick, Jerry Wills, Kevin N. Johnston, Ronald LaCaria, Benjamin Minot, Ric San Nicholas, Dickie Stanley (Stunts); Kim Burke (Head Wrangler); George Abos, Robin Baldwin, Joseph "J.P.S." Brown, Brad Clark, Holly Edwards, John Fearn, Jr., Gary Gang, Bill Getzwiller, Joseph Getzwiller, Ron Grayes, J.T. Hall, Clinton James, J. Chris Knagge, Robin C. Larson, Ron Mitchell, Harold Clay Scott, Brenda Sue Wadsworth, Byron Wilkerson, Ivan "Red" Wolverton, Kip Wolverton, Wendy Wolverton (Wranglers).

130 minutes; Released December 25, 1993

Westerns had been in a long death spiral at the box office, but the mini-series *Lonesome Dove* captured the attention of TV audiences in 1989. Hollywood took notice and decided that perhaps it was time to revisit the genre. Westerns made a resurgence in the early 1990s when Kevin Costner's *Dances with Wolves* (1990) and Clint Eastwood's *Unforgiven* (1992) took home

Best Picture Oscars. Eastwood's aged gunman William Munny was a stone-cold brutal killer who would have been an ideal match for Mitchum 10 or 15 years earlier when David Peoples wrote the script. With the renewed interest in cowboys, Kevin Costner and Kurt Russell took on competing Wyatt Earp-O.K. Corral projects. Both films were star-laden affairs that were rushed into production attempting to beat the other to the screen to tell the story of the Dodge City marshal turned Tombstone, Arizona, lawman and his tubercular friend Doc Holliday. Mitchum became attached to Russell's Earp film *Tombstone*, with screenwriter Kevin Jarre handpicking the cast and originally handling the directorial chores.

Problems surfaced early in the production which filmed on location at Old Tucson and its sister site Mescal near Benson, Arizona, in the summer of 1993. The biggest problem was that Jarre had never directed a film. His inexperience behind the camera was immediately apparent, and he was resistant to advice on how to speed up his process. He spent valuable time trying to set up John Ford shots. "I knew from the third day Kevin couldn't direct," co-star Sam Elliott told *Entertainment Weekly*. "He wasn't getting the shots he needed." The producers fired Jarre four weeks into filming, and the entire film was in danger of being permanently shut down. Star Kurt Russell kept the behind-schedule, over-budget production afloat as George P. Cosmatos was brought in with scant preparation to direct the rest of the film. The brash Cosmatos immediately butted heads with esteemed cinematographer William Fraker, who quit the film more than once. Russell bluntly told *True West* magazine that the experience was "the hardest work of my life." With the production schedule shuffled about, several scenes were abandoned altogether, including dozens of pages of Jarre's outstanding script. Mitchum's role as bearded, whiskey-swigging patriarch Newman Haynes Clanton and his complicated Skeleton Canyon Massacre scene was one of the casualties of the cuts. Mitchum's dialogue was assumed by Powers Boothe's character Curly Bill Brocius to retain some of Jarre's rich lines.

"I was to play Old Man Clanton," Mitchum told *Trail Dust Magazine,* "but I was having trouble with my back. I had it x-rayed and the doctor forbade me to do it because in the second scene I'm lying there with a horse on top of me! So, I had to beg off… [T]hen they asked me to narrate it." Some reports claim Mitchum suffered the back injury when he fell from the horse on set. This is incorrect. Mitchum thought he could manage bringing the horse down through a rocky canyon for his scene, but the segment was never filmed. Mitchum's bad back gave the producers the easy out to drop the costly scene altogether. They simply couldn't afford to wait for him to feel better. Mitchum was never in wardrobe. Western film aficionado Frank Stallone proudly wore the boots in the film that had originally been set aside for Mitchum. Chris Mitchum confirms that his dad was not hurt during filming. "He never injured his back," Chris says. "He never made it to the set…. They had a contract they had to pay my dad, so they had him do the voiceover."*

"I black out if I lean over to tie a shoe," Mitchum told *The National Enquirer* in describing his current physical condition after years of stunts and horseback riding. The body had grown battered, but the rich baritone remained solvent despite the years of physical abuse. It became his calling card in these later years, with Lee Server writing, "It had come to sound like the Voice of the West, of frontier values, masculine values, and the sound of when men were men." Mitchum's words open *Tombstone* with dialogue over black and white images of stars Russell and Val Kilmer intercut with vintage footage from the silent films *The Great Train Robbery* (1903) and *The Bank Robbery* (1908). Mitchum's narration over the beginning and closing credits adds a fitting sense of legend to *Tombstone* as he initially explains the hostilities existing in the post–Civil War region and the lead-up to the gunfight at the O.K. Corral. His closing line regarding Earp's 1929 funeral—"Tom Mix cried"—is memora-

---

*Chris Mitchum (e-mail correspondence, May 2018).

ble. *Variety* found his narration added "credible continuity" to the film. Mitchum did the entire looping session in one hour for the full fee contracted for his acting part.

Charlton Heston, Harry Carey, Jr., Don Collier, Buck Taylor, Billy Bob Thornton and Pedro Armendariz, Jr., have small roles in a large cast that includes a bit for Chris Mitchum as Heston's ranch hand. Glenn Ford was to have appeared, but health issues prevented him from taking a role. Hugh O'Brian, TV's Wyatt Earp in the 1950s, filmed a scene under Jarre's direction, but it did not make the final cut. O'Brian later expressed interest in doing the narration, but the job went to the senior Mitchum who was already being paid for doing nothing on the film. Chris Mitchum told *Psychotronic Video*: "Most of my work was cut out. They cut about 42 pages of stuff out of the script to downplay the other characters and place emphasis on Kurt Russell's character. So instead of this beautiful epic film, they cut it down to just a good action western."

Roughhewn character actor Don Collier was originally going to portray Tombstone photographer C.S. Fly, the future sheriff of Cochise County. However, Collier only briefly appears as a high-rolling gambler in the finished film. If one blinks, they might miss the veteran western player entirely. Collier wasn't aware that Mitchum was originally going to play Old Man Clanton, the character Walter Brennan memorably brought to life in John Ford's *My Darling Clementine* (1946). According to Collier, "I moved out to Tucson in 1983. Los Angeles got too big for me. I did two little parts in *Tombstone*. In one scene I was a photographer, but after they shot it, all you saw was the back of my head. So Kurt Russell said, 'Let's use Don for this other part too.' They filmed it very quickly. Everything was rushed on that."*

Rambling and imperfect, the $25 million *Tombstone* resonated with macho males and western aficionados. *True West* called it one of the top five westerns ever made. *Entertainment Weekly* named it one of the 25 greatest westerns of the last 25 years. Philip Armour placed it in *The 100 Greatest Movie Westerns of All Time*.

John Farkis detailed its entire history in *The Making of* Tombstone: *Behind the Scenes of the Classic Modern Western*.

Beating Costner's Earp film to the theaters before Christmas 1993, the picture did decent box office business before exploding as a popular video rental. It's now a treasured part of western fans' film libraries, a story they can watch again and again featuring endlessly quotable dialogue and a cast of performers at the top of their game. Russell handled himself well in the part of Earp, and Kilmer stole the film as the dying Doc Holliday. Sam Elliott, Bill Paxton, Powers Boothe, Stephen Lang and Michael Biehn as Johnny Ringo add to the western flavor in memorable roles. *Tombstone* is tough, exciting, and never boring. It's a shame Mitchum didn't get to play Old Man Clanton. It was a part Kirk Douglas, Gregory Peck and Jack Palance had all been considered for.

Mitchum's services remained in demand, but more so as a crusty and rumpled character player. "If phlegm sold for 20 cents a pound, I could retire," Mitchum told *True*. He had colorful cameos in *Mr. North* (1988) and *Scrooged* (1988) and performed admirably as a shady CIA operative in the TV movie thriller *Brotherhood of the Rose* (1989). He impressively stepped in for an ailing Edward Woodward to headline two 1987 episodes of the action series *The Equalizer*. However, few of the roles he now assumed seemed worthy of his longtime standing in the business: a homeless man in the short-lived sitcom *A Family for Joe* (1990), a psychiatrist in the minor thriller *Midnight Ride* (1990), a business tycoon phoning in a weekly cameo in the cable series *African Skies* (1992–1994), a cigar-smoking God in the French sketch comedy *Seven Deadly Sins* (1992), a lawyer in the Bo Derek drama *Woman of Desire* (1994), and a fire marshal in the lowbrow comedy *Backfire!* (1995).

Yakuza director Sydney Pollock once likened Mitchum to a powerful and lazy horse who needed to be spurred into performing to his full capabilities. Mitchum was too often content to lope along the easiest path. He did do a solid cameo with choice lines as a wily cop in a re-

---
*Don Collier (phone conversation, May 2018).

Shading his lawman character with a western hat in Universal's 1991 remake of *Cape Fear*.

make of *Cape Fear* (1991) for director Martin Scorsese, and bemusedly watching Robert De Niro turn his original Max Cady character into a violent cartoon caricature. Mitchum turned down the Irish drama *The Field* (1990); his friend Richard Harris was nominated for an Oscar as the towering Bull McCabe. Mitchum also said no to a part in Oliver Stone's conspiracy-laden *JFK* (1991) and dropped out of the high-quality TV movie *In the Line of Fire: Manhunt in the Dakotas* (1991). Rod Steiger took over the showy part of an anti-government white supremacist fighting the Feds. Director Budd Boetticher and co-producer Burt Kennedy wanted Mitchum to portray showman P.T. Barnum in *A Horse for Mr. Barnum*, about three American cowboys sent to Spain to bring back an Andalusia horse for the title character. In 1994, Mitchum, Bruce Boxleitner, James Coburn, Jorge Rivero and Henry Silva were announced for the $20 million film. It never got made.

The work he did accept during this period wasn't overly demanding. He was host-narrator for the 1986 historical TV series *The Entrepreneurs* and the 1988 documentary *John Huston: The Man, the Movies, the Maverick*. He also narrated the World War II TV series *Eyes of War* (1989). In 1992, Mitchum landed a high-profile commercial job as the spokesman for the American cattle industry's "Beef: It's what's for dinner" campaign. The message from the Beef Council was simple and direct, and Mitchum was the perfect red-blooded western male to deliver the voiceover pitch. He was resistant to commercials as an A-list movie star, but now that he was doing character parts, he didn't object to selling product. He even promoted Glad trash bags and Nuveen investment portfolios. There was more cowboy and western imagery used in Mitchum's voice spots for GM Motors and their Pontiac Trans Sport tagline: "Life is more exciting in Montana."

Mitchum served as an on-screen narrator for the documentary *100 Years of the Hollywood Western* (1994) along with Kurt Russell, James Coburn, Charles Bronson, Gene Hackman and James Garner. In the film, Mitchum says, "Every performer in Hollywood wanted to be in [a western]" over a humorous clip of himself in *Girl Rush* (1944). The voice jobs paid well and was welcome work for the aging film legend. Not that it was always easy for Mitchum to clear the airways. He was still smoking Pall Malls and drinking Jose Cuevo tequila with semi-regularity.

Mitchum continued along his directionless late career path, now dividing his time between Santa Barbara and Paradise Valley, Arizona, where he lived on Mockingbird Lane along the equestrian trails in the foothills of the Phoenix Mountains. The area was once known as Windy Gulch. Nearby, at the base of Mummy Mountain, sat the world-famous Camelback Inn and its pueblo-styled casitas. Coincidentally, the western-themed resort featured the Hopalong Cassidy College for Kids as one of its attractions, as well as a small faux ghost town for its guests. To the immediate south of Camelback Mountain was the area once known as the film set Cudia City, which served as the main location for the TV western *26 Men* (1957–1959). As for his decision to move semi-permanently to Arizona, Mitchum liked wintering in the dry climate where he had made so many films and personal appearances. The rugged landscape fit his image. He could watch the sun rise over the vast Superstition mountain range and the Four Peaks Wilderness. To the north was Pinnacle Peak and a famous patio steakhouse built around an Old West facade. Arizona gave him a chance to rest and relax. Mitchum's mother and sister had relocated to the state, as well as Jim and his children. After a string of low-budget direct-to-video films, Jim Mitchum finally said adios to an acting career and moved into the real estate and construction business. Like his dad, he began breeding horses.

In the Grand Canyon State, Robert Mitchum took in Arabian horse shows and classic car events for Barrett-Jackson on the rodeo grounds of Scottsdale's Westworld. In the early 1990s, he visited Westworld's Festival of the West when his son Chris appeared. He stretched out in the shadow of Camelback Mountain telling tall tales at the El Chorro Lounge and Trader Vic's and the Rusty Spur in Old Town Scottsdale, a retro shopping and art district billed as "the West's most western town." Another establishment he visited near his home was Scottsdale's Handlebar J Saloon, where authentic cowboy hats hung from the ceiling and leather saddles and bull skulls adorned the walls. Down the street, Mitchum's pal Rory Calhoun once owned a cowboy bar called The Crystal Pistol that became a western-themed hamburger joint known as The Chuck Box.

Arizona was happy to have a star of Mitchum's magnitude making his home there and promoting a western lifestyle to the public. *The Arizona Republic* reported during the making of *Nightkill* at Sky Harbor Airport in 1980 that a smiling Mitchum was warm and obliging to a crowd gathered around him, even offering hugs and kisses to his fans. "The big man, who most often is a villain in films, proved to be only a charming softy," they wrote. In recognition of the many films he had done in Arizona, the Metro Phoenix Film Board presented him with their Crystal Phoenix Award in 1988. It was a minor and somewhat trivial award, but Mitchum was happy to accept. Event publicist Phil Strassberg recalled Mitchum at the ceremony for *The Mesa Tribune*: "He was very amiable. He was the same kind of laidback presence that we are all familiar with. He was quite unassuming."

Arizona stuntman–horse trainer Rodd Wolff got his start in westerns with a saddle fall on an episode of *Death Valley Days*. From there he worked on *Duel at Diablo* (1966), *Rio Lobo* (1970) and *The Outlaw Josey Wales* (1976). In *Charro* (1969), he served as Elvis Presley's riding double. Wolff performed stunts on the Phoenix-made Mitchum film *Nightkill* (1980) and worked in the transportation department on *Tombstone*. He got to know Mitchum after the cowboy legend moved to Arizona:

> Robert Mitchum was my neighbor in Paradise Valley. He had horses, and I went over a few times to visit him. We'd have lunch and then we'd ride his horses around the property together. We did that three or four times. He liked to talk about horses, not so much about movies. The best way to get close to people like that is to talk about subjects other than movies, so Bob and I talked about horses. I remember I did tell him that my favorite movie of his was *Blood on the Moon* that he made up in Sedona with Barbara Bel Geddes, and he did say that was one of his favorites as well. Not *the* favorite, but one of them.
>
> I have some pictures of Bob and I at the Golden Boot Awards together. I never took a camera with me to his house. His hair was always a little ruffled and half the time he didn't shave. I doubt if he would have been too pleased with me bringing over a camera. I did ask him about working with Jane Russell. He said he enjoyed working with her. I remember he winked and said he enjoyed working with all his leading ladies. Back then, people were very guarded because so many stories were being sold to *The National Enquirer*. With people like Bob Mitchum, I knew him and talked to him, but three meetings didn't make me an intimate friend. I wish I could have worked with him more back in the 1960s. I would have liked that. I thought he was a neat guy.*

Rodd Wolff's sentiments were echoed by Hollywood train consultant Jim Clark, who worked with Mitchum on *War and Remembrance* and provided vintage rail cars for *Wild*

---

*Rodd Wolff (phone conversation, September 2017).

Wild West (1999) and *The Lone Ranger* (2013) in addition to organizing the Tombstone Western Film Festival from 2000 to 2005:

> I wish I could have worked with Bob on a western. I first recognized him when I was a kid in Hoppy movies. I was born in 1943. I liked his laidback cool, but slightly menacing way about him. My grandmother, who I lived with, was a big fan of Hoppy and introduced me to him over Roy and Gene (Rogers and Autry). On *War and Remembrance,* he was his usual cool self, and I thought he and Polly Bergen were good together. He always made a good military man because he reeked authority. However, nothing tops his film noir portrayals in black and white films as in *Night of the Hunter* and *Out of the Past*. As far as westerns go, *El Dorado, 5 Card Stud, The Way West* and others proved he could hold his own with everything from heroes to villains, a war drama to a western, and still play a clever detective in the shadows. No one has ever been quite like him.*

Neil Summers had the opportunity to work on Mitchum's *El Dorado* and *Young Billy Young* before distinguishing himself as one of the industry's top stuntmen in everything from *The Outlaw Josey Wales* (1976) to *Appaloosa* (2008). He made a name for himself as a character player in the westerns *The Life and Times of Judge Roy Bean* (1972), *My Name Is Nobody* (1973) and *Bad Girls* (1994). He was a western fan who took delight in collecting memorabilia and meeting boyhood idols like John Wayne on *Rio Lobo* (1970). Summers published the collectible books *Candid Cowboys* and *Unsung Heroes,* full of stunt action photos. In 1989, Summers and fellow stuntman Richard Farnsworth were invited to B-Western cowboy Monte Hale's 80th birthday party in Santa Barbara and ran into Mitchum there. "Bob showed up and was looking great," Summers says. "He was in a talkative mood and had questions for me about some of the guys he'd lost track of or hadn't heard anything about for years. Once people showed up and settled in, of course, everyone wanted Bob's time, so he sat down and held court for a while. My personal opinion is that Mitchum was for real; friendly when he wanted to be and aloof when it got too much for him. He was one of Hollywood's greats and his legacy will last as long as there are movies."†

Recognition for his lifetime of work began to be sent Mitchum's way. In 1983, he appeared at a San Francisco film festival commemorating him. To the *San Francisco Chronicle* he attributed his long career to the mere ability "to walk and talk and do my own stunts." The following year he received a star on the Hollywood Walk of Fame, and in 1992 he was awarded the prestigious Cecil B. DeMille Award at the Golden Globes. In humbly accepting the DeMille Award, Mitchum stated he disliked using the word *career,* professing it was simply the progression of a job which he was fortunate to have. To be noticed and rewarded by his peers was something he was "truly, honestly, sincerely grateful for." The self-deprecating humor remained. When asked by *The Today Show*'s Gene Shalit what he'd like to be remembered for, Mitchum suggested *Hoppy Serves a Writ*. Mitchum notched Career Achievement Awards from the National Board of Review in 1991, the Hollywood Foreign Press Association in 1992, and the San Sebastian Film Festival in 1993. One of the more notable of these honor ceremonies for Mitchum was the 1994 Golden Boot Award given to him for his contribution to the western genre. He was originally to receive the cowboy honor in 1989, but filming schedules conflicted.

The Golden Boot was given to the top western stars, stuntmen, writers, directors and character actors working in the field; men Mitchum knew well like Ben Johnson, Richard Farnsworth, Budd Boetticher, Burt Kennedy, Harry Carey, Jr., and Pierce Lyden. It was the cowboy Oscar. William Boyd, Clint Eastwood and Jack Palance were booted the previous year. *The Magnificent Seven*'s James Coburn was acknowledged alongside Mitchum, whose *Young Billy Young* female lead Angie Dickinson presented him the award on stage at the Beverly Hilton Hotel. The encounter was described as a touching reunion between the former co-stars. The event was cowboy casual with Mitchum

---

*Jim Clark (e-mail correspondence, September 2017).
†Neil Summers (written correspondence, May 2018).

wearing a blue western shirt, gray blazer and bolo tie. The Golden Boot was not Mitchum's sole western recognition. In 1994, the Lone Pine Film Festival celebrated the 50th anniversary of Mitchum's first starring role at an event featuring John Mitchum, Ruth Terry, Barbara Hale, Kay Aldridge, John Ericson, Pierce Lyden, Anne Mitchum, Loren Janes, William Witney and Charles Champlin. Mitchum was unable to attend because of a commitment in Oslo, Norway, for *The Sunset Boys* (1995), but he filmed a video interview for the ceremony. It was a lot of fuss for a guy between trains.

Dead Man (Miramax, 1995)

Cast: Johnny Depp (William Blake); Gary Farmer (Nobody); Crispin Glover (Train Fireman); Lance Henriksen (Cole Wilson); Michael Wincott (Conway Twill); Eugene Byrd (Johnny "The Kid" Pickett); John Hurt (John Scholfield); Robert Mitchum (John Dickinson); Iggy Pop (Salvatore "Sally" Jenko); Gabriel Byrne (Charlie Dickinson); Jared Harris (Benmont Trench); Mili Avital (Thel Russell); Jimmy Ray Weeks (Marvin); Mark Bringelson (Lee); John North (Mr. Olafson); Peter Schrum (Drunk); Mike Dawson (Old Man); Billy Bob Thornton (Big George Drakoulious); Michelle Thrush (Nobody's Girlfriend); Gibby Haines (Man in Alley); Richard Boes (Man with Wrench); George Duckworth (Man at End of Street); Thomas Bettles (Young Nobody #1); Alfred Molina (Trading Post Missionary); Daniel Chas Stacy (Young Nobody #2); Todd Pfeiffer (Man #2 at Trading Post); Leonard Bowechop, Cecil Cheeka, Michael McCarty (Makah Villagers); Steve Buscemi (Bartender).

Crew: Jim Jarmusch (Director); Karen Koch, Demetra J. MacBride (Producers); Jim Jarmusch (Screenplay); Robby Muller (Photographer); Neil Young (Music); Ted Berner (Art Director); Jay Rabinowitz (Editor); Al Jones (Stunt Coordinator); Tori Bridges, Erik Stabenau (Stunts); Red Wolverton, Kip Wolverton, Margery Wolverton (Wranglers).

121 minutes; Released May 5, 1996

"The only job you're going to get is pushing up daisies from a pine box," a shotgun-wielding Mitchum informs transported Cleveland bookkeeper Johnny Depp in the offbeat, daringly different western *Dead Man*. Hip New Yorker Jim Jarmusch's eerie black-and-white art film has many fans due to the sheer style, but it confused most critics and mainstream audiences with its audacious execution of an 1870s Pacific Northwest journey into the Hereafter. Mortally wounded and sporting a derby and a fur coat, the meek, quirky Depp is one of the least stereotypical western gunmen to grace the screen.

As John Dickinson with his shotgun in the avant-garde western *Dead Man* (1995).

The fact that he has a bullet lodged in his heart during the story, yet becomes deadly proficient with a pistol, intensifies the feeling that Jarmusch's entire film is a fantasy. As Mitchum's final western, it seems appropriately mysterious, bizarre, and hard to get a handle on. Violent and even sexually explicit, it's 180 degrees from his Hopalong Cassidy debut, although it is fitting that Mitchum portrays a bad guy in both. A meditation on death, the film sustains a weird, dream-like aura throughout the course of its two-hour running time, peopled with eccentric characters played by an odd assortment of real-life personalities ranging from Crispin Glover to Billy Bob Thornton and Iggy Pop. A harsh, jarring guitar soundtrack by Neil Young haunts the film. It's an acquired taste, to be sure.

Mitchum portrays John Dickinson, a feared metal works industrialist who reigns over the disorienting, black smoke–enshrouded, clanging-loud western town of Machine. The craggy, crazed Mitchum hires a trio of gunmen (Lance Henriksen, Michael Wincott and Eugene Byrd) to track down injured protagonist William Blake (Depp), the man responsible for shooting his no-account son Gabriel Byrne. Most importantly, Mitchum wants the return of the Pinto horse Depp has taken. The gunmen are a fearsome lot, but they can't hold a candle to the physical power of the aging lion Mitchum, whose deeply creviced face now looks like one of the western landscapes he once traversed. Chomping on a cigar and brandishing a shotgun, Mitchum makes Dickinson as dangerous as he is profane in his two scenes. He's peculiar to a degree. When meeting the gunmen, Mitchum ignores them, choosing instead to deliver his dialogue to a giant stuffed grizzly bear standing above him. It's a surreal moment in what has been termed a postmodern "acid western."

Dead Man shot exteriors primarily in the Coconino National Forest outside of Flagstaff and Sedona, Arizona, as well as parts of Nevada, Oregon and Washington State. The town that Mitchum rules was built in the desert at the Cowtown set outside of Phoenix near the Agua Fria Wash. However, Mitchum's scenes were all performed on an interior set within the span of a few days in the fall of 1994. The 77-year-old actor tore into the cameo role. He didn't bother with a great deal of motivation for the character. A self-assured minimalist, he found the frightening power of the man easily enough. Jarmusch, a protégé of Nicholas Ray at New York University, told *The New York Times* that Mitchum was the only actor he ever found intimidating.

In the film's press material, producer Demetra MacBride explains that the filmmakers were hopeful they could find a Robert Mitchum type with a strong and threatening presence to portray Dickinson. The choices for that type of performer were so limited (Oliver Reed, James Coburn, Jack Palance, Richard Harris, William Smith, Charles Napier) that they ultimately decided to approach Mitchum himself. They were pleasantly surprised to find him at least somewhat receptive. "He's this gruff, kind of commanding man," MacBride explains. "He's-been-there-and-done-that 50 times before. He's the elder statesman. He's epic. That's all there is to it." MacBride told the *Houston Chronicle*, "Mitchum's a legend. We were all completely in awe and reverence. We used to joke that it looked like he strangled that bear to death. He really is the American man. He was quite spectacular."

Jarmusch flew to Santa Barbara to have lunch with Mitchum, an event the director recalled on *Charlie Rose* as "one of the more amazing afternoons of my life." Jarmusch was not a fan of traditional western films, but he did like *Blood on the Moon* because it was so different. As usual, Mitchum was reluctant to commit but, according to *The New York Times*, by the end of the extended meeting he announced, "Okay, I'll do your damn movie."

Jarmusch then went about finding an appropriate 12-gauge double-barreled shotgun for Mitchum to brandish in the film. He did his period research and presented Mitchum with options to choose. Mitchum didn't care. Whatever shotgun Jarmusch wanted him to carry. He was the director. Considering that he needed to hold it throughout his scenes, Mitchum finally opted for the lightest of the bunch. He was, after all, a senior citizen. Unlike many actors who improvise on the set, Mitchum preferred to stick to Jarmusch's scripted words. Jarmusch was extremely reluctant to present Mitchum with any last-minute script changes. Once he got to know Mitchum, Jarmusch told *The Guardian* in a British Film Institute interview, "He's a very self-effacing, really funny, intelligent man, and it was a real honor to work with him."

Mitchum's casting was fine with star Johnny Depp. Like many emerging actors the likes of Liam Neeson, Michael Madsen and Benicio Del Toro, Depp was a Mitchum fan. In press releases, an awestruck Depp said of Mitchum, "He was about seven feet tall and in great shape.... He was a tough guy." In a Q&A with *YM Magazine,* Depp revealed:

> If I could have been a different person, I would have wanted to be Robert Mitchum in *Night of the Hunter.* He was incredible. I admire him quite a bit. I hate the fact that Hollywood needs to label people "bad boys" or that stupid used-up word "rebel," When Robert Mitchum first came around, he did whatever he wanted to do, and he was busted and labeled a bad boy. But he was a normal guy who happened to be an actor who didn't want to change his lifestyle for Hollywood. I think he was the original "independent." He didn't care what anyone else thought. Now there are people who do that just because they think it's cool.

It took *Dead Man* time to find its audience, but the picture now has a cult following. *Variety* called Mitchum's appearance "a relatively colorless cameo." *Sight and Sound* liked him better, tagging him "inspired and deranged." *Time Out* wrote that he was "glorious, however briefly, as an irascible factory baron." *Screen International* opined, "Robert Mitchum is excellent in his all-too-brief appearance," and *Empire* added, "There's plenty to enjoy from the rest of the all-star cast as well, in particular, the dangerously dotty Mitchum who really should do comedy more often." *The Arizona Republic* called him, "a strong presence, as always," while the *Chicago Tribune* tagged him "the great Bob Mitchum—in a part you only wish were bigger." *Renegade Westerns* noted that Mitchum remains "every inch the rough individualist—oozing that famed masculine menace."

Mitchum proved he wasn't ready to be put out to pasture, as he donned the western wardrobe to be suited and booted one last time. There would, however, be no horseback riding for Mitchum in the film. His extended hiatus from the western genre was telling. It had been over 25 years since he'd been on a true western location. The cowboy stuntmen and wranglers Mitchum befriended in the old days were out of the business.

A veteran rodeo hand turned horse-wrangling stuntman, Harry McCrorey moved into the transportation department to drive trucks on *Dead Man* as he witnessed the business change and move away from cowboy flicks. In the late 1950s, 700 wranglers worked in Hollywood on films and television. By the early 1990s, about 35 were actively making a living. Few westerners had the ability to replace them or the resources to sustain themselves even if they could. The same change was happening in front of the camera. McCrorey worked on *Rio Lobo* (1970) as well as on the TV shows *The High Chaparral, Bonanza* and *Gunsmoke.* "I can't think of many actors who can do a western," McCrorey told the *Indianapolis Star* in 1989. "Perhaps Sam Elliott. Perhaps Tom Selleck. I did *The Sacketts* with them. But Ben Johnson and people like him can't play the young gunslingers any more. Coming up with an actor who can sell himself is hard to do. I guess cowboys are cowboys and actors are actors. Cowboys can't act, and actors can't ride."

"The young fellas haven't had the chance to be around as much livestock as we did," veteran stuntman Richard Farnsworth told the *Ocala Star-Banner* in 1989. "The wagon drivers and horsemen are harder to find. There are still some good horseback stuntmen around, but not as many as there used to be because they're not making westerns any more." Ben Johnson readily agreed with his old friend Farnsworth. He told Darrell Arnold of *Western Horseman,*

> It's hard to find young people in the business who know anything about the Real West. Most actors can't ride well enough to get in and out of a scene.... When they made *Heaven's Gate,* they invested 50 or 60 million dollars in it, and it busted all those people. They called it a western, so after that, any time somebody mentioned a western, they all ran backwards. It's very expensive to make an authentic western. It's almost

impossible to afford to have 1000 head of cattle in a movie. It is just very difficult to finance, produce, direct and act out a good western.

But Mitchum managed two of them against the odds.

Despite revisiting the western genre, Mitchum's overwhelming status as a noir icon was still paramount in the minds of fans. Famed mystery novelist Robert B. Parker admitted in interviews that he wrote his signature private detective character Spenser with a young Mitchum in mind. *Dead Man* star Johnny Depp's brother Daniel Depp was moved enough by Mitchum's legendary presence to base a literary character on him, an ex-cowboy stuntman and rodeo veteran named David Spandau, in the novel *Loser's Town*. Journalist turned crime novelist Dick Lochte, who interviewed Mitchum in the 1970s, wrote a prospective screenplay for the star. It was a modern noir featuring Mitchum as ex-con Dave "Mace" Mason, readjusting to life in a changing Los Angeles. Mitchum ultimately passed on the project, but Lochte retooled the story into a younger Mitchum character for the novel *Blues in the Night*.

Mitchum's strong influence can also be seen in the western print genre. Horse wrangler-cowboy stuntman Ben Miller, the rodeo-roping nephew of Ben Johnson, had a violent western story in development for several years entitled *Mescal*. Unable to make it into a film, Miller novelized the story. The death-dealing renegade Arizona lawman character Frank Haggard reads like a classic crazed Mitchum bad guy. Brian Garfield, popular author of the novels *Death Wish* and *Wild Times,* blatantly likens a main character in his modern story *Necessity* to Mitchum. Garfield's many older westerns, especially his mixed-breed deputy Jeremiah Tree who matches up with Wyatt Earp in *Sliphammer,* seem to use Mitchum as a blueprint in their physical description, manner, speech pattern and choice of words. Garfield revealed himself in an interview with Ralph D. Gardner about the writing process when asked about the possibility of making his 1969 Golden Spur Award nominated book *Arizona* into a movie. "If I were to make this film today," Garfield says. "I think my first choice for that role would be Robert Mitchum, who I think is one of our great screen actors."

After *Dead Man,* Mitchum portrayed lawman Jeff Fahey's father in a 1995 episode of the modern-western TV series *The Marshal*. When asked by interviewer Ellen Gray if he planned to watch the episode, a sardonic Mitchum replied, "If I live 'til Monday, I may look at it." He filmed a cameo as director George Stevens in the underwhelming biopic *James Dean: Live Fast, Die Young* (aka *James Dean: Race with Destiny*) (1997). Now in his late 70s, Mitchum preferred not to work, though the film's associate producer Dan Sefton recalled in the *Houston Chronicle,* "Fire came to his eyes when the cameras began rolling." The film starred Mitchum's granddaughter Carrie and her husband Casper Van Dien. Mitchum took those roles because they asked. There was little financial incentive for Mitchum to make a late career turn into a "Buckshot Bob" scene-stealing western cameo player. He was turning down roles during this period to the apparent benefit of grizzled character player James Gammon, whom the trade publication *Variety* dubbed "the poor man's Robert Mitchum." Gammon appeared in colorful roles in *Silverado* (1985), *Wyatt Earp* (1994), *Wild Bill* (1995) and the TV mini-series *Streets of Laredo* (1995). It was a lot of work for an old man, reasoned Mitchum; and too much dust and dirt in his spent lungs. *Dead Man* was his last western and his final theatrical feature.

Adios, Amigo

As life and career wound down, Mitchum began to relax his guard with a couple of journalists. Mitchum and the family had long been opposed to an autobiography ("The Los Angeles Police have it all on file," Mitchum told Mike Tomkies), and he tended to look on anyone new in his life with a degree of suspicion and a raised eyebrow. Researcher Jerry Roberts was determined to chronicle Mitchum's life historically, and Mitchum granted a lengthy interview over cups of coffee to clarify many previously documented inaccuracies and half-truths. The interview and thorough research resulted in two invaluable Mitchum resources in the forms of the books *Robert Mitchum: A Bio-Bibliography* and *Mitchum: In His Own Words*. In Arizona, Mitchum befriended writer-publicist Pierre O'Rourke and informally discussed his career in western films. O'Rourke ultimately recapped their conversations in a memorial penned to the actor in the pages of *The Arizonan*. "I learned that Robert Mitchum's biting mannerism was his way of acceptance, eventually his embrace," O'Rourke says of their time together.

Writer David Fury became a friend of veteran western star Chuck Connors from TV's *The Rifleman* and ultimately released a fine biography on the actor and sportsman, *The Man Behind the Rifle*. Fury also created an old-fashioned western plot for Connors to star in as a nostalgic TV movie entitled *The Final Showdown*. Then Connors became ill and passed away from lung cancer in 1992. Fury considered that with retooling the script and the character of retired marshal Jake Taylor might be perfect for Robert Mitchum. He sent the screenplay on spec to Mitchum in 1994 with faint hope that he would ever receive a response. In many cases when stars receive an unsolicited screenplay at their home address, they promptly deposit it in the trash without a second thought. That's simply the way it is. Fury was surprised that within ten days of mailing his screenplay, he received a hand-written return letter from Mitchum explaining that he needed some time to "thaw out" after having returned from Toronto for his work on *African Skies*. Fury's screenplay was never heard from again, but the writer treasured the fact that Mitchum took the time and effort to send a personal reply. It showed the film legend's true character.

Prolific western fiction writer Robert Vaughan wrote a screenplay entitled *Colorado's Raid* about a pair of aged Texas lawmen whose decades-long feud is set aside to clear the name of their mutual granddaughter's husband. Vaughan wrote the script with Mitchum and Dale Robertson in mind, and this screenplay found more traction than Fury's. Mitchum liked the premise and committed to strapping on his six guns one last time opposite his old friend Robertson. The film went into pre-production in San Antonio, Texas, with Al Frakes serving as the director and Simon Williams-Channing producing for London's Imagine Films. Mitchum's health was faltering, but he hoped that for this old-fashioned western, he could rally his strength and go out with guns blazing. But Mitchum took a turn for the worse and the project never went into principal photography. Vaughan, who sometimes wrote westerns under the pen name Hank Mitchum, ended up rewriting the story and publishing it as the novel *The Lawmen*.

The end of the trail was not smooth. Mitchum

was diagnosed with lung cancer and emphysema that severely affected his ability to breathe. It was a permanent noose around his neck. Mitchum deadpanned to *The National Enquirer*, "Well, you gotta die of something!" After Christmas 1996 he fell at home and fractured a hip. The aging tough guy pulled himself into a chair and begged off being taken to the hospital. He finally acquiesced at Dorothy's request. Briefly. Mitchum's condition prompted Ernest Borgnine, Charlton Heston and Clint Eastwood to lobby the Motion Picture Academy with letters of support for an Honorary Oscar for Mitchum. "If ever anybody deserved some kind of lifetime achievement Oscar, it was Bob Mitchum," Borgnine wrote in his autobiography. Borgnine's effort was to no avail. Mitchum had shunned the awards ceremony back in 1945 and the Academy never forgot the slight. The stoic Mitchum seemed resigned to his fate, even if he hated being coddled and attached to an oxygen tank. Always the rebel, he continued to down an occasional drink and unhook himself from his oxygen for cigarettes. Nobody was going to deny him those enjoyments. Regarding the cumbersome oxygen tank, Mitchum said, "I only need it to breathe."

Mitchum had a couple of final phone interviews, including a piece by film buff Elwy Yost regarding Hopalong Cassidy for TV-Ontario. Mitchum spoke regularly on the phone with Anthony Caruso but was reluctant to let his friend see his weakening condition. Actor pal Charles Napier, a rough-hewn TV cowboy on the series *The Oregon Trail* and *Outlaws*, had been introduced to Mitchum in the early 1970s by Richard Egan. Napier visited Mitchum for a final marathon drink and bull fest at Mitchum's Santa Barbara home. When a frustrated Mitchum was satisfied that no more could be said, he hurled his walker against the wall and bid Napier goodbye. It was the last Napier saw of his friend. "Those few days in Santa Barbara became a blur, filled with booze and bullshitting," Napier wrote in his memoir. "When it was time to leave, there were no hugs or sentiments between the two of us. Bob just said, 'Get the fuck out of here.'"

Mitchum died in his sleep at home on July 1, 1997, at the age of 79. Chris Mitchum reported there was a final drink and stubbed-out cigarette near the bed; Mitchum still seeking a relaxing blur before the everlasting darkness. Shortly before his death, brother John Mitchum arranged a Them Ornery Mitchum Boys Celebration in Stockton, California, in May 1997. The event was attended by western figures Jack Elam, James Drury, Stuart Whitman, Jane Russell, Walter Reed, Peggy Stewart, Anne Jeffreys and banjo-playing TV cowboy Jon Locke. After Robert Mitchum's death, John told Stockton's *Record Net*:

> He was the most generous man I have ever known. I consider him one of the finest individuals I've known in my life. I have beautiful memories.... Courageous, profoundly brilliant, tender. He could be very fierce when the occasion demanded. He was an enormous talent—he wrote poetry, he wrote music—but he rose above that from a standpoint of ego. He never allowed ego to enter the talent field.... He is truly a great man. I feel elevated having known him that long. I can't put it any other way.

Robert Mitchum couldn't make the Stockton ceremony, but he managed a phone call to the event to offer his thanks. His mind remained sharp to the last sunset. "I never did anything

As the good guy in *The Good Guys and the Bad Guys* (1969).

to glorify myself or improve my lot," he told *Parade* somewhat wistfully in 1994. "I took what came and did the best I could with it." Mitchum accepted his fate, even if he was upset that he didn't have the strength to go out swinging like his alter ego, the wild man known to the industry and the world as Big Bad Bob. He'd no doubt have preferred to perish in a final bruising bar fight, a gun-blazing street shootout, or atop a bucking bronc like his character Jeff McCloud in *The Lusty Men*. He always claimed he was prepared for death, telling Dick Lochte it was "just one more hangover" further on up the road. In a phone interview conducted with the *Record Net* for the Celebration Days event, Mitchum reflected simply, "It's been worth it. I did it, and I'm done." To his friend Pierre O'Rourke in *The Arizonan*, Mitchum said: "I learned from it all—took it all to the screen. Regrets? Aw, hell. That I didn't do more."

"He was the best tequila-drinking, two-fisted tough guy around," Ernest Borgnine said in a eulogy for *E-Online*. Mitchum's leading lady Jane Russell, star of Howard Hughes' notoriously risqué western *The Outlaw* (1943), told the same news outlet, "Mitchum was one of the best actors that ever walked. He always knew his lines, was very calm, always on time. He always came through." Old Tucson Studios owner Bob Shelton told the *Tucson Citizen*, "We've lost one of the great western 'he man' hero types." Republic cowboy star Rex Allen, a buddy of Mitchum's from Arizona, added, "He was one hell of a guy. He was a man's man. He was a great guy to be around, a good friend. We're going to miss him." Record producer Snuff Garrett, another Arizona pal, commented to the *Tucson Citizen*, "He'll be missed. I'm sorry he's gone. Everybody should be; he was a good guy.... We always had a good time when he was around." Veteran western player Harry Carey, Jr., told Lee Server, "It's over 50 years later and I still haven't met another guy like that in my life."

Bob Fenster of *The Arizona Republic* wrote, "We'll remember him as a battler; went his own way, fought, won, never gave in. Mitchum was one of the toughest Hollywood produced, on or off the screen." Writer Boots LeBaron proclaimed Mitchum one of his favorite bad-to-the-bone characters, penning that Mitchum "wore his soul like a bulletproof vest over his barrel chest." Charles Champlin in *The Los Angeles Times* wrote, "There are undoubtedly new generations of hell-raisers coming along, but none of them is going to replace Robert Mitchum, or to create the marvelous body of work he did when he wasn't hell-raising." Dick Lochte chimed in: "Mitchum was the genuine article—the Hollywood tough guy as hard-boiled as the heroes he played.... He created a unique and extremely popular on-screen image. Somehow, he managed to be both cool and reckless, heroic and vaguely sinister, laconic to the point of inertia, yet still a man of action. And above all, he was tough. Today's movie stars don't even come close."

Fellow cowboy actor and beloved movie icon James Stewart died the day after Mitchum. These were significant deaths for the last bastions of classic-loving Hollywood to absorb. Somehow it was fitting that the always reticent Mitchum would share his final stage. *American Cowboy* wrote,

> The day before Stewart died, actor Robert Mitchum also crossed over that river. That week marked a sad and reflective occasion for many Americans, especially those who knew those two well from the performances they gave us while in the prime of their careers. They were the last of a breed, and their passing heralds the end of an era. Even if Hollywood were capable of again making movies like those, there wouldn't be men such as these to cast as characters.

Janet Maslin of *The New York Times* added, "Stewart and Mitchum spoiled their audiences with great, unmannered performances that would be virtually impossible to equal in today's filmmaking atmosphere.... Stewart and Mitchum were quintessentially American heroes who embodied a rock-solid moral code, deeply resonant ideas about good and bad. And the world that shaped and cherished that code is also gone." *San Francisco Chronicle* entertainment writer John Stanley weighed in, writing in his book *The Gang That Shot Up Hollywood*: "Two of the finest western stars of all time, dying within hours of each other. I saw this image of them riding side by side across the desert, six-shooters strapped to their waists, Winchester '73 repeating rifles slid into their scabbards. Riding out to avenge new wrongs. Heroes to the very end." Twenty years after their deaths, Gregory Monro directed a documentary about the western icons entitled *James Stewart & Robert Mitchum: The Two Faces of America* (2017). Publicity for the 52-minute film declared that the actors "incarnated the American spirit for more than half a century," and that Mitchum was "the lovable rogue everyone would like to have as a partner."

On *The Larry King Show*, Burt Reynolds discussed the respect that actors of his generation had for these two men. "They worshiped them," Reynolds said. "I spent my early years at the feet of Mitchum and Jimmy…. Worshiped them." After the passing of Mitchum and Stewart, Mitchum's son Chris shared a story among friends about the two actors meeting St. Peter over a campfire on their way to Cowboy Heaven to continue running herd with the ghost riders in the sky. He called it "Rider Coming In." Former *Sugarfoot* western TV star Will Hutchins put Chris' story in print for *Western Clippings*. "To me, Bob was more of a humorist, a philosopher with deep Irish humor, than an actor," Hutchins wrote in setting up the story. "He seemed to say in each role, 'Nothing matters all that much. And most things don't matter at all.' The consummate pro, he placed himself at the service of his co-workers and the story. He knew the picture was the star. Always has been. His style was practically invisible and practically universal…. He is one of our best actors and human beings."

Even in death, Mitchum refused to be boxed in. His ashes were scattered into the Pacific Ocean off the coast of Montecito, California. The family borrowed friend Fess Parker's schooner for the occasion. There was no memorial, no large wake. Mitchum didn't want any of that fuss. Simply get rid of him and be done with it. There was no need to sit around talking about his life. Mitchum's voice continued to be heard on television in his beef ads months after his death. He was eventually replaced by the distinctive, drawling sound of fellow western actor Sam Elliott. Mitchum's GM Motors' Montana spots were assumed by his *War and Remembrance* co-star and friend Charles Napier.

People moved or passed on. Brother John Mitchum died from cancer in 2001 at the age of 82, after releasing a book of poems entitled *An American Boy Grows Up* with heartfelt odes to cowboys, stuntmen and Ben Johnson. Sister Julie died in 2003 at 88. Mitchum's forever patient and forgiving widow Dorothy lived until 2014, dying in hospice care at the age of 94. Jim Mitchum retired to a horse ranch in Skull Valley near Prescott, Arizona. Chris Mitchum served several years on the board of the Screen Actors Guild and spent two years as the vice-president. After an unrealized attempt to produce a remake of the classic western *High Noon*, he moved into California politics as a conservative Republican. Chris was involved in many charitable causes including celebrity rodeos and the annual Hollywood Benefit Horse Show. He continued to act, portraying a lawman in his son Bentley's western short *Judgement* (2017).

Daughter Petrine wrote a book on the history of movie and television horses, *Hollywood Hoofbeats*. Regarding her father, Petrine told *Rozaneh Magazine*,

> I came to know my father better through writing this book and came to have an even greater respect for him. I also became quite angry that he wasn't still around so I could ask him about his experiences that I just sort of took for granted as a kid. But I did hear wonderful stories about him, particularly from the wranglers who worked with him because he was the kind of guy who liked to hang out with the wranglers. That was a gift when writing this book.

Interviewed by the *Knoxville News*, Jim Mitchum commented on his dad:

> I miss him more as a guy that I knew, than maybe as a father figure. He and I became very good friends. He may have had some shortcomings as a father, but he was a great guy. Very thoughtful and considerate. He did a lot of great things for people that never got publicized. He was a very charitable guy. But never wanted recognition for that. He was a very bright guy. He wasn't the kind of guy to give you fatherly advice. If he told you something, it was usually kind of obtuse and you had to figure out what he was talking about.

To biographer Mike Tomkies, Jim commented on his dad's western screen image: "The American ideal of the rugged individual which is depicted by men like John Wayne, Gary Cooper, and by my father is a very real thing. He certainly represents that." In Herb Fagen's *White Hats and Silver Spurs*, Chris Mitchum wrote:

> The people who love doing westerns, with whom I've come into contact, are good, decent people. They embody the spirit of the American cowboy. What is that spirit? It is the ability to stand up for what's right, the readiness to take personal responsibility and the holding of positive values along with a moral code. They are people who care and who treat others with respect. They are the kind of people you want your son or daughter to marry.

Chris saw those qualities in his dad, even if the elder Mitchum often sought to keep that part of his character hidden. After his father's death, Chris told *People* magazine: "He was a very thoughtful, caring, generous person…. And it was hidden behind this crusty exterior that he developed to protect himself."

John Mitchum's daughter Cindy Azbill has kept the cowboy spirit exhibited by her father and Uncle Bob alive by filming interviews for a *Them Ornery Mitchum Boys* tribute and releasing a John Mitchum *Legacy* CD at a 2016 Paramount Ranch event where a host of western figures read her dad's cowboy poetry. According to Cindy,

> Dad and Uncle Bob grew up with horses on a Delaware farm, but they didn't know how to western ride. They had no idea what a cowboy was. They learned it, though. Dad tolerated horses, but Uncle Bob really did come to love horses. He had two or three horse farms of his own. He was a fabulous rider, and so was my cousin Chris. Uncle Bob started with the Hoppys, but towards the end of his career wasn't doing any more westerns. He'd been on too many horses at that point. He'd say whenever a script came his way and it said, "a lone cowboy rides off in the sunset," he'd immediately close it.
>
> My dad and Uncle Bob were certainly friends with the stuntmen and the wranglers. They always had a group of interesting characters around them. I caught an episode of the TV western *Cimarron City* the other night. There was Myron Healey, Dan Blocker, Dad, Richard Farnsworth and Lennie Geer on the screen. The TV set literally looked like our living room when I was a kid. All those guys were there. Everyone from wranglers to John Wayne, it didn't matter. But then we lived in the Valley. Uncle Bob's house in Bel Air was different. It was a little more highbrow…. Dad and Uncle Bob had totally different personalities. Bob a bit standoffish, probably due to his fame. Dad, well, he was just the opposite. Everyone wanted be John Mitchum's friend. They were close, though, great drinking buddies…. As a character actor, Dad said he got more work without his teeth than he did with his teeth. Uncle Bob would never have taken his teeth out. They both wore dentures from the time they were in their teens. Dad and Uncle Bob were funny boys. I try to keep their memory alive.*

A decade and a half after Mitchum's death, there remains continued interest in his career as a big-screen cowboy. His films play regularly on the cable channel Encore Westerns with the occasional Six Gun Salute bunching them together into a Mitchum Marathon. In July 2011, UCLA hosted a Robert Mitchum Western Festival entitled "Tracking the Cat: Robert Mitchum in the West" at the Billy Wilder Theater in Westwood, California, that featured a dozen of his oaters. Promoting the films, UCLA's press release stated, "Mitchum's enigmatic presence, at once rugged and sensuous, was the crucial, alchemical element in a number of auteur-driven classic Westerns that redefined the genre in the postwar years." In reviewing the series of films, *The Los Angeles Times* wrote, "Looking at Mitchum through the lens of the western offers an intriguing window on his talent, on the easy naturalism of his acting style and the cool way he used those famously heavy-lidded eyes to project an intensely masculine presence."

At his Internet site *Jeff Arnold's West,* blogger Jeff Arnold wrote of Mitchum's cowboy output: "Occasionally he turned in a blisteringly good performance. He was right for the genre, being tall, rangy, craggy-faced, tough and taciturn, and he suited the part of lonesome drifters. He's one of my favorite Western actors." At the site

---

*Cindy Azbill Mitchum (phone conversation, September 2017).

Great Western Movies, fellow blogger Nicholas Chennault wrote, "Robert Mitchum could be very good in westerns, and some of his earlier work isn't seen as much as it deserves.... Even when he was a good guy, he seemed on the verge of becoming a bad guy, and that possibility added an edge to his performances." Western film blogger Colin at the site *Riding the High Country* added, "Mitchum was the kind of actor for whom the phrase 'undervalued performer' might have been specially coined.... Mitchum was often, and to an extent still is, unfairly criticized for his apparent non-acting, but he was a master of underplaying and everything is there in the eyes and the face."

In 2013, Mitchum received a posthumous Western Heritage Award from the Hall of Great Western Performers, formerly known as the Cowboy Hall of Fame. He took his rightful place alongside such giants of the western genre as John Wayne, Randolph Scott, Joel McCrea, Ben Johnson, Richard Farnsworth, Clint Eastwood and Gary Cooper, among others dating all the way back to Tom Mix and William Boyd. According to the organization's publicity, this honor is bestowed to actors "who have made significant contributions to the western film, radio or theater. Through a solid body of work in motion pictures, radio or stage, the inductee must project the traditional Western ideals of honesty, integrity and self-sufficiency."

Beginning in 2014, the Western Film Preservation Society in Raleigh, North Carolina, showed *Nevada, West of the Pecos* and *Man with the Gun* to appreciative audiences. The following year, the Pendleton Real West Festival in Oregon screened a print of *The Lusty Men.* In 2017, the Film Society of Lincoln Center held a 24-film Mitchum Centenary retrospective at the New York Film Festival with showings of the westerns *Pursued, Blood on the Moon, The Lusty Men, River of No Return, Track of the Cat, The Wonderful Country, El Dorado* and *Dead Man.* Publicity for the event trumpeted, "The magnetic figure he cut into the screen has endured as a paragon of timeless cool, and his spot on the Mount Rushmore of American actors is undeniable." The Lone Pine Film Festival held a Mitchum Centenary celebration in what would have been his 100th year, showing *Nevada* and hosting a panel with western historian Ed Hulse and William Wellman's son William, Jr. In the spring of 2018, the American Film Institute held a Robert Mitchum Retrospective, showing *Pursued, Blood on the Moon, The Lusty Men* and *The Sundowners* among its dozen titles. The Toronto International Film Festival joined in with a Mitchum retrospective featuring more than a half dozen of his oaters.

The small Arizona city of Kingman named a street after Mitchum, as it did for other cowboy heroes of the silver screen. In the same Walleck Ranch neighborhood as Robert Mitchum Drive are Gene Autry Drive, John Wayne Drive, Will Rogers Way, Roy Rogers Way, Rex Allen Drive, Alan Ladd Drive and Andy Devine Boulevard. At Gallup, New Mexico's El Rancho Hotel, where Mitchum stayed while filming *Pursued* in 1946, there's a room named after him. The Thunder Road Steakhouse in Albuquerque, New Mexico, has walls adorned with Mitchum memorabilia from his cult film. In the small town of Trappe, Maryland, Mitchum's Steakhouse celebrated the life of the state's former resident and was named "Favorite New Steakhouse" in 2011. The restaurant ultimately closed but reopened in 2018 as the similarly themed Mitchum's Tavern.

Mitchum's popularity wasn't limited to the U.S. In Nikko, Japan, the theme park Western Village featured a robotic Robert Mitchum alongside life-size animatronic cowboy figures of John Wayne, Clint Eastwood and Charles Bronson throughout the 1990s and into the early 21st century. The Milltown House in Dingle, Ireland, boasts the Robert Mitchum Bar, while the menu of the legendary pub Stagger Lee in Berlin, Germany, offers a drink called the Robert Mitchum. The order consists of a full tumbler of tequila, a Lucky Strike cigarette and a match. Musician Julian Cope performs the song "Robert Mitchum," its lyrics exclaiming, "You're such a dude; you're such a guy." The alternative Belfast music band the Sons of Robert Mitchum tours Europe to wide acclaim playing songs like "Build My Gallows High." Country musician–actor Mark Collie modeled himself after Mitchum and Johnny Cash, even recording Mitchum's "Ballad of Thunder Road" on his CD *Born and Raised in Black and White.*

Mitchum's own singing voice appeared alongside that of Marty Robbins and Frankie Laine in the CD compilation *Riders in the Sky: Scenes from the American West,* an El Records homage to the music of cowboy cinema. Mitchum croons "Danny Boy" from *Pursued.* A music video fashioned from Mitchum clips in *The Lusty Men* made its way around the Internet to the accompaniment of the Johnny Cash rodeo song "Bull Rider." The Mitchum image and Cash vocals perfectly complement one another.

In 2017, Burt Reynolds starred in *The Last Movie Star* as Vic Edwards, an actor in his twilight years appearing at a low-rent film festival in his honor in Nashville. One of the films in which Vic starred is *Siege at the Alamo* with Robert Mitchum's Davy Crockett dying in his arms on screen. That same year, Sam Elliott starred in writer-director Brett Haley's *The Hero,* about a faded cowboy actor with a terminal cancer diagnosis attempting to land one last film of significance. Clouding his path are his own history of aberrant behavior and misdeeds, including serial womanizing and a daily regimen of drinking and doping. Press materials state the Elliott character Lee Hayden was written specifically for the actor and was based on hard-living screen cowboys who came before him including Robert Mitchum, Lee Marvin, Sterling Hayden and James Coburn.

In an interview with *The Guardian,* Elliott declares himself a fan of the western classics *Red River* (1948), *Shane* (1953) and *The Searchers* (1956). Elliott said,

> There was a particular time in Hollywood where the western was the bread and butter for everybody in town. In the early days, there was a bunch of really good western actors that were all you needed to make a good western. There were horses all around town. And wagons. And now all that stuff has moved on…. It's just a whole industry that has disappeared. There's a simplicity to that form that has always spoken to me. There's a pretty well-defined morality to the characters; the good, the bad…. Not a lot of gray area.

Author James Scott Bell wrote an entire book extolling the manly virtues of Robert Mitchum,

As the eternal drifter at Sedona's Red Rock Crossing in *Blood on the Moon* (1948).

and contending that the cowboy star's sense of adventure, demonstrations of bravery and do-right heroism are now missing in society. Lee Server's 2001 Mitchum book rates as one of the most popular celebrity bios, and John Mitchum's *Them Ornery Mitchum Boys* is a collector's item. "Both books read like wild fiction," notes *Sight and Sound*. "But just possibly, it's all true." Over a period of several years, documentary filmmaker Bruce Weber revealed snippets of a highly anticipated, three-decades-in-the-making film on Mitchum entitled *Nice Girls Don't Stay for Breakfast* (the title derived from a Julie London song). "I met Bob almost 25 years ago," Weber told *The Hollywood Reporter* in 2013. "It took a little bit of time to get him to do it, but once he said yes, he was a man of his word. He was a real gentleman like that." The film was finally finished in 2018, and *The Hollywood Reporter* called it "[a] cinematic valentine to one of the on-screen greats. This is a warm, jazzy homage to a much-celebrated but also very complicated man whose complexity nonetheless remains forever just out of reach." So there remains a sustained interest in Mitchum's career as a cool cultural icon, as well as a man associated with westerns and the cowboy lifestyle.

Mitchum was a maverick, a man's man who lived life on his own terms but respected the Cowboy Code. A rawhide-tough loner and drifter who radiated quiet machismo. His best screen roles reflect facets of the man himself. He became a fine horseman and a top enactor of celluloid saloon brawls. He performed nearly all his own stunts in *Blood on the Moon*, which features a fight widely regarded as one of the best in a western. He hardened the cowboy myth. As a professional, he always strove to be real. Nobody would ever catch him acting. He did the back-breaking work and his actions as a big-screen cowboy were honest. In many ways, he represents the manly ideal: broad-shouldered, deep-voiced, self-confident, with appeal to men and women alike. Mitchum portrayed independent men with a backbone who rose to the occasion. In Bruce Weber's documentary, Clint Eastwood said that Mitchum "was not afraid of any type of failure."

Mercurial and unpredictable, Mitchum was the black hat and he was the white hat. Good guy. Bad guy. He believably conveyed both sides of the proverbial coin. "The concept of the noir western is almost unthinkable without Robert Mitchum," writes Imogen Sara Smith in *Bright Lights Film Journal*. Through viewing Mitchum's canon of films, specifically his westerns, one can come closest to getting an overall picture of what and who he was. Mitchum's Zen is the eternal lone wolf who must keep moving; forever drifting with the wayward wind. Home is wherever he hangs his hat, and many nights it's sleeping under the stars. He was named as one of the Greatest Western Actors by *American Cowboy* magazine and ranked in the top ten western icons in a 2017 History Channel poll. Viewing a handful of his best films will show this to be true. He stood tall and never backed down. He is the western screen's ultimate highwayman and defiant non-conformist who lived on the edge and beyond. A legend of the screen, "Hollywood's Cowboy Rebel" Robert Mitchum gave life one hell of an interesting ride.

Bibliography

Books and Articles

Aaker, Lee. *Television Western Players, 1960–1975*. Jefferson, NC: McFarland, 2017.

Abbott, E.C., and Helena Huntington Smith. *We Pointed Them North: Recollections of a Cowpuncher*. Norman: University of Oklahoma, 1955.

Abrams, Simon. "Sam Elliott: My Security Comes from the Fact I've Never Done a Job for Money." *The Guardian*, June 7, 2017.

"Acting is Great… It Sure Beats Working." *National Enquirer*, March 1, 1983.

"Actor Mitchum Reflects on His Movie Adventures." *Evansville Courier and Press*, February 16, 1986.

"Actor Robert Mitchum Dies at 79." *Houston Chronicle*, July 2, 1979.

Adams, Andy. *The Log of a Cowboy*. New York: Grossett & Dunlap, 1903.

Albert, Dora. "Dual Personality." *Screenland*, May 1946.

Allen, Michael. *Rodeo Cowboys in the North American Imagination*. Reno: University of Nevada Press, 1998.

Alpert, Don. "Mitchum's Bad, Bad, Bad World." *The Los Angeles Times*, December 19, 1965.

Anderson, Bob. "Hal Baylor: The Winner and Still the Champ." *Trail Dust*, Spring 1996.

Anderson, George. "*Blazing Saddles* Writer Shoots Down Criticism." *Pittsburgh Post-Gazette*, March 11, 1974.

Anderson, Janette Hyam. "I'll Go Anywhere for a Free Lunch." *Trail Dust*, Summer/Fall 1994.

Anderson, Janette Hyam. "Lucky Me." *Trail Dust*, Summer/Fall 1996.

Andrews, Geoff. "I Have Two Acting Styles: With or Without a Horse." *Time Out*, June 29–July 6, 2005.

"Angie Lays Down the Law." *Variety*, August 21, 2008.

Archerd, Armand. "Typecasting—Mitchum for Mitchum." *Medina County Gazette*, February 7, 1966.

Arkatov, Jackie. "Ryan a Heavy Again." *The Los Angeles Times*, December 25, 1989.

Armour, Philip. *The 100 Greatest Western Movies of All-Time*. Guilford, CT: Two Dot, 2011.

Armstrong, Stephen B. *Andrew V. McLaglen: The Life and Hollywood Career*. Jefferson, NC: McFarland, 2011.

Arnold, Darrell. "Ben Johnson." *Western Horseman*, August 1989.

Arnold, Darrell. *The Cowboy Kind*. Missoula, MT: Mountain Press, 2001.

Bacon, James. "After 27 Movie Years Producer Has First Ulcer." *Victoria Advocate*, October 8, 1960.

Bacon, James. *Made in Hollywood*. Chicago: Contemporary, 1977.

Badham, John, and Craig Modderno. *I'll Be in My Trailer*. Studio City, CA: Michael Weisse, 2006.

"*Bandido* Bob." *Silver Screen*, August 1956.

Baskette, Kirtley. "Lucky Bum." *Modern Screen*, October 1945.

Bawden, James, and Ron Miller. *Conversations with Classic Film Stars: Interviews with Hollywood's Golden Era*. Lexington: University of Kentucky Press, 2016.

Beck, Henry Cabot. "The Western *Godfather*." *True West*, October 2006.

Beck, Marilyn. "TV Closeup." *Daily Reporter*, August 28, 1968.

Bell, James Scott. *Manliness the Robert Mitchum Way*. Woodland Hills, CA: Compendium, 2016.

Belton, John. *Robert Mitchum*. New York: Pyramid, 1976.

Bennetts, Leslie. "3 Mitchums Starring in a New CBS Movie." *The New York Times*, October 14, 1985.

Berg, Lucas. "Unruly and Unabashed." *The Los Angeles Times*, August 17, 1947.

Bishoff, Don. "Robert Mitchum—Man of Many Faces." *Eugene Register Guard*, June 10, 1966.

Blake, Michael F. *Hollywood and the OK Corral: Portrayals of the Gunfight and Wyatt Earp*. Jefferson, NC: McFarland, 2006.

"Bob Mitchum Prides Himself on Being Different." *Australian Women's Weekly*, May 10, 1947.

"Bob Mitchum Tries Living as a Hermit." *Arkansas Gazette*, January 26, 1969.

Boetticher, Budd. *When in Disgrace*. Santa Barbara, CA: Neville, 1989.

Bogdanovich, Peter. *Who the Devil Made It?* New York: Ballantine, 1997.

Borgnine, Ernest. *Ernie: The Autobiography*. New York: Citadel, 2008.

Bowers, Larry. "Deciphering Fact from Fiction of *Thunder Road*." *Cleveland Daily Banner*, January 2, 2016.

Boyle, Hal. "Design for Loafing." *Repository*, March 15, 1957.

Boyle, Hal. "Mitchum Outlives His Past." *Lawrence Journal-World*, August 23, 1972.

Breck, Peter. "Cut 'Em Off at the Pass!" *Wildest Westerns* #4, 2002.

Breck, Peter. "Westerns, Learn to Like 'Em or Else!" *Wildest Westerns* #3, 2001.
Brooks, Jane. "Robert Mitchum: The Bad Boy from Felton." *The Morning News*, March 3, 1983.
Brown, David G. "Golden Boot Awards Honor the Stars of Hollywood Westerners." *American Cowboy*, Nov/Dec. 1994.
Brown, David G. "Last of a Breed." *American Cowboy*, October 1995.
Brown, Geoff. "Powerful Presence Gives the Lie to a Myth." *The Times of London*, May 26, 1984.
Brown, J.P.S. *The Outfit: A Cowboy's Primer*. Lincoln, NE: IUniverse, 2008.
Browning, Norma Lee. "First Role in a John Wayne Film Makes Name for Chris." *The Chicago Tribune*, June 16, 1968.
Buck, Jerry. "Slim Pickens: Still Enjoying a Fat Career." *Times-Picayune*, October 15, 1981.
Buscombe, Edward. *The BFI Companion to the Western*. London: Atheneum, 1988.
Buscombe, Edward. *100 Westerns*. London: BFI Screen Guides, 2006.
Calder, Jenni. *There Must Be a Lone Ranger*. London: Hamilton, 1974.
Callan, Michael Feeney. *Richard Harris: Sex, Death & the Movies: An Intimate Biography*. London: Robson, 2003.
Canford, Tom. *Baker's Daughter, Miller's Son*. Hollow Square Press, 2015.
Canutt, Yakima, and John Crawford. *My Rodeo Years: Memoir of a Bronc Rider's Path to Hollywood Fame*. Jefferson, NC: McFarland, 2009.
"Captain of *G.I. Joe*: Unknown Horse Opera Specialist Mitchum Gets Break in Pyle Film." *San Francisco Chronicle*, August 18, 1945.
Capua, Michelangelo. *Deborah Kerr: A Biography*. Jefferson, NC: McFarland, 2010.
Capua, Michelangelo. *Jean Negulesco: The Life and Films*. Jefferson, NC: McFarland, 2017.
Capua, Michelangelo. *William Holden: A Biography*. Jefferson, NC: McFarland, 2010.
Carducci, Joe. *Stone Male: Requiem for the Living Picture*. Centennial, WY: Redoubt, 2016.
Carey, Harry, Jr. *Company of Heroes: My Life as an Actor in the John Ford Stock Company*. Metuchen, NJ: Scarecrow, 1994.
Carr, Howie. *Hitman—The Untold Story of Johnny Martorano*. New York: St. Martin's, 2013.
Champlin, Charles. "Mitchum: Hollywood's Enduring Bad Boy." *Los Angeles Times*, July 2, 1997.
Champlin, Charles. "Robert Mitchum: Interview." *Los Angeles Times*, October 2, 1994.
Chapman, Art. "Movies Desert Wranglers." *Indianapolis Star*, December 14, 1989.
Chappell, Helen. "Robert Mitchum Slept Here." *Tidewater Times*, January 2013.
Charles, Arthur L. "Trouble Ahead for Mitchum." *Modern Screen*, December 1949.
Cobb, Chris. "*Agency*: The $5 Million Movie." *Ottawa Journal*, July 19, 1979.
Collins, Steve. "A Hunter Pilot's Story: Robert Mitchum Movie Star." *Rod & Rifle*, November/December 2016.
Combs, Richard. *Robert Aldrich*. London: BFI, 1978.
Connolly, Mike. "Barry Nelson Plays Role of Angel in New TV Series." *Marietta Daily Journal*, December 13, 1964.
Conrad, Barnaby. *Name Dropping: Tales from My Barbary Coast Saloon*. Sanger, CA: Write Thought, 1997.
Copeland, Bobby J. *Roy Barcroft: King of the Badmen*. Madison, NC: Empire, 2000.
Copeland, Bobby J. *Trail Talk*. Madison, NC: Empire, 1996.
Crowther, Bruce. *Mitchum: The Film Career of Robert Mitchum*. London: Robert Hale, 1991.
Cuthbert, David. "Jim Davis Wonders, 'What Happened to the Western Renaissance?'" *Times-Picayune*, April 25, 1976.
Darrach, Brad. "The Last of the Iron-Assed Loners." *Penthouse*, September 1972.
Davidson, Bill. "The Many Moods of Robert Mitchum." *Saturday Evening Post*, August 25/September 1, 1962.
Davis, Ivor. "The Fellow Who Took the Sweat Out of Acting." *San Francisco Chronicle*, April 20, 1986.
Dimona, Joseph. "Last of the Tough Guys." *The Town Talk*, August 25, 1985.
"Director Boss with Mitchum." *Trenton Evening Times*, November 14, 1954.
Downing, David. *Robert Mitchum*. London: W.H. Allen, 1985.
Dunne, Mike. "Battle of the Chili Champs." *Sacramento Bee*, October 28, 1980.
Dyke, Scott. "Meandering the Mesquite: Hobos in Hollywood—Remembering the Mitchum Brothers." *Green Valley News*, August 27, 2014.
Earle, Anitra. "Mitchum: Once the Cameras Start Rolling, There's No Way Out." *San Francisco Chronicle*, July 9, 1972.
Ebert, Roger. "How Mitchum's Garden Vegetates." *Chicago Sun Times*, October 12, 1969.
Ebert, Roger. "Passions Run Deep for James Caan." *Chicago Sun Times*, October 2, 1988.
Ebert, Roger. "Robert Mitchum: How High Are We?" *Chicago Sun Times*, July 1, 1973.
Ebert, Roger. "Robert Mitchum: One of the Greatest Movie Stars was Rin Tin Tin." *Chicago Sun Times*, October 2, 1993.
Eells, George. *Robert Mitchum: A Biography*. New York: F. Watts, 1984.
Errico, Marcus. "Two Mitchum Films Still to Come." *E-Online*, July 2, 1997.
Evans, Max. *Now and Forever: A Novel of Love and Betrayal Reincarnate*. Albuquerque: University of New Mexico Press, 2003.
Eyles, Alan. *The Western: An Illustrated Guide*. London: Zwemmer, 1967.
Eyman, Scott. *John Wayne: The Life and Legend*. New York: Simon & Schuster, 2014.
"The Face on the Cutting Room Floor." *Milwaukee Journal*, November 21, 1959.
Fagen, Herb. *Encyclopedia of Westerns*. New York: Checkmark, 2003.
Fagen, Herb. *White Hats and Silver Spurs: Interviews with 24 Stars of Film and Television Westerns of the Thirties Through the Sixties*. Jefferson, NC: McFarland, 1996.
Farkis, John. *The Making of Tombstone: Behind the Scenes of the Classic Modern Western*. Jefferson, NC: McFarland, 2018.
Farkis, John. *Not Thinkin' … Just Remembering … The*

Making of John Wayne's The Alamo. Albany, GA: BearManor, 2015.

Fenady, Andrew J. "Robert Mitchum—The Ice Man." *Trail Dust,* Winter/Spring 1997.

Fenster, Bob. "Mitchum Always Went His Own Way." *The Arizona Republic,* July 6, 1997.

Ferguson, Ken. "Heaven Knows, Mr. Mitchum, and So Does Deborah Kerr." *Photoplay,* February 1985.

Ferretti, Fred. "Ensemble Acting Buoys *That Championship Season.*" *The New York Times,* December 19, 1982.

Ferrier, Dave. "Top Ten Villains of the West." *Wildest Westerns #3,* 2001.

Field, Sally. *In Pieces.* New York: Grand Central, 2018.

Fields, Sidney. "The Mitchum Manner." *New York Daily News,* June 20, 1972.

Fitzerald, Michael, and Steve Kiefer. "Gary Gray: Child Star/Western Star." *Wildest Westerns.* #7, 2005.

"5 Card Stud ... Cold Time in Hot Mexico." *The Evening Capital,* August 24, 1968.

Flick, A.J. "Obituary." *Tucson Citizen,* July 2, 1997.

Frank, Jeff. "Taylor No Stranger to North County." *San Diego Union-Tribune,* March 26, 2011.

Freeman, Alex. "TV Closeup." *Daily Reporter,* January 12, 1967.

Freeman, Don. "Point of View." *San Diego Union,* January 25, 1983.

Frizzell, Helen. "Mr. Mitchum Full of Surprises." *Australian Women's Weekly,* October 14, 1959.

Fury, David. "Last of the Tough Guys." *Movie Collectors World,* August 8, 1997.

Gagliasso, Dan. "Liberal Blacklist Couldn't Stop Chris Mitchum." *Breitbart News,* March 31, 2012.

Gardner, Hy, and Marilyn Gardner. "Glad You Asked That." *Springfield Union,* June 14, 1981.

Gardner, Ralph D. *Writers Talk to Ralph D. Gardner.* Metuchen, NJ: Scarecrow Press, 1989.

Garmon, Ron. "Michael Parks." *Worldly Remains* #1, 2000.

Garnier, Philippe. "Border Crossing." *Film Comment,* November/December 2014.

Gazdik, Tanya. "GM Goes to Montana." *Ad Week,* October 19, 1998.

Gehman, Richard. "Robert Mitchum: Star Who Hates Hollywood." *True Magazine,* October 1962.

Gentry, Charles. "Robert Mitchum Real G.I. Joe." *Detroit Times,* August 3, 1945.

Gentry, Kenneth B. *Pioneertown, USA.* CreateSpace, 2018.

Gidlund, Carl. "Cowboy Classic." *Spokesman Review,* July 28, 2007.

Gilchrist, Roderick. "The Gypsy in Robert Mitchum's Soul." *Daily Mail,* June 17, 1974.

Goldrup, Tom, and Jim Goldrup. *Feature Players: The Stories Behind the Faces.* Ben Lomond, CA: Self, 1992.

Goldrup, Tom, and Jim Goldrup. *Growing Up on the Set: Interviews with 39 Former Child Actors of Classic Film and Television.* Jefferson, NC: McFarland, 2002.

Gorman, Earl J. *Fire Mission: The World of Nam, A Marine's Story.* Clarendon Hills, IL: Red Devil Press, 2008.

Graham, Harry L. "Stuntman Recalls Friend Up for an Academy Award." *Orange County Register,* March 25, 1979.

Grant, Kevin, and Clark Hodgkiss. *Renegade Westerns: Movies That Shot Down Frontier Myths.* Surrey, England: FAB Press, 2018.

Gray, Ellen. "Mitchum Discusses (Sort of) Role in *The Marshal.*" *Spokesman Review,* September 25, 1995.

Greenberg, Abe. "Voice of Hollywood: Of Howard Hawks' Heroes." *Hollywood Citizen-News,* June 30, 1967.

Griffin, Mark. *A Hundred or More Little Things: The Life and Films of Vincente Minnelli.* Cambridge: De Capo, 2010.

Grobel, Lawrence. *The Hustons: The Life and Times of a Hollywood Dynasty.* New York: Skyhorse, 2014.

Haber, Joyce. "70 Films a Lot of Work for One Lazy Cowpoke." *Los Angeles Times,* March 23, 1969.

Hamilton, Judy. "Being a Heavy Can Be Easier." *Augusta Chronicle,* September 13, 1974.

Hanfling, Barrie. *Westerns and the Trail of Tradition: A Year-by-Year History, 1929–1962.* Jefferson, NC: McFarland, 2010.

Harbinson, W.A. *Bronson!* London: Pinnacle, 1975.

Harrington, Cliff. "My Tokyo Interviews." *Forty Stories of Japan.* Fine Line Press, 2015.

Harrison, Fletcher. "Remembering Those N.M. Days with Robert Mitchum and Stewart." *Albuquerque Tribune,* July 10, 1997.

Hayes, Steve. *Googies: Coffee Shop to the Stars.* Albany, GA: BearManor, 2008.

Heffernan, Harold. "Bob Mitchum Got Start in Commercial Short." *Repository,* November 18, 1946.

Heffernan, Harold. "Bob Mitchum Shuns Work and Worry." *Toledo Blade,* November 29, 1965.

Helfer, Ralph. *The Beauty of the Beasts: Tales of Hollywood's Wild Animal Stars.* New York: Harper, 1990.

Helmick, Paul A. *Cut, Print, and That's a Wrap: A Hollywood Memoir.* Jefferson, NC: McFarland, 2001.

Hendrickson, Paul. "Robert Mitchum." *The Washington Post,* January 3, 1983.

Herdy, Amy. "*Tombstone* Rides On." *American Cowboy,* January 2015.

"Here's the True Face of Robert Mitchum." *The Detroit Times,* September 23, 1959.

Herzog, Buck. "On Amusement: Robert Mitchum." *Milwaukee Sentinel,* May 1, 1949.

Hewitt, Bill. "Robert Mitchum: Classic Cool." *People,* July 14, 1997.

Hickerson, Charles. "The Rhinestones Show, I Took the Blows, and Did It My Way: Manuel Cuevas on a Lifetime of Design." *Native,* November 2014.

Hickey, William. "Robert Mitchum: They Broke the Mold." *Plain Dealer,* January 20, 1983.

Hinterberger, John. "Mitchum: The Actor and His Reputation." *Seattle Daily Times,* June 28, 1966.

Hirschberg, Lynn. "The Last of the Indies." *The New York Times,* July 31, 2005.

Hitt, Jim. *The American West from Fiction (1823–1976) Into Film (1909–1986).* Jefferson, NC: McFarland, 1990.

Hofstede, David. "100 Best Westerns Ever Made." *Cowboys & Indians,* January 2002.

Holland, Dave. *On Location in Lone Pine.* Granada Hills, CA: Holland House, 2014.

Holmes, Sue Major. "Old West's Stars Live Again at New Mexico Watering Hole." *Los Angeles Times,* May 28, 1989.

Honeycutt, Kirk. "Robert Mitchum Rolls Merrily Along

Despite the Vehicles." *The New York Times*, April 9, 1978.
Hopper, Hedda. "Bob Mitchum: Cooling It at Malibu." *Chicago Tribune*, July 25, 1965.
Hopper, Hedda. "Bob Mitchum: Horse Opera Past, Fillies in the Future." *Los Angeles Times*, November 24, 1965.
Hopper, Hedda. "Looking at Hollywood." *Springfield Union*, January 16, 1955.
Hopper, Hedda. "Mitch Stars in Three Films." *News and Courier*, March 26, 1961.
Hopper, Hedda. "Mitchum Clowns at Interview." *Los Angeles Times*, March 23, 1947.
Hughes, Mike. "Robert Mitchum: This Is One Roustabout Who Likes Privacy." *Bellingham Herald*, February 6, 1983.
Hulse, Ed. *Filming the West of Zane Grey*. Burbank: Riverwood Press, 2016.
Humbird, Alma Massey. *The Humbird's Reel Stories*. Portland, OR: Richard Mort, 1998.
Hunt, James. "Why Can't Mitchum Behave?" *Photoplay*, March 1954.
Hunter, Stephen. "Icon, Iconoclast Robert Mitchum Dies. Imperturbable Star Was 79." *The Washington Post*, July 2, 1997.
Hunter, Thomas O'D. *Memoirs of a Spaghetti Cowboy*. Self, 2015.
Huston, John. *An Open Book*. London: Macmillan, 1981.
James, Clive. *North Face of Soho: Unreliable Memoirs*. London: Picador, 2009.
James, Nick. "The Big Stealer." *Sight and Sound*, August 2005.
Jensen, Richard D. *The Nicest Fella: The Life of Ben Johnson*. New York: IUniverse, 2010.
"Jim Jarmusch *Guardian* Interview at the BFI." *The Guardian*, November 15, 1999.
"Jim Mitchum Tired of Hearing About His Dad." *Danville Bee*, October 22, 1962.
"Johnny Be Bad." *YM Magazine*, May 1990.
Johnson, Erskine. "For Bob Mitchum, A Serious Role." *Park City Daily News*, July 22, 1963.
Johnson, Erskine. "In Hollywood." *Daily Sun*, April 19, 1955.
Johnson, Erskine. "Looking at Hollywood." *Lima News*, May 1, 1946.
Johnson, Erskine. "No Rocking Chair for William Powell." *Tacoma Daily Ledger*, December 5, 1954.
Johnson, Erskine. "Robert Mitchum Satisfied to Follow Bogart, Tracy." *San Bernardino County Sun*, December 16, 1954.
Jones, Kent. "Hidden Star: Richard Widmark." *Film Comment*, May/June 2001.
Jones, Malcolm. "Being Robert Mitchum." *Newsweek*, March 21, 2001.
Jones, Preston Neal. *Heaven and Hell to Play With: The Making of 'Night of the Hunter.'* New York: Limelight, 2002.
Joyner, C. Courtney. *The Westerners: Interviews with Actors, Directors, Writers & Producers*. Jefferson, NC: McFarland, 2009.
Kass. Carole. "Mitchum Is Extended Belated Recognition." *Richmond Times Dispatch*, October 26, 1980.
Kennedy, Harlan. "Robert Mitchum: An Interview." *Film Comment*, July/August 1992.

Kilday, Gregg. "Bruce Weber Returns for 25th Anniversary of His Chet Baker Doc." *The Hollywood Reporter*, September 2, 2013.
Kilgallen, Dorothy. "20th Century Picks Mitchum for *The Day Custer Fell*." *Arkansas Gazette*, October 16, 1964.
King, Larry. "People." *USA Today*, March 25, 1991.
King, Susan. "On the Sunny Side." *Los Angeles Times*, October 18, 2008.
Kitses, Jim, and Greg Rickman. *The Western Reader*. New York: Limelight, 2004.
Kleiner, Dick. "Bob Mitchum Has Wild, Wooly Night." *Delaware County Daily Times*, August 27, 1966.
Kleiner, Dick. "Mitchum Makes a Masterpiece in *Eddie Coyle*." *Indiana Gazette*, July 14, 1973.
Kleiner, Dick. "Westerns Always Good, Popular." *Childress Index*, June 20, 1970.
Klemesrud, Judy. "Another Mitchum, Another Wayne." *New York Times*, June 20, 1971.
LaFaille, David. *Edge of Reason*. Xlibris, 2013.
Lammers, Tim. "Film Legend's Daughter Rides High with *Hollywood Hoofbeats*." *Rozaneh Magazine*, Sept/Oct. 2006.
Langella, Frank. *Dropped Names: Famous Men and Women as I Knew Them*. New York: HarperCollins, 2012.
LaSalle, Mick. "Mitchum Was One Tough Act: A Working-Class Hero of the Silver Screen." *San Francisco Chronicle*, July 2, 1997.
Lawrence, Tom. "Just a Fella: Wilford Brimley Reflects on Long Career." *Powell Tribune*, March 20, 2014.
Lawrenson, Helen. "The Man Who Never Got to Speak for National Youth Day." *Esquire*, May 1964.
Lea, Tom. *Tom Lea: An Oral History*. El Paso: Texas Western Press, 1995.
LeBaron, Boots. *The Human Race*. CreateSpace, 2013.
Leeds, Lila, and Lyle Leeds. *Bad Girl of Hollywood: The Lila Leeds Story*. Self, 2017.
Leider, Emily. *Myrna Loy—The Only Good Girl in Hollywood*. Berkeley: University of California, 2011.
Levy, Emanuel. *Vincente Minnelli: Hollywood's Dark Dreamer*. New York: St. Martin's, 2013.
Lewis, Dan. "Mitchum Just Doesn't Want Work." *Morning Star*, August 23, 1972.
Lewis, Grover. "Robert Mitchum: The Last Celluloid Desperado." *Rolling Stone*, March 15, 1973.
Lilley, Tim. *Campfire Conversations*. Akron, OH: Big Trail, 2007.
Lilley, Tim. *Campfire Conversations Complete*. Akron, OH: Big Trail, 2010.
Lochte, Dick. "Hell, I Look Like I've Changed Five Million Tires." *Los Angeles Free Press*, July 6, 1973.
Lochte, Dick. "Just One More Hangover." *Los Angeles Free Press*, June 29, 1973.
Lochte, Dick. "Just One More Hangover." *Salon Magazine*, July 11, 1997.
Lodge, Stephen. *And… Action!* Rancho Mirage, CA: Mirage, 2008.
Lousararian, Ed, and Joe Wallison. "Ridin' the Range with Frank Stallone." *Wildest Westerns*. #6, 2003.
Love, Damien. *Robert Mitchum: Solid, Dad, Crazy*. London: B.T. Batsford, 2002.
Lyden, Pierce, and Mario DeMarco. *Camera! Roll 'Em! Action!* Self, 1986.

Lyden, Pierce, and Mario DeMarco. *Pierce Lyden: The Movie Badmen I Rode With*. Self, 1988.
Lyden, Pierce, and Mario DeMarco. *Those Saturday Serials*. Self, 1989.
MacAdams, Lewis. "Robert Mitchum: Lemme Tell You How Films Are Made." *L.A. Weekly*, April 16–22, 1982.
Maddrey, Joseph. *The Quick, the Dead, and the Revived: The Many Lives of the Western Film*. Jefferson, NC: McFarland, 2016.
Magers, Boyd. "The A-Westerns of Robert Mitchum." *Western Clippings* #135, Jan/Feb 2017.
Magers, Boyd. "Cowboy Quotes." *Western Clippings* #146, Nov/Dec 2018.
Magers, Boyd, and Michael G. Fitzgerald. *Ladies of the Western: Interviews with 50 Leading Ladies of Movie and Television Westerns from the 1930s to the 1960s*. Jefferson, NC: McFarland, 2006.
Mann, Roderick. "Mitchum Out of Step with Style and Aplomb." *Los Angeles Times*, October 8, 1978.
Mann, Roderick. "Robert Mitchum Feels Thrills of Fear." *Boston Herald*, June 12, 1973.
Manners, Dorothy. "At Last He Is a Hero." *Los Angeles Herald Examiner*, January 12, 1964.
Manners, Dorothy. "Mitchum Doing Well, Unconsciously." *Los Angeles Herald Examiner*, October 13, 1968.
Marrill, Alvin H. *Robert Mitchum on the Screen*. New York: A.S. Barnes, 1978.
Martin, Deana, and Wendy Holden. *Memories Are Made of This: Dean Martin Through His Daughter's Eyes*. New York: Three Rivers, 2004.
Martin, Mick. "Jim Mitchum Another John Wayne, Clint Eastwood?" *The Express*, April 22, 1976.
Masley, Ed. "Swing Along with Mitchum." *Pittsburgh Post-Gazette*, May 15, 1996.
Maslin, Janet. "Stewart, Mitchum and a Nation's Character." *The New York Times*, July 13, 1997.
Maynard, John. "All the Wrong Answers." *Motion Picture*, February 1949.
McCormick, Brett. "Christopher Mitchum." *Psychotronic Video* #22, 1996.
McCoy, Brian. "Robert Mitchum's Brother in Lode Recalls Bond." *Stockton Record Net*, July 3, 1997.
McDowall, Roddy. *Double Exposure, Take Two*. New York: Morrow, 1989.
McPherson, Virginia. "Bob Needs a Place to Change His Pants." *Newark Star Ledger*, December 21, 1946.
McQueen, Max. "Mitchum Remembered for More Than Movies." *Mesa Tribune*, July 3, 1997.
"Medicine Man Just a Quack." *Detroit News*, December 29, 1946.
Meuel, David. *The Noir Western—Darkness on the Range, 1943–1962*. Jefferson, NC: McFarland, 2015.
Meyerson, Ed. "The Richest Bum in Town." *Photoplay*, December 1956.
Miller, Ben. *Mescal*. Writer's Cramp, 2013.
Miller, Ron. "Horseman Parlays Stunt Work into Successful Acting Career." *Ocala Star-Banner*, September 15, 1989.
Millner, Cork. *Portraits*. Santa Barbara, CA: Fithian, 1994.
Mills, Bart. "Hulking, Grunting, Engaging Mitchum." *Chicago Tribune*, June 24, 1973.
Minnelli, Vincente, and Hector Arce. *Vincente Minnelli's I Remember It Well*. New York: Berkley, 1975.
Mitchum, Chris. "Act and Act Fast." *Fighting Stars*, June/August 1975.
Mitchum, Dorothy. "My Bob." *Photoplay*, July 1954.
Mitchum, John. *Them Ornery Mitchum Boys*. Pacifica, CA: Creatures at Large, 1989.
Mitchum, Julie. "My Brother Is a Fake!" *Modern Screen*, July 1948.
Mitchum, Petrine Day, and Audrey Pavia. *Hollywood Hoofbeats: The Fascinating Story of Horses in Movies and Television*. New York: 15, 2014.
"Mitchum Pictured with Nude Causes Row with Spouse." *Durham Morning Herald*, April 5, 1954.
Mitchum, Robert. "Do It Again? Sure, Admits Bob Mitchum." *Desert Sun*, July 3, 1961.
Mitchum, Robert. "Globe-trotting Robert Mitchum Is Ready to Stop Dreaming." *Bristol Daily Courier*, September 10, 1959.
Mitchum, Robert. "Mitchum Is Willing to Swap Places with Movie Horses." *Columbus Daily Enquirer*, September 22, 1952.
Mitchum Robert. "Not So Tough Guy." *Memories*, Fall 1988.
Mitchum, Robert. "Now I'll Talk." *Modern Screen*, July 1949.
"Mitchum's Son Much Like Father." *The Spokesman Review*, November 24, 1962.
Monahan, Ione. "Lunch with Mitchum Like a Dream." *The Montreal Gazette*, December 15, 1978.
Moritz, Charles. *Current Biography Yearbook*. New York: H.W. Wilson, 1971.
Morse, Barry, Anthony Wynn and Robert E. Wood. *Remember with Advantages: Chasing 'The Fugitive' and Other Stories from an Actor's Life*. Jefferson, NC: McFarland, 2007.
Mosby, Aline. "Grocery Store Cowboys Run Business for Ill Proprietor." *Richmond Times Dispatch*, December 2, 1947.
Mosby, Aline. "Robert Mitchum Pictured as Big Cut-Up on Film Set." *Spokane Daily Chronicle*, February 6, 1952.
Muir, Florabel. "What Now for Mitchum?" *Photoplay*, April 1949.
Munn, Michael. *John Wayne: The Man Behind the Myth*. New York: New American, 2003.
Murray, Jim. "Mitchum on the Run with Quarter Horses." *The Arizona Republic*, July 14, 1973.
Nevins, Francis M. *The Films of Hopalong Cassidy*. Waynesville, NC: World of Yesterday, 1988.
Nevins, Francis M. *Hopalong Cassidy: On the Page, On the Screen*. Lone Pine, CA: Riverwood Press, Museum of Lone Pine Film History, 2008.
"New Image for Hal Baylor: He Gets the Girl." *Daily Herald*, October 27, 1969.
Nogueira, Rui. "Robert Wise at RKO." *Focus on Film*, Winter 1972.
O'Halleran, Bill. "He's the Only Gary Cooper Still Alive." *TV Guide*, January 29, 1983.
Oppenheimer, Peer J. "The Mellowing of a Hollywood Roughneck." *Family Weekly*, January 2, 1966.
O'Rourke, Pierre. "Robert Mitchum Rides into the Sunset." *The Arizonan*. Vol. 1, #6, July 6, 1997.
O'Sullivan, Majella. "I Was So Innocent in the 60s, but Robert Mitchum Corrupted Me." *The Independent*, March 19, 2016.
Otterburn-Hall, William. "Mitchum Goes Religious for *The Wrath of God*." *San Francisco Chronicle*, January 16, 1972.

Otterburn-Hall, William. "Robert Mitchum: 'See the Scars on Me? That's the Hard Way.'" *San Francisco Chronicle*, November 26, 1967.
Parfrey, Adam. "Budd Boetticher Ends Up Near Ramona." *San Diego Reader*, September 17, 1992.
Parish, James Robert. *The Tough Guys*. New Rochelle, New York: Arlington House, 1976.
Parrish, Robert. *Hollywood Doesn't Live Here Anymore*. Boston: Little, Brown & Co., 1988.
Parsons, Louella. "Robert Mitchum Keeps Sense of Humor in Hard Work." *News and Courier*, August 3, 1947.
"The Passing of an Era." *American Cowboy*, Sept./Oct. 1997.
Pernokas, Nick. "Joe Pepper and the Most Abused Saddle in the World." *Shop Talk*, September 2017.
Perry, James A. "The Real Fall Guy." *Times-Picayune*, June 26, 1982.
Persico, Joyce. "Shattering the Mitchum Myth." *Trenton Evening Times*, December 13, 1970.
Persico, Joyce J. "Star of *Cocoon* Enjoys Gruff Image." *Cleveland Plain Dealer*, November 25, 1988.
Pitts, Michael R. *Western Movies: A Guide to 5,105 Feature Films*. Jefferson, NC: McFarland, 2013.
Prelutsky, Burt. "Stardom Meaningless to Robert Mitchum." *Arizona Republic*, December 8, 1970.
"A 'Q' and 'A' with Actor James Mitchum." *Knoxville News*, June 15, 2008.
"Quarter Horses Are Actor Mitchum's Real Interest." *Tucson-Daily Citizen*, October 22, 1965.
Raffetto, Francis. "Earthy Mitchum Talks Life, Films." *Dallas Morning News*, June 21, 1972.
Rainer, Peter. "Mitchum Has Come Long Way from Hopalong Films." *Boston Herald*, April 29, 1983.
Rassmussen, Fred. "Maryland Was Home to Tough Guy Actor." *The Baltimore Sun*, July 20, 1997.
Rawson, Greg. "Unromantic Horse Got Hungry, Ate Scenery." *The Sun*, June 10, 1948.
Ray, Nicholas. *I Was Interrupted: Nicholas Ray on Making Movies*. Berkeley: University of California Press, 1993.
Reid, John Howard. *Great Hollywood Westerns: Classic Pictures, Must-See Movies & B-Films*. Morrisville, NC: Lulu, 2006.
Rendle, Georgina Warrington. *Thank You, Georgina: Kindly Leave the Stage*. Kibworth Beauchamp, Leicester, UK: Troubador, 2017.
Reynolds, Burt, and Jon Winokur. *But Enough About Me*. New York: G.P. Putnam's Sons, 2016.
Robb, Brian J. *Johnny Depp: A Modern Rebel*. London: Plexus, 2007.
"Robert Mitchum: A Star Admits He's Still Loser." *Desert Sun*, February 9, 1968.
"Robert Mitchum Dies After Lengthy Illness." *Los Angeles Daily News*, July 2, 1997.
"Robert Mitchum Enjoys Vacation." *The Bend Bulletin*, March 26, 1949.
"Robert Mitchum, Film and TV Star to Present Feature Race Award." *Hobbs Daily News-Sun*, August 30, 1963.
"Robert Mitchum is a Journeyman Cook." *San Bernardino County Sun*, December 27, 1970.
"Robert Mitchum Named Den Father of Cub Scouts." *Arkansas Gazette*, January 15, 1950.
Roberts, Jerry. *Mitchum: In His Own Words*. New York: Limelight, 2000.
Roberts, Jerry. *Robert Mitchum: A Bio-Bibliography*. Westport, CN: Greeenwood Press, 1992.
Roberts, John. "The Western Robert Mitchum." *Favorite Westerns & Serial World*, #32/52. 1989.
Robson, Lloyd. *Oh Dad! A Search for Robert Mitchum*. Cardigan: Parthian, 2008.
Rose, Bob. "Cabot Ponders Politics." *Corpus Christi Caller Times*, March 2, 1969.
Ross, Don. "Mitchum, an Actor Who Doesn't Like to Talk." *New York Herald-Tribune*, October 25, 1955.
Rothel, David. *The Singing Cowboys*. South Brunswick, NJ: A.S. Barnes, 1978.
Rothel, David. *Those Great Cowboy Sidekicks*. New York: Scarecrow Press, 1984.
Rowland, Noni. "Six Shearers Get Film Trip." *Australian Women's Weekly*, January 13, 1960.
Sandell, Scott. "The Quotable Robert Mitchum." *The Los Angeles Times*, August 4, 2017.
Sandford, Christopher. "Missing Robert Mitchum." *The American*, September 4, 2017.
Sante, Luc, and Melissa Holbrook Pierson. *OK You Mugs: Writers on Movie Actors*. New York: Pantheon, 1999.
Scott, John L. "Mitchum's Mobile Cabin Takes Him into Wilds He Really Loves." *Los Angeles Times*, August 24, 1952.
Scott, Vernon. "He's a Chip Off the Old Mitch." *Playground Daily News*, January 27, 1976.
Scott, Vernon. "Mitchum Is Target of Brawlers." *Battle Creek Enquirer*, April 10, 1965.
Scott, Vernon. "Mitchum's 'Good Ride.'" *The Hollywood Reporter*, July 1, 1997.
Seile, Andy. "A Pro with a Powerful Presence." *USA Today*, July 2, 1997.
Sellers, Robert. *Don't Let the Bastards Grind You Down: How One Generation of British Actors Changed the World*. London: Cornerstone, 2011.
Server, Lee. *Ava Gardner: Love Is Nothing*. New York: St. Martin's, 2006.
Server, Lee. *Robert Mitchum: Baby, I Don't Care*. New York: St. Martin's, 2001.
Seymour, Jr., James W. "Rough, Tough, & Rowdy Robert Mitchum." *People*, February 14, 1983.
Sharp, Kathleen. "A Star in Spite of Himself." *Parade*, June 12, 1994.
Shearer, Lloyd. "Hollywood's Most Underrated Actor: Robert Mitchum." *Independent Star-News*, February 19, 1961.
Shipp, Cameron. "Movie Menace." *Collier's*, February 21, 1948.
Shipp, Cameron. "Off-Trail Hombre." *Photoplay*, February 1946.
"Shoot First (Ask Questions Later)." *Entertainment Weekly*, December 24, 1993.
Simpson, Claudette. "Carol Adams." *Prescott Courier*, February 19, 1981.
Simpson, Paul. *The Rough Guide to Westerns*. London: Penguin, 2006.
Siringo, Charles A. *A Texas Cowboy: Or 15 Years on the Hurricane Deck of a Spanish Pony*. Chicago: Siringo & Dobson, 1886.
Slatta, Richard W. *The Cowboy Encyclopedia*. New York: W.W. Norton & Co., 1996.
Smith, Alan. "Robert Mitchum: I'm Dying." *National Enquirer*, August 20, 1996.
Smith, Cecil. "Robert Mitchum as Pug Henry in

Wouk's Epic *Winds of War*." *San Francisco Chronicle*, March 22, 1981.

Smith, Imogen Sara. "Homeless on the Range: *The Lusty Men* and 'The Great American Search.'" *Bright Lights Film Journal*, July 2008.

Smith, Imogen Sara. *In Lonely Places: Film Noir Beyond the City*. Jefferson, NC: McFarland, 2011.

Smith, Imogen Sara. "Past Sunset: Noir in the West." *Bright Lights Film Journal*, October 2009.

Soifer, Jason. "Silver Screen Legend's Son Prefers Horses to Today's Tinsel Town." *Prescott Daily Courier*, June 26, 2005.

Sparks, Howard. "Roughin' It." *Wichita Eagle*, October 27, 1968.

Spivey, Donald. *If You Were Only White: The Life of Leroy 'Satchel' Paige*. Columbia: University of Missouri Press, 2012.

Stack, Dennis. "He's Looking for Action." *Kansas City Star*, November 14, 1971.

Stack, Peter. "Hollywood Legend: Robert Mitchum Wows the Film Festival Crowd." *San Francisco Chronicle*, April 25, 1983.

Stanley, John. "Another Mitchum Who Makes a Career Out of Being a Character." *The San Francisco Chronicle*, July 18, 1976.

Stanley, John. *The Gang That Shot Up Hollywood*. Pacifica, CA: Creatures at Large, 2011.

Stern, Daniel. "The Return of Hugh O'Brian." *Photoplay*, December 1957.

Stromberg, Gary, and Jane Merrill. *The Harder They Fall*. Center City, MN: Hazeldon, 2007.

Sullivan, Paul. "Our 26th Player Award Goes to Mike Torrez." *Boston Herald*, August 20, 1980.

"*The Sundowners* Australian Bush Saga." *Australian Women's Weekly*, March 22, 1961.

Taylor, Louis. *Ride Western: A Complete Guide to Western Horsemanship*. New York: Harper & Row, 1968.

"Tennessee Ernie Ford Hits Stardom on CBS Network." *Columbus Dispatch*, March 21, 1954.

Tessel, Harry. "Slim Pickens: Nobody Ever Proved That I Was an Actor." *Advocate*, June 29, 1979.

"This Singin' Cowboy Still Plays That Swing." *Albuquerque Journal*, August 10, 1986.

Thomas, Bob. "Another Mitchum Bobs Up." *Boston American*, May 18, 1961.

Thomas, Bob. "Few Like Him: Robert Mitchum Is an Endangered Species." *Yuma Sun*, September 10, 1985.

Thomas, Bob. "Mitchum Isn't a Tax Dodger." *World Herald*, December 11, 1960.

Thomas, Bob. "Mitchum Takes a Dim View of Tours." *Oregonian*, April 12, 1965.

Thomas, Bob. "On the Hollywood Scene." *Daily Reporter*, November 29, 1967.

Thomas, Bob. "*River of No Return* Had Location Trouble." *Columbus Dispatch*, September 27, 1953.

Thomas, Bob. "Robert Mitchum—The Sleepy-Eyed Tough Guy." *Deseret News*, March 25, 1993.

Thomas, Nick. "Chris Mitchum's Journey to Hollywood." *Mesquite Local News*, March 6, 2015.

Thomas, Tony. *The Best of Universal*. Lanham, MD: Rowman & Littlefield, 1997.

Tomkies, Mike. *Backwoods Mates to Hollywood's Greats*. Scotland: Whittles, 2009.

Tomkies, Mike. *The Robert Mitchum Story: It Sure Beats Working*. New York: Ballantine, 1973.

Toohey, Mark. "Bullrider Makes Movies." *Seguin Gazette*, December 13, 1984.

"Top Loafer." *South Coast Ties*, January 11, 1954.

Turan, Kenneth. "Saddling Up with Mitchum." *The Los Angeles Times*, July 7, 2011.

Tyler, Tim. "Hero Bum Gets Knocked Down and Gets Up with a Grunt." *San Francisco Sunday Examiner & Chronicle*, April 19, 1970.

Ustinov, Peter. *Dear Me*. Harmondsworth: Penguin, 1978.

Wade, Jack. "His Kind of Man." *Modern Screen*, January 1953.

Wagner, Robert. "Mitchum Most Non-Complexed." *Times-Picayune*, October 26, 1955.

Ward, Robert. "Mr. Bad Taste and Trouble Himself Robert Mitchum." *Rolling Stone*, March 1, 1983.

Warren, James. "Rugged Robert." *Screen Thrills Illustrated*, July 1963.

Warshow, Robert. *The Immediate Experience*. New York: Doubleday, 1962.

"Wayne's Stuntman to be Honored." *Desert Sun*, February 20, 1979.

Weaver, Tom. *Wild Wild Westerners*. Duncan, OK: BearManor, 2012.

Wellman, Jr., William. *Wild Bill Wellman: Hollywood Rebel*. New York: Pantheon, 2015.

White, Ron. "Mitchum." *San Antonio Express and News*, July 23, 1972.

Wills, Gary. "Mitchum, Stewart Remembered." *Advocate*, July 12, 1997.

Wilmington, Michael. "Tall in the Director's Chair: Budd Boetticher Made Some of the Best Remembered Westerns of the 50s and 60s." *Los Angeles Times*, November 29, 1992.

Wilson, Earl. "Mitchum Tops Tallulah's Talking." *Morning Star*, July 1, 1972.

Wilson, Earl. "Mitchum Was First Hippie." *Beaver County Times*, June 29, 1968.

Wilson, Earl. "Quotable Mr. Mitchum." *Los Angeles Herald Examiner*. January 19, 1971.

Winner, Michael. "I've Known a Few Drunks in My Time." *Daily Mail*, December 2, 2009.

Wolf, William. "Celebrity Soapbox." *Arkansas Democrat*, October 22, 1972.

Wolverton, Red Cloud. *To the Far Corners*. Victoria, BC: Trafford, 2006.

"Worst Dressed Man on Screen." *Dubbo Liberal and Macquarie Advocate*, June 11, 1949.

Yarbrough, Tinsley. *Those Great Western Movie Locations*. Greenville, NC: Tumbleweed, 2015.

Zeismer, Jerry. *Ready When You Are*. Lanham, MD: Scarecrow Press, 2003.

Zinnemann, Fred. *A Life in the Movies*. New York: Scribner's, 1992.

Zollo, Paul. *Hollywood Remembered: An Oral History of Its Golden Age*. Lanham: MD: Taylor, 2011.

Zollo, Paul. *More Songwriters on Songwriting*. Boston: De Capo, 2012.

Websites

Center for Cowboy Ethics and Leadership. http://www.cowboyethics.org.

Darol Dickinson. http://www.texaslonghorn.com.

Great Western Movies: The Best of Wild West Film and History by Nicholas Chennault. http://the greatwesternmovies.com/.
Jeff Arnold's West Film Review Site. http://JeffArnoldblog.blogspot.com/.
John Wayne Congressional Gold Medal Hearing. http://dukefanclub.weebly.com/congressional-gold-medal.html.
Mitchell Ryan. http://www.mitchellryan.net.
NBBI James Caan Interview. http://www.nationalboard.org.
Riding the High Country Western Reviews and Ramblings. http://livius1.wordpress.com/.
Robert Mitchum Retrospective: Lincoln Center Film Society. https://www.filmlinc.org/nyff2017/sections/retrospective/.
Western Writer Ron Scheer's Blog. http://buddiesinthesaddle.blogspot.com/.
Yaphet Kotto. http://facebook.com.

Archived Interviews/Radio-TV Shows

What's My Line?, 1957 (Mitchum).
Dick Cavett, *The Dick Cavett Show*, 1971 (Mitchum).
French TV interview, 1971 (Mitchum).
Richard Schickel, *Sound on Film*, 1971 (Mitchum).
Johnny Carson, *The Tonight Show*, 1978 (Mitchum).
WEDU TV Interview, early 1980s (Mitchum on Marilyn Monroe).
Barbara Walters, *The Barbara Walters Special*, 1983 (Mitchum).
William Holden: The Golden Boy. 1989.
Reflections on the Silver Screen. 1991. (Mitchum segment).
Robert Mitchum: The Reluctant Star. 1991.
100 Years of the Hollywood Western, 1994 (Mitchum narration).
Carole Langer, 1997 (Mitchum *Youtube* interview).
The Larry King Show, 1997 (Burt Reynolds).
Dick Dinman, WMPG Radio (Stanley Rubin & Michael Anderson, Jr.).
Robert Mitchum: Hollywood Greats, 1999.
Robert Mitchum: Poet with an Axe, 2001 (A&E Biography).
KNPR Studio/Nevada State Historical Society (Herbie McDonald Interview).
James Stewart, Robert Mitchum: The Two Faces of America, 2017 (Greg Monro film).
Nice Girls Don't Stay for Breakfast, 2018 (Bruce Weber film).

Index

Numbers in bold italics indicate pages with illustrations

Abbott, E.C. 60
Aberbach, Julian 68
Acapulco, Mexico 97, 98
Acosta, Rodolfo 97
Adair, Bobby 191
Adams, Andy 154
Adams, Carol 74
Adams, Peter 120
The Adventures of Kit Carson (TV) 43
The Adventures of Spin and Marty (TV) 9, 95
Aerial Gunner (1943) 23
African Skies (TV) 201, 209
Agee, James 17
Agency (1979) 181, 192
Agoura, CA 65
Agua Fria Wash 206
Aguirre, the Wrath of God (1972) 174
Ahern, Daniel 10
Akins, Claude 40, 91, 92
Akridge, Eddy 73
Alabama Hills 21, 27, 30, 31, 38
The Alamo (1960) 39, 87, 119, 120, 131
The Alamo Inn 186
Alberta, Canada 76, 83
Albright, Lola 134
Albuquerque, NM 171, 214
Alcoholism: America on the Rocks (1973) 185
Aldrich, Robert 45, 90, 149
Aldridge, Kay 205
Allen, Barbara Jo 34
Allen, Henry Wilson "Heck" 156
Allen, Michael 74
Allen, Rex 73, 211, 214
Almeria, Spain 145
The Ambassador (1984) 180–181
Ambler, Jerry 73
Ambush at Dark Canyon (2012) 162
Ambush Bay (1966) 163
America, Why I Love Her 36, 95
An American Boy Grows Up 212
American Commandos (1986) 164
American Film Institute 214
American Humane Association 169, 174

Ames, Preston 112
The Ames Brothers 50
The Amsterdam Kill (1977) 180
Anchor Ranch 31
Anderson, Broncho Billy 70
Anderson, Buddy 162
Anderson, John 148, 158, 159
Anderson, Judith 47
Anderson, Michael, Jr. 115, 116, 117
Angel Face (1952) 68, 82
The Angry Hills (1959) 45, 90, 100
Antelope Valley Inn 192
Anthony, Pat 77
Antler's Bar 114
Anzio (1968) 145
Apache (1954) 45
Apache Junction, AZ 162, 163
Appaloosa (2008) 204
Archainbaud, George 19
Archerd, Army 125
Ardrey, Robert 103
Arizona 208
Arizona Raiders (1965) 162
Armendariz, Pedro 102
Armendariz, Pedro, Jr. 201
Armour, Philip 64, 201
Armstrong, Garry 7, 16, 17, 29, 50, 55, 61, 78, 79, 105, 110, 126, 135, 140, 152, 169, 184, 186
Armstrong, Stephen B. 142
Arness, James 196
Arngrim, Stefan 135
Arnold, Darrell 44, 207
Arnold, Eddy 68
Arnold, Jeff 88, 213
Arruza, Carlos 119
Asner, Ed 125, 126, 128, 129
Aston, Sam 107
Atascadero, CA 154
Athabasca River 77
Atlantic City (1980) 181
Aubrey, James 175, 176, 179, 180
Autry, Gene 39, 42, 43, 68, 99, 198, 204, 214
Azbill, Cindy 7, 142, 213

Bacharach, Burt 160, 161
Backfire! (1995) 201
Backstage Bar 189
Bacon, James 118, 183

Bad Girls (1994) 204
Badham, John 25
Baker, Norma Jean 80
Baker, Stanley 180
The Ballad of Cable Hogue (1970) 172
The Ballad of Josie (1967) 119
"The Ballad of Marshal Flagg" 169
"Ballad of Thunder Road" 50, 214
Balsam, Martin 167
Bandido! (1956) **96**–100, 107, 136, 143, 173
Bandolero! (1968) 57, 95, 152
Bane, Holly 43
Banff National Park 77
Banff Springs Hotel Bar 80
The Bank Robbery (1908) 200
Banks, Ronnie 191
Banner (horse) 99
Bar 20 (1943) 27–**28**, 31
"The Bar 20 Boys" 16, 30, 32
Barcroft, Roy 17–18, 29, 139
Bare Knuckles (1977) 146
Barney's Beanery 57
Barnum, P.T. 202
Baron, Lita 83
Barry, Don "Red" 108
Barry, Joe 91, 93
Bartlett, Sy 108
Bass, Sam 84
Batjac Prods. 87, 90, 91, 128
Baxter, Alan 73
Baxter, Anne 71
Baylor, Hal 78, 189
The Beat Generation (1959) 163
Behrman, Paul 57
Bel Geddes, Barbara 60–**62**, 64, 203
Bell, Hank 48
Bell, James Scott 215
Belmont Farm 108–109, 133, 153
Belmont Scare (horse) 114, 191
Belton, John 22, 43, 77, 83, 100, 107, 113
Bend, OR 134, 141
Benham, H.N. 132
Benson, AZ 200
Benteen, Frederick 120
Bergen, Polly 135, 204
Betty Ford Clinic 195

225

226 Index

Beyond the Last Frontier (1943) 25–27, 32
Bezzerides, A.I. "Buzz" 87
Biehn, Michael 201
Big Jake (1971) 80, 164
The Big Land (1957) 106
Big River, Big Man 119, 121
The Big Showdown 90
The Big Sky (1951) 17, 56, 122, 133, 134
The Big Sleep (1978) 3, 181, 185
The Big Steal (1949) 57
The Big Trail (1930) 50
The Big Valley (TV) 87, 105, 189, 192
Bigfoot (1969) 164
Billy the Kid 163, 164, 179–180
Billy the Kid (ballet) 65
Billy the Kid (1930) 47
Bimini Girl 132
Bingo (horse) 39
Birth of a Nation (1913) 20
Bishop, Norman 80
Bitter Creek (1954) 40
Black Diamond (horse) 86, 87
Black Horse Canyon (1954) 86
Black Saddle (TV) 105
Blade Runner (1982) 181
Blake, Denis 117
Blazing Saddles (1974) 179, 186
Blocker, Dan 95, 213
Blood Alley (1955) 87, 90, 91
Blood Hunt 195
Blood on the Moon (1948) 3, **4**, **5**, 48, 52–53, 56, 58–65, 101, 162, 203, 206, 214, **215**, 216
The Bloody Spur 90
Bloom, Claire **194**
Blues in the Night 208
Boardner's 57
Boetticher, Budd 91, 118, 119, 131, 134, 187, 202, 204
Bogart, Humphrey 11, 74, 82, 141
Bogdanovich, Peter 126, 131
Bonanza (TV) 48, 71, 95, 150, 189, 193, 207
Bondi, Beulah 85, 88
Boomtown Benefit Party 103, 192
Boone, Richard 132, 140, 180, 185, 189, 196
Boothe, Powers 200, 201
Border Patrol (1943) 13–17, 22
Borgnine, Ernest 40, 190, 191, 195, 196, 210, 211
Born and Raised in Black and White 214
"Botany Bay" 117
Bouchey, Willis 162
Bourne, Merle 113
Bow Falls/River 77
Bowie, James 74, 119
boxing 10–11, 29, 47, 77
Boxleitner, Bruce 202
Boyd, William 12–16, **18**–20, 29–**32**, 190, 196, 204, 214
Boyle, Hal 174
Boyle, Peter 181
Boynton Pass 61

Brackett, Leigh 123
Brand, Max 43, 93
Brand, Neville 188
Branded (TV) 121, 150, 196
Brandon, Henry 97
The Brave Bulls 101
Bray, Robert 59
Breakheart Pass (1976) 80, 145, 186
Breakthrough (1979) 181, 187
Breck, Peter 105, 163
Brennan, Walter 60, 61, 64, 158, 201
Bretherton, Howard 25
Brewer's Saloon 16
Brewster, Jim 80
The Bridge on the River Kwai (1957) 27
Brimley, Wilford 193
Britton, Layne "Shotgun" 98
Brocius, Curly Bill 200
Brodie, Steve 11, 31, 47, 53, 197
Bronson, Charles 49, 95, 142–145, 147, 185, 190, 202, 214
Bronson Canyon/Cave 21
Brooks, Mel 179
Brotherhood of the Rose (1989) 201
Brown, Harry 44, 123
Brown, Johnny Mack 23, **24**
Brown, JPS "Joe" 179, 193
Brown, Robert 159
Brown, Wally 34
Brynner, Yul 94, 142–144, 148
Buccella, Maria Gracia 142, 144
Buck, Jerry 44
Buckaroo Buffet 70
Bucket of Blood 16, 21
Bucko, Ralph 16
Bucko, Roy 16
Buffalo Bill (1944) 39
"Build My Gallows High" 214
"Bull Rider" 215
Bull's Eye Bee (horse) 156, **168**
Buono, Victor 173, 174, 176
Bureau of Indian Affairs 137
Burk, Jim 137
Burnette, Smiley 25, 26, 38
Burns, OR 134
Burraston, Jack 117
Burton, Richard 132, 181
Busch, Niven 47
Buscombe, Edward 104
Butch Cassidy and the Sundance Kid (1969) 98–99
Butler, James 194
Buttram, Pat 68
Buzzy Rides the Range (1940) 128
Byrd, Eugene 206
Byrne, Gabriel 206

Caan, James 124–126, 128, 130
Cabeen, Boyd 53, 55, 70, 83, 196
Café del Sol 190
Calder, Jenni 142
Calhern, Louis 65
Calhoun, Rory 70, 78, 80, 83, 203
California Studios 29
"Calypso Is Like So" 50
Camelback Inn 202

Camelback Mountain 202–203
Cameron, Rod 190
Candid Cowboys 204
Canford, Tom 176
Cannes, France 89
Canutt, Tap 169, 170
Canutt, Yakima 15, 29, 75, 169
Cap Gun (horse) 136, 154–155, 169
Cape Fear (1962) 79, 88, 121, 135, 150
Cape Fear (1991) **202**
Capua, Michelangelo 55
Cardinale, Claudia 108
Carducci, Joe 49
Carey, Harry 48
Carey, Harry, Jr. 47, 139, 161, 189, 190, 201, 204, 211
Carey, Olive 47, 130, 190
Cargo, David 168, 170
Carney, Alan 34
Carr, Howie 181
Carradine, David 159, 160, 162, 167–170, 195
Carradine, John 164, 165, 169, 170
Carroll, Len 80
Carson, Johnny 19, 183
Carson, Sunset 44
Carter, Forrest 179
Caruso, Anthony 11, 13, 69–70, 105, 106–107, 195, 210
Casa Grande, AZ 193
Cascade River 77
Cash, Johnny 58, 100, 149, 191, 195, 214, 215
Cass, Dave 7, 159, 160, 162–163, 170, 171
Cassidy, Butch 98
Castellana Hilton 144
Castro, Fidel 98
Cat Ballou (1965) 119, 120
Cathedral Rock 61
Cattle Queen of Montana (1954) 84
Cavett, Dick 19, 31, 183
Chama, NM 168–171
Chama River 169, **171**
Champion (horse) 99
Champlin, Charles 14, 21, 31, 205, 211
Chandler, John Davis 169
Chandler, Lane 48, 73
Chandler, Raymond 3
Charles, Ray 181
Charlie Rose 206
Charro! (1969) 163, 203
Chasen's 176
Chateau Marmont 53
Chennault, Nicholas 100, 214
Cheyenne (TV) 132, 189
Chez Jay 189
Chief Owanahee 136
Chihuahua, Mexico 100
"Chilly Winds" 75
Chisum (1970) 95, 125, 163, 196
Christmas Valley Lodge 140
The Chuck Box 203
Chupaderos, Mexico 148
Churubusco Studios 149

Index

Cimarron City (TV) 213
Cimarron Strip (TV) 7, 146, 169, 189
Clanton, Billy 156
Clark, Jim 203–204
Clark, Roydon 137
Clarke, Richard 26
Clarke, Robert 34
Clarksville, TX 110
Classic Movie Fight Scenes 29, 31, 61, 126, 169
Claxton, Bill 150
Cleary, Jon 115
Cleopatra (1963) 120
Clifford, Terry 195
Clift, Montgomery 48
Clothier, William 86, 87, 134, 142
Clouse, Robert 180
Clyde, Andy 13, **15**, 17, 20, 21, 29, **30**, 38
Coburn, James 129, 179, 180, 202, 204, 206, 215
Cocaine (horse) 107
Cock 'n' Bull 57, 183
Coconino National Forest 63, 206
Code of the West 43
Code of the West (1947) 96
Cody, Buffalo Bill 75
Cody, Iron Eyes 64
Coe, Peter 53
Coe, Tucker 174
Coffee Pot Rock 61
Cohen, Larry 121
Cohen, Ronald M. 169
Cohn, Nudie 38, 191
Coleman, George 90
Colicos, John 173
Colin 214
Collie, Mark 214
Collier, Don 7, 129, 149, 150, 157, 161, 201
Collins, Max Allan 90
Collins, Steve 195
Colorado Springs, CO 76
Colorado Sunset (1939) 39
Colorado Territory (1949) 50
Colorado's Raid 209
Colt Comrades (1943) 21–23
The Comancheros (1961) 39
Combs, Richard 45
Comes a Horseman (1978) 53
commercials 185, 202, 212
Conagher (1991) 140
Confessions of an Acting Cowboy 150
Connolly, Mike 121
Connors, Chuck 83, 121, 125, 128, 161, 189, 209
The Conqueror (1956) 84
Conrad, Barnaby 188
Conrad, Joseph 10
Coogan's Bluff (1968) 57
Cook, Glenn 27
Cool Hand Luke (1967) 132, 167
Cooper, D.B. 193
Cooper, Gary 3, 5, 39, 70, 99, 116, 117, 165, 213, 214
Cope, Julian 214
Copeland, Bobby 17, 32

Copland, Aaron 65
The Copper Room 141
Corbett, Ben 16, 48
Corbucci, Sergio 145
Corey, Wendell 158
Cornthwaite, Robert 11
Corrigan, Ray "Crash" 24
Corriganville 24, 25, 190
Corvette K-225 (1943) 23, 58
Cosa Nostra Asia (1974) 164
Cosmatos, George P. 200
Costner, Kevin 199–201
Cotton, Carolina 68
The Covered Wagon 108
Cowan, Lester 45
The Cowboy Club 61
Cowboy Code 1, 43–44, 155, 216
Cowboy Hall of Fame 214
The Cowboys (1972) 111
Cowpoke 71, 74
Cowtown 206
Crabbe, Buster 39, 190
Crawford, Johnny 83, 125
Crescent Heights Market 53
Crocetti, Dino 152
Crockett, Davy 74, 119, 215
Cromwell, John 71
Crooked River Gorge 134, 140
Crosby, Bing 56
Crosby, Floyd 102
Crossfire (1947) 52
Crowther, Bosley 51, 68, 74, 88
Crowther, Bruce 75, 104, 172
Crump, Pete 73
Cry Havoc (1943) 23
Crystal Phoenix Award 203
The Crystal Pistol 203
Cudia City 202
Cuernavaca, Mexico 97, 174
Cuevas, Manuel 191
Cumbres Pass 168
Cumbres Toltec Railroad 168
Curtis, Dan 186, 194
Curtis, Dick 53
Curtis, Tony 106, 121
Curtiz, Michael 71
Custer, George Armstrong 120
Custer of the West (1967) 120

Dallas (1950) 70
Dallas (TV) 61, 110
Dallas, TX 74, 110, 193
Dalroy, Rube 16
Dan Tana's 189
Dances with Wolves (1990) 199
"Danny Boy" 50, 215
Darby, Kim 155
Dark City (1950) 148
Darrach, Brad 183
Da Silva, Howard 71
Daves, Delmer 71
Davies, W.H. 10
Davis, Del 80
Davis, George 112
Davis, Jim 110, 128, 129, 189
Davis, Wee Willie 66
Dawson, Gordon 135
The Day Custer Fell 120

Dead Man (1995) **205**–208, 214
The Deadly Peacemaker 91
The Dean Martin Show (TV) 152
Deane, Howard 169
Dean's Place (TV) 153
Death Scenes 16, 19, 21, 22, 31, 45, 64, 72, 86, 110
Death Valley, CA 13
Death Valley Days (TV) 11, 27, 150, 162, 169, 191, 203
Death Wish (1974) 208
Decca Records 56
DeCorsia, Ted 91, 92, 148
The Defiant Ones (1958) 106
DeFrance, Steve "Bunker" 7, 159, 162, 170
Dekker, Albert 102
Del Toro, Benicio 207
DeMille, Cecil B. 19, 20, 204
De Niro, Robert 202
Denver, CO 71, 103
Depp, Daniel 208
Depp, Johnny 50, 205–208
Derek, Bo 201
Dern, Bruce 181
Deschutes National Forest 134
Deschutes River 134
Deuel, Geoffrey 164
The Devil Horse (1926) 15
Devine, Andy 38, 214
Devona Flats 77
Dew, Eddie 25
De Young, Joe 60
Diaz, Rudy 57
Di Bona, Dominic 169
Dick Powell Theatre 121
Dickinson, Angie 79, 129, 157, 158, 159, 160, 161, 166, 190, 204
Dickinson, Darol 191
Dillard, Art 16
DiMaggio, Joe 80
DiMona, Joseph 20
Dinman, Dick 117
Dirty Harry (1971) 174
The Distant Drummer (1970) 185
Django (1966) 145
Dmytryk, Edward 46, 52, 94
Doc (1971) 185
Dodd, Jimmie 75
Dodge City (1939) 27, 31, 38, 39, 52, 136
Doeke, F.A. 118
Dollarhide, Ross 73
Dollarhide, Sandy 141
Dollor (horse) 99
Domergue, Faith 68
Don Guerro (horse) 191
Donner, Robert 125
Dortort, David 70, 71
Doughboys in Ireland (1943) 23
Dougherty, Jim 80
Douglas, Gordon 34
Douglas, Kirk 51, 56, 95, 106, 121, 131, 134, 135, 137, 139, 140–142, 149, 167, 179, 201
Dow Motel 16, 21
Downing, David 24, 45, 57, 104, 110
Drago, Harry Sinclair 20

Drake, Oliver 25
drinking 32, 82, 83, 104, 107, 112, 125, 130, 153, 172, 174, 175, 180–185, 194
A Drinking Life 185
The Driver (1978) 181
DRM Prods. 97, 101, 108
Drum Beat (1954) 106
Drury, James 95, 210
Dry Creek Basin 61
Duel at Diablo (1966) 162, 174, 203
Duel in the Sun (1946) 46
Dumbrille, Douglas 29
Duncan, Thomas W. 119
Dundee and the Culhane (TV) 163
Durango, Mexico 100, 104, 106, 107, 148, 150, 151, 153, 164, 167, 179, **190**
Durgom, George "Bullets" 133, 188
Dylan, Bob 188

Earp, Wyatt 156, 200, 201, 208
Easton Bros. Gym 47
Eastwood, Clint 3, 5, 95–96, 105, 119, 145, 165, 169, 173, 179, 181, 186, 190, 199, 200, 204, 210, 214, 216
Ebert, Roger 35, 55, 60, 64, 141, 153, 184
The Ed Sullivan Show (TV) 50
Edwards, Blake 179
Eells, George 11, 20, 31, 53, 183
Egan, Richard 105, 163, 197, 210
Eisenhower, Dwight D. 58
El Chorro Lounge 203
El Dorado (1967) 4, 75, 89, 120, 122–131, 136, 150, 152, 156, 157, 162, 169, **187**, 204, 214
El Matador 188
El Mirador Hotel 98
El Rancho Broke-O 11, 13
El Rancho Hotel/Resort 52, 70, 114, 214
Elam, Jack 137, 161, 189, 190, 210
Eldredge, George **24**
Elkhorn Lodge 168
Elliott, Bill 24, 38, 190
Elliott, Sam 140, 200, 201, 207, 212, 215
Ely, Ron 187
Empire (TV) 105
The Enemy Below (1957) 46, 100
The Entrepreneurs (TV) 202
Epper, Tony 189
The Equalizer (TV) 201
Ericson, John 205
Escort West (1958) 108
Estes Park, CO 73
Eugene, OR 54, 134, 137, 141
Evans, Gene 161
Evans, Gentleman Jack 16
Evans, Vicki 57
The Executioner Part 2 (1984) 164
exercise 10, 11, 47, 77, 135
eyes, appearance 28
Eyes of War (TV) 202
Eyles, Allen 3
Eyman, Scott 89, 196

F-Troop (TV) 95
Factor, Max 45
Fagen, Herb 23, 43, 93, 99, 130, 172, 177, 188, 213
Fahey, Jeff 208
False Colors (1943) 28–**30**
A Family for Joe (TV) 201
Fancher, Hampton 181
Fapp, Daniel 149
The Far Side of Jericho (2006) 136
Farber, Manny 74
Farewell, My Lovely (1975) 3, 180
Farkas, John 201
Farnsworth, Richard 44, 53, 73, 204, 207, 213, 214
Farnum, Dustine 27
Farrow, Mia 155
Fast, Howard 54
Father Murphy (TV) 129
Fellows, Robert 83, 95, 196
Felton, Earl 97–99
Fenady, Andrew J. 196
Fenster, Bob 141, 211
Fenton, Frank 83
Ferrer, Mel 101
Ferrier, Dave 152
Fidler, Jimmie 66, 84
Fieberling, Hal 78
The Field (1990) 202
Field, Sally 137, **138**
Fier, Jack 35
fight scenes 18, 23, 29, 31, 34, 39, 40, 49, 50, 54, 55, 60, 61, 64, 69, 74, **116**, 117, 125, 147, 160, 216
"Fighting Stallions" 125
film festivals 30, 89, 121, 203–205, 214
Film Society of Lincoln Center 214
The Final Showdown 209
Fire Down Below (1956) 50, 100, 101, 175
First Blood (1982) 181
Fischer, Carl 121
Fisher, Clay 156
Fisk, Jim 84
fistfights 31, 44, 52, 76, 95, 117, 125, 141, 186–188
A Fistful of Dollars (1964) 96, 145
"5 Card Stud" 158
5 Card Stud (1968) 80, 99, 148–156, 160, 166, 167, 173, **190**
Fix, Paul **158**, 160
Flagstaff, AZ 62, 63, 206
Flap (1970) 150
Fleischer, Richard 97, 120, 179
Fleming, Rhonda 70
Flicka (horse) 86
Flying Leathernecks (1951) 94
Flynn, Errol 39, 52, 82, 108, 112, 136, 144
The Fog Cutter 70
Foley, Red 84
Follow the Free Wind 123
Fonda, Henry 94, 95, 101, 121, 190
"Foolish Pride" 56
For a Few Dollars More (1966) 96, 145
Ford, Bob 70

Ford, Glenn 70, 93, 95, 130, 131, 136, 155, 190, 201
Ford, John 13, 14, 21, 47, 94, 102, 128, 130, 134, 150, 179, 187, 200, 201
Ford, Robin "Danny" 57
Ford, Tennessee Ernie 50, 83, 84
Foreign Intrigue (1956) 97, 100
Formosa Café 189
Fort Apache (1948) 87, 102, 150
Fort Rock, OR 134
Fort Worth, TX 74, 110
48 Hrs. (1982) 181
Foster, Fred 50
Foster, Norman 54
Foster, Stephen 34
Four Faces West (1948) 22
4 for Texas (1963) 119, 149
Four Peaks Wilderness 203
Fowley, Douglas 21, 27, 53, 97, **168**, 169
Foy, Bryan 70
Fraker, William 200
Frakes, Al 209
Francis (mule) 86
Francisco, Don 191
Frank, Harriet 111
Frederick, Fred 45
Frederick, Reva 76, 133
Freeman, Alex 139
Freeman, Joel 132
Freese, Marty 7, 157
The French Connection (1971) 174
Friedkin, William 181
The Friends of Eddie Coyle (1973) 105, 180–182, 184
From Here to Eternity (1953) 69
Frontier Village 140
Fuller, Lance 84
Funny Girl (1968) 131
Fury, David 209

Gable, Clark 39, 82, 111, 120, 128
Galiban (horse) **67**
Gallup, NM 47, 48, 52, 162, 214
The Gambler (1980) 159
The Gambler's Moon 70
Gammon, James 208
Gammons Gulch 161–162
Gammons, Jay 129–130, 161
Gammons, John 129
Garden of the Gods Club & Resort 114
Gardner, Ava 80, 106, 161
Gardner, Ralph D. 208
Garfield, Brian 26, 43, 51, 64, 74, 142, 189, 208
Garfield, John 51
Garmes, Lee 71
Garner, James 108, 161, 202
Garrett, Pat 44, 179
Garrett, Snuff 211
Gates, Nancy 37, 40
Gates Pass 123
Gatlin, Jerry 149, 159, 162
Gaulden, Ray 148
Geer, Lennie 95, 197, 213
Geisler, Jerry 57

Index

Gentry, Charles 45
George, Christopher 125, 128
Gerlock, Bob 114
Giant (1956) 94, 109
The Gift of Cochise 70
Gilmore, William S., Jr. 174, 176
Girl Rush (1944) 32–35, 37, 53, 202
Girls Town (1959) 163
"Git Along Little Doggie" 23
Givot, George 20
Glory Gulch 148
The Glory Guys (1965) 117, 124
Glover, Crispin 206
Go Tell the Spartans (1978) 181
Going Home (1971) 175
Golan-Globus 181
Golden Boot Awards 161, 203–205
Golden Boy 55
Golden Gate Mountain 123
Golden Oldie (horse) 191
Goldman, William 98
Goldwater, Barry 131, 191
Goldwyn, Samuel, Jr. 91, 93
Gone with the Wind (1939) 20, 31
The Good Guys and the Bad Guys (1969) 136, 161, 162, 164, 167–173, 179, **210**
The Good, the Bad, and the Ugly (1966) 96, 145
Goodhue, Jim 113
Googies 108
Gordon, Leo 40, 91–93, 108, 188
Gordon, Waxey 10
Gorilla Pictures 69, 90
Gorman, Earl J. 132
"Gotta Travel On" 51
Gower Gulch 15, 16, 20, 22, 94
Graham, Fargo 7, 170–171
Graham, Fred 39
Graham, James 174
Graham, Mac 80
Graham, Sheilah 84
Grahame, Gloria 69
Grainger, Edmund 70
Grand Canyon Massacre (1964) 120, 145
Granger, Stewart 120
Grant, James Edward 70
Grant, Kevin 3
Grant, Kirby 85
The Grass Is Greener (1960) 119
Gray, Ellen 208
Gray, Gary 54, 56
Great Day in the Morning (1956) 70
The Great Silence (1968) 145
The Great Train Robbery (1903) 200
Greer, Jane 3, 52
Grey, Zane 5, 34, 37, 39, 41, 43, 45, 46, 155
Griffin, Mark 110, 111
Griffith, D.W. 20
Griffith Park 21
Gringo Gulch 172
Grizzly Adams (TV) 43, 193
Grobel, Lawrence 104
"The Grocery Store Cowboys" 53
Guadalajara, Mexico 192
Guadio, Tony 65

Guanajuato, Mexico 176
Guerra, Enrico 99
Gun Belt (1953) 106
Gun Fury (1953) 199
Gunderson, Gustave Olaf 108
Gundown 180
The Gundown (2011) 162
Gunfight at the OK Corral (1957) 101, 119
Gung Ho! (1943) 23, 58, 106
Gunman's Chance 59
guns 93, 99, 128
Gunsmoke (TV) 27, 29, 95, 108, 129, 134, 146, 150, 158, 159, 162, 169, 189, 193, 196, 207
Guthrie, A.B. "Bud" 133, 134

Haas, Thomas 99
Haber, Joyce 143
Hack, Herman 16
Hackman, Gene 181, 202
Haggerty, Dan 43, 193
Haggerty, Donald Paul 43
Hale, Alan 52
Hale, Barbara 42, 43, 205
Hale, Monte 190, 204
Hale, Wanda 113
Haley, Brett 215
Hall, Arch 121
Hall, Thurston 42
Hall, William 141
The Hallelujah Trail (1965) 162
Hamill, Pete 185
Hamilton, George **109**, 110, **111**, 112
Hamilton, John 127
Handlebar J Saloon 203
The Hangout 53
The Hangover 11
Hannan, Chick 169
Harbinson, W.A. 145
Hardin, John Wesley 144
Hardin, Ty 121
Hardrock 70
Hardy, Phil 23, 25, 83, 88
Harlan, Russell 17, 27
Harper, Tess **194**
Harrington, Cliff 184
Harris, Harry 34
Harris, Richard 180, 181, 185, 186, 202, 206
Harrison, Mark 113
Hart, William S. 16
Harvey, Laurence 119
Haskell, Molly 127
Hassayampa River 114
Hathaway, Henry 120, 148–150, 152, 153, 155, 156, 166, 179
Have Gun—Will Travel (TV) 27, 95, 120, 134, 140, 141, 189
Hawaii (1966) 132
Hawks, Howard 4, 5, 57, 122–126, 128–131, 133, 152, 158, 164, 179
Haworth, Joe 85, 105, 106
Hayden, Sterling 76, 91, 172, 190, 196, 197, 215
Hayes, Chester 102, 107
Hayes, Gabby 38
Hayes, Steve 108

Hayward, Chuck 142, 149
Hayward, Susan 71–73, 76, 84
Hayworth, Rita 173, 175, 176
Healey, Myron 213
Heaven Knows, Mr. Allison (1957) 46, 50, 100, 116, 119, 120
Heaven with a Gun (1969) 155
Heaven's Gate (1980) 180, 207
Hecht, Harold 133
Hee Haw (TV) 189
Heffernan, Harold 45, 154
Heflin, Van 87
Heisler, Stuart 70
Helfer, Ralph 15, 77
Heller in Pink Tights (1960) 119
Helmick, Paul 82, 131
Hemingway, Ernest 11
Henabery, Joseph 20
Hendrickson, Paul 35, 183
Henriksen, Lance 206
Henry, Buzz 128
Henry, Will 156
Hensley, Gene 114
Henson, Chuck 7, 129
Here Come the Brides (TV) 159
Hernandez, Chema 99
The Hero (2017) 215
Herzog, Werner 174
Heston, Charlton 71, 95, 120, 135, 173, 180, 193, 201, 210
"Hey, Mr. Cottonpicker" 84
Hickey, Dave 93, 95
Hidalgo (2004) 136
Higgins, Jack 174
The High Chaparral (TV) 27, 71, 120, 129, 146, 150, 157, 159, 162, 207
High Noon (1952) 5, 115, 212
High Plains Drifter (1973) 95, 105
High Sierra (1941) 50
High Voltage (horse) 75
Hildyard, Jack 116
Hill, George Roy 98, 132
Hill, Walter 181
Hill, Weldon 108
The Hills Run Red (1966) 145
Hilton, Les 86, 87
Hinterbeyer, John 138, 139
His Kind of Woman (1951) 68, 69, 77
Hitchcock, Alfred 11
Hitching Post Theatre 35
Hitt, Jim 88
Hodgkiss, Clark 3
Hoffman, Henryk 3, 51, 103
Holden, Barbara 190
Holden, William 54, 55, 119, 130, 131, 141, 166, 179, 181, 190, 196
Holliday, Doc 200, 201
Hollywood Greats 22, 58, 196
Hollywood Hoofbeats 212
Hollywood in the Desert (1993) 150
Hollywood's Makeup Magic 45
Holmes, Bill 141
Holmes, Earl 191
Holt, Charlene 125, 127, 128
Holt, Jack 36
Holt, Jennifer **24**

Index

Holt, Tim 36, 46
Hombre (1967) 111, 162
Home from the Hill (1960) 39, **109**–114, 119, 166
Hondo (1953) 40, 70, 92, 107
Hondo (TV) 150, 159, 196
Honeycutt, Kirk 20
The Honkers (1972) 129
Hopalong Cassidy College for Kids 202
Hopper, Dennis 164
Hopper, Hedda 53, 67, 105, 106, 112, 115
Hopper, William 85, 86
Hoppy Serves a Writ (1943) 16–19, 22, 204
Horn, Tom 44
Horne, Victoria 106
A Horse for Mr. Barnum 202
Horse Opera 97
horseback riding 14–15, 39, 41, 48–49, 62, 87, 107, 118, 160, 170
horses 39, 66–67, 99, 107, 113, 114, 136, 153, 154, 174, 191, 196
Horton, Johnny 184
Hough, Emerson 108
Houston, Norman 37
Houston, TX 74
How the West Was Won (1962) 77, 155
How the West Was Won (TV) 129, 150
Howard, Trevor 98, 180
Howe, James Wong 47
Hoy, Robert "Bob" 80, 150, 155
Hud (1963) 111
Hudkins Bros. Ranch 193
Hudson, Rock 94
Huff, Butch 7, 186
Hugenberger, Art 136
Hughes, Howard 58, 69, 70, 74, 84, 108
Hull, Henry 92
Hulse, Ed 41, 214
The Human Comedy (1943) 22
Humbird, Alma Massey 140
Humbird, William "Smokey" 140
Humphrey, William 109
Hunnicutt, Arthur 70, 74, 84, 124, 165
Hunt, Terry 77
Hunter, Jeffrey 120
Hunter, Tab 85–88
Hunter, Thomas 145–146
Hurst, Paul **33**
Huston, John 82, 101, 120, 121, 132, 181, 187, 197
Hutchins, Will 212
Hutchison, Ken 173, 174, 176, 180

"I Got Spurs" 46
In Harm's Way (1965) 163
In the Line of Fire: Manhunt in the Dakotas (1991) 202
Indian Creek Corrals 86
Ingram Ranch 23, 190
International Chili Society 191

The Invincible Six (1970) 164
Invitation to a Gunfighter (1964) 94
Inyo Mountain Range 21
Ireland, Jill 144
Ireland, John 57, 69, 145, 190, 197
The Iron Mistress (1951) 106
The Iron Sheriff (1957) 91
Ironsides (horse) 129
Irwin, Ron 132
Is Paris Burning? (1966) 132
Iverson, Jack 23
Iverson Ranch 25, 57, 190

Jackpot 181
Jacks, Robert L. 97
Jaeckel, Richard 148, 163
Jagger, Dean 47
Jake Spanner, Private Eye (1989) 196
James, Clive 184
James, Jesse 70, 84
James, John "Dusty" 11, 53
James Dean—Live Fast, Die Young (1997) 208
James Stewart & Robert Mitchum: The Two Faces of America (2017) 45, 212
Janes, Loren 205
Jarmusch, Jim 205, 206, 207
Jarre, Kevin 200, 201
Jarre, Maurice 142, 148
Jasper National Park 77
Jasper Park Lodge 80
Javier, Jorge 151
Jaws (1975) 181
Jeffreys, Anne 37, 38, 40, 60, 210
Jeffries, Herb 106
Jennings, Waylon 58
Jensen, Richard 40
Jenson, Roy 79, 80, 149, 180, 188
JFK (1991) 202
Jim Kane 179
JL Ranch 196
Jochim, Laurence Lee 190
Joe Kidd (1972) 186
John Huston: The Man, the Movies, the Maverick (1988) 202
Johnny Guitar (1954) 76
Johns, Glynnis 110
Johns, Larry 11
Johnson, Ben 39, 40, 44, 73, 121, 131, 165, 190, 191, 197, 204, 207–208, 212, 214
Johnson, Erskine 43, 88, 91
Johnson, Lyndon 193
Jones, Buck 13
Jones, Elmer Elsworth 83, 124
Jones, Fat 39, 86, 193
Jones, Gordon Graham 128
Jones, L.Q. 189
Jones, Malcolm 95
Jordan, Richard 181, 182
Jory, Victor 17, 18, 20, 21, 27, 31
Joyner, C. Courtney 169, 189
Judgment (2017) 212
The Jungle 119
Junior Bonner (1972) 75

"Just Like Me" 56
Justice, Katherine 148

Kael, Pauline 123
Kanab, UT 162, 193
Kane, Joseph 66
Keith, Brian 180
Keller, Helen 181
Kelly, Jack 160
Ken Murray's Shooting Stars (1979) 139
Kendall, Cy 34
Kennedy, Arthur 71, 74, 75
Kennedy, Burt 91, 156, 159, 160–162, 167, 168–170, 172, 202, 204
Kennedy, George 167, 169, 170, 172
Kennedy, Harlan 144
Kern River Valley 13
Kernville, CA 13, 16, 19, 30
Kerr, Deborah 115, 116, 119
Kerwin, Lance **192**
Ketchum, Cliff 136
The Keys 186
Kilgore, Merle 149
A Killer in the Family (1983) **192**, 193
The Killing (1956) 97
Killy, Edward 38, 40
Kilmer, Val 200, 201
Kinds of Love, Kinds of Death 174
King (1978) 193
King, Charlie "Blackie" 21
King, Larry 144, 183, 212
King of the Mountain 165
Kingman, AZ 214
King's Pistol (horse) 169
Kirby, Jay 13, **15**, 21, 27
Kiss Me, Deadly (1955) 90
Kittredge, Linda 141
Kleiner, Dick 123, 139
Knagge Ranch 157
Kon Tiki Lounge 156
Kona Coast (1968) 132
Kortman, Bob 16
Kotto, Yaphet 150, 151, 152
Kramer, Stanley 106
Kristofferson, Kris 58, 180
Kruschen, Jack 161
Kubrick, Stanley 97
Kulik, Buzz 143, 144

La Cucaracha Cantina 104
La Fuente Restaurant 156
La Luz, Mexico 174, 176
Ladd, Alan 61, 69, 70, 76, 93, 106, 108, 214
Lagrimas (horse) 102–**103**
Laine, Frankie 55, 100, 215
Lake Louise 77
L'Amour, Louis 43, 70
Lancaster, Burt 95, 99, 120, 121, 133, 153, 173, 179, 181
Lane, Allan "Rocky" 23–24, 38
Lang, Stephen 201
Langella, Frank 173, 174, 176
Langer, Carole 97
Langford, Frances **33**–35
Laramie Street 169

Laredo (TV) 188
The Larry King Show (TV) 212
LaRue, Lash 86
Las Cruces, NM 165
Las Vegas, NV 70, 185
LaShelle, Joseph 77
Last Bus to Banjo Creek 121
The Last Hard Men (1976) 129, 164, 180, 186
The Last Movie (1971) 164
The Last Movie Star (2017) 215
The Last of the Fast Guns (1958) 102
The Last Picture Show (1971) 40
The Last Ride of the Dalton Gang (1979) 150
"The Last Roundup" 23
Last Stand at Saber River (1997) 169
The Last Time I Saw Archie (1961) 121
The Last Tycoon (1976) 192
The Last Wagon (1956) 71
Laszlo, Ernest 97
Laughton, Charles 88, 148
Laurel Canyon 57, 179
Laurenz, John 46
Law of the 45's (1935) 38
Law of the Land (1976) 189
The Lawmen 209
Lawrence of Arabia (1962) 27
Lea, Sarah 103
Lea, Tom 101–103, 107
Lean, David 131
"Leaning on the Everlasting Arms" 50
Leather Burners (1943) 19–22
LeBaron, Boots 211
Lee, Allen 169
Lee, Bruce 189
Lee, Kenneth 169
Leeds, Lila 57, 58
Legacy 213
The Legend of Caleb York 90
Legend of Custer (TV) 120
Leider, Emily 67
Lennart, Isobel 119
Leonard, Elmore 169
Leonard, Terry 174
Leone, Sergio 96, 144, 145, 147
LeRoy, Mervyn 31, 33
Lesser, Sol 70
Levy, Emmanuel 110, 112, 113
Lewis, Grover 181
The Life and Legend of Wyatt Earp (TV) 27
The Life and Times of Judge Roy Bean (1972) 80, 129, 161, 162, 204
Li'l Abner's Steakhouse 156
Lilley, Tim 127
"Lime Juice Tab" 117
The List of Adrian Messenger (1962) 121
Little Big Man (1970) 169
Little Horse Park 61
Little House on the Prairie (TV) 129
"Little Ole Wine Drinker Me" 50
Little Sky, Dawn 136
Little Sky, Eddie 136
Livingston, Bob 26

Lochte, Dick 50, 183, 208, 211
Locke, Jon 95, 210
Lockheed Aircraft 11, 12, 25, 27, 35, 80, 100
Lodge, Stephen 189
The Log of a Cowboy 154
Lomax, Bliss 20
London, Jack 10, 11, 196
London, Julie *101*–104, 106, 107, 216
"Londonderry Air" 50
Lone Hand (1953) 70
Lone Pine, CA 19, 21, 27, 29, 31, 38, 40, 41, 43, 121, 205, 214
The Lone Ranger (TV) 11
The Lone Ranger (2013) 204
The Lone Star Trail (1943) 23–27, 32, 35
Lonely Are the Brave (1962) 169
The Loners (TV) 121
Lonesome Dove (1989) 199
Long Beach Players Guild 11
The Long Summer of George Adams 108
The Long Wire 84
The Longest Day (1962) 46, 121
The Loretta Young Show (TV) 55
The Losers 74
Loser's Town 208
Lost Canyon (1942) 14
Loughran, Tommy 10
Love, Damian 88, 113, 177
Lovering, Otho 158, 169
Lowe, Jane 157
Loy, Myrna 65–67
Lucas, Nick 68
Lucey's 57
Lumet, Sidney 181
Lundigan, William 135, 136
Lupton, John 92, 93
The Lusty Men (1952) 3, 68–76, 107, 171, 211, 214, 215
Lyden, Pierce 13, 14, 16, 22, 29, 30, 53, 94–95, 190, 204, 205
Lyles, A.C. 22
Lynn, Diana 85, 86, 88
Lytess, Natasha 81–82

Macao (1952) 68, 71
MacBride, Demetra 206
MacDonald, John D. 132
MacKenna's Gold (1969) 57
MacLaglen, Andrew V. 87, 90, 134, 135, 139, 141, 152, 164, 180, 181
MacLaine, Shirley 119, 121
MacMurray, Fred 51
Maddrey, Joseph 5
Madison, Guy 46, *182*
Madrid, Spain 145–147
Madsen, Michael 207
Magers, Boyd 3, 7, 23, 25
The Magnificent Seven (1960) 27, 99, 108, 144, 204
The Magnificent Seven Ride! (1972) 179
Mahoney, Jock 102
Majestic Theatre 74
Major Dundee (1965) 117, 135, 169
Majors, Lee 192

Malcolm, Derek 53
Malle, Louis 181
Mallory, John 73
The Man Behind the Rifle 209
A Man Called Horse (1970) 185
The Man from Snowy River (1982) 121
The Man in the Middle (1964) 121
Man O' War (horse) 191
The Man Who Shot Liberty Valance (1962) 14, 87
The Man Who Would Be King 132
Man with the Gun (1955) 5, 90–96, 149, 161, 214
Mandeville Canyon 69, 140
"The Mandeville Canyon Gang" 69
Mann, Anthony 71
Mann, Roderick 136, 184
Manne, Shelly 158
Manners, Sam 163
Mannix, Eddie 32
March or Die (1977) 181
Margret Ann 132
Maria's Lovers (1984) 192
Marrill, Alvin H. 23, 82, 103, 116
The Marshal (TV) 208
Martin, Dean 122, 123, 126, 132, 148–*154*, 158, 160, 161, 167, 179, 197
Martin, Deana 158, 160, 162
Martin, Mick 165
Martin, Richard "Chito" *36*, 38, 40–41, 42, 43, 46
Martin, Strother 189
Martorano, Johnny 181
Marvin, Lee 120, 121, 131, 136, 173, 179, 180, 188, 197, 215
Masley, Ed 184
Maslin, Janet 211
Mate, Rudolph 71
Matilda (1978) 181
Mature, Victor 33, 108
Maunder, Wayne 120
Maverick (TV) 160
The Maverick 71
Maverick Motel 139
Maynard, Kermit 26
Mazatlan, Mexico 172
McCarthy, Todd 126
McClelland, Doug 113
McClintock! (1963) 129, 134, 159, 161, 162
McCoy, Horace 71
McCrea, Jody 120
McCrea, Joel 39, 40, 50, 56, 76, 86, 88, 95, 120, 214
McCrory, Harry 207
McDonald, Herbie 70
McDowall, Roddy 148, *149*, 155, 156
McGraw, Charles 61, 102, 105, 107, 189, 196
McKim, Harry *37*
McKim, Sammy 40
McNeill, Joe 64
McQ (1974) 186
McQueen, Steve 75, 108, 126, 144, 155, 188
The Mean Machine (1973) 164
Meeker, Ralph 90

Index

Menger Bar 74
Merlin, Jan 121
Merrill, Gary 102
Merton, John 34
Mescal 208
Mescal Movie Ranch 171, 200
Meuel, David 49
Mexico City, Mexico 97, 149–151, 174
The Mexico Courts 104
Midnight Plus One 174
Midnight Ride (1990) 201
Midway (1976) 105, 181
Mifune, Toshiro 120
Miles, Peter 65, 66
Milestone, Lewis 45, 65
military/military roles 45–46
Millard, Joe 169
Miller, Arthur 120
Miller, Ben 208
Miller, Charlie 48
Miller, Don 20, 26, 41, 43
Miller, Lorraine 26
Miller, Tom 176
Millner, Cork 18, 88
Milltown House 214
Minesweeper (1943) 23
Minnelli, Vincente 109–113
The Misfits (1961) 82, 119, 120
Missing Men 16
Missouri Legend 70
The Missourian 121
Mr. Horn (1979) 150
Mr. Moses (1965) 121
Mr. North (1988) 201
Mitchell, Darwin 136
Mitchum, Anne 9, 127, 205
Mitchum, Bentley **194**, 195, 212
Mitchum, Bonnie 188
Mitchum, Carrie 208
Mitchum, Chris 7, 14–15, 85, 108, 114, 127, 161, 163, 164, 169, **194**, 195, 200, 201, 210, 212, 213
Mitchum, Dorothy Spence 10, 11, 56, 57, 70, 85, 89, 98, 133, 153, 166, 172, 174, 195, 210, 212
Mitchum, Hank 209
Mitchum, James Thomas 9
Mitchum, Jim 11, 50, 85, 105, 119, 120, 145, 163–165, 169, 196, 203, 212, 213
Mitchum John 9, 14, 16, 28, 36, 73, 80, 89, 94, 95, 124, 127, 139, 141, 142, 145, 164, 165, 186, 188, 189, 195, 196, 205, 210, 212, 213, 216
Mitchum, Julie "Annette" 9, 212
Mitchum, Petrine "Trina" 84, 87, 114, 165–166, 212
The Mitchum Droolettes 40
The Mitchum Ramble 35
Mitchum Rock 57
Mitchum Steakhouse 214
Mitchum Tavern 214
Mix, Tom 13, 38, 53, 200, 214
Mojave Desert 13
Monahan, Kasper 41
Monogram Ranch 63
Monro, Gregory 212

Monroe, Marilyn 3, **77**–83, 160
The Monroes (TV) 117
Monstroid (1980) 165
Monte Walsh (1970) 105, 129, 131, 172, 173
Montecito, CA 212
Montecito Mountain 190
Montgomery, Jack 48
Monty, Harry 80
Monument Records 50
Monument Valley 39
Moonrunners (1974) 164
Moore, Roger 181
"Moreton Bay" 117
Moriarty, Steve 186
Morrison, Marion 50
Morrison Ranch 65
Morse, Barry 194
Morse, L.A. 196
Mosby, Aline 72, 73
Moser, Earl 14, 22
Mount Bachelor 134
Mount Rainier National Park 86
Mount Whitney 31
Muir, Florabel 45
A Mule for the Marquesa 120
"Mule Train" 55
Mulford, Clarence E. 12
Mummy Mountain 202
Munn, Michael 126, 131
Munro, Tom 53
Murphy, Audie 93, 100, 136, 162, 187
Murphy, Billy "Red" 83, 163
Murphy, Charlie 14, 19, 22
Murphy, Eddie 181
Murray, Jim 191
Murray, Ken 130
Murray, Zon 60
Mustin, Burt 71
Musuraca, Nicholas 35, 59
My Darling Clementine (1946) 201
My Forbidden Past (1951) 80
My Name Is Nobody (1973) 204
Myers, Stevie 136

Napier, Charles 206, 210, 212
Native Americans 136–137
Necessity 208
Needham, Hal 134, 136
Neeson, Liam 207
Negulesco, Jean 79
Nelson, Ralph 173–176
Nelson, Willie 58
Nettleton, Lois 169
Network (1976) 181
Nevada (1927) 5
Nevada (1935) 39
Nevada (1944) 5, 35–42, 65, 214
Nevada Smith (1966) 126, 155
Nevins, Francis M. 21
Newbury, Mickey 58
Newlan, Paul 34
Newman, Paul 99, 111, 161, 162, 179
Newton, Stacy 162
Nice Girls Don't Stay for Breakfast (2018) 216
Nicholson, Jack 174

The Night Fighters (1959) 100, 118
Night of the Hunter (1955) 50, 54, 88, **89**, 148–150, 152, 153, 173, 204, 207
Night Riders 100
Nightkill (1980) 193, 203
Nimeth, Mike 16
Niver, Kemp 70
Nolte, Nick 181, 188
None But the Brave (1965) 132
Norris, Chuck 189
North, Alex 91, 102
North and South (TV) 195
North to Alaska (1960) 119, 120, 131, 155
Not as a Stranger (1955) 90
Nugent, Carol 74
Nyby, Christian 47

Oak Creek Tavern 61
Oakie, Jack 106
O'Brian, Hugh 93, 201
O'Brien, George 36
The Oceana 172
"Oh, Susanna" 34
O'Hara, Maureen 190
"O-He-O-Hi-O" 56
Ohmart, Carol 71
Ojala, Arvo 93
The Old Breed 167
The Old Dick 196
Old Ironsides (horse) 129
The Old Place 188
Old Tucson Studios 7, 120, 123, 128, 129, 150, 156, 157, 159–163, 170, 171, 200, 211
Once Upon a Time in the West (1969) 144, 147
100 Years of the Hollywood Western (1994) 202
One Minute to Zero (1952) 76, 89, 94, 105
One Shoe Makes it Murder (1982) 161
O'Neal, Ryan 179
Onstatt, Cedric 83
Oppenheimer, Peer J. 57
Orbison, Roy 50
The Oregon Trail (TV) 210
O'Rourke, Pierre 122, 209, 211
Osborne, Robert 183
O'Toole, Peter 181
Otterburn-Hall, William 76, 183
Out of Retirement 195
Out of the Past (1947) 3, 52, 64, 134, 139, 204
The Outcasts of Poker Flat (1952) 106
The Outfit: A Cowboy's Primer 193
The Outlaw (1943) 211
The Outlaw Josey Wales (1976) 95, 179, 203, 204
Outlaws (TV) (1960s) 150
Outlaws (TV) (1980s) 193, 210
The Outrage (1964) 162
Owen, James P. 43
Owens, Cliff 129
Owens, Kimo 128–129

Owens, Ray 190
The Oxbow Incident (1943) 87

Paige, Leroy "Satchel" 105, 106
Paint Your Wagon (1969) 95
Palance, Jack 40, 61, 120, 131, 180, 187, 201, 204, 206
Pale Rider (1985) 169
Palo Bolero Falls 98
The Palomino 156
The Palomino Club 189
Pancho (horse) 107
Paradise Valley, AZ 202–203
Paramount Ranch 191, 213
Paris, Texas 112
Parish, James Robert 57
Parker, Ed 188
Parker, Eddie 23
Parker, Eleanor 110, 113
Parker, Fess 190, 212
Parker, Robert B. 208
Parker, Tom 105
Parkinson, Cliff 14
Parkinson, Michael 183
Parks, Michael 186–187
Parrish, Robert 4, 71, 101–104, 107, 175
Parsons, Louella 46
The Pass System 29
Pat Garrett and Billy the Kid (1973) 179
Patten, Luana 110
Patton (1970) 174
Patton, George S. 132
Paxton, Bill 201
Payne, John 79
"Peace in the Valley" 83
Peck, Gregory 39, 69, 95, 101, 120, 131, 172, 179, 180, 190, 193, 201
Peckinpah, Sam 121, 135, 143, 144, 147, 166, 167, 169, 172, 174, 179, 180, 188
Pendleton, OR 71
Peoples, David 200
Peppard, George **109**–113, 180
Pepper, Joe 136
Perils of the Wilderness (1956) 94
Perrine, Valerie 181
Persico, Joyce 100
Peters, Charlotte 103
The Petrified Forest 11
Phillips, Alex 102
Phillips, Rusty 195
Phoenix, AZ 71, 202, 203, 206
Pickens, Slim 44, 73, 129, 165, 189
Pickett, Bill 75
Pie (horse) 99
Pike's Peak, CO 114
Pine Street Saloon 189
Pinnacle Peak 203
Pioneer Village 150
Pioneertown 53
Pitts, Michael R. 26, 64, 94, 100, 110, 172, 177
A Place in the Sun (1951) 27
Placerita Canyon 25
Planet of the Apes (1968) 27
Playa Hotel 172

Plaza de Toros de Las Ventos 144
Plunkett, Walter 109
Pocket Money (1972) 162, 179
Poitier, Sidney 106
Police Story (TV) 193
Pollock, Lew 34
Pollock, Sydney 201
Polo Lounge 173, 189
Pomeroy, Allen 49
Poore, Dan 73
Pop, Iggy 206
Post, Ted 181
Powder River (1953) 83
Powell, Dick 84, 105, 119, 121
Powers, Mala 70
The Prairie (1946) 73
Prelutsky, Burt 172
Preminger, Otto 77, 79, 82, 181
Presley, Elvis 47, 105, 150, 163, 203
Preston, Robert 59–61, 64, 76, 190, 197
Pritchett, Paula 174
The Professionals (1966) 119, 120
Promises to Keep (1985) 150, **194**
Puerto Vallarta, Mexico 172
Pursued (1947) **4**, 46–54, 56, 64, 104, 136, 159, 214, 215
Pyle, Denver 73, 110, 148, 154

The Quick and the Dead (1995) 129
Quinn, Anthony 97, 101, 150

"Rachel" 56
Rachel and the Stranger (1948) 50–52, 54–58, 135, 137, 141
The Racket (1951) 68, 71
Rafter Six Guest Ranch 80
Ragan, Mike 43
Raiders of Sunset Pass (1943) 26
Rampage (1963) 15, 121
Ramrod (1947) 50
Randall, Glenn 65
Rangitikei Pub 195
The Rare Breed (1966) 134
Rattlesnake Pass 157
Ravetch, Irving 111
Rawhide (1951) 137
Rawhide (TV) 95
Rawhide Western Town 192
Ray, Nicholas 71–76, 206
Reagan, Ronald 84, 95, 131, 191
The Rebel (TV) 196
The Rebel Outlaw Josey Wales 179
Red Dust (1932) 132
The Red Pony (1949) 45, 53, 65–68
Red River (1948) 17, 52, 128, 145, 215
Red River (1988) 196
Red Rock Canyon 30, 47
Red Rock Crossing **4**, **59**, 61, **215**
Redford, Robert 99
Redigo (TV) 105
Redwing, Rodd 93, 128
Reed, Marshall 73
Reed, Oliver 180, 206
Reed, Ray 84
Reed, Walter 210
Reeves, George 17, 20, 21, 27, **28**
Reeves, Jim 68

Reid, John Howard 83
The Reluctant Star 32, 45, 46, 52, 53
Remington, Frederick 123
Remuda Dude Ranch 114
Renard, Ken 110
Rettig, Tommy **78**, **81**, 83
The Return of Josey Wales (1986) 186
Return to Thunder Road 165
Reunion at Fairborough (1985) 119
Reynolds, Bernie 76, 186
Reynolds, Burt 148, 173, 186, 212, 215
Reynolds, Craig 38
Ricco (1973) 164
Richards, Bob 169
Richards, Dick 180, 181
Rickey, Carrie 64, 141
Ride Lonesome (1959) 91, 187
Ride the High Country (1962) 94, 158, 169
Ride the Wild Surf (1964) 163
Riders in the Sky: Scenes from the American West 215
Riders of the Deadline (1943) 30–**32**
The Rifleman (TV) 83, 125, 128, 158, 189, 209
Righter, Carroll 11
Riley, Elaine 34–35, 43
"Ring of Fire" 149
Ringo, Johnny 144, 201
Rio Bravo (1959) 17, 119, 120, 122, 123, 129, 131, 152, 157, 158, 161
Rio Grande (1950) 39
Rio Lobo (1970) 129, 131, 136, 137, 157, 161, 164, 203, 204, 207
Riste, Arthur 86
Ritter, Tex 23, **24**, 46
The River Bottom 189
"River of No Return" 83–84
River of No Return (1954) 3, 50, 76–86, 136, 137, 149, 150, 160, 180, 214
Riverboat (TV) 95
Rivero, Jorge 131, 202
Roarke, Adam 125
Robards, Jason, Jr. 152, 153, 172, 188
Robbins, Marty 100, 117, 215
The Robe (1953) 33
Roberson, Chuck 73, 89, 102, 105–107, 113, 128, 192, 196
"Robert Mitchum" 214
The Robert Mitchum Bar 214
Roberts, Gerald 73
Roberts, Jerry 19, 64, 113, 180, 209
Roberts, Marguerite 148
Robertson, Cliff 120
Robertson, Dale 113, 153, 191, 209
Robotham, George 149
Robson, Mark 69
Rocco, Alex 181
Rodney, John 47–50
Rogell, Sid 34
Rogers, C.B. "Bird Dog" 114
Rogers, Kenny 159
Rogers, Roy 23, 42, 87, 99, 190, 204, 214
Rogers, Will 38, 44, 86, 185, 214
Roland, Gilbert **96**, 97, 99, 100

Roosevelt, Teddy 74
Rooster Cogburn (1975) 155
Rose, Bob 154
Rosebud (1975) 181
Rosson, Harold 123
Rothel, David 25, 35, 40
Rothwell, Robert 83
Rough Company 74
Rough Night in Jericho (1967) 152, 162
Roughshod (1949) 69
The Rounder 107
The Rounders (1965) 162
"Roving Gambler" 51
Ruarke, Robert 108
Rubin, Stanley 82–83
Ruidoso Downs, NM 114
Run for the Sun (1956) 98
Runyon, Thomas 188
Russell, Jane 58, 68, 70, 83, 105, 108, 190, 203, 210, 211
Russell, Kurt 200–202
The Rusty Spur 203
Ryan, Mitchell 105, 163
Ryan, Robert 47, 52, 70, 79, 95, 120, 121, 153, 180, 187, 196
Ryan's Daughter (1970) 131, 169, 174, 176

Saboteur (1942) 11
The Sacketts (1979) 129, 140, 150, 207
The Saga of Cali York 90
Salmon River 77
Salt, Waldo 54
San Antonio, TX 74
San Fernando Valley Saddlery 136
San Francisco Peaks 63
San Juan Mountains 168
San Miguel de Allende 103
San Ysidro Ranch 190
Sanborn, Les 73, 75
Sanderson, Harold 117
Sands of Iwo Jima (1949) 163
Santa Barbara, CA 190, 195, 196, 202, 204, 206, 210
Santa Fe, NM 168, 170–172
Santa Fe Trail (1950) 52
Santa Ynez Valley 190
The Saratoga 57
Saskatchewan (1954) 76, 80, 106
Saturday Night Live (TV) 196
Schary, Dore 56
Scheer, Ron 51
Scheider, Roy 181
Schickel, Richard 126–127, 135
Schiller, Brian 118
Schlom, Herman 33, 34
Scorsese, Martin 202
Scott, George C. 120
Scott, Randolph 39, 49, 58, 66, 88, 91, 95, 131, 136, 155, 190, 214
Scott, Vernon 188
Scott, Zachary 97, 99, 100
Scottsdale, AZ 192, 203
Scrooged (1988) 201
The Searchers (1956) 21, 47, 94, 97, 107, 128, 215

Second Chance (1953) 61, 77
Secret Ceremony (1968) 155
Sedona, AZ 4, 59, 63, 64, 71, 203, 206, **215**
Sedona Lodge 61
Seebe Guest Ranch 80
The Seekers (1979) 193
Sefton, Dan 208
Selander, Lesley 16, 27
Selleck, Tom 169, 207
Sellwood, Neville 117
Selznik, David O. 53
Server, Lee 34, 40, 47, 64, 87, 93, 95, 97, 103, 106, 111, 122, 125, 154, 176, 180, 187, 200, 211, 216
Seven Deadly Sins (1992) 201
Seven Men from Now (1955) 91
Shalit, Gene 204
Shane (1953) 40, 93, 94, 215
Shane (TV) 170
Share Benefit Organization 192, 195
Sharpe, Dave 36
Sharpe, Karen 92, 93, 95
Shaw, Robert 120, 181
Shay, John "Jack" 11
She Wore a Yellow Ribbon (1949) 39, 47, 128
Shearer, Lloyd 30
Shelton, Al 191
Shelton, Bob 128, 157, 159, 211
Shenandoah (1965) 134
Sherman, Harry "Pop" 12–14, 16, 19, 20, 22, 27, 29, 31, 90
Sherman, Teddi/Lois 22
Sherwood, Robert E. 11
"Shifting Sands" 134
Shipp, Cameron 53
The Shootist (1976) 180
Short, Luke 59
Shosone Indians 136
Shoulders, Jim 73
Shryack, Dennis 169
Siegel, Don 57, 119, 180
Sierra Madre 148, 153, 174
Silva, Henry 40, 202
Silva, Simone 89
Silver Phantom (horse) 117
Silverado (1985) 176, 208
Silverton, CO 168
Simmons, Jean 68, 82
Simpson, Paul 3
Simpson, Russell 13, **15**
Sinatra, Frank 120, 121, 130, 132, 149, 185, 195
Siringo, Charles A. 182
Sitting Bull 120
6-B Ranch 154, 196
"16 Tons" 83
Skeleton Canyon 200
Ski (horse) 86
Skull Valley 212
Sky King (TV) 85
Slate, Jeremy 148
Slattery, Desmond 83
Slaughter on Tenth Avenue (1957) 105
Sliphammer 208

Sloane, Everett 110
Smith, Cecil 193
Smith, Charlie 191
Smith, Dean 128
Smith, Imogen Sara 43, 216
Smith, Jaclyn 193
Smith, William 188, 189, 193, 206
Smithlin, Smokey 108
Smoke Bellew 196
Snake River 71
Snowy River 117
Socorro, NM 168
Sombrero Peak 157
Sonora, Mexico 100, 174
The Sons of Katie Elder (1965) 117, 152, 153, 155, 169
The Sons of Robert Mitchum 214
The Sons of the Pioneers 84
Sorcerer (1977) 181
Spartacus (1960) 139
Spearman, Frank H. 70
Spielberg, Stephen 181
The Spikes Gang (1974) 179
Spillane, Mickey 90
Spivey, Donald 106
The Spoilers (1942) 23, 49, 66
Spokane, WA 71
The Sportsmen's Lodge 189
Springfield, OR 54
Stack, Robert 70
Stader, Paul 97
Stagecoach (1939) 5, 13, 61, 128
Stagecoach (1986) 180
Stagedoor Bar 186
Stagger Lee 214
Stalag 17 (1954) 94
The Stalking Moon (1969) 172
Stallone, Frank 200
Stanford, Dok 84
Stanley, John 211–212
Stanush, Claude 71
Stanwyck, Barbara 84, 190
Stark, Ray 130–131
Stark, Richard 174
Starr Pass Trail 157
The Stars in Their Courses 123
Steel (horse) 39, 41, **42**, 169
Steel, Tom 23–24
Steele, Bob 13, 39
Steiger, Rod 181, 202
Steinbeck, John 65
Steiner, Max 47
Stephens, Blackie 73
Sterling, Jan 91–93
Sterling, King 50
Sterling, Robert 69
Stevens, George 94, 208
Stevens, Inger 148
Stevens, Stella 196
Stewart, James 40, 45, 60, 95, 99, 131, 134, 136, 152, 211
Stewart, Peggy 210
Stoltz, Eric **192**
Stone, N.B. "Bo" 94
Stone, Oliver 202
The Story of G.I. Joe (1945) 45, 64, 73, 87, 163
Stout, Bud 162

Index

Stradling, Harry, Jr. 156, 158, 169
Strang, Harry **24**
Strange, Glenn 29, 73
The Stranger Wore a Gun (1953) 40
Strassberg, Phil 203
A Streetcar Named Desire (1951) 68
"Streets of Laredo" 50
Streets of Laredo (1995) 208
Streisand, Barbra 131
Strode, Woody 120
Stross, Raymond 118
Strudwick, Shepperd 66
stuntmen 24, 30, 39, 61, 69, 76, 81, 125, 149, 150, 157, 162, 170, 192
stunts 16, 18, 19, 21, 24, 29, 50, 98, 147
Sturges, John 101
Sugarfoot (TV) 212
Summers, Dirk 193
Summers, Neil 7, 162, 204
"Sunday Morning Coming Down" 180
The Sundowners (1960) 3, **6**, 50, 113–122, 166, 214
The Sunset Boys (1995) 205
Sunset Pass (1946) 46
Superstition Mountains 203
Support Your Local Gunfighter (1971) 161
Support Your Local Sheriff (1969) 137, 161
Swayze, Patrick 195
Switzer, Carl "Alfalfa" 86

Tackett, Dale 196
Tackett Stock Farm 154
Tales of Wells Fargo (TV) 113
Taliaferro, Hal 16, 21
Talbot Prods. 108, 156, 162, 163
Tall Dark Stranger 51
Tall in the Saddle (1944) 39
The Tall T (1957) 40, 91, 187
Taylor, Buck 201
Taylor, Dub 110
Taylor, Duke 57
Taylor, Elizabeth 195
Taylor, Robert 98, 128
Taylor, Rod 119, 121, 132, 193, 195
Teal, Ray 48
Ten Eyck, Melissa 112
Tepotzlan, Mexico 98
Terhune, Bob "Terrible" 169, 189
A Terrible Beauty 100
Terry, Ruth 205
The Texan (TV) 83
Texas Law 16
Thackery, Bud 25
That Championship Season (1982) 192, 195
That Man 51
Thaxter, Phyllis 61
Them Ornery Mitchum Boys 14, 16, 28, 80, 213, 216
They Live By Night (1948) 71
Thiess, Ursula 70, 97–99
Thirty Seconds Over Tokyo (1944) 31
This Man Is Mine 74
Thomas, Bob 82, 114, 119, 153, 181, 184

Thomas, Kevin 123
Thompson, Glen 49
Thompson, Hank 68
Thompson, Hunter S. 50
Thompson's Last Run (1986) 193
Thomson, David 21, 75
Thornton, Billy Bob 201, 206
Thousand Oaks Chili Cookoff 191
3 Godfathers (1948) 47, 102
3:10 to Yuma (1957) 95, 106
Three Violent People (1956) 71
Thunder Over Texas (1934) 38
Thunder Road (1958) 50, 85, 98, 100, 104, 105, 107, 120, 150, 163
Thunder Road Steakhouse 214
Thurston, Helen 80
Tibbs, Casey 73, 197
Tidewater Inn 133
Till the End of Time (1946) 46, **182**
Timonium State Fair 114
Tiomkin, Dimitri 117
Tison, Gary 193
To the Last Man (1933) 39
The Today Show (TV) 204
Tom Horn (1980) 80, 129
Tom Sawyer 132
Tombstone (1993) 140, 150, 199–205
Tomkies, Mike 14, 17, 39, 40, 52, 67, 77, 89, 142, 143, 150, 155, 172, 184, 209, 213
Tonge, Philip 85
The Tonight Show (TV) 19, 122, 183
"Too Ra Loo Ra Loo Ral" 50
Top Gun (1955) 91
Torvay, Jose 97
Tourneur, Jacques 52, 70
Towne, Robert 143, 147
Track of the Cat (1954) **85**–90, 214
Trackdown (1976) 164
Tracy, Spencer 31, 116
Trader Vic's 203
The Train Robbers (1973) 125
The Tramplers (1965) 120
Trappe, MD 114, 214
Trigger (horse) 87, 99
Triple R Ranch 114
Tropico Gold Mine 191
The Troubadour 180
The Troubleshooter 94
True Grit (1969) 148, 150, 155, 166
Tucker, Forrest 131, 189
Tully, Jim 10
Tully, Tom 59, 60, 64
Turk's Tavern 189
Turner, Lana 108
Turner, Rodney 117
26 Men (TV) 202
Two for the Seesaw (1962) 63, 121
Two Mules for Sister Sara (1970) 119
Tyler, Tim 156
Tyler, Tom 39, 60, 61

Ulzana's Raid (1972) 45
The Undefeated (1969) 136, 150
Underwater (1955) 105
Unforgiven (1992) 199
The Unforgiven (1960) 101, 119
Union Pacific (1939) 50

Unsung Heroes 204
Untamed (1955) 105
Ustinov, Peter 116

Vague, Vera 34
Valley of Fire 120
Van Cleef, Lee 179, 190
Van Dien, Casper 208
Van Tilburg Clark, Walter 85
Vasquez Rocks 191
Vaughan, Robert 209
Vera Cruz (1954) 45, 99
Victor's 57
The Victors (1963) 163
Vietnam 132–133
Viharo, Robert 7, 142, 146–147
Villa, Jose Trinidad 149
Villa, Pancho 142, 143, 147, 149
Villa Capri 70
Villa Rides! (1968) 136, 142–148, 173
Vincent, Jan-Michael 164
Virginia City (1940) 52
The Virginian (1946) 50
The Virginian (TV) 60, 95, 150, 189
voice characteristics/work 26, 200, 202, 212
Volkie, Ralph 71
Von Sternberg, Josef 71
Vye, Murvyn 78–80

Wagner, Wende 164
Wagon Train (TV) 50, 135, 150
Wakely, Jimmy 25, 35
Wald, Jerry 73, 75
Wales, Wally 16
Walker, Charlie 50
Walker, Clint 132, 189
Walker, Robert 31
Walker, Robert, Jr. 156, **157, 159**, 162
Walker Ranch 25
Wallace, Tim 61, 80, 83, 85, 94, 98, 105, 170
Walleck Ranch 214
Wallis, Hal 148, 150
Walsh, Raoul 47, 48, 50, 71, 179, 188
Walters, Barbara 188
Wanderer 172
Wanderers of the Wasteland (1945) 46
Wanted—Dead or Alive (TV) 108
War and Remembrance (1988) 46, 150, 186, 193, 196, 203, 204, 212
The War Horses 132
The War Wagon (1967) 126, 139, 150
Ward, Blackjack 16
Ward, Brad 121
Ward, Robert 183
wardrobe 14, 22, 46, 60, 71, 135
Warlock (1959) 94
Warm Springs Reservation 140
Warner, Jack L. 50
Warren, Charles Marquis 108
Warren, James 46
Warshaw, Robert 122
Washington International Horse Show 114
Waterhole #3 (1967) 80
Watson, Wylie 118

Way of a Gaucho (1952) 70
The Way West (1967) 9, 17, 48, 131–142, 204
Wayne, John 3–5, 22, 23, 29, 35, 36, 39–41, 43, 48, 50, 61, 64, 66, 70, 76, 79, 84, 87, 89–91, 94–96, 99, 107, 118–131, 134, 136, 139, 141, 149, 152, 153, 155–157, 159, 161, 163–167, 169, 179–181, 186, **187**, 189, 190, 196, 204, 213, 214
Wayne, Patrick 164
We Pointed Them North: Recollections of a Cowpuncher 60
Weaver, Tom 34
Webb, Roy 71
Weber, Bruce 216
Weisbart, David 120
The Well at Ras Daga 108
Wellman, William 45, 86, 87, 90, 134, 179
Wellman, William, Jr. 214
Wells, Orson 63, 94, 174
West of the Pecos (1945) 41–46, 65, 214
Western, Johnny 100
Western costume 135
Western Film Preservation Society 214
Western Heritage Award 214
Western Village 214
The Westerner (1940) 5, 60
The Westerner (TV) 121
Westlake, Donald 174
Westward the Women (1951) 87
Westworld 203
We've Never Been Licked (1943) 23
What a Way to Go (1964) 121
What's My Line? (TV) 101
"Wheels" 51
"When I'm Walkin' Arm and Arm with Jim" 34
When the Legends Die (1972) 179
When There's Sumpthin' to Do 131
Where Danger Lives (1950) 68
"Whipporwill" 50
Whispering Smith (1948) 61, 70, 79
Whispering Winds Ranch 154
Whitaker, Slim 48

White Hunter, Black Heart (1990) 181
White Stallion Ranch 157
White Witch Doctor (1953) 76, 153
Whitman, Stuart 7, 120, 161, 164, 195, 210
Who Rides with Kane? 156
Who Rides with Wyatt? 156
Wickenburg, AZ 114
Widmark, Richard 69, 71, 119, 134, 137, 139, 141, 142, 161, 179, 190
Wieghorst, Olaf 125
Wild Bill (1995) 208
The Wild Bunch (1969) 99, 135, 166, 174, 179
"The Wild Colonial Boy" 117
The Wild Geese (1978) 181
The Wild River 70
Wild Rovers (1971) 179
Wild Times (1980) 140, 208
The Wild West (1977) 190
The Wild Wild West (1999) 136, 204
The Wild Wild West (TV) 189
Wildhorn Guest Ranch 114
Wildside (TV) 193
Wilkins, Paul 11, 12, 17, 32, 34
Will Penny (1968) 80, 172, 173
Willamette River 134, 137
Williams, Bill 42, 43, 46, **182**
Williams, Guinn "Big Boy" 38, 39, 42, 110
Williams, Paul 192
Williams, Tex 84
Williams-Channing, Simon 209
Williamson, Thames 70
Wills, Henry 27, 162
Wilson, Earl 35, 183, 188
Wilson, Michael 27
Wilson, Richard 91, 93, 94
Wilson, Terry 49, 50
Wincott, Michael 206
The Winds of War (1983) 5, 46, 150, 164, 186, 193, 194
Windy Gulch 202
Winner, Michael 181, 185
The Winston Affair (1964) 121
Wisbar, Frank 73
Wise, Robert 59, 61, 63, 64
Witney, Michael 136, 140

Witney, William 205
Wohler, Edward 112
Wolf, William 137
Wolfe, Thomas 10
Wolff, Rodd 7, 203
Woman of Desire (1994) 201
The Wonderful Country (1959) 4, 99–108, 128, 136, 162, 191, 214
Woods, Harry 25, 26, 29, 42
Woodward, Edward 201
Woodward, Morgan 189
Wooley, Sheb 73, 100
Wranglers 14, 99, 129, 170–171, 207
The Wrath of God (1972) 99, 155, 173–177, 180, 185
Wright, Teresa 47, **48**, **51**, 85
Wyatt Earp (1994) 200–201, 208
Wynn, Keenan 121

The Yakuza (1975) 180, 182, 185, 201
Yaltapec, Mexico 97
Yarbrough, Glemm 169
Yates, Peter 180
Ye Coach & Horses 57
Yellow Sky (1948) 87
The Yellow Tomahawk (1954) 83
Yost, Elwy 210
Young, Jack 7, 107, 128, 159, 163, 170
Young, Loretta 54, 55
Young, Neil 206
Young, Robert 52
"Young Billy Young" 158
Young Billy Young (1969) 51, 79, 129, 136, 155–167, 170, 204
Young Guns of Texas (1962) 120
The Young Riders (TV) 129, 150
Yucca Valley, CA 53
Yukon, Oklahoma 114

Zacatecas, Mexico 151
Zane Grey Theatre (TV) 91
Zanuck, Darryl F. 79
Zeismer, Jerry 176
Zemo, Nic 113
Zinnemann, Fred 115, 116, 119, 120
Zip Cochise (horse) 129
Zollo, Paul 11